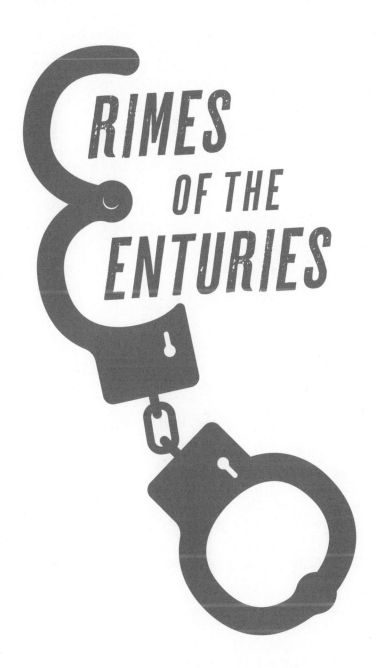

CRIMES OF THE CENTURIES

EQUAL JUSTICE UNDER LAW

CRIMES OF THE CENTURIES

The Cases That Changed Us

AMBER HUNT

UNION SQUARE & CO.
NEW YORK

UNION
SQUARE
& CO.
NEW YORK

UNION SQUARE & CO. and the distinctive Union Square & Co. logo
are trademarks of Sterling Publishing Co., Inc.

Union Square & Co., LLC, is a subsidiary of Sterling Publishing Co., Inc.

ISBN 978-1-4549-4910-7
ISBN 978-1-4549-4911-4 (e-book)

For information about custom editions, special sales, and premium purchases,
please contact specialsales@unionsquareandco.com.

Printed in China

2 4 6 8 10 9 7 5 3 1

unionsquareandco.com

Cover design by Igor Satanovsky
Interior design by Kevin Ullrich

For picture credits see page 357

To Amy Wilson and Amanda Rossmann,
my partners on the A-Team

CONTENTS

Part 4
FORENSIC ADVANCES

Part 5
UNSOLVED WITH IMPACT

Preface

History was never my favorite subject in school. The emphasis was always on events, and I had trouble getting myself to care about things that happened decades or even centuries before I was born. The people involved didn't feel real, as if they were fictional characters from a stodgy play set in an unfamiliar time period to which I couldn't relate. I didn't get it.

This didn't make sense, professionally speaking. I am a journalist. I have been one since founding my middle school's newspaper more than thirty years ago. I've been paid to professionally write for newspapers since my junior year of high school, when I showed up at the local metro paper and asked for a job, and, much to my surprise, they gave me one. Since then, I've never worked outside of a newsroom except for one year, when I did a journalism fellowship. Reporting is in my blood, so it felt like an inexplicable—even shameful—disconnect: What kind of journalist doesn't *get* history?

And then came an "aha" moment. To be clear, this was the first in a succession. I wish I were the type of person for whom the heavens part just once, but I'm a bit thick for that, so bear with me: When I began researching my book *The Kennedy Wives: Trials and Triumphs in America's Most Public Family*, I hit a wall. The words wouldn't come. Even with help from a coauthor, I found myself unable to connect with these women whose lives were so different from mine. While reading history books and existing biographies, I felt my eyes glaze over just as they did back in school. It all felt so academic. But then, frustrated by my lackluster word count, I dug into newspapers. I found tidbits written by journalists just like me, but from decades prior. These weren't front-page stories, typically, but filler pieces stuck inside, taking up space in an era when insatiable newsprint demanded to be filled. One such story that stuck with me was about Joan Kennedy's hair—how she told a reporter that she and her sisters-in-law used "falls," or wefts of artificial hair to make natural locks appear fuller. Jackie and Ethel were annoyed by Joan's candor and reportedly asked her to backpedal to the press. I could relate on two fronts: 1) I, like Joan, have been known to share details that others wish I'd suppress; and 2) even in pre-Instagram days, women have felt pressured to appear effortlessly gorgeous. This was one of the first times that I remember feeling like I could see behind the curtain—I caught a glimpse of the relatable humans behind the headlines. From then on, no matter the story I wrote, I turned to the archives, which in the newspaper world are dubbed "morgues." I wanted to wrap my head around how those similar events affected the people of the time.

Fast forward to the pandemic. My boss sent me home from the *Cincinnati Enquirer* newsroom in March 2020, supposedly a three-week work-from-home hiatus to stop the spread of COVID-19. I felt utterly lost, a disquieting mix of panic and numbness. I tried to find my footing but failed. So I did what comes naturally to me: I researched the hell out of the 1918 pandemic. I read story after story, trying to mine the past to make sense of what was happening in the present, and perhaps shed a little light on what might play out as this horrifying thing unfolded. So much of what was written sounded disturbingly familiar in that it was maddeningly contradictory: It's not the flu, some stories insisted; it's merely weaklings exaggerating their colds. It *is* the flu, but no worse than previous bouts. It's an awful flu whose victims can be tallied four figures at a time. It will never end. It has ended already. People are panicking needlessly. People aren't panicking enough.

Businesses used the mysterious illness to sell life insurance and throat remedies and "the best accident and health policy ever written." I dare say the flu-inspired poetry was some of my favorite:

> **Don't spit, don't crowd, don't cough, don't sneeze;**
> **Use goose-grease every time you wheeze;**
> **Eat solid food and sleep some, too;**
> **You'll never die of Spanish "flu."**[1]

As nonsensical and chaotic as the Spanish flu coverage was, I felt a strange sense of relief wash over me: We've been here before, in a situation quite similar, and we were idiots about it then, too. Yet we came out the other side. We can do it again. I pictured a journalist one hundred years in the future finding the same solace in the stories I was writing about COVID, and that's when everything clicked.

We're all just people stuck in a glorified time loop. So much changes around us—technology, fashion, language, art—but at our core, we're the same people we've always been. We love our families and raise our children and yearn for security and have our hearts broken. We think we know everything even if we know nothing, we blame politicians when it suits us, we look for medical miracles in the classified ads. We are scared of aging and death, yet routinely flout our very mortality.

As sure as all of that is true, so is this: Some of us endure or are witness to unfathomable hardships that seem destined to define our whole lives, and maybe the lives of others—maybe entire generations, in fact—that inevitably, somehow, fade into background noise when given enough time. The newspaper morgues bear this out. Pick any day in history, and if there's a newspaper still around that had been published that day, I guarantee you'll find a story that changed someone's life. I chose two dates at random: On December 5, 1750, the *Maryland Gazette* wrote:

> **On Tuesday night a barbarous murder was committed at the seaside, near this town [Yarmouth, UK], on the body of Robert Bullen, about eighteen years of age, son of a farmer at Thrandeston in Suffolk.[2] [Bullen was stabbed more than 20 times.]**

March 12, 1800, in the *Lancaster Intelligencer*, beneath the headline "SHOCKING MURDER!":

> **On Saturday last, a most shocking Murder was committed in Preston, on the body of a child of Mr. Leonard, aged about 18 months.[3] [A woman named Marcey Bump strangled the child and threw "it" down a well.]**

Dust off the dated language, and any one of these tales could be fodder for an episode of *Dateline*. Flesh out the stories with some context about the era in which they occurred, and you've got yourself a history lesson.

So that's what I did. By the end of 2020, I had launched the podcast *Crimes of the Centuries* through the Obsessed Network—so now I'm not only teaching myself the history lessons that just never seemed to stick back in school, but I get the privilege of sharing these lessons with tens of thousands of listeners every week. Each episode explores a case that had lasting impact in some significant way but whose participants—most notably, the victims—have since been largely forgotten. Few people know today that the first documented murder trial in America centered on a young woman named Elma Sands, whose suspected killer was represented by Alexander Hamilton *and* Aaron Burr four years before Burr killed Hamilton in a duel. Few know that the first time anyone pleaded temporary insanity in America involved the murder of the beloved son of Francis Scott Key, lyricist of "The Star-Spangled Banner." Not every morbid headline of yore had such lasting impact, but more did than you probably realize.

Every law in place today has an origin story. Somewhere down the line, a crime was committed (or at least alleged) that highlighted a weakness in our legal system, and that case prompted change. Maybe the change was clear and direct, resulting in a law we have today. Or maybe that change was more subtle—a shift in consciousness that, when combined with other societal factors, ultimately set the stage for new rights and protections. This book aims to tie like cases together by grouping them thematically. To that end, I've chosen five cases to flesh out each of these five categories: Civil Rights Catalysts, Law Changers, Forensic Advancers, Societal Shifters, and Unsolved with Impact.

But I don't want this book to be an academic exercise. At the heart of each case are the people who were involved—people not unlike you or me, who never imagined that their stories would end up in such an anthology. To tell these stories, I am indebted to the journalists who chronicled them first. Even in instances in which I reference work by another author, that work was invariably made possible by the journalists who, as the adage goes, wrote the first drafts of history. They might not have had any clue that the crime they were covering was destined to have the impact it had, but because they did their jobs, we're able today to follow the breadcrumb trail back into time, make the past come alive, and use it to find our footing for the future.

Part 1

LAW CHANGERS

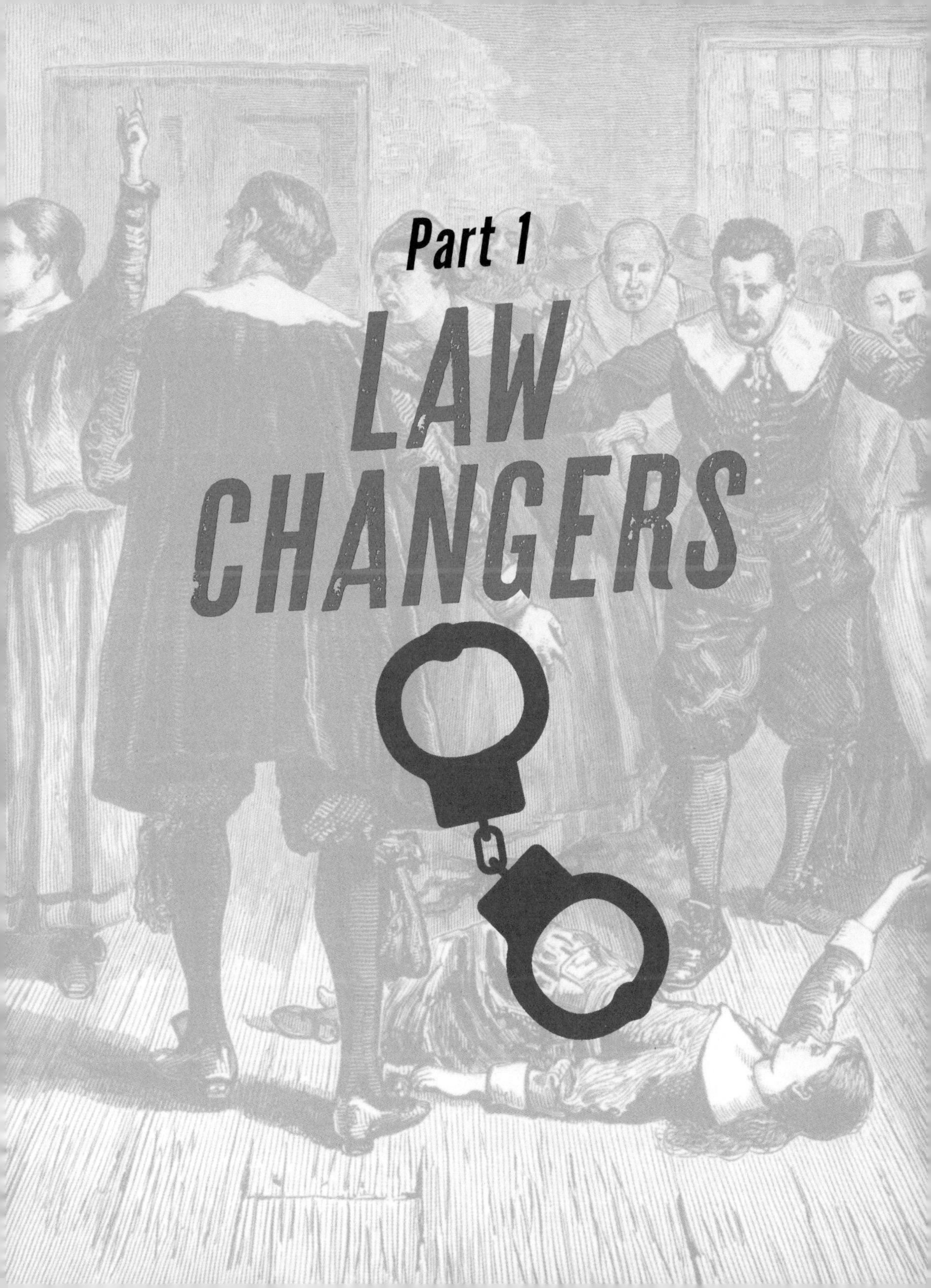

Witch House
ANTIQUES

1

Lessons Learned from the Salem Witch Trials

(1692–93)

To Thomas Putnam in 1692, spirits were as real as the livestock he cared for and the lashings he doled out on his children and servants if they did not pray to keep soil-spoiling demons at bay. So when his twelve-year-old daughter Ann Putnam Jr. began thrashing about and convulsing, her eyes rolling back while her mouth spewed utter gibberish, Putnam's mind leapt easily to spiritual possession as a possible cause. Doctors and ministers alike came to examine the child, as well as the Putnams' similarly afflicted seventeen-year-old maid, Elizabeth Hubbard. When those trained in medicine failed to find an answer for the perplexing behavior, those trained in theology offered their take instead: The girls must be bewitched, they concluded.

Young Ann agreed, then expounded, pointing a trembling finger at neighbor Sarah Good as the cause of her recent torment. *Good's been sending her spirit to me, demanding that I sign the devil's book*, Ann insisted. Elizabeth agreed, and to onlookers it made sense: Sarah Good was known throughout the village as an ill-tempered nuisance. She would even snap at people who tried to come to her aid. If folks in 1692 Salem were asked to make a list of likely witches in their midst, quite a few of the tallies would be topped with the name Sarah Good.

The point of the accusation, of course, was to isolate the trouble and quiet the woes, but the opposite happened: neighbor after neighbor fell victim to similar symptoms. Soon, more than two hundred people would face

OPPOSITE: A view of what is now a museum known as the Witch House, in Salem, Massachusetts, from a photograph taken in 1901. It was the former home of Judge Jonathan Corwin, one of the judges involved in the Salem witch trial of 1692.

accusations that they, like Sarah Good, had discovered the means to sic their spirits on innocents.

Because the Salem witch trials of 1692 continue to be such a source of fascination, many assume that the events there were unique to Salem (actually Salem Village, see opposite page), but that isn't the case. In Massachusetts alone, people charged with witchcraft prior to 1692 numbered more than fifty, fourteen of whom were executed for the crime.[1] Those scenarios usually involved just a few accused at a time, but in neighboring states—Connecticut for example—larger-scale "outbreaks" had been documented, resulting in dozens of deaths. Salem's story continues to resonate so strongly some 330 years later not because it was an outlier but for other reasons—specifically, the impact that the trials had on the nascent American judicial system, due in part to the profound regret that at least some of the accusers carried with them for the rest of their lives.

The story began with four girls: Ann and Elizabeth on one side of the village, and Betty Parris and Abigail Williams on the other. Betty was the nine-year-old daughter of the Rev. Samuel Parris and his wife, while Abigail was Betty's orphaned cousin. Like the girls in the Putnam house, Betty and Abigail "were bitten and pinched by invisible agents," documented the Rev. John Hale, a minister from the neighboring town of Beverly who traveled three miles by horse to observe the girls. "Their arms, necks, and backs turned this way and that way, and returned back again, so as it was impossible for them to do of themselves, and beyond the power of any epileptic fits or natural disease to effect," Hale wrote.[2]

While the Rev. Parris sent his daughter, Betty, away to stay with relatives elsewhere, the other three afflicted girls stayed. After weeks with no relief, four men from Salem Village traveled about five miles southeast to

A fragment from Abigail William's testimony of May 18, 1692, claiming that she had "been almost killed by the apparition of a man named John Willard."

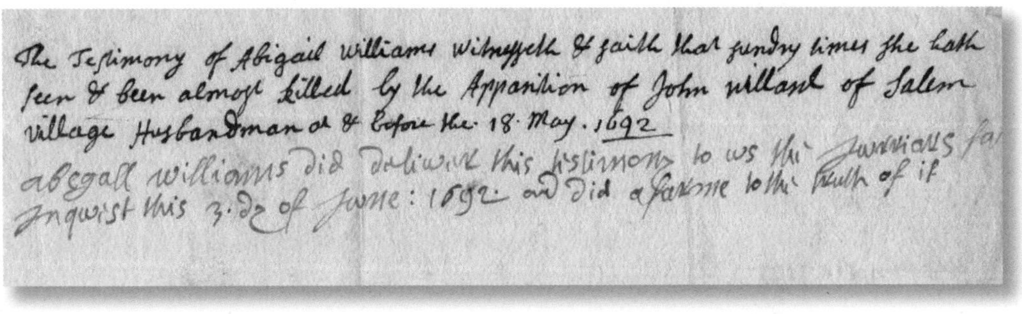

The Testimony of Abigail williams witnesseth & saith that sundry times she hath seen & been almost killed by the Apparition of John willard of Salem village Husbandman at & before the 18. May. 1692

abegall williams did deliver this testimony to us the Jurrors for Inquest this 3. dy of June: 1692 and did afarme to the truth of it

Salem Town to begin legal proceedings against the people they believed were responsible for their loved ones' woes. The date was Monday, February 29, 1692. Today, the village is a town called Danvers. In 1692, it didn't qualify as a town. Salem Village served as the rural counterpart of Salem Town. Each had its own personality, but not its own political structure or parish. The biggest schisms between the two centered on class and money. Those who lived in the village were farmers; those in the town were the seventeenth-century equivalent of city folk. The latter looked down upon the former, who resented the condescension. It was *their* toiling that put food on everyone's tables. For years, whoever served as minister of the Puritan church that serviced both sides of Salem found himself caught in the middle of the feud because the two factions had to unite to pay his salary and provide him wood to endure Massachusetts' brutal winters. Briefly, a minister named George Burroughs held the post. He'd been lured to bring his family to Salem and settle down in the church-provided home that came with the position, but the townsfolk and villagers squabbled over his salary, which they simply stopped paying. Burroughs left town, after which Samuel Parris took over. Like Burroughs, the Rev. Parris routinely found himself caught in the middle of the sparring sides of Salem, his salary often the casualty. Like his parishioner and ally, Putnam, he believed that ill-tempered spirits were not only real but were responsible for the worst of Salem's woes. "If ever there were witches, men and women in covenant with the devil, here are multitudes in New England," he said from the pulpit.[3] After all, he reasoned, there was one devil among the twelve disciples, "so in our churches God knows how many Devils there are."

Evidence of the devil took myriad forms—as sickness sweeping through the town, as drought threatening the crops, or, apparently, as epileptic-type fits, as was the case in the Parris and Putnam homes. The men of the house resolved to flush out the witches causing the suffering. Accompanied by his brother, Edward, as well as fellow villagers Joseph Hutchinson and Thomas Preston, Putnam headed to Salem Town, where the four presented legal complaints to magistrates Jonathan Corwin and John Hathorne, men respected as wealthy merchants and politicians in colonial New England. Neither had official legal training, which was perhaps fitting, considering the New World had a newly imported legal system. What the Putnam quartet

reported—"suspicion of witchcraft"[4]—sparked not only concern but triggered a chain of events that is still routinely referenced today whenever someone invokes the term "witch hunt" to suggest that allegations against someone are hasty, biased, or flat-out wrong.

The Putnam clan's complaints triggered the quick interrogations of two women named as suspected witches. There was, of course, Sarah Good, who'd been born in 1653 to Elizabeth and John Solart.[5] Solart, an innkeeper nicknamed the "Frenchman," was a man of means, but when he died in 1672[6], his considerable estate got tied up in probate court for years. Whatever had been left to his wife, Elizabeth, quickly fell into the hands of her second husband, Ezekiel Woodward, a much younger man whom she married within months of John's death[7], and who apparently envisioned other uses for his new wife's money. Most of John's daughters inherited nothing.

This left Sarah with limited marriage prospects, which threatened her social status—a fear realized when she married a former indentured servant. That husband died in debt in 1682, after which she married William Good. Sarah and William were held responsible for Sarah's late husband's debts and had some of their land seized and sold to satisfy creditors. By the time Sarah was accused of witchcraft, they had sold the rest of their land and still couldn't make ends meet. They were a cranky, destitute pair who rented rooms from neighbors with their four-year-old daughter, Dorothy (identified in some documents as Dorcas). Sarah was also pregnant.

According to Ann Putnam Jr.'s allegations, Sarah had begun sending her specter—her spirit—to pinch and harass her in its efforts to force the girl to sign the devil's book, thereby forming a covenant with Satan. Normally, accusations made by a tween girl against an adult wouldn't have carried much weight, but Ann was pointing the finger at a woman already disenfranchised and disliked by much of the community. Sarah Good was an easy target, and Ann's weren't the only allegations plaguing her. Elizabeth, the teenage maid in the Putnam house, said that Good had sent a wolf to stalk her. Elizabeth also said another Sarah—this one surnamed Osburne[8]—was tormenting her as well. Osburne, like Good, was already side-eyed by the villagers and townsfolk because she had upset the status quo in Salem Village after the death of her first husband, Robert Prince, who was related to the Putnam family by marriage. Prince had left property to his sons, but

Osburne remarried an indentured servant, and the couple decided to keep the inheritance for themselves. The situation overall wasn't dissimilar to what had happened with Sarah Good's inheritance, but the jilted heirs in this case were males that had been born to a respectable family. That their mother would dare to keep money for herself rather than bequeath it to her sons was scandalous.

Not that Osburne was living it up on her late husband's dime. When the allegations struck that she was tormenting Hubbard, Osburne was so sick she was largely bedridden. It was plain to those questioning her that she wasn't physically capable of the attacks ascribed to her, but a specter has no corporeal form. Her accusers insisted that her spirit was spry and accompanied by a "short hairy thing with two legs and two wings." As the tormented girls gave their testimony, they would point skyward and describe the hideous sights in such frightening detail that the magistrates believed the tales over their own unseeing eyes. This was by no means the first time that spectral evidence—or testimony in which witnesses claimed the accused appeared to them in spirit form and did them harm—had been admitted in court, though it more often had been presented in British courts, not the

A nineteenth-century engraving depicting a scene from the Salem witch trials.

colonies. Even so, it rarely had been given so much weight. Once it was deployed, it eviscerated any presumption of innocence.[9]

"Why do you hurt these children?" Magistrate Hathorne asked Osburne. "I do not hurt them," she replied. Unsatisfied, Hathorne pressed: "Who do you employ then to hurt them?"[10] Osburne insisted she was not doing anything to harm them. Hathorne asked the accusing children to stand up and identify Osburne as one of their tormenters. Each did. Osburne tried to reason with the magistrates, pointing to her own ailments as proof that she was "more likely bewitched than a witch."[11] Still, she was ordered to stand trial and sent to jail to await it with Sarah Good.

The girls on the other side of town, Betty and Abigail, had blamed a different woman for their woes—one whose involvement in their ordeal had apparently been borne of concern. Tituba Indian—possibly a South American indigenous person—was an enslaved house servant owned by Rev. Parris; she was believed by villagers to be the wife of another slave owned by Parris, John Indian. In hopes of flushing out whoever was causing the girls' fits, the couple baked a loaf of rye bread mixed with some urine from Betty and Abigail. The idea was that whoever had possessed the girls would have left behind traces of herself, which would in turn be passed onto the witch cake, as it was called. The loaf was then fed to the family dog, which was supposed to reveal the identity of the witch afflicting the girls. It didn't, but word spread that Tituba had performed this bit of counter-magic in an effort to unmask the girls' tormenter, and soon the girls claimed that it had been Tituba afflicting them all along.

Tituba was tortured and, being an enslaved person, may have been better equipped to understand that she was at the mercy of her accusers. While

The apprehension warrant for Tituba Indian and Sarah Osburne for suspicion of witchcraft, February 29, 1692, signed by John Hathorne.

Salem Febr the 29th day. 1691/2
33
Whereas Mrs Joseph Hutcheson Thomas Putnam
Edward Putnam and Thomas Preston Yeomen
of Salem Village in ye County of Essex personally
appeared before Us, And made Complaint on
behalfe of Theire Majesties against Sarah

Sarahs Good and Osburne denied wrongdoing, Tituba soon did what the magistrates asked of her: she confessed. It was clear from the questions posed to her by Hathorne that anything else would have been rejected. Rather than being asked what happened so that the narrative flowed from her freely, she was asked what evil spirit she had contacted. The devil made her do it, she told the court, and all of Salem was at risk. Both the town and village were teeming with witches—including Sarah Good and Sarah Osburne, who Tituba claimed were her partners in tormenting Betty, Abigail, Elizabeth, and Ann. Sarah Good tried to deflect: maybe it was Osburne alone, she offered. But the more Good denied the girls' charges, the more afflicted they seemed, their bodies writhing in pain as agonized screams escaped their lips. Even Good's husband, William, seemed ultimately convinced. He said, "I may say with tears that she is an enemy to all good."[12]

A nineteenth-century engraving of William Phips, the first governor of the Province of Massachusetts Bay, from 1692–94.

While Tituba's confession spared her from charges, her ordeal was far from over: She was to serve as the star witness against the two Sarahs, whose spirits she would claim had been sent after her to attack and blind her. She would also continue to provide authorities details about her rendezvous with witches, devils, and familiars, describing the devil's book that she said she had signed in blood. She saw others' names in the book, too, she insisted. In all, Tituba said nine witches were in the Salemites' midst. The terrified residents began eyeing each other with suspicion, and more accusations soon followed.

As mentioned on page 4, allegations of witchcraft were not uncommon in Massachusetts prior to 1692, but there were key differences between those instances and this new purported outbreak. For starters, the state was on the cusp of overhauling its legal system. Spring of 1692 brought with it the first royally appointed governor of the Province of Massachusetts Bay, William Phips, and a new charter that invalidated all the existing laws and courts that had been created in the colony. A new court was to be established as well, but not until June. With some forty people facing witchcraft charges by May, Phips decided faster action was necessary. He created a Court of Oyer and Terminer (from the Anglo-French, "to hear and determine"), the template for which was imported from England—which in turn had been inherited from northern France. This was an emergency court to deal with what the people of Salem truly felt was an emergency situation: an outbreak of witches. The hearings that followed bore some resemblance to trials of today. They were presided over by a panel of magistrates rather than a single judge, and while a jury also heard the presented evidence, the magistrates weren't constrained from opining in jurors' presence. The notion of confirmation bias—a tendency to favor information that confirms one's beliefs—didn't exist. Also, there were no prosecutors and no defense lawyers. The magistrates posed leading questions crafted from a presumption of guilt, and no witnesses were called on defendants' behalf to counter that presumption. The only defense the accused had against the charges was their own word.

Just as much of these procedures had been imported from across the pond, so too had the punishment for witchcraft. Some of the earliest documented witch trials were in England in the early fifteenth century. In one, a woman named Margery Jourdemayne was burned alive at the stake in 1441 after providing the duchess of Gloucester a potion in hopes of aiding conception. A century later, King Henry VIII officially codified the crime of witchcraft as not just a felony, but a capital offense, in his Witchcraft Act of 1541. A supposed witchcraft outbreak kicked off with the death of an infant in the late 1500s in a small German settlement near present-day Trier. The execution of the suspect in that case, a woman named Eva, was meant to stanch the spread, but that effort clearly failed. In a twenty-year span, approximately five hundred people—nearly one-quarter of the settlement's residents—were killed for witchcraft.[13] In the late sixteenth to early seventeenth century, King James I of Britain was such a believer in witches that he aided in hunts and wrote a book called *Daemonologie*, first published in 1597. A popular read of the time, the book declared that it was necessary to expose, try, and execute witches. The book likely informed William Shakespeare's depictions of the three witches in *Macbeth*[14], along with the high-profile trial of a young Englishwoman named Anne Gunter—who in 1606 confessed that she'd lied about three women cursing her with witchcraft.[15] One hundred years later, the beliefs espoused in that book would serve as a backdrop for the Salem trials.

In hindsight, the events in Salem unfurled quickly—the entire ordeal was over within a year's time—but it must have felt agonizingly slow for those caught amid the panic. Accusations trickled out day after day. What began with four girls accusing three marginalized women soon ballooned close to Trier levels. The pool of accusers broadened as well, making it tougher for the skeptics in Salem to voice their doubts. One was a man named John Proctor,[16] a landowner and farmer. By 1692, he'd fathered some nine children and was married to his third wife, Elizabeth. From the onset of the witchcraft allegations, he'd been dubious. He told neighbor Samuel Sibley: "If those girls were allowed to continue, we should all be devils and witches quickly. They should rather be had to the whipping post."[17] When Proctor's servant, Mary Warren, began showing signs of affliction, Proctor threatened to beat the spirits out of her. Described as a huge man, stocky in build, Proctor's threat was no doubt terrifying to the girl, though it shouldn't have mattered much to Satan. Thus, when Mary's symptoms suddenly abated, Proctor's skepticism was bolstered. Then accusations started coming from more respected members of the community–including the elder Ann Putnam, mother of one of the original accusers. Other adults, women and a few men, claimed to be stricken with the same limb-stiffening, voice-stealing affliction that had struck the original girls. Proctor's ridicule put his family in the crosshairs. His servant's symptoms returned, and Mary soon joined the younger Ann in accusing Proctor's wife, Elizabeth, of afflicting them. John was outraged, and during the court hearing to determine whether Elizabeth should face trial, several of her accusers also accused him. Elizabeth was ordered to stand trial, and John was arrested. Even the Proctors' two children would be accused before the spate was over. The message sent to other doubters was clear: Speak up, and you just might be labeled a witch. The same was true for accusers who rescinded their allegations, as happened with Mary Warren. When she attempted to walk back her accusations by saying that she and the others were faking their symptoms, she prompted the afflicted to accuse her of sending her specter to torment them. She retracted her retraction.

"IF THOSE GIRLS WERE ALLOWED TO CONTINUE, WE SHOULD ALL BE DEVILS AND WITCHES QUICKLY. THEY SHOULD RATHER BE HAD TO THE WHIPPING POST."

It's telling that even one of the accusers at the time was willing, however briefly, to say not only that she was faking but that she was sure everyone else was, too. That fuels one of the theories behind what caused the baffling symptoms all those centuries ago: jealous revenge. Many of the accusations came from young girls who worked as servants and were afforded very little control in their day-to-day lives. It was common for employers to beat their workers, and girls had it worse than most. Their only hope for a better life was to marry into one, yet there was a shortage of young men in Salem, making the pickings slim. Imagine how it must have felt for them to finally feel heard in this society, to finally have a semblance of power.

Other possible causes for the confounding symptoms that swept through Salem have been posited over the centuries since, including ones rooted in medical issues, such as ergotism, a toxic condition produced by eating grain infected with ergot fungus. Supporters of the theory point to the hallucinogenic effects of ergotism, which could explain the visions the afflicted described of seeing spirits and their animal helpers floating over judges' heads during trial. To Salem historian and author Emerson Baker, however, the explanation falls short because documentation suggests symptoms came and went, which isn't typical of ergot poisoning, and also didn't hit everyone in the household, as likely would be the case if the affected food were a staple such as bread.[18]

Another possible cause—one that Baker deems more likely—was what we'd today call post-traumatic stress disorder. Some of the girls afflicted had come to Salem as refugees from elsewhere in New England, where battles raged between settlers and Native peoples. Some had been orphaned in vicious conflicts marred by horrific atrocities—rapes, beheadings, scalpings. It's possible some of the girls' initial symptoms were physical and psychological manifestations of PTSD, which sparked conversion disorder, or a mass psychosis, in others, once it was labeled witchcraft. In his book *A Storm of Witchcraft*, Baker also argues that at least some of the two hundred-plus allegations must have been deliberate acts of fraud:

> **The fact that someone was afflicted by a psychological disorder that was beyond his or her control does not rule out the possibility that some of that person's actions were deliberate and willful acts of calumny and deception.[19]**

Three months after the panic began, the stakes became clear. Osburne, who'd been sick when she entered jail, died in her cell. Her fate was predictable, as the conditions in the jail were dismal. As the months passed and the number of accused went from a handful to scores, conditions grew even worse. Prisoners sat amid their own waste, feces clinging to their clothes and skin, their bodies crawling with lice and fleas. Many fell sick with respiratory illnesses. In the seventeenth century, it was common to find soap made of lye in one's home, but such a luxury wasn't afforded to inmates—who, incidentally, were charged for their disgusting, sickness-spreading room and board. Sarah Good gave birth in this cesspool, and, not surprisingly, her infant died soon after. Her daughter, Dorothy, was accused and jailed alongside her mother. Though she ultimately survived, the psychological damage done to Dorothy was said to have scarred her beyond repair. She would die poor and homeless by age sixteen.

Proctor's arrest was in April 1692. At this point, a couple of people had died in the jail, but no one had been executed for heresy. That wouldn't happen until June, with the public hanging of Bridget Bishop. She was a thrice-married woman accused of tormenting young Ann Putnam, Mary Walcott, Elizabeth Hubbard, and Mercy Lewis. "She calls the Devil her god!" Ann screamed. Bewildered, Bridget replied, "I never saw these persons before, nor was I in this place before. I am as innocent as the child unborn. I am innocent of a witch." Unfortunately for Bridget, this wasn't the first time she'd faced allegations of witchcraft. Her first husband had died after six years of marriage, after which she remarried, this time to a man who would die just one year later. People thought two husbands dying within two years was too much, so she had been tried for bewitching her second husband after his death. Despite being acquitted for lack of evidence, Bridget had lived for 20 years with a cloud of suspicion hanging over her head. The stench of the previous allegations stubbornly clung to her. When accused, Bridget's third husband, Edward Bishop, joined the chorus that maligned her. The Rev. Cotton Mather wrote at the time: "There was little occasion to prove the witchcraft, it being evident and notorious to all beholders." On June 10, 1692, Bridget Bishop was the first person accused of witchcraft to be hanged in Salem. The hanging apparently prompted one of the special court's judges to resign in protest, which allowed subsequent hangings to happen at a faster clip. Eleven people—including John Proctor—would die in three public hangings between then and August.

The Rev. George Burroughs—the minister who'd left Salem because parishioners stopped paying his salary—had been hanged alongside Proctor on August 19. Burroughs had long moved away from the town, yet some of the afflicted claimed his spirit returned to them regularly to torment them. Not only that, but his accusers said in court that they could see the ghosts of four people Burroughs had murdered. As Baker wrote: "They were the ghosts of Burroughs's first two wives, as well as the wife and daughter of Reverend Deodat Lawson, another former Salem Village minister who happened to be present in the courtroom."[20] Burroughs's denials struck the judges as exactly what a witch would say. He was convicted and hanged despite his impassioned pleas of innocence, which included a perfect recitation of the Lord's Prayer—a feat believed impossible for a witch. The sight of a once-beloved community member—and a man of God, no less—dangling lifeless from the end of a rope rattled some onlookers, but it didn't stop the allegations.

The turning point in public opinion came with the particularly gruesome death of Giles Cory, an eighty-year-old man who was accused of witchcraft with his wife, Martha. To underscore how powerless servants were at the time, Giles previously had been convicted of brutally and fatally beating a teenage servant about fifteen years prior to the Salem trial, for which he was only fined. Once accused of witchcraft, he risked a hangman's noose, which he devised a plan to avoid. The law at the time stated that a person faced trial only after entering a plea of guilty or innocent to a capital crime, so Cory chose to stand mute on the charge. Judge Jonathan Corwin was adamant that Cory not escape justice, so he heeded a suggestion from Thomas Putnam and used a method that had originated in France called *peine forte et dure*—meaning "hard and forceful

A c. 1874 engraving depicting two men offering pen and paper to Martha Cory, for her to write her confession as a witch. She was hanged on September 22, 1692.

punishment." Giles was stripped naked and forced to lay in the street. Atop his body were placed heavy boards, and atop the boards were placed stones. As the weight accumulated, Giles was implored to enter his plea. He refused. At one point, the pressure from the stones crushing his body was so great that his eyes bulged and from his mouth he thrust his tongue, which Corwin shoved back in with his cane. It took two days of unfathomable torture for Giles Cory to finally die.

Though Giles didn't save himself, the gruesomeness of his slow and painful death on September 19 prompted a shift in public sentiment. That shift seemed solidified three days later with the final batch of Salem hangings, a spectacle that included Giles's wife, Martha. The Rev. Increase Mather, who was president of Harvard College at Cambridge, wrote in his 1693 book *Cases of Conscience Concerning Evil Spirits*, that it would be better to let ten witches go free than shed the blood of even one person wrongly accused of witchcraft.

And therein lies the real legacy of the Salem witch trials beyond the hefty body count (nineteen people were hanged, one was pressed to death, and five more died in jail). Some of the people responsible for the situation regretted what they had done and publicly repented. "What I did was ignorantly, being deluded by Satan," the younger Ann Putnam wrote in a confession read publicly fourteen years after the fervor subsided. "I desire to lie in the dust, and to be humbled for it, in that I was a cause, with others, of so sad a calamity and earnestly beg forgiveness of God, and from all those unto whom I have given just cause of sorrow and offense, whose relations were taken away or accused."[21]

While Ann did not place blame at her father's feet, some historians have wondered how much of Thomas Putnam's personal vendettas helped fuel the accusations of his daughter (and wife, as the elder Ann also leveled witchcraft allegations as the "outbreak" unfolded). Both parents died of an unknown illness within weeks of each other in 1699, seven years before young Ann's confession. They, like so many others, went to their graves making no such confession. Most of the judges who had enforced death sentences denied wrongdoing as well. But Ann Putnam's repentance was bolstered by that of Samuel Sewell, one of the judges. He, too, publicly confessed, then set aside a day each year for the remainder of his life to fast and pray forgiveness. He continued the practice until his death in 1730.

Legal Legacy

The ripple effects of the horror unleashed in Salem are reflected in the changed judicial system that formed in its wake, including:

- Spectral evidence (or testimony in which witnesses alleged the accused appeared to them in spirit form) was prohibited from being admitted into courts.
- While our current doctrine evolved over the centuries, Salem underscored doubts and sparked discussion about the reliability of hearsay evidence—specifically rumors, assumptions, and gossip.
- The Salem cases helped shape the concept of "innocent until proven guilty," a cornerstone of American jurisprudence. The opposite was true during the trials: many of those who died were killed because they weren't able to prove that they weren't witches.
- While it took centuries for our judicial system to officially embrace a defendant's right to counsel in most cases, Salem underscored the importance of representation and the ability to cross-examine witnesses. No longer are judges allowed to serve as prosecutor, defense lawyer, judge, and executioner.

2

The Dream Team Representing Levi Weeks

(1800)

Gulielma Sands was a nobody when her life began in 1777. The daughter of a Quaker preacher who had died in England when she was young, Gulielma—reported by newspapers of the time as called Juliana, but known to her friends as Elma—maintained an "amiable and irreproachable character"[1] in Manhattan, where she lived for a time with her sickly mother. Soon, however, Elma found herself pawned off on relatives as her mother's health declined. By the time she was twenty-two years old, Elma had lived for several years with a married couple named Catherine and Elias Ring, identified in some accounts as Elma's aunt and uncle, in others as her cousins, and in others still as more distant family. Whatever the case, the Rings ran a boarding house on Greenwich Street in Manhattan, where Elma lived and fell in love—and from which she disappeared one frigid evening in December 1799.

The country at this point was still young, as was its legal system, though big strides had been made since the days of the Salem witch trials. For starters, prosecutors existed, though they weren't always hired. Victims tended to represent themselves in court, but that of course wasn't possible if said victim had been slain. In that situation, an attorney would be brought in to represent those who couldn't represent themselves. Defense lawyers were even less common. Typically, a defendant would defend himself. As English barrister William Hawkins wrote in *A Treatise of Pleas of the Crown*—a 1716 publication that informed the American judicial system—the thinking was that any innocent defendant should have no trouble representing themselves. Hawkins wrote, "It requires no manner of skill to make a plain and honest defense."[2]

The gruesome death of Elma Sands would challenge that thinking, as the suspect in the case deployed the nation's first-ever legal dream team—one that included founding father Alexander Hamilton and the man who would kill him in a duel just a few years later, Aaron Burr.

The Rings' boarding house was one of hundreds of such establishments dotting New York. As the eighteenth century drew to a close, New York's population was around 60,000—a miniscule amount compared to today, but nearly double the number of people who'd lived there even just ten years prior. The exploding growth, coupled with a spate of conflagrations, left the area with a housing shortage that boarding houses helped remedy. As such, the Rings' home served as refuge to a variety of people, mostly men, who typically were passing through town or were otherwise in transition, perhaps waiting for homes of their own to be built somewhere nearby. Elma was one of the few single women who lived at the boarding house, and she helped Catherine and Elias care for their guests—one of whom swept Elma off her feet.

Levi Weeks was a talented house carpenter who worked with his brother, Ezra. The two came from a large family—there were eleven children born to their parents, ten of whom lived past infancy, surprisingly—but they were closest with each other, and their eventual career interests aligned enough that they became business partners as adults. Ezra would oversee

An 1810 drawing of Greenwich Street on the lower west side of Manhattan by Anne-Marguérite-Henriette Rouillé de Marigny depicts the area much as it would have looked around the time Elma lived there.

construction projects that Levi would work on. Ezra, as the brains of the business, made good money, while Levi was the lesser-paid brawn of the duo. Still, to a young woman like Elma of decidedly modest means, Levi had pedigree. Even more important to the charming young woman, he had heart—and he made it plain that her name was etched on it. In the fall of 1799, when the nation was barely older than Elma herself, the couple's love grew. Levi hadn't been the first boarder to become smitten with Elma, but he was the first to hold her attention in return. In early December, Elma shared a secret with Catherine's sister, Hope. She and Levi were set to steal away on December 22 to be married, she excitedly shared, making Hope promise not to tell a soul. Hope had seen the attraction blossoming between the two and was elated to hear that vows were in the future. She began helping Elma make the arrangements.

For weeks, she kept her promise to keep the plans a secret, but on December 21—the day before the nuptials—she couldn't hold it in any longer. She told Catherine about Elma's impending plans. Catherine, of course, had witnessed the relationship's genesis. At first, she hadn't been happy. She felt protective of Elma, and she worried that Levi's intentions weren't honorable. Catherine had even taken to sneaking up on the two from time to time. She would take her shoes off to tiptoe to Elma's door, where she'd spy on Levi in the young woman's room. Each time she'd done so, she'd been impressed with Levi's behavior. He seemed respectful and genuinely concerned for Elma. Eventually Catherine was comfortable enough that she didn't worry about leaving Elma and Levi together in the house while she visited family for six weeks.[3] Granted, others were around—including Elias, Catherine's husband—to make sure nothing untoward happened, but Catherine was impressed by how close the two had seem to grow during her absence. "After my return, I paid strict attention to their conduct and saw an appearance of mutual attachment, but nothing improper," Catherine would later say.[4] For a spell, Elma had fallen sick, and it was endearing to Catherine how worried Levi seemed to be about her. He was clearly smitten, enough so that when Hope spilled the secret about the planned elopement, Catherine was only upset with the *how* of things, not the *what*. She gently confronted Elma the next day and tried to persuade her to have a proper wedding. Elma said that wasn't possible. Levi wanted to keep the marriage plans a secret, especially from his brother Ezra, so the two had to elope. Given their mixed stations in life, this wasn't a huge surprise. Ezra Weeks was wealthy, after all, and it made sense to Catherine that he'd want his younger brother to marry someone with money and status, too. Elma didn't have money, but she was a fine girl, "virtuous and modest,"[5] who loved Levi, so Catherine relented in her opposition and hoped that Ezra would warm to Elma just as she had warmed to Levi.

Much of December 22 was mundane. Catherine tended to her boarders while sneaking side conversations with Elma about the evening's big plans. Around noon, Levi returned from visiting his brother Ezra with an injured knee. Elma came to his aid, dressing his knee in a bandage. This caught Catherine's attention because the injury at first seemed bad enough to threaten the wedding.

"Levi, you won't be able to go out today," Sylvanus Russel, a fellow boarder, said, though he was ignorant that anything special was on the docket that evening.

"I am determined to tonight," Levi replied.[6]

Catherine saw this exchange as sweet evidence of the plans to which she had to play dumb. Later that night, she quietly helped Elma get dressed in her chosen wedding clothes while saying nothing to her husband, Elias, and betraying no insider knowledge to Levi. It would be a cold night in New York and Elma didn't have a hand warmer, so she borrowed a fur muff from a neighbor and promised to return it. Just shy of 8:00 p.m., Elma began watching the front door. Catherine fretted. She told Elma that she worried Levi wouldn't show. Elma was "perfectly cheerful," and said she didn't fear. She knew he'd come at eight as promised. Levi did arrive, though a few minutes late. He entered a room where he found Elias, Catherine, Elma, and two boarders sitting. They visited a few minutes before the boarders went to bed, after which Catherine pinned a shawl on Elma, who seemed paler and more agitated than she had all day. Catherine gently assuaged what she assumed were natural pre-wedding jitters and wished her well. Next Catherine heard whispers and rustling sounds and then the opening and closing of the front door. She would never see Elma alive again.

Catherine found it odd that Levi had come home around 10:00 p.m. that night to stay in his room, and odder still that he'd asked Catherine if Elma had gone to bed.

"No," Catherine replied. "She is gone out, at least I saw her ready to go and have good reason to think she went."

"I'm surprised she should go out so late at night and alone," Levi said.

"I've no reason to think she went alone," Catherine answered. It was a confusing exchange, to be sure, but she didn't press him.[7] The wedding had been a secret, after all, and the couple might have sound reasons for wanting to spend their wedding night apart. Maybe it had to do with the way they intended to tell Ezra. Or maybe they'd postponed the plans. Either way, Catherine didn't feel she could ask questions about a situation she wasn't supposed to know anything about. Catherine lit a candle and searched the house, thinking maybe Elma had quietly returned. Twice she approached Levi's closed door but stopped short of knocking. Instead, she went to bed and hoped that the next day would bring clarity.

The morning unfolded with such regularity that Catherine's nerves quieted even though she still wasn't sure where Elma had gone. It wasn't unusual for the young woman to stay the night with friends in town. Catherine began to piece together scenarios in her mind: Perhaps Levi had gotten cold feet and Elma was too heartbroken or embarrassed to return to the Rings' home. Levi, for his part, came to breakfast as usual. No one mentioned Elma in the morning. Hours later, Levi returned after being out a while and again asked if Elma had returned. Catherine said no.

"Have you sent anywhere for her?" he asked Catherine.

"No," she replied, explaining that she hadn't thought of sending for her because she kept expecting her to return at any moment. Finally, Catherine came clean. "Levi," she said, "to tell thee the truth, I believe she went thee, she told me she was to."

Levi looked surprised. "If she'd gone with me, she would have come [home] with me," he said.[8]

Later in the day, Catherine learned that Elma's friends hadn't seen her after all. No one had seen her since the night of the twenty-second. This is when the panic crept in. Hope, Catherine's sister, confronted Levi, demanding to know where Elma had gone. Levi said he had no idea: "Do you think if

I knew where she was I would not tell you?" Seeing how agitated Catherine was, the next morning his approach softened. "Mrs. Ring, don't grieve so," he said. "I am in hopes things will turn out better than you expect."[9]

Finally, on the twenty-fourth, Catherine's unease turned to dread. She filled her husband in on the wedding plans, which prompted Elias to angrily confront Levi and demand to know what had happened after he and Elma left the house the previous night. Levi again claimed ignorance.

"Stop, Levi, this matter has become so serious. I can stand it no longer," Catherine said. She told him she knew that his and Elma's plans had been to marry the other night, and that she'd only been as patient as she'd been because she trusted him so much. As she spoke, Levi turned pale and started to tremble. He clasped his hands together and began to cry.

"I'm ruined! I'm ruined!" he wailed. "I'm undone forever, unless she appears to clear me—my existence will be only a burden!"[10]

"I'M RUINED! I'M RUINED! I'M UNDONE FOREVER, UNLESS SHE APPEARS TO CLEAR ME—MY EXISTENCE WILL BE ONLY A BURDEN!"

After he regrouped, he stammered that it simply wasn't true. There had been no wedding plans, he insisted. He would never marry without his brother's approval. The Rings didn't know what to think. Elias began organizing search parties. He and Catherine felt sure that Levi knew something he wasn't sharing, but without any evidence that something bad had happened to Elma—something beyond her leaving town a heartbroken mess—there wasn't much they could do. Another day passed, and then another, with no word. The tension in the house was thick, the mood, heavy. Levi saw Catherine worrying with friends and, in an ill-advised attempt to assuage her concerns, approached her.

"Give her up," he said of Elma. "She is gone no doubt, and all our grieving would do no good." His tone was meant to comfort, but his words had the opposite effect. Catherine asked him what he meant. "Mrs. Ring, it's my firm belief she's now in eternity; it certainly is, therefore make yourself easy, for your mourning will never bring her back."[11] Word spread across town about the missing girl and her lover's strange certainty that she'd died. Elias ordered that the docks near his home be dragged, but the search proved fruitless. Just as Christmas had come and gone with no answers, so too did New Year's Eve and Day. Finally, on January 2, an earlier discovery made by some boys in what was then called Lispenard's Meadows (in what is now Tribeca) came to light. It'd been about a week since the boys had noticed an

A nineteenth-century engraving of Lispenard's Meadows near present-day Canal Street in New York City, where boys discovered Elma's body in the Manhattan Well.

odd item floating in a well, which they'd fished out of the murky water and taken home. It was a handwarmer—*the* handwarmer that Elma had borrowed that cold night in December when she was last seen. The boys led authorities to the stone well, at the bottom of which was Elma's bruised and battered body. Her clothes were ripped, and her neck had seemingly been broken. The coroner determined that, contrary to rapidly spreading rumors fueled by the supposedly secret marriage plans, Elma wasn't pregnant. The cause of death was officially declared murder.

Levi Weeks was immediately a suspect. It didn't help that witnesses stepped forward to say they'd noticed a single sleigh carrying two men and one woman tearing through the meadow near the well. It had stood out because the sleigh didn't have bells attached to it, which made it dangerously stealthy on a dark night predating reliable electric light bulbs by eighty years. While the sleigh had been moving too quickly for anyone to get a good look at its occupants, its description matched that of a horse and sleigh belonging to Ezra Weeks. Not only that, but Susanna Broad, an elderly neighbor of Ezra's, said that she heard the gate to his lumberyard fly open around 8:00 p.m., followed by the sound of his single-horse, bell-less sleigh disappearing into the night. Other witnesses reported hearing a young woman scream, "Murder, murder!" and "Oh, Lord have mercy upon me!" between 8:00 and 9:00 p.m. on December 22.[12]

As soon as Elma's body was found, Ezra Weeks knew things looked bad for his brother. In the days after the grisly discovery, however, something unusual happened that worried Ezra further: Elma's body was put on display in an open casket in front of the Rings' boarding house. While viewing unpreserved bodies wasn't unusual in this era before embalming practices were widely accepted, bodies that had endured trauma weren't typically displayed. So upset were the Rings, however, that they presented the remains of their surrogate daughter publicly. Thousands of people filed by to view for themselves the scrapes on her hands, marks on her neck, bruises on her breasts. Word had spread that her neck had been broken, though a couple of physicians in town took it upon themselves to examine her corpse and found her neck intact. However, one of her collar bones was another matter altogether. In the end, Elma's injuries outraged onlookers and fueled public interest in the case.

Levi asked his brother to serve as his counsel. This wasn't unusual for the time. When the nation was new, neither the defense nor the prosecution typically retained lawyers to represent them. English criminal procedure, which is what the colonists transplanted in America, was designed differently, often with the victim of the crime arguing the case to a court. Because that couldn't happen in this scenario, that role was filled instead by the well-known, well-respected lawyer Cadwallader David Colden, who'd been named after his grandfather, the former royal lieutenant-governor of New York. The younger Colden studied with one of New York's premier attorneys before being admitted to the bar in 1791. By decade's end, he'd been appointed district attorney for New York City—and from 1818 to 1821, served as its mayor.

Levi and Ezra Weeks were understandably worried about their chances facing off against such a learned legal foe, so Ezra tapped some of his high-profile clients, one of whom just so happened to be Founding Father and first secretary of the treasury Alexander Hamilton. Ezra had been building a mansion for Hamilton, whose bills weren't up to date. That likely played into his decision to represent Levi Weeks, as was the fact that at this point in his life, his once-bright star was waning. Just three years earlier, he'd endured

Portraits, from left to right, of the first legal dream team: Alexander Hamilton, Aaron Burr, and Henry Brockholst Livingston; all engravings c. 1902.

the biggest scandal of his life—one that essentially ended any presidential aspirations—when he admitted having an affair with a young married woman named Maria Reynolds.

Hamilton wouldn't defend the accused alone. Aaron Burr was also a lawyer, and in 1800—the year this case would unfold—he was running for president on what was then the Democratic-Republican ticket. (He would lose to Thomas Jefferson, but he was elected vice president.) Hamilton and Burr worked with one more accomplished lawyer. Though his name isn't as well known today, at the time, he was as big a star as were his partners. Henry Brockholst Livingston had been a captain in the Continental Army after graduating the College of New Jersey, later renamed Princeton. After the Revolutionary War, he studied law and entered the New York bar in 1783, where he kept a private practice for the next two decades while also serving in the state assembly.

He was not only a high-profile lawyer, but he was one of thirteen children born to William Livingston, who'd served as the first governor of New Jersey.[13] This was a man who, in 1789, had delivered the first Independence Day speech with George Washington in the audience. Livingston also had served on the staff of General Philip Schuyler, whose daughter Eliza was married to Hamilton.

These were legitimate celebrities in New York. Hamilton and Burr were among the founders of the Manhattan Company, which had financed the Manhattan Well—part of a new water supply system—in which Elma's body was found. Burr had also built the road leading up to it.[14] Together with

Livingston, the trio formed the country's first legal dream team—which led to such nationwide interest in the outcome that it marked the first murder trial in US history for which transcripts were saved.

During the trial, Levi didn't testify on his own behalf, as was far more common than it is nowadays. Rather, his team of lawyers did what we consider standard now: they focused on arguing that prosecutors had too weak a case for the jury to convict Levi Weeks. This seemed a risky approach because Colden had a good bit of evidence. He not only had the damning testimony of Catherine and Elias Ring, as well as Ezra's neighbor Susanna Broad, but he had a woman named Catherine Lyon who testified that she saw Elma—whom she knew personally—and spoke to her just after 8:00 p.m. near the well, after which she'd sworn she heard her friend scream "Oh, save me!"[15] This was important because it countered one of Levi's main defenses—namely, that it was possible Elma had killed herself by jumping into the well.

An illustration from *Frank Leslie's Illustrated Newspaper*, entitled "Aaron Burr's Stratagem at the Weeks Trial," 1882.

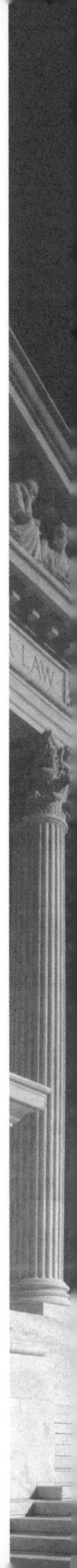

Levi's lawyers worked to dismantle the evidence against him. They pointed out that though Catherine Ring *thought* she heard Elma and Levi leave the boarding house together, she didn't actually see them leave. She'd assumed it was them when the front door opened and closed because she'd watched them getting ready to leave minutes earlier. The people who reported seeing a single-horse sleigh barreling through the night didn't get a good look at the occupants because it was well after sunset and the sleigh was traveling too quickly. They couldn't even say for sure what color the horse was, aside from it being dark hued. And Broad's testimony crumbled on cross-examination when she said that she'd heard Ezra's gate open and his bell-less sleigh depart a few days after Christmas rather than before.[16]

Levi's team also attacked the victim's character—a once-taboo approach that, again, is commonplace today. They called as a witness neighbor Joseph Watkins, who said that while Catherine Ring was away in the country for her six-week vacation, he heard loud, scandalous noises coming from Elma's room. He could hear two voices, a man's and a woman's, and while the woman's was too quiet to hear, he thought the man's was Elias. He could tell the difference between Elias and Levi's voices, he said, because "Ring's is a high-sounding voice, that of Week's a low soft voice."[17] He said he'd mentioned as much to his own wife as they listened to the "shaking of the bed."

"I told my wife that girl will be ruined," Watkins testified.[18] He heard similar bed-rattling sounds between eight and fourteen times over a few weeks' span. He said the noises stopped once Catherine Ring returned from her sojourn.

Not content to merely paint Elma as a possible hussy, they also suggested she might be a drug addict. They called witnesses who testified that Elma was overly reliant on a popular drug called laudanum, a diluted form of opium used as a painkiller and cough suppressant. Elma reportedly was fond of it and had a high enough tolerance to it that people were surprised by the dosage they saw a doctor administer to her.

While Livingston, Hamilton, and Burr called witnesses to craft such an unflattering portrait of Elma, the witnesses called on Levi's behalf described him as trustworthy, industrious, reputable, and friendly. His brother Ezra provided his alibi. He swore that Levi had been with him until 8:00 p.m., then away for fifteen minutes, then with him again until nearly 10:00. If true, that would have left him only a quarter-hour window to go to the boarding house, meet Elma, return to his brother's to borrow a sleigh, speed to the Manhattan Well, kill Elma, and return the sleigh to reunite with his brother.

Hamilton and company didn't solely rely on tarnishing Elma's reputation and offering a brother's alibi. They also offered alternate suspects. After the neighbor suggested an illicit affair between Elma and Elias Ring, his name was of course floated. Next, the defense suggested one of the Rings' boarders—a man named Richard David Croucher. Croucher was a British immigrant, which, so soon after the Revolutionary War, was hardly an applauded trait, especially not in a room full of war veterans. A cloth merchant,[19] Croucher had also taken a particular interest in the case, passing out pamphlets and spreading gossip that declared Levi the killer. On the stand, Croucher seemed all too eager to implicate Levi further. Of Levi and Elma, he said that "at a time when they were less cautious than usual, I saw them in a very intimate situation."[20] He also, unwisely even if true, placed himself at the crime scene, according to a woman who chatted with him soon after. She relayed that Croucher said he went past the Manhattan Well almost

A view of New York's City Hall (center, now Federal Hall) and the surrounding buildings, as it looked in 1797, three years before the Weeks trial was held there.

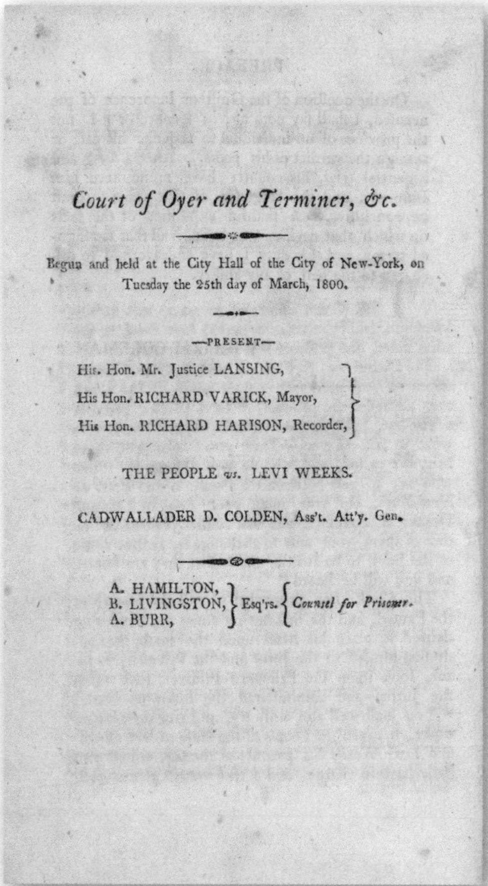

Court of Oyer and Terminer, &c.

Begun and held at the City Hall of the City of New-York, on Tuesday the 25th day of March, 1800.

—PRESENT—

His. Hon. Mr. Justice LANSING,
His Hon. RICHARD VARICK, Mayor,
His Hon. RICHARD HARISON, Recorder,

THE PEOPLE *vs.* LEVI WEEKS.

CADWALLADER D. COLDEN, Ass't. Att'y. Gen.

A. HAMILTON,
B. LIVINGSTON, Esq'rs. *Counsel for Prisoner.*
A. BURR,

A page from a report on the Weeks trial published by a stationery shop across the street from City Hall in 1800, listing the attorneys in the case.

every day and had even been there the day of the murder. He lamented being there at the wrong time to save Elma.

Croucher seemed so determined to pin murder on Levi that, on cross-examination, Aaron Burr dramatically bellowed: "And where, sir, was you on the night of the twenty-second of December, 1799?" Croucher offered an alibi: He was dining with a rich lady on Bowery Lane who'd invited some friends over because it was her son's birthday. He admitted he'd gone in and out, but the rich lady testified that she was certain he was with her between 8:00 and 11:00 p.m. If Burr had hoped for a tortured confession on the stand, he didn't get it. Still, they did what would become a mainstay tactic for defense lawyers: they muddied the waters enough. After testimony from seventy-five witnesses over the two-day trial, the jury stepped out at 2:26 a.m. At 2:30 a.m., they returned with their verdict: it took them four minutes to decide Levi was not guilty.

Livingston, Hamilton, and Burr had done something unprecedented: they'd joined forces as a legal team to nail an acquittal for their client. Catherine Ring was devastated. She was not only certain that Levi Weeks had bought his freedom with high-priced lawyers, but she'd watched Elma's reputation be destroyed in the process. She reportedly approached Hamilton and said: "If thee dies a natural death, I shall think there is no justice in Heaven."[21]

As it turned out, none of the key players in this case seem to have fared well in the aftermath. For starters, Elias Ring appears to have run out of money around 1820 because he was listed as insolvent in the *New-York Evening Post*. One of the justices who weighed the case was lost at sea.

Burr infamously killed Hamilton in an illegal duel in 1804, just four years after they probably celebrated the win in this case. While Burr escaped prosecution, he spent the rest of his life an outcast. Levi Weeks did, too. The popular sentiment was that he was the only person with motive to kill Elma Sands, so he must have done it. Even worse, he'd gotten away with it because his rich brother was able to buy his freedom by not just hiring fancy lawyers, but by straight-up changing the process that most accused people had faced under English-turned-American law. Levi moved first to Massachusetts, and then, in 1809, to Mississippi, where he married a woman named Ann Greenleaf and had three children. He earned a reputation as a noted architect there. On September 20, 1819, he died at age forty-three of yellow fever, leaving behind his pregnant wife and three children. One of the children died at age five on November 5, less than four weeks from the date Ann gave birth to Levi's last child—a boy she named Levi Hinckley.

In hindsight, it turned out that Croucher was perhaps as villainous as Levi's lawyers believed, based on tidbits gathered from various newspaper archives. Just three months after Levi Weeks was acquitted, Croucher was accused of raping a thirteen-year-old girl. A story in the *Lancaster Intelligencer* read: "The prisoner is a man of about 40, with every mark on his face of a crafty, unprincipled villain. The girl . . . told her story with artlessness, and in tears. The horror of the diabolical scene seemed still fresh in her memory. . . . The criminal had no other apology than that she was a whore."[22] He was convicted on July 8, 1800, and sentenced to life in prison. Three years later, the *Evening Post* wrote that he'd been pardoned by George Clinton, New York's first governor, who'd later become the United States' fourth vice president. Clinton thought Croucher was mentally ill and, because of that, his punishment had been too severe. Croucher doesn't appear to have been reformed, however. According to the *Evening Post*, after he was released, Croucher robbed a man. He fled back to England, where, according to a book written by one of Hamilton's sons in 1865, Croucher committed another "heinous crime" and was executed.

Elma Sands could never have imagined the impact her death would have on the American judicial system. She'd been a quiet, essentially orphaned nobody in life who simply wanted to marry the man she loved. Instead, she bundled up on that cold winter night more than 220 years ago to greet her killer, whose identity officially remains a mystery to this day.

Legal Legacy

After the formation of America's first legal dream team, the approach to defending people accused of crimes forever shifted. Among the changes:

- Defendants recognized that representing themselves in court, as had long been typical, wasn't necessarily ideal. Outside attorneys schooled in law were seen as an important asset to making one's case.
- The schism between haves and have-nots in court was solidified: defendants with the financial means began hiring better attorneys who not only were well-educated but who also could perform well in courtrooms.
- Because the case was so well-documented, the defense lawyers' tactic—muddying the waters by accusing someone else of committing the murder—became standard fare.

3

Daniel Sickles's Claim of Temporary Insanity

(1859)

Philip Barton Key II stood in Washington, DC's Lafayette Square, waving his handkerchief in the air, hoping to catch the eye of his lover. It was Sunday, February 27, 1859, and he'd last seen Teresa on Wednesday. She would be expecting his signal. The two had only managed to stay apart a few days at a time for more than a year, so hungry were they for each other.

Key pulled from his pocket a pair of opera glasses he used to watch for Teresa's signals from the window of her home, but she didn't appear. This was unusual, but Key had plenty to do in DC's storied square. He was a high-profile figure, having been appointed US District Attorney six years earlier by President Franklin Pierce. It was an important post, representing the government in cases heard in federal court—a post that had previously been held by his late father, Francis Scott Key, a prominent lawyer who is most remembered today for having written the lyrics to "The Star-Spangled Banner." Soon, the younger Key ran into Samuel F. Butterworth, another renowned lawyer, and the two exchanged chitchat before Key's eye was caught by another political celebrity heading his way. Key knew Daniel Sickles so well that he extended his hand in greeting. Sickles pulled a gun and shot a bullet through that hand. "You have dishonored my bed and family, you scoundrel—prepare to die!" he screamed.[1]

If Key had known that his friend Sickles had spent the previous night sleepless and sobbing, he might not have greeted him in such a friendly way, for Key's lover—the woman whose attention he'd been trying to catch all morning—was Sickles's young wife, Teresa. After months of subterfuge, their affair had been disclosed to Sickles by way of an anonymous letter. Key would be fatally shot through the chest before he'd learn the details of what had led to his death—details the rest of the world would soon become all too familiar with, thanks to a salacious and well-publicized criminal trial that was also the first in America to introduce a defense of temporary insanity.

It's a dubious mark to leave on history, one that no one of the era could have predicted for any of the people involved in the case, least of all the victim. Philip Barton Key II had been raised in one of the most prominent families in the nation's capital city. His father had taken part in some of the biggest criminal cases of the time, including defending two civilians who had been implicated in the Burr-Wilkinson seditionist conspiracy plot in 1807.[2] Francis Key and his wife, Mary, had four children. The oldest was Philip Barton Key II, named after Francis's history-making uncle, who'd served as a US circuit judge nominated by President John Adams and, later, as a US representative from Maryland.

An engraved portrait of Philip Barton Key II, after a photograph by Mathew Brady, published in *Harper's Weekly* on March 19, 1859.

Barton—as he was called—followed in the footsteps of both his father and his great-uncle namesake, becoming a renowned lawyer himself. He married a woman named Ellen Swan, with whom he also had four children. When Ellen died suddenly in 1855, Barton was heartbroken, telling reporters he'd loved her like no woman on earth and doubted he could ever be happy with anyone else.[3] That didn't keep him from trying, however. Barton was considered the most handsome man in Washington society, and he was famously flirtatious and known to sleep with other politicians' wives. Truth was, though, that many of the men whose wives he bedded were sleeping with mistresses of their own, and everyone seemed to keep busy enough on that front that no one got too worked up about Barton's dalliances.

About two years after Ellen's death, Barton met Sickles, a newcomer to DC who'd been raised by his real-estate investor father and overattentive mother. They weren't of the same quality stock as the Key family, but they prized education and strove to give Daniel the best they could afford, which included sending him to a prestigious academy about two hundred miles north of their home in Manhattan.[4] Sickles wasn't the most disciplined student, however, and he quickly butted heads with the school's headmaster After one particularly potent confrontation, Sickles left in a rage.[5] Instead of returning home to face his disappointed parents, Sickles got work at the local newspaper instead in a gig known as a "printer's devil."[6] His job was to lay out letters onto a plate that would then be used to print the day's news onto newsprint. During this job, which he held for about a year and a half, Sickles read copious news reports and found himself enamored with politics. When he returned home, he took his first steps toward entering that world himself by stumping for presidential candidate Martin Van Buren. His first political speech was endorsing the fellow New Yorker who, like Sickles, had descended from Dutch immigrants.

When Sickles went to college, his parents arranged for him to move in with the scholarly family of a man named Lorenzo Da Ponte—a former priest turned famed librettist for Mozart—who'd been chased out of Italy thanks to repeated sex scandals before landing in Manhattan. Lorenzo's son by the same name oversaw Sickles's admission into the University of the City of New York (present-day New York University)—both Lorenzos were members of the faculty. It was through the Da Ponte family that Sickles would meet his eventual wife, Teresa, though their meet-cute was questionable at best. Teresa was the elder Lorenzo's granddaughter—Lorenzo the younger's niece—and she was just a toddler when Sickles first encountered her as he began his college career.

Lorenzo the elder died at age eighty-nine in August 1838 and his son would die suddenly two years later, abruptly halting Sickles's university career. Sickles found his professional footing soon afterward though. In 1843, after studying law under Benjamin Franklin Butler, attorney general for Presidents Andrew Jackson and Martin Van Buren, twenty-four-year-old Sickles opened a law office on Nassau Street in Manhattan and quickly made a name for himself. As his future wife-to-be learned her school lessons, Sickles began rubbing elbows with politicians while spending his free time at a brothel run by a worldly and poetic woman known as Fanny White—who fell in love with her client. Fanny doted on Daniel—referred to by Fanny's servants simply as "her man." She bought him expensive suits and took him to New York's finest restaurants. It seems Daniel returned her affection and refused to hide their relationship, even as people told him it'd ruin his political career. In 1846, he ran for the New York Assembly and won, bringing Fanny to Albany, where he gave her a tour of the state capitol. Bringing a sex worker as his plus-one caused quite a scandal, though Sickles got away with it because those who objected weren't vociferous about it—lest they be asked to explain in detail how they knew Fanny's occupation.

Getting married was never in the cards for Fanny and Daniel, so he technically remained a bachelor—and a philandering one at that. He stayed in touch with the Da Ponte family and watched with interest as Teresa matured. She was the only child of parents Maria Da Ponte and composer Antonio Bagioli, who ensured she got the best education their considerable wealth could buy. By the time Teresa was a teenager, she was multilingual and urbane, speaking eloquently on music, philosophy, and art. Additionally, newspaper stories commented on her beauty, referencing her "Italian lustre and depth of eye."[7] This all proved too much for Sickles to resist apparently. In 1852, he and Teresa would marry in a hurry, and their one and only offspring, a daughter named Laura Buchanan Sickles, would arrive seven months later.

From *the Harper's Weekly* series of engravings, a portrait of Teresa Bagioli Sickles, also after a Brady photograph.

Fanny White reportedly beat Sickles with a bullwhip when she learned he'd gotten married,[8] though their relationship continued for a few more years. Its demise came in the mid-1850s after Teresa and Laura joined Sickles to live in DC as he settled into his new role as a senator from New York state. It wasn't that Sickles's eye stopped roving upon their arrival, but Fanny, at least, wasn't willing to stay on the sidelines. In a few years, she would finally marry and do what few sex workers of the era ever managed: reform her reputation.

When Sickles met Barton Key, the two struck up a fast friendship and political alliance. Key had been appointed by Pierce, who was ousted as president after a single term by challenger James Buchanan, for whom Sickles had served as an assistant when Buchanan was appointed United States Minister to the United Kingdom. Buchanan surprised everyone by winning the primary. Key expected he'd be ousted by the new guy, but Sickles suggested Buchanan keep him on, and, because Buchanan so valued Sickles's input, he agreed. Sickles and Buchanan were surely close enough that the former could have expected some kind of appointment by the latter come inauguration, but Sickles wasn't content to ride on anyone's coattails. He ran for the Senate instead. After he won the election, he found a two-story white house near the White House known as Ewell House because it'd been built

by Dr. Thomas Ewell, a Navy surgeon. Sickles hired Key to negotiate the lease of the home,[9] after which he moved in with his wife and daughter.

It made sense that Key and Sickles hit it off straight away. They had a lot in common—they were about the same age, they were both lawyers and Democrats, and they both routinely had affairs with other men's wives. For some reason, that last shared attribute never seemed to give Sickles any pause, but it should have. Especially when it became apparent to everyone in DC that Key had become smitten with Teresa. Exactly when that occurred isn't quite clear, but it's likely they met at one of the many parties Teresa hosted at the Ewell House for her husband's well-connected friends. Key and Teresa were soon inseparable, a fact that friends and colleagues raised to Sickles on occasion, but he batted away the rumors. The two said their friendship was platonic, and Sickles apparently chose to believe that was true. People who paid attention, however, noticed a pattern: When Sickles would work late or leave town, both of which were often thanks to his job, Teresa would have her carriage driver swing by Key's place to pick him up. The two would take back streets to get where they were going. Teresa's parties weren't limited to when her husband was home, and when he wasn't, Key was by her side.

What Teresa saw in Keys isn't hard to imagine. He not only was professionally accomplished, but he was considered "Apollo in appearance," known for his foppish attire, such as white leather tights and high boots."[10] He was witty and clever, with "a sad but handsome face" and "easy, fashionable air." He had an effortless rapport with women especially and was "a favorite with every hostess of the day."[11] On top of that, Teresa wrote letters to her husband that highlighted how lonely she felt at times. "I want to be with you as much as possible," she wrote. "I wish to be near and with you. I hate the idea of your going away without me and know that I would not have you if it were in my power."[12] But Sickles did go away, and often. The attention Teresa hoped he'd give her was too frequently spent on other men's wives instead. Key, meanwhile, seemed enraptured. During an auction of his belongings after his death, bidders realized that the only art that had adorned the walls of Key's home was a framed image of a famous ballerina of the era—a woman who bore a remarkable likeness to Teresa.[13]

The genesis of the affair was a stolen kiss here and there in the Sickles's home. "I think the intimacy commenced in April or May 1858," Teresa would later write.[14] The two "had connection" on the parlor sofa around then. Teresa worried that the servants would catch on, so Key hatched a plan. He reached out to a man named John Gray with a house to rent on 15th Street near Lafayette Square. Gray found the query odd. Here was a US attorney asking about his property, supposedly on behalf of some congressman who might need a place to stay. Gray told Key the home would cost $50 a month. Rather than connecting Gray to the tenant, Key paid the monthly bill himself—and was the only man ever seen visiting it in the weeks that followed. He rarely visited alone. A woman dressed in black, wearing a veil over her face, often met him there.

It's ironic that the couple decided it safest to rent the 15th Street house, when it was that very choice that ensured their affair would become known. Key, a public figure and widower, drew far more attention visiting a rented home with a veiled woman than he ever would have had visiting a married woman in her own home. Rumors spread around the Club House, a private home that served booze to the town's fashionable movers and shakers. Key at first denied the rumors, but as the weeks passed, he seemed to grow bolder, eventually admitting the affair. From the *New York Herald*:

> **Key had been time and again warned by his friends that something dangerous would grow from his criminal attachment. He was accustomed, however, to treat these friendly admonitions with an air of haughty bravado. He would listen to no remonstrance from any quarter.[15]**

On February 24, 1859, a messenger handed Sickles a yellow envelope, which Sickles thought nothing of. He shoved it into his pocket and headed to a hotel near the Capitol for his version of a happy hour gathering, dubbed a "nightly hop." Teresa and Key were there together; Key dutifully left when Sickles arrived. Teresa and her husband stayed late as brass band music entertained the booze-laden crowd. It was only later, after the couple had returned home and Teresa retired for the night, that Sickles remembered

the letter he'd dismissed earlier. In a few days' time, newspapers nationwide would reprint its contents verbatim:

> **Dear Sir: With deep regret I inclose [sic] to your address the few lines but an indispensable duty compels me so to do seeing that you are greatly imposed upon.**
>
> **There is a fellow, I may say, for he is not a gentleman by any means by the [name] of Philip Barton Key & I believe the district attorney who rents a house of a negro man by the name of Jno. A Gray situated on 15th street between K and L streets for no other purpose than to meet your wife Mrs. Sickles. He hangs a string out of the window as a signal to her that he is in and leaves the door unfastened and she walks in and sir I do assure you he has as much the use of your wife as you have.**
>
> **With these few hints I leave the rest for you to imagine.**
>
> **Most respectfully**
> **Your friend R. P. G.[16]**

The next morning, when Sickles approached a longtime friend to ask his help confirming the details of the distressing letter, it was clear he'd had a sleepless night. George Wooldridge was a controversial character who'd founded newspapers that pridefully peddled in stories about grisly accidents, gruesome crimes, and torrid affairs. As the founder of a rag called the *Sunday Flash*, he'd been named a defendant in New York City's first obscenity trial. He'd spared himself by testifying against his colleagues, but he moved onto another risky print venture and found himself sued time and again for obscenity and defamation. He'd finally taken a job as doorkeeper of the New York State Assembly, which is how he'd met and befriended Sickles. Sickles knew that if anyone could help him flush out the truth purported in the R.P.G. letter, it was Wooldridge. As Sickles discussed the pros and cons of a Naval Appropriations Bill at the Capitol, Wooldridge began questioning neighbors of the rental home on 15th Street. The early intel pointed to Key using the home as a love nest, but the identity of the woman was still unclear. Neighbors only had descriptions of her clothing, not her face, and Sickles was buoyed when told that one placed the most recent rendezvous as Thursday. Teresa's whereabouts were accounted for that whole day, and the woman who arrived for trysts with Key never varied, which would rule out Teresa. Still, he wanted to be sure, so Wooldridge rented a room from a woman across the street from John Gray's house while Sickles placed a classified ad asking R.P.G., "who recently addressed a letter to a gentleman in this city," to "confer a great favor upon the gentleman . . . by granting him an early, immediate and confidential interview."[17] No one replied to the ad.

As Wooldridge babysat the house, he conducted further interviews and concluded that the early info he'd received about the latest encounter being Thursday was erroneous. The consensus was that Key and the woman had last met on Wednesday, meaning that Teresa wasn't ruled out after all. Wooldridge conveyed this to Sickles, who took the news hard, sobbing uncontrollably. Clearly, the hope he'd held out had hinged entirely on this, for once it was clarified, Sickles no longer questioned the validity of the accusations. It was true: Teresa had been having an affair with Key.

He confronted his wife Saturday night, two days after the letter arrived. He swatted away her initial denials by providing her with the specifics he'd gleaned over the past few days of sleuthing. Teresa was so overcome that she fainted. When she came to, she cowered in fear of her husband, but he assured her he was no threat. He believed she'd been conned by a scoundrel, but he did insist that she detail the whole affair in a written confession.[18] Overcome by shame and guilt, she did so. Soon, the tawdry contents of that confession would be reprinted in newspapers around the world:

> **I have been in a house in Fifteenth street with Mr. Key; how many times I don't know; I believe the house belongs to a colored man; the house was unoccupied; commenced going there the latter part of January; have been in alone and with Mr. Key; usually stayed an hour or more. There was a bed in the second story–I did what is usual for a wicked woman to do. The intimacy commenced this winter, when I came from New York, in that house–an intimacy of an improper kind; have met half a dozen times or more at different hours of the day; on Monday of this week, and Wednesday also; would arrange meetings when we met in the street and at parties. Never would**

"I HAVE BEEN IN A HOUSE IN FIFTEENTH STREET WITH MR. KEY. . . . THE INTIMACY COMMENCED THIS WINTER, WHEN I CAME FROM NEW YORK, IN THAT HOUSE—AN INTIMACY OF AN IMPROPER KIND."

speak to him when Mr. Sickles was at home, because I knew he did not like for me to speak to him. Did not see Mr. Key for some days after I got there; he then told me he had hired the house as a place where he and I could meet. I agreed to it. Had nothing to eat or drink there. The room is warmed by a wood fire. Mr. Key generally goes first. Have walked there together, say four times–I do not think more; was there on Wednesday last, between two and three. I went there alone; Laura was at Mrs. Hoover's; Mr. Key took her and left her there at my request. From there I went to Fifteenth street to meet Mr. Key; from there to the milk woman's. Immediately after Mr. Key left Laura at Mrs. Hoover's I met him in Fifteenth street. Went in by the back gate. Went in the same bedroom, and there an improper interview was had. I undressed myself. Mr. Key undressed also. This occurred on Wednesday, 23d of February, 1859. Mr. Key has kissed me in this house a number of times. I do not deny that we have had a connection in this house last spring, a year ago, in the parlor, on the sofa. Mr. Sickles was sometimes out of town and sometimes in the Capitol. I think the intimacy commenced in April or May, 1858. I did not think it safe to meet him in this house, because there are servants who might suspect something. As a general thing have worn a black and white woolen plaid dress, and beaver hat trimmed with black velvet. Have worn a black silk dress there also; also a plaid silk dress, black velvet cloak trimmed with lace, and black velvet shawl trimmed with fringe. On Wednesday I either had on my brown dress or black and white woolen dress, beaver hat and velvet shawl. I arranged with Mr. Key to go in the back way, after leaving Laura at Mrs. Hoover's. The arrangement to go in the back was either made in the street or at Mr. [Senator Stephen] Douglas', as we would be less likely to be seen. The house is in Fifteenth street, between K and L streets, on the left hand side of the way; arranged the interview for Wednesday in the street, I think, on Monday. I went in the front door. It was open; occupied the same room; undressed myself and he also; went to bed together. Mr. Key has ridden in Mr. Sickles' carriage, and has called at his house without Mr. Sickles' knowledge and after my being told not to invite him to do so, and against Mr. Sickles' repeated request.

> This is a true statement, written by myself, without any inducement held out by Mr. Sickles of forgiveness or reward, and without any menace from him. This I have written with my bedroom door open, and my maid and child in the adjoining room, at half past eight o'clock in the evening. Miss [Octavia, a friend] Ridgeley is in the house, within call.
>
> Teresa Bagioli[19]

That night, the Ewell House was filled with the tormented cries of both husband and wife. Teresa was so upset and ashamed that she wouldn't let herself be comfortable in a bed. She slept on the floor in a separate room from her husband. Sickles wailed all night long.

The next morning, Sickles recruited a few trusted friends, including attorney Samuel Butterworth, to discuss what he should do next. It was during this discussion that he so happened to look out a window and saw Key twirling a handkerchief in the air. Because of Teresa's detailed confession, Sickles now knew that this was one of the ways the two arranged their trysts. Furious, he solicited his comrades' opinions on how to handle things. Butterworth said he didn't have good advice but added that, really, there was only one thing a man of honor could do anyway. Butterworth left the house and engaged Key in idle chitchat while Sickles grabbed and loaded three guns. When Key spotted Sickles walking toward him on Pennsylvania Avenue, within sight of the White House, he had no idea that he was reaching out his hand to greet a man who'd been obsessing over him for days.

The first bullet went through his outstretched hand, prompting Key to back up. "Murder!" he screamed. "Murder! Don't shoot me!" Key normally would have been armed, but it so happened that he'd left his gun at home that day. Instinctively, he reached into his pocket and found only the opera glasses with which he'd spy Teresa in a window. He threw those, hitting Sickles without effect. Sickles fired again. This bullet went into Key's thigh. Key staggered back, falling to the ground. Sickles kept advancing and fired again at the closest range yet with the gun pointed straight into Key's chest. Key was mortally wounded, but Sickles tried nonetheless to fire a final bullet into his head. This time, the gun misfired. By then, witnesses had gathered and closed in around Key, whom they carried to the nearby Club House.

They could tell he was dying and asked if he had any message he wanted delivered to his children, but Key was gone. He died without saying another word.

Reporters who descended on the scene were aided by an invention that had recently been fine-tuned enough to be a godsend for this type of story: the telegraph. This enabled writers to send their stories swiftly to editors across the country, ensuring that the Key-Sickles affair became the most-covered event in human history up until that point. The story had all the elements: rich and powerful players, forbidden sex, and murder. It also had a plot twist: normally the crime would have been prosecuted by the US District Attorney in DC, but that man was the victim in the case, and because he was indisposed, his replacement would have to be appointed by the president, who was the defendant's close friend, James Buchanan.

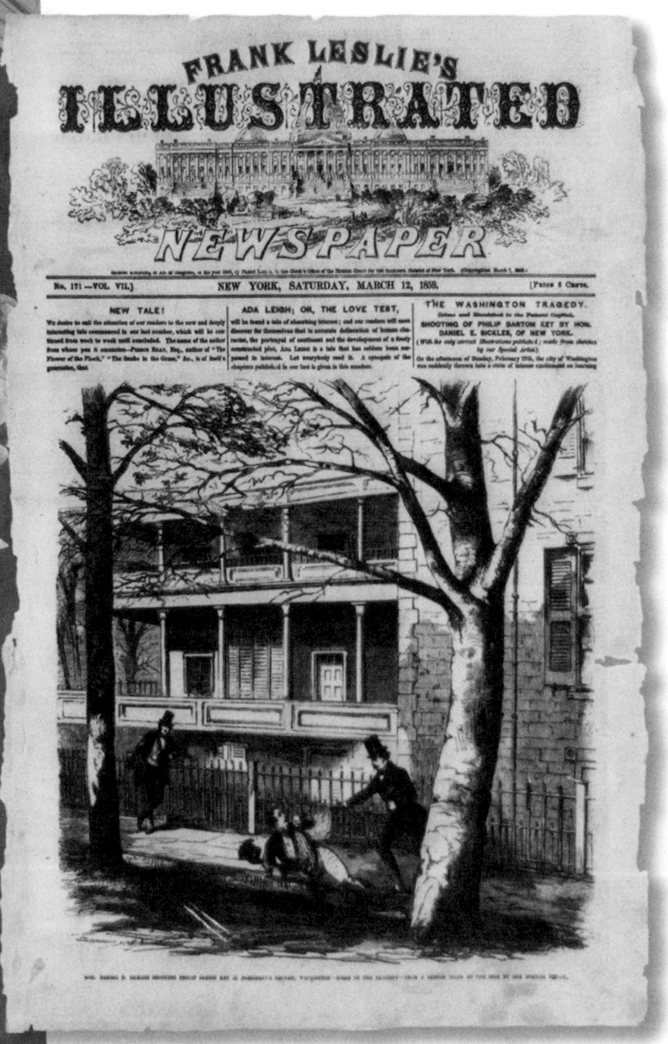
FRANK LESLIE'S
ILLUSTRATED
NEWSPAPER

No. 171.—VOL. VII.] NEW YORK, SATURDAY, MARCH 12, 1859. [PRICE 6 CENTS.

NEW TALE!

ADA LEIGH; OR, THE LOVE TEST,

THE WASHINGTON TRAGEDY.

SHOOTING OF PHILIP BARTON KEY BY HON. DANIEL E. SICKLES, OF NEW YORK.

The March 12, 1859 front page of *Frank Leslie's Illustrated Newspaper* featured this engraving titled "Hon. Daniel E. Sickles shooting Philip Barton Key, in President's Square, Washington."

To his credit, Robert Ould didn't seem interested in pulling any punches. He fought to keep Key's affair with Teresa out of the courtroom, arguing to the judge that Sickles's motive didn't matter. You can't just kill someone because you're mad at them, he said. The judge ruled against him on most matters, save one important one: he agreed that Teresa's confession letter should not be admitted into evidence. Sickles's lawyers wanted the tawdry details known, however, because they figured they would help their client, so they leaked the letter to the press, who sent it via telegraph it to newsrooms worldwide. Newspapers in the United

Kingdom that hadn't even written much about the trial beforehand saw fit to print the confession word for word.

Sickles had talented defense lawyers in his courtroom, including James T. Brady, who was considered among the most brilliant lawyers in all of New York,[20] and Edwin Stanton, who would go on to serve as Abraham Lincoln's secretary of war during the Civil War. They had learned of a novel defense deployed in the United Kingdom involving a Scottish man named Daniel M'Naghten, who'd traveled to London to kill the prime minister because he said Tories in his country were harassing and plotting to murder him in 1843. In an effort to put a stop to it all, M'Naghten fired a gun when he thought he spied Prime Minister Robert Peel, but the bullet's recipient was actually Peel's secretary, Edward Drummond. M'Naghten pleaded insanity, but it was a different type than the courts had usually recognized because M'Naghten wasn't stark-raving mad. He could clearly articulate why he'd set out to kill his victim, but at the same time, he was clearly delusional. A new test was born to gauge insanity: 1) Did the defendant know what he was doing when he committed the crime? Or 2) Did the defendant understand his actions were wrong?[21] It was called the M'Naghten Rule (or Test), and Sickles's lawyers argued that while he was fine up until the RPG letter arrived, and fine again after shooting Key, he was legally insane at the moment he pulled the trigger.

From the moment the story hit the newspapers, it was clear that public sentiment was on Sickles' side. In one paper, the report noted:

> **The community was thrown into an intense state of excitement today by the killing of Philip Barton Key, U.S. District Attorney for the District of Columbia, by Daniel E. Sickles. According to the report, Mr. Sickles, being convinced of the truth of certain scandalous rumors involving his wife, resolved to redress his wrongs.**[22]

And in another:

> **Sickles justifies himself by saying he had performed a duty which he owes to himself and society. The sympathy seems to be generally with him.**[23]

Legal Legacy

The Daniel Sickles trial tallied several "firsts" in the US, including:

- Telegraphs had recently been fine-tuned enough for reporters to send stories swiftly to editors nationwide, making the tawdry trial the most-covered criminal case in history up until that point.
- This development also marked one of the first times defense lawyers were able to use the press to garner sympathy for their client by having his wife's confession letter admitting to adultery—which had been kept from jurors—printed verbatim in papers.
- Defense lawyers, including James T. Brady and Edwin Stanton, brought a new defense to the US based on a UK murder case involving a man named Daniel M'Naghten, deemed delusional at the time of his crime but not permanently insane. With that case, the M'Naghten Rule was born to gauge whether a defendant knew what they were doing when committing a crime and/or understand that their actions were wrong.

That was true of the general public, but more pointedly, of the twelve men who'd heard the case. They decided Sickles had been driven temporarily mad by a man who'd violated the so-called Unwritten Law—a never-codified rule that allowed man to kill in defense of the sanctity of his home or the virtue of his woman. For about a century after the trial, juries routinely gave men the right to kill their wives' lovers up until the 1950s.

Sickles eventually lost the public's goodwill, though, largely because he and Teresa reconciled after his acquittal. He forgave her; the two stayed married and they reunited in New York with their daughter. He defended his reasoning by saying that he couldn't let the mother of his child be forever shunned by society. She'd earned too much notoriety to be able to remarry, and if he didn't forgive her, he'd be ensuring that she and their daughter, Laura, would be outcasts. Those with whom the reconciliation sat poorly saw things differently: if the affair was so trivial that Sickles could forgive his cheating wife, how could it have also been so terrible that Barton Key had to die for it?

Regardless, it turned out that sparing Teresa from a tragic fate wasn't within Sickles's power. Eight years after her love life made international headlines, she died of consumption at just thirty-one years old. Her daughter, Laura, didn't fare much better. She became an alcoholic and died at age thirty-eight in 1892 of cirrhosis of the liver.[24] Sickles, on the other hand, lived a long and celebrated life. The Key affair temporarily derailed his political career, but his stint as a noted general for the Union in the Civil War largely rehabilitated his reputation and landed him back in politics decades later—though he was down one leg thanks to the Battle of Gettysburg. He lived until 1914, dying at age ninety-four of a cerebral hemorrhage.[25]

4

The Slaying of Stanford White and the Trial of the Century

(1906)

The crowd that had gathered on the roof of Madison Square Garden the evening of June 25, 1906, had settled in for the second act of a new musical called *Mam'zelle Champagne*. The revue was a light affair consisting "chiefly of music, comedy, girls and lingerie," as one news brief put it.[1] "It is one of those bubbling, effervescent, breezy things, which are always due in the good old summer time."

The high-society folk attending the premiere were in an appropriately jovial mood while listening to the chorus of a deceptively risqué number called "I Could Love a Million Girls" when something strange began to unfold near the front of the audience. Stanford White, one of New York City's most famous architects, seated comfortably while enjoying the silly tune, seemed unaware that a strange-looking man had haltingly approached his table. The man looked out of place, as he was wearing a heavy winter coat despite the hot June weather. His gaze fixated on White, the man pulled a pistol from his coat, steadily aimed it, and fired three shots.

The performers on stage froze. For a split second, the crowd went silent as the audience tried to rationalize that what they were seeing was part of the performance. Someone even laughed. But one of the bullets had torn White's face off, and once that sight began to register in their confused minds, people panicked. They screamed and scattered as the gunman raised the pistol over his head to show he was no threat to anyone else. "That man ruined my wife!" he yelled by way of explanation.

So began one of the most bizarre and scandalous crimes of the early twentieth century—one with a trial of such a high profile that it would be the first time in American history that a judge would opt to sequester the empaneled jury out of fear they'd be unfairly swayed by the notoriety the case was getting in the media.

On the surface, the case has similarities with the Key-Barton affair from nearly fifty years earlier: at its center was a love triangle featuring two wealthy and prominent men and a younger, dark-haired woman whose beauty was described as almost otherworldly. In this case, that woman was Evelyn Nesbit, the first of two children born to Winfield Scott Nesbit, a lawyer, and his home-maker wife, Evelyn Florence (née McKenzie), in Tarentum, Pennsylvania.[2] The year of Evelyn's arrival was either 1884 or 1885, the ambiguity owing to destroyed county records and some fibbing about her age in subsequent years. What's agreed upon is that she was born on Christmas Day and was adored by her father, who was rather progressive in how he treated his daughter. Winfield encouraged Evelyn to study and stocked a small library for her in their modest home. While girls of the era were routinely pressured to focus on becoming faithful wives, Evelyn's father told her that her fate was to attend Vassar College.[3] When Evelyn's brother, Howard, came along a few years later, he didn't supplant her position as the apple of her father's eye. Howard was a mama's boy, while Evelyn was very much a daddy's girl.

She was also a performer. As Paula Uruburu writes in *American Eve*, Evelyn was "a vivacious and free-spirited child" who "bounced headfirst into all activities, particularly those she thought would please her father—singing, dancing, drawing, reciting from her books, playing the piano."[4] She impressed all who met her as unusually bright, ambitious, and destined for more than was typically expected for a middle-class girl from a steel town in the Pittsburgh region.

In 1896, the world that Evelyn knew—and the one she'd been raised to anticipate down the road—came crashing down around her. Her father died suddenly at age forty, leaving the family impoverished. The traumatized girl watched as repo men came to the home she once considered a sanctuary and hauled their belongings from within. The books that she had treasured, given to her by her father, were among the first items to go. The displaced family began moving from one boarding house to another while Mrs. Nesbit, a talented but self-taught seamstress, found work at Wanamaker's, one of the country's first department stores. She got her children jobs there, too, by lying about their ages so they'd be old enough to be hired.

The stress on the family was palpable. Mrs. Nesbit regularly broke down in tears, throwing herself onto her bed and crying, "What will become of us?" There wasn't much room for the children's grief to surface without triggering an outburst from their mother, so they learned to bottle their own emotions. Their lives were unmoored. Even though all three in the family worked, they often had only enough money to split a single meal a day. Mrs. Nesbit sometimes shuttled the children off for weeks or months at a time to live with distant relatives. She'd reclaim them once she found some sort of financial footing. Once, Christmas and Evelyn's birthday came and went while they were at a virtual stranger's house. Evelyn found a stray cat and pretended that it'd been given to her as a gift to salve the sting of spending the day alone and forgotten.[5]

Later, at a point when Howard was off with relatives while Evelyn and her mother were reunited and living in Philadelphia, Evelyn happened to pause while walking down the street to gaze in a shop window. An elderly woman inside stared back. The woman introduced herself as Mrs. Darach and asked if Evelyn would like to pose for a portrait. Evelyn had been admired previously for her looks, but that admiration had never brought with it potential pay. She told Mrs. Darach she'd ask her mother about the proposal. Mrs. Nesbit approved, and the next thing Evelyn knew, she earned her first day's wage—one dollar—sitting for hours at a time as an artist's model. "I was as proud as though I myself combined all the genius of Michelangelo and Rosa Bonheur," Evelyn would later write about that first day's wage.[6] The experience changed her life virtually overnight. It also completely changed the modeling industry, for Evelyn became the first "It Girl" of the twentieth century—or, as Uruburu put it, the prototype of what's known today as a supermodel.[7] One 1901 wire story read: "New York artists declare that Miss Evelyn Florence Nesbit is the prettiest girl of fifteen years who has ever posed for them. Artists such as Beckwith, Wildes, Levy, Church and Phillips declare her an almost perfect type of maidenly beauty."[8] Alongside that write-up in the *Marion Star* newspaper was an etching of Evelyn peering directly at the viewer with thick, tousled hair and a detached gaze.

"I WAS AS PROUD AS THOUGH I MYSELF COMBINED ALL THE GENIUS OF MICHELANGELO AND ROSA BONHEUR."

Artists who worked with Evelyn marveled at how she could manage to look both innocent and seductive, both aloof and alluring, at the same time. She seemed a chameleon: When she wore makeup and tied her hair up, she

Portrait of Evelyn Nesbit, c. 1900.

could look like a charming socialite. Down and mussed, she could be a peasant girl.

"Miss Nesbit has a mobile face, yet she can change her personality in looks, gesture and effect quicker than anyone else I have ever seen," photographer Ryland W. Phillips once remarked. "She can change her whole expression instantly from sorrow to gladness, every feature adding to the total transformation."[9]

The pay wasn't earth-shattering—$1 in 1901 translates to about $35 in 2023—but it certainly outpaced what the whole family was earning at the store.

"When I saw that I could earn more money posing as an artist's model than I could at Wanamaker's, I gave my mother no peace until she permitted me to pose for a livelihood," Evelyn later said. "Her objections crumbled under the force of necessity.[10]

Soon, Evelyn's face was everywhere, either photographed or painted or etched. She appeared on beer trays, cigarette and tobacco cards, fans, wallpaper, playing cards, cigar labels, and pocket mirrors. She served as the face of Prudential Life Insurance, Pompeian face cream, and Coca-Cola. She peered out from fine art paintings, too, often as an angel or some other ethereal being. She even inspired music, such as a piece titled the "Nesbit Waltz" written by Vincent Spadea, whose sheet music featured Evelyn dressed in a kimono on the cover. As her fame grew, so did her rates, albeit modestly. She could charge $5 for a half-day's work and $10 for a full day (about $350 in 2023). While it wasn't enough money to catapult the family into wealthy-elite status, it did provide them with stability and a permanent home. It also gave Evelyn the opportunity to pursue an interest she'd had since she was little: performing on stage. As early as 1901, stories about Evelyn's modeling career included mention of her theatrical aspirations. Her fame in photos didn't afford her any shortcuts on stage, however. Her debut was as a "Spanish maiden" in a musical comedy called *Florodora*, which had debuted in London in 1899 and done well there; it then opened at the New York Theatre in October 1901. It ran on Broadway for 552 performances, the third-longest run on Broadway at the time. Evelyn made sure rehearsals and shows could work around her schedule so she could continue to model, which paid the family's bills. In theater, she was destined to remain a chorus girl, where, as one reviewer of the time described it, she "contribute(d) what baseball players would call good team work."[11]

Despite being a background player, however, Evelyn did manage to stand out. During the *Florodora* run she caught the eye of Stanford White, a worldly forty-six-year-old architect. Evelyn was just sixteen at the time. White was well known throughout the city, having recently rebuilt the University of Virginia Rotunda, which originally had been designed by Thomas Jefferson but was gutted by a fire in 1895. White's redesign, which wisely included a fireproof tile dome, was finished in 1899. After seeing Evelyn on stage as a Florodora Girl several times, he approached her. Old enough to be

Stanford White, photographed c. 1900.

her father, he at first seemed interested in playing the role of a surrogate.

"My first experience of Mr. White was that he was very unprepossessing, that he was very kindly, and that he was safe," Evelyn later recalled. "He did not treat me with any great ceremony, but he was courteous, attentive and took an interest in my life. . . . He exercised an almost fatherly supervision over what I ate and was particularly solicitous as to what I drank. He was mildly reproving, gently bantering, a man who kept one smiling with his own good humour or interested in his own experience. Everybody had spoken so well of him, and he was undoubtedly a genius in his art. He had met my mother and knew something of our history, and he was keenly interested in my adventures in the artistic world."[12]

White took great interest in Evelyn's career and well-being, lavishing her with gifts and praise. He seemed to delight in her innocence, her naivete. He invited her to one of his apartments that he had tucked away in the city, a place that from the outside looked plain and even rundown but was anything but once inside. "The sudden plunge from that dingy street entrance into these room was breathtaking. The predominating color was a wonderful red, a shade I have always called Italian red. Heavy red velvet curtains shut out all daylight. There was plenty of illumination—yet I could find no lights anywhere. Stanford White, you see, was the first man to conceal electric bulbs so that you could get only their glow. Indirect lighting is a common thing today, but then it was a startling innovation. Fine paintings hung on the walls; an exquisite nude I particularly remember by Robert Reid."[13]

Evelyn sat shyly at an antique, intricately carved table. She was one of three others invited to a luncheon with White that day. "I tasted champagne for the first time. I was permitted one glass, no more," she recalled. She found the attention far more intoxicating than the wine. After the meal, White escorted Evelyn upstairs to a room of deep forest green. From the ceiling hung a "gorgeous swing with red velvet ropes around which trailed green smilax, set high in the ceiling at one end of the studio." As a little girl would, Evelyn jumped onto the swing. White pushed her while encouraging her to kick at a "large, multicolored paper Japanese parasol suspended by an undetectable string," Uruburu wrote in *American Eve*.

> **The closer she got, the happier he seemed. He clapped and shivered with delight each time Evelyn's dainty foot pierced the gaily decorated paper. As the colorful parasol twirled like a kaleidoscope before her eyes, again and again a giggling Evelyn broke the thin membrane of the paper until another had to be put in its place. White always made sure he had a replacement on hand.[14]**

White soon moved Evelyn into a finely adorned apartment with her mother. He was their kindly benefactor. He even paid for Howard's schooling. Mrs. Nesbit adored this man who doted on her children as though they were his own. She delighted when he offered to pay for her to take a trip to visit relatives, ensuring she'd be away for more than a week, during which he'd step in and supervise Evelyn. Mrs. Nesbit didn't question his intentions, but she should have.

Back when it happened, what White did to Evelyn was considered an attack on her honor. Today we would not hesitate to call it rape. One night, he plied the virgin with alcohol that caused "a curious sensation," waited for her to pass out, and then raped her as she lay incapacitated. When she regained consciousness, White was naked next to her. She later remembered that she "let out one suppressed scream. I know I started to cry. I was utterly confused, still a bit dizzy and terribly embarrassed and afraid."

"Don't cry, Kittens," White said as he pulled her to his knee, kissing her cheeks and neck. "Please don't. It's all over. Now you belong to me."[15]

Evelyn was in no position to report her rapist. In the prudish Victorian era, to admit what had happened to her would ensure the end of her career, and by this point, her entire family was financially beholden to White. He had, in today's parlance, groomed her. Additionally, Mrs. Nesbit had made clear many times that Evelyn was to do as White said. With this in mind, Evelyn did not feel safe turning to her mother in the wake of her assault. For days, she moved through the motions of life aimlessly as if in a trance.

Stanny, as she'd come to call White by then, tried to calm her, to convince her that what "they" had done was wicked—as though she'd been a participant to, rather than a victim of, the act—but also natural and commonplace. Everyone did it, and he was morally better than most because he at least admitted its wickedness. He warned her that she should not tell anyone lest her reputation be ruined. No one would marry a spoiled girl.[16]

Just as Evelyn had done after losing her father, Evelyn went into survival mode. She suppressed the intense emotions raging within her and accepted what White told her—she surrendered any pretext of power. She became his mistress.

Later, in court, she would describe how he'd push her on the red velvet swing in his apartment while she wore nothing but the pearl-drop necklace he'd given her as a gift.[17] She didn't really piece together that he had a pattern of pursuing other young showgirls and was, certainly by today's standards, an outright pedophile, though there were clues—similar pictures of other young girls shot in the same backgrounds as he was arranging for Evelyn, for example. She looked past all that because he was charming and generous, and Evelyn would eventually feel something she assumed was love for him.

As naive as she seemed to be about his pattern with young girls, she did notice that he paid attention to other women, and like most insecure people in their first big relationship, she didn't like it. So she occasionally would try to make him jealous. She had a brief romance with John Barrymore—Drew Barrymore's grandfather, who would go on to become a famous actor but was just an editorial cartoonist from a rich family when he met Evelyn at one of White's parties. The two dated enough that they were mentioned in the gossip columns. This didn't upset White as hoped, but it bothered Mrs. Nesbit, who considered Barrymore a playboy and leech. To stop that relationship, she sent Evelyn away to a private school for a spell—for which White helped foot the bill.

When Evelyn returned to New York, she found herself again in demand, both in acting and modeling. Her relationship with White was briefly resurrected, though, at age seventeen, she was reaching the upper age limit of his interest threshold. Their relationship soon quickly fizzled. Just as that happened, she realized she'd caught the eye of another theater lover, Harry Kendall Thaw, who began pursuing her with disconcerting zeal. He began sending her letters purporting to be a man named Mr. Munroe, and using that identity, managed to convince her to meet him for lunch. At their first meeting, he dropped to his knees and kissed the hem of her dress. Evelyn at first found Thaw silly and weird, but she was flattered nonetheless—especially since her head was still spinning from the trauma White had inflicted upon her.

Thaw, the son of a coal and railroad baron, was just as wealthy as White but eighteen years younger, making him a far more appropriate romantic match, at least on paper. Eventually, Evelyn learned Thaw's real name, but not his full identity. He'd had a history of mental health issues. His father, William, had died when Thaw was eighteen, after which his mother, Mary, doted on him to an unhealthy degree. He would routinely get himself into trouble, inviting chorus girls to apartments he rented and then beating the girls with dog whips, handcuffing them, and pouring boiling water on their bodies, supposedly to teach them valuable life lessons about the importance of purity and chastity in girls and women. His mother repeatedly bailed him out of the resulting legal troubles.[18]

He also had been obsessed with Stanford White, a man who'd been accepted in New York's high society, from which Thaw had been kept at arm's length because of his peculiar behavior. Thaw, over the years, had twisted meaningless coincidences into evidence that White was plotting to keep him shunned from elite circles. He seemed not to consider that his shunning might have been self-imposed by incidents White had nothing to do with—like the time Thaw chased down a cab driver with a shotgun because he thought he'd been bilked of 10 cents, or when he was expelled from Harvard for threatening students and teachers. From Thaw's perspective, he was an absurdly wealthy man—one whose mother gave him a mind-boggling $80,000 ($3 million in 2023) annual allowance a year after his father's death—who felt ostracized by the other elites, and for reasons known only to him, it was the fault of Stanford White.[19]

Harry Kendall Thaw in a portrait from c. 1895.

Rumors about White's private proclivities helped fuel Thaw's ire. Thaw's criminal mistreatment of chorus girls notwithstanding, he considered himself an upstanding, moral person, one who fell in line with the rantings of Anthony Comstock, the anti-vice crusader who used his post as special agent of the US Postal Service to block people from mailing things he deemed less than virtuous. Thaw was sure that White's rumored affinity for young girls warranted Comstock investigation, and he sent myriad letters suggesting as much.

Thaw hired private investigators to dig up whatever they could on White, so it had come to his attention that White was considered Evelyn's benefactor. Thaw decided it was his job to free the girl from the clutches of this awful man—and subject her to his talons instead. He proposed marriage.

At first, Evelyn dismissed Thaw—or Mr. Munroe, as she knew him first, a facade he creepily dropped after a few meetings. She and her mother both deemed Thaw a bit too odd for their liking. But Evelyn fell ill. It began with dull stomach pains that progressively became so searing that she started to throw up. Mrs. Nesbit tried to reach White for help but couldn't locate him. In desperation, she reached out to Thaw instead. Thaw arranged for one of the country's best doctors to rush to Evelyn's aid, who arrived just in time to save Evelyn from dying from a burst appendix. After that, he took Evelyn and Mrs. Nesbit on a European trip, supposedly so Evelyn could heal. During the trip, he worked quickly to physically separate mother and daughter, allowing him unfettered access to the recuperating girl. He broached the subject of marriage again. Evelyn, however, had by this time heard Thaw's views on chastity and knew he would not condone the relationship she'd had with White. Still, he persisted.

"I realized that I could not marry any man unless he knew everything there was to know about me," Evelyn later wrote. "This was a matter of common honesty."[20]

One night in Paris, Evelyn told Thaw the true extent of her relationship with White. He began to pace and sob. He decided that the champagne White had given Evelyn the night of the rape must have been drugged, and he demanded that she sign a written document saying so. Evelyn wasn't positive this was true—it was feasible that she passed out from the alcohol—and, besides, her own emotions about White were complicated, and she refused to sign the statement. Thaw viciously beat her. Had Evelyn's mother been near, they might have been able to flee together, but the teen at that point was alone, penniless, and recuperating from invasive surgery. She was at Thaw's mercy. Luckily, his fury seemed to subside. Evelyn, meanwhile, had struggled with her own feelings of guilt about her rape and subsequent affair, and, in the way that women often do when they're mistreated, she wondered if Thaw's reaction wasn't fair. Maybe she deserved a thrashing for the wicked things she had allowed to happen.

About two weeks after she'd told Thaw the truth, in the wake of a pleasant dinner at a castle Thaw had rented them in Bavaria, Evelyn went to bed only to be awakened by Thaw beating her again with a riding crop. As he screamed about sinfulness and indecency, he raped her. Eventually, she made it back home to New York, where she detailed Thaw's abuse in an affidavit to a lawyer hired by White. She tried to avoid both men, but they had effectively driven a wedge between her and her mother, and she was lost and confused. Both pursued her. For a while, Evelyn steered clear of Thaw and returned to White, but the latter's treatment of her was so mercurial that Thaw's constant love letters finally broke through. She married him in 1905, two years after telling police he beat her. If Evelyn had hoped this development would finally put an end to Thaw's obsession with White, however, she was sorely disappointed. If anything, his fixation heightened.

After the two had been married more just more than a year, they ended up atop the Madison Square Garden—the second structure to bear that name—which at the time was one of the tallest buildings in New York. Standing thirty-two stories and opening in 1890, it had been built by White's firm; he also kept an apartment there. Atop the roof in an open-air restaurant called Café Martin, *Mam'zelle Champagne* was having its New York debut.

Evelyn and Thaw were about to head to Europe on vacation, but before they left, Thaw had bought tickets for the show. White wasn't supposed to be there that night. He'd planned to be in Philadelphia on a business trip, but his plans were scuttled and, at some point during the show, he arrived and was seated near the stage. Restaurant patrons later said they'd noticed Thaw glaring at White, but no one thought much of it when his coated figure crept closer to White's table. It's never been established if Thaw was triggered by the suggestive song "I Could Love a Million Girls," or if the lyrics by Edgar Allan Woolf were just coincidentally perfect for the occasion:

I've heard men say so often they could love their wives alone
But I think such prudish men must have hearts made of stone
Now my heart is made of asphalt and grows soft at each warm glance
A pretty girl may cast at me while eyeing me askance.[21]

Whatever the case, Thaw fished out a pistol from his coat and opened fire. Certain he'd fatally shot White, Thaw held the pistol over his head and emptied the remaining bullets before walking across the room to his wife.

"Good God, Harry," Evelyn said, the space around her erupting in chaos. "What have you done?"

"It's all right, dear," he calmly replied. "I have probably saved your life."

Thaw was arrested and held in the "Tombs" jail in Lower Manhattan, in a wing called Murderers' Row, but he was no ordinary prisoner. A photo exists of Thaw in his jail cell, dining at a cloth-covered table, his tie tucked into his buttoned-up shirt to keep it clean. Several plates full of food are laid before him, as well as a crystal pitcher and silver teapot. Over his shoulder there should be a jail cot, but instead, you can see a brass bed with extra blankets.

Harry Kendall Thaw dining in luxury in his cell at the Tombs jail in Lower Manhattan, 1906 or 1907.

When word spread about the murder, it spread in conjunction with Thaw's reported justification—that White had not only had a sexual relationship with the young and lovely Evelyn Nesbit, but that he'd raped her while she was unconscious. This shaped his defense. His lawyers pleaded him not guilty by arguing he'd followed the unwritten law requiring a man to protect his wife. Key to that defense was what Thaw had learned about White from Evelyn, so she was his star witness. It made for salacious headlines on front pages across the country. People were so desperate for news about every minor development in the case that a Western Union office was set up next to the courthouse so reporters could file nationwide.

Even the process of jury selection was breathlessly reported. It was covered overseas, with one London publication devoting five to six columns a day to the trial as it unfolded in February 1907.[22] "No trial for murder ever was accorded half the attention," read a wire story.[23] Reporters made special note of the countless female spectators drawn each day to the courthouse. Though only people who had business in the court were supposed to be admitted, "through methods which were not disclosed," hundreds managed to find seats, with women being the most insistent and successful.[24] It was such a high-profile case that the judge ordered the jury to be sequestered.

When White was first killed, public sentiment was on the victim's side, especially because White had been the more prominent and respected of the two men. But once Thaw's motive was explained, the sympathy shifted. The thinking was as simple as it was misogynistic: what honorable husband wouldn't gun down a man who'd slept with his wife? Harry Thaw became an American hero. He explained why he had killed White by saying: "For the sake of wife and home." Soon after, a popular song was released by that name.

The first jury hearing the case against Thaw sat through weeks of testimony but couldn't quickly reach a verdict, which, given the unrelenting newspaper coverage of the case, posed a dilemma for Judge James Fitzgerald. On April 10, 1907, the jury began deliberating just after 5:15 p.m. Fitzgerald waited a spell, then headed to his club uptown, where he had posted outside "an automobile in readiness to make a trip to the court house should he be needed."[25] Hours passed and it was clear the jurors struggling. Fitzgerald called and spoke with court officers, who in turn asked jurors whether there was any hope for a verdict yet that night. "The reply from the jury

Showers tonight and Wednesday.

The Washington Times

LAST EDITION

NUMBER 476. WASHINGTON, TUESDAY EVENING, JUNE 26, 1906. PRICE ONE CENT.

HARRY THAW KILLS STANFORD WHITE IN JEALOUS RAGE OVER ACTRESS WIFE

INSANE PATIENT FOUGHT FIERCELY WITH 3 GUARDS

MISSOURI FORBIDS TRUST TO COLLECT ADMITTED CLAIMS

TRAGIC CLIMAX ON ROOF GARDEN BEFORE CROWD

Millionaire Slayer Claims Famous Architect Ruined His Wife Before His Marriage to Her—Held for Murder by Coroner.

Thaw Tells Own Story Of the Killing of White

In Broken Sentences He Indicates Motive to Have Been Jealousy and Revenge—Declares Dead Man Ruined His Wife.

MRS. THAW ALONE WALKS TO COURT TO SEE HUSBAND

Police Had Made An Unsuccessful All Night Search For Her.

The front page of the *Washington Times* from June 26, 1906—the day after Harry Kendall Thaw murdered Stanford White—was devoted almost entirely to the scandal, as were most major metropolitan newspapers across the country.

room was strongly negative," read a wire story. "The jury was said to be almost hopelessly divided and none of those connected with the case would express the hope tonight of anything better than a disagreement as a climax of the long drawn out and expensive trial."[26] Fitzgerald made his decision by phone: the jury would need to stay overnight in a hotel.

The trial ended with seven jurors voting for murder in the first degree and five voting for acquittal. The case was leveled again, however, and after five days of testimony and twenty-five hours of deliberation, Thaw was found not guilty by reason of temporary insanity in 1908. He was spared life in prison, but he was sent to the Matteawan State Hospital for the Criminally Insane in Fishkill, New York. On August 17, 1913, he escaped; according to the *New York Times*, he "brushed past the milkman, jumped into a waiting automobile, and did not stop until he was arrested in Canada" two days later.[27]

Thaw was eventually brought back to the United States by Canadian immigration officials the following month.

Evelyn visited him at Matteawan for years. In 1910, she gave birth to her one and only son, Russell Thaw. She said he was conceived during a conjugal visit. Harry Thaw, however, disputed this. Regardless, Evelyn made raising her son a front-and-center priority. She didn't want to make the same mistakes her mother had made with her, so she devoted herself to protecting and nurturing Russell, who eventually became a renowned pilot.[28]

Harry Thaw was released from the asylum in 1915, and he and Evelyn divorced. Two years later, he was arrested for horsewhipping a young high school boy named Fred Gump. The Thaw family paid the Gumps $100,000 in damages,[29] and Thaw went back to an asylum for seven years. He was released in 1924 for good and died of a heart attack in 1947.

Meanwhile, Evelyn's mother—who had remarried, to a businessman named Charles Holman—was forever tarnished by the ordeal. Public opinion was that she had basically whored out her daughter and that she'd put Evelyn in danger in order to live a more lavish lifestyle. As early as 1906, Mrs. Nesbit was defending herself to reporters. In a letter to the *Pittsburgh Press*, she wrote: "I never introduced my daughter to Stanford White. I never took her to the theater managers. I accompanied her, as I would not permit her going alone. I have been maliciously misrepresented."[30] Evelyn and her mother had a falling out, but they eventually reconciled. Mrs. Nesbit died in 1944.

Evelyn wrote two memoirs—one in 1914, the other in 1934—which provided some much-needed income to a woman whose once-lucrative career was destroyed by the scandal. In 1955, she was paid $30,000 for her life story, which led to the Joan Collins movie *The Girl on the Red Velvet Swing*. The year the movie came out, Nesbit gave an interview in which she said White was "the most wonderful man I ever knew," and that she'd never loved Harry Thaw—in fact, she hated him, she said. "It would have been better if he had never been born," she said. "Too much money spoiled him young."[31] She remarried once, to her dance partner, Jack Clifford, in 1916—that, too, ended in divorce—and mounted a few attempts at comebacks, such as in the 1930s when she'd sing at clubs.

But the public could never quite separate her from the scandal, and her comeback never materialized. Everywhere she went, she was recognized

Legal Legacy

Aside from being one of the most thoroughly covered trials in America's history, the Thaw trial remains noteworthy for several reasons:

- While the earlier Sickles-Key affair (see chapter 3), and subsequent murder trial, marked the first time temporary insanity was used as a defense in America, it was still novel and was used differently in the Thaw case. Whereas Sickles had killed a man who was actively pursuing his wife for an affair, Thaw's insanity was said to have been sparked by a relationship that predated his and had been known to him for years.
- The eventual verdict—not guilty by reason of temporary insanity—was a return to the prevalence of the so-called "Unwritten Law," whereby men were acquitted for murders of those who besmirched the virtue of a wife, sister, or daughter.

Evelyn Nesbit Thaw hiding her face from a photographer on a street in White Plains, New York, 1909.

and mobbed, but she only got the headache that came with fame and none of the financial security or the fun. In 1922, she was evicted for not paying her rent and attempted suicide by poison. Four years later, she tried again. She once said: "Stanny White was killed but my fate was worse. I lived."[32]

In fairness, though, Evelyn was a survivor. Her life was marred by a series of tough situations, but she seemed to overcome every obstacle thrown her way. Her modeling career—consisting of untold hours holding awkward poses—led to back issues, for which she developed a morphine addiction that she eventually overcame. She was a single mother in an era where that was taboo. Eventually, she settled in Southern California, where she became a sculptor and ceramics teacher and lived her remaining days near her son, his wife and, eventually, their three children. When she was in her seventies and someone asked her about her the scandal, she'd reply, "Oh, yeah, that was when I rocked civilization."[33] Evelyn died quietly in a nursing home in 1967 at age eighty-two.[34] Her tombstone in Culver City, California, makes no reference of her modeling career or her role in one of the biggest scandals of the twentieth century. It describes her simply as: Mother.[35]

5

The Coerced-but-True Confession in the Hix-Snooks Case

(1929)

Even to those who knew her, Theora Hix was a mystery. She was unusually smart, pursuing a medical degree at a time when women comprised only about 4 percent of American physicians. Her girlfriends, who called her Teddy, said she didn't like to talk about herself much, as protecting her privacy seemed paramount. Though her two roommates saw her every day, they gave up making small talk with her because she rarely answered any of their conversation-making questions. She wasn't rude about it, so they just smiled and nodded. *That's Teddy for you.*

When the world learned her name in 1929, Hix would quickly come to represent a new type of woman in America—and not just because she wore her hair in a pixie cut and pursued what was deemed a man's career. She'd grown up fiercely independent, with a wit as sharp as her intellect. Born in 1904, she was still a teenager when women got the right to vote. Anti-vice crusader Anthony Comstock (see page 52) was not only dead, but many of the laws he had championed had been rolled back since his passing. The country had changed drastically over the previous generation or so, and women like Hix were determined to make sure the clock was never turned back. She belonged to no one; her story was hers and hers alone.

At least until Hix was murdered at age twenty-four in a high-profile case that exposed to the world her deepest, most personal secrets—and challenged whether the United States judicial system would respect the agency newly bestowed upon its women citizens by punishing the man who took Hix's life.

It was a fate her parents never could have predicted. Theora's father, Melvin Hix, was a school principal and textbook author who'd been trying for years to conceive a child with his homemaker wife, Joanna. The couple

A detail of Theora Hix from a 1929 group photo of the Alpha Epsilon Iota sorority, a sorority for women in medicine.

had finally resigned themselves to being childless when, at age forty-one, Joanna learned she was pregnant. The daughter they raised in Brooklyn, New York, didn't want for much growing up. Her father made a respectable living[1] and valued education above all else. He was the type of man to write the *New York Times* to applaud the launch of its all-essay magazine[2] and give speeches touting the importance of literacy at teachers' conventions.[3]

In 1923, with Theora's high school graduation past them and Melvin Hix's retirement ahead, the family moved to Bradenton, Florida, after Melvin and Joanna spotting a billboard advertising the place as "The Friendly City."[4] The home they bought at the corner of Prospect Avenue and Mango Street included space for Theora, though she was soon off to Ohio to begin college. She enrolled as an undergraduate at Ohio State University and then, upon graduating, went straight into the College of Medicine.

Theora was ahead of her time in a lot of ways, particularly when it came to sex. She was open and experimental with the men in her life. A former boyfriend would later say she not only initiated all kinds of positions with him, but she also suggested they try various drugs for sexual enhancement.[5] That Theora was a woman having sex before marriage wasn't unique—about half of the women enrolled in college in this era were sexually active according to polls of the day—but her openness was less common. This was an era in which oral sex had just started to emerge as a mainstream sexual technique and was, in fact, illegal in many places.[6]

Marion Meyers was one of Theora's boyfriends at Ohio State. She was unlike any girl he'd met before—smart, witty, adventurous, and, of course, very sexual. He loved all of that, though he was less fond of the fact that she wasn't interested in being exclusive. That, to her, reeked of a bygone era. Meyers tried not to let it bother him. The year before Theora died, the couple met in his car on a lover's lane along the Scioto River for a rendezvous. The police showed up, tapped on the steam-fogged window and fined the couple $20 apiece—which translates to nearly $350 in today's money. The lovebirds gave the cops fake names and paid their fines.[7]

Meyers wanted to make things official—and monogamous—so after he landed a job with the Ohio Department of Agriculture, he asked Theora to marry him, but her reaction wasn't what he'd hoped. She laughed.[8] Heart-broken, he ended their relationship and moved to Bono, Ohio, about 130 miles north of Columbus—though he'd sometimes swing back in town to visit his former fraternity. A year later, when two teenage boys found Theora's body lying face down in a field, Meyers was the investigators' first suspect.

Theora was supposed to come home after a date on June 13, 1929. She lived in an apartment on Neil Avenue in Columbus with two sisters, Alice and Beatrice Bustin. Alice, at age twenty-nine, was the older of the two. She'd found Theora through a classmate of hers in the university's medical school. She thought Theora appropriately studious and responsible. The only aspect of their new roommate that gave the sisters pause was her tendency to shy away from answering personal questions, but they did manage to at least glean that she was seeing a man in Columbus. The vagueness of it all fueled their imaginations, but not in a sinister way. When Theora didn't come home on June 13, the sisters didn't worry. The next afternoon, however, they began to feel uneasy enough that they went to the police station to report her missing.

Not long after, teenage boys—Milton Miller and Paul Krumlauf—had gone to the New York Central Railroad rifle range for target practice. While getting ready to start, one of them noticed a bundle of clothing in the weeds and went to investigate. As they got closer, they recognized the shape of a body garbed in a high-end brown dress with a white collar. Her right hand tightly grasped a handkerchief covered in blood. The boys summoned police without touching the body, so they mercifully weren't the ones to roll over the corpse and discover that her head had been crushed by what looked like a ball-peen hammer. Her throat had also been slit through both the carotid artery and the jugular. Whoever had attacked the woman had made damn sure she was dead.

Armed with this discovery, police circled back to the Bustin sisters and peppered them with questions about their missing roommate. With each answer, it became clear that the dead girl in the field and the roommate were one and the same. To be certain, police brought out some of the personal belongings found with the victim—specifically a watch she always wore, which the sisters recognized. Word spread rapidly about Hix's death, prompting tips to pour into the local police department. Almost as soon as they learned about Theora's jilted ex-boyfriend, Marion Meyers, the man himself called the police and offered to tell them everything he knew.

A fraternity brother had told him the news, he explained, but he thought he was perhaps being pranked. Police invited him to come talk—then promptly arrested him.

Today, this move rightly seems premature, but in the 1920s and 1930s, arrests on mere suspicion charges were commonplace in America. It wasn't until 1991 that the US Supreme Court ruled and insisted on probable cause and a forty-eight-hour time limit for warrantless arrests.[9] Meyers was held on a suspicion charge and immediately questioned. When he denied any knowledge about Theora's death, investigators ushered him to the morgue and insisted he look at his handiwork. They pulled back a sheet exposing Theora's brutally disfigured corpse. Meyers sobbed at the sight and nearly collapsed. He insisted he never could have done anything like that to her, nor could he imagine anyone who would—though he did mention another of her lovers—a man whose entanglement with a student would ignite a nationwide scandal.

James Howard Snook was a prominent OSU veterinary professor who had previously been a member of the US Olympic pistol team, with which he won a gold medal in the men's 30-meter team military pistol event in the 1920 Olympics in Belgium. In the years since, he'd kept up pistoleering as a hobby while earning a respectable living teaching and also inventing tools for his trade. His best-known invention was a device called a Snook Hook that aided in the neutering and spaying of cats and dogs. The hook is still used in procedures today.

Snook did not seem a likely match for Theora. He was in his early forties but looked even older, and he appeared to be happily married to his wife, Helen, and they had recently had a baby girl. He had Christian roots and a conservative bent, was an upstanding citizen, and was a member of the King Avenue Church. None of this precluded an affair, of course, but it all made Theora specifically seem like an odd pick. Still, Meyers had relayed a lot of specific and personal details about Theora's relationship with the man, so officers showed up at Snook's house on West Tenth Avenue to ask some questions. Snooks had been eating breakfast with Helen when the officers knocked, and he seemed annoyed by the interruption. He flippantly asked to finish his meal, prompting the cops to say that they would tell his wife why they were questioning him, and he could show up at the station whenever he saw fit. Snook realized he didn't have the upper hand in the situation and agreed to leave then with the officers.[10]

Once in an interrogation room, Snook said the cops had gotten bad intel if they thought Theora was anything more than a mere acquaintance to him. He only knew her because she'd done a bit of work for him, he said. While her parents were comfortable and sent her money now and then, she was

OPPOSITE: James Snook posing with a revolver, c. 1920s; Snook was part of the US pistol team that won a gold medal in the 1920 Belgium Olympics.

BELOW: The front page of the *Columbus Evening Dispatch*, June 15, 1929, the day after the body of Theora Hix was found on a rifle range five miles northwest of Columbus, Ohio.

THE WEATHER
Fair and slightly warmer tonight and Sunday.

Columbus Evening Dispatch.
OHIO'S GREATEST HOME DAILY

PUBLICATION OFFICE
34 South Third Street
Telephone—ADams 6161

VOL. 58, NO. 350 *** COMPLETE EDITION SATURDAY, JUNE 15, 1929. SIXTEEN PAGES PRICE TWO CENTS

UNIVERSITY INSTRUCTORS HELD IN CO-ED SLAYING

Slain Girl Not "Kiss, Tell" Type

Psychologist Says Miss Hix "Just Perfectly Normal Girl."

MARKED ABILITY

Victim Had No Mental Aberrations, But Was Reserved.

FIGURES AND SCENE OF CO-ED MURDER

JAMES H. SNOOK. MILTON MILLER. PAUL KRUMLAUF. THEORA HIX. MARION T. MEYERS.

VETERINARY PROFESSOR AND AGRICULTURE DEPT. ATTACHE QUIZZED IN RANGE MURDER

Slated on Technical Charge of Investigation After Two-Hour Questioning in Probe of Death of Theora Hix.

ACQUAINTANCES OF GIRL

Prof. Snook, Once Champion Pistol Shot of World, and M. T. Meyers, Extension Service Agent, Taken Into Custody.

Two men, one a professor in the college of veterinary medicine at Ohio State university, the other a farm agent connected with the college of agriculture, were being held by city police, Saturday, on technical charges of investigation, pending further questioning in connection with the brutal murder of Miss Theora K. Hix, medical student at the university, Thursday night.

They are Prof. James H. Snook, of the college of veterinary medicine, of 349 West Tenth avenue, and former world champion pistol shot, and Marion T. Meyers, who resides at the Gamma Alpha fraternity house at 1501 Neil avenue.

DISCLAIM CONNECTION WITH MURDER

Both were taken into custody, Saturday morning, by city police, and questioned for two hours by Chief of Detectives Shellenbarger at city prison, before being slated. Both disclaim any connection with the murder, although admitting that they had been acquainted with the young woman and had taken auto rides with her.

Meyers, who is working on state corn borer work, told police that he was in Columbus, Thursday night, but spent the evening at his fraternity house and left Friday morning for Bono, Ohio, in Lucas county. He was notified of the

Extra Election Board Meeting Looms on Gas

Ordinance Certification Must Be Ready by Tuesday as Hearings Clash.

Flyers Test Yellow Bird; Delay, Take-Off for Paris

Gas for Refueling Is Rushed to Beach at Comillas, Spain, Though French Trio and American Stowaway Take Their Time at Completing Jump to Le Bourget.

Croxton to Retire as Fund Director Nov. 1

Has Been at Head of Organization Since Establishment in 1921.

by no means a spoiled trust-fund baby, so she worked menial jobs around the university to support herself.[11] That included the types of gigs grad students fill on occasion to help out pampered professors. Investigators were dubious, though, so they kept asking questions. Snook got a bit more detailed: he had been alone with Theora, but just once, and only because he'd offered her a ride when he'd seen her walking in the rain.

The police pressed more, and Snook's story shifted. He said that after he'd once offered Theora a ride in the rain, the two became friendly—and that friendliness evolved into a three-year sexual affair. He'd taken her target shooting before, too, at the very gun range where her body was discovered. Police now had two viable suspects—a jilted ex-lover who perhaps became obsessed with Theora after she rejected his marriage proposal, and a current lover who maybe worried that his affair might be exposed, thereby threatening his marriage and livelihood. Many in law enforcement leaned toward Meyers being the more likely suspect. After all, Theora seemed a free-love type who didn't seem to make the types of demands on her lovers that a married man would find burdensome. She didn't want exclusivity. But Meyers did. Meanwhile, Snook seemed a measured, well-to-do man who, despite his affair, loved his wife and daughter. Meyers was asked for an alibi, and he admitted he was in Columbus the night Theora was killed. His old fraternity was throwing a party, he explained, and he'd attended. Several of his frat brothers confirmed that he'd been with them all night, never leaving the party.[12]

Snook, meanwhile, said he was working in his university office until after 9:00 p.m. His wife said she heard him come home at about 9:30. The banging of the screen door alerted her. Helen called out to him, but he didn't answer, though that wasn't unusual. She was busy with the baby anyway and didn't pay him much mind. A couple of hours later, she finally went downstairs to check on Snook, and she found him in the kitchen eating a sandwich.

Neither alibi was bulletproof, but they were both pretty strong. Police needed more information. "PROFESSOR, STATE EMPLOYEE HELD IN MURDER OF GIRL," read an all-caps, above-the-fold headline in the *Dayton Daily News* on June 15, 1929.[13] Some tips trickled in, including one from a taxi driver who said he had picked up a woman matching Theora's description the night of the murder. He said the woman seemed distracted and agitated and had him drive in circles looking for someone who seemed to be standing her up. Theora bummed cigarettes off the cabbie twice, though she was so nervous that she only took a couple of puffs from each one.[14] Another tip came from a local hospital where Theora had been working the night she'd disappeared. She'd left her job answering phones to take a break, telling her supervisor she was running out for a date but would be back shortly. The supervisor was miffed when she never returned—until he learned the next day that she'd met a gruesome fate.[15]

Police also heard from a woman who said she recognized James Snook and Theora Hix from the photographs of them that ran in the papers. She knew them as a married couple who'd been renting a room from her, though she didn't know them by the names the newspaper printed. The man was Howard Snook, a traveling salesman, she said, and the woman was his wife. Mr. Snook paid weekly for the rented room, the woman explained, and she'd only seen the wife one time, but she remembered her appearance because of the notable age difference between her and her "husband." Police brought the landlady to the station to see Snook in person. Following today's protocols for identification procedures, this would have been fertile ground for a defense lawyer come trial. Lineups are the preferred methods for witness identifications, but the landlady's positive ID in this case was bolstered by Snook himself. He admitted that he did rent a room from her. He played dumb about the significance of his admission—and the fact that he'd not volunteered the existence of a rented love nest without provocation.[16]

Prosecuting attorney John J. Chester Jr. decided there surely was more that Snooks wasn't volunteering. On the second day after Snooks's arrest, Chester decided it was time for Snooks to confess—and in 1929, there weren't many ground rules dictating what lengths police could go to in hopes of getting a suspect to crack. Snooks told Chester he had nothing to do with Theora's death, and he was physically beaten in response. At one point, Chester grabbed Snooks and began slapping his face back and forth with both hands, leaving red welts on his cheeks. Snook asked for his lawyer, but Chester—in a world that predated *Miranda* rights by more than three decades—downright refused. Snook's lawyer, E. O. Rickets, stood outside the detective bureau where Snook was being questioned and literally banged on the door but wasn't admitted. This was legal because at the time, the Sixth Amendment

guaranteeing a defendant's right to counsel only applied to federal criminal matters. It wasn't extended to all felonies until 1963 with the Supreme Court's ruling in *Gideon v. Wainwright*, which held that "the Fourteenth Amendment creates a right for criminal defendants who cannot pay for their own lawyers to have the state appoint attorneys on their behalf."[17]

With Snook's denials falling on deaf ears and his lawyer shut out, Chester decided to take him to the rented "love nest," as the couple's rendezvous room had been dubbed in the press, as well as to the murder scene. Reporters tagged along and described how Snook seemed unaffected by both locations, save for a slight shudder when he looked at the grass where Theora had bled out. As the story kept generating headlines, Snook's employers took action. He was fired from Ohio State University for having an affair with a student. The dean of the veterinary school was also deemed responsible and forced to resign. Snook's life was crumbling around him. Finally, one full week after Theora's death, Chester announced to reporters that Snook had signed a full confession. He worried that the tactics he'd used might be scrutinized, so he'd cleverly arranged for reporters to meet with the sleep-deprived, physically assaulted suspect without his lawyers present. In a stupor, Snook told the journalists what he'd told Chester, which was printed subsequently in newspapers nationwide. Chester's thinking was that when Snook's attorneys challenged the confession in court, the prosecutor would be able to agree to set aside the official confession and instead present to jurors what Snooks told reporters instead. That story was this: [18]

Snook and Theora had met when she started working for him in 1926. At the time, Snook was reeling emotionally. The nearly two-year-old daughter he'd had with wife Helen wasn't their first child. The couple actually had a son first, but the boy died in 1925. When the second baby came, Helen was focused on keeping that baby as healthy and happy as possible, so she and the baby shared a room while she and her husband began drifting apart.

Meanwhile, he was running into Theora a fair amount. She was part of the stenography pool; it was her job to take notes and dictation. It so happened that Snook wrote a ton, meaning that they worked together quite often. What he'd told police about giving Theora a ride on a rainy day was true—he'd actually given her and a friend that ride. But a week later, he offered her a solo ride in the country, during which they talked about personal stuff, like marriage and relationships. The solo rides continued, and the discussions became more risqué. Eventually they began talking about the philosophy espoused in a book titled *Companionate Marriage* by Benjamin Barr Lindsey, a famous judge of the era. The book talked about the importance of sex in a marriage for reasons outside of procreation. It espoused using birth control. The discussion prompted Snook to lament his sexless marriage, which in turn prompted Theora to mention that she didn't like dating guys her own age because they were inexperienced.

"Our friendship developed rapidly, and our auto rides increased in frequency," Snook told reporters. "I took a very strong liking to the girl, but I do want it understood that ours was not a silly little love affair. I still love my wife and baby and want to see them happy."

"I TOOK A VERY STRONG LIKING TO THE GIRL, BUT I DO WANT IT UNDERSTOOD THAT OURS WAS NOT A SILLY LITTLE LOVE AFFAIR. I STILL LOVE MY WIFE AND BABY."

Their connection wasn't about love; it was about pleasure. The two met up at least once a week, sometimes renting rooms by the day or, when the weather cooperated, finding secluded spots outdoors. Theora liked being able to scream with abandon, and Snook kept a blanket in his trunk for such meetups. The gun range was a regular stop for liaisons, but Theora had also taken an interest in shooting, so the two went there for target practice as well. Snook taught her how to handle pistols and rifles and eventually gave her a .41 caliber double-barrel Derringer pistol to carry in her purse, even though it was illegal to carry a concealed weapon in Ohio at the time.

The affair paused twice—once when Theora moved to New York briefly, and again for a few weeks in early 1928 when Snook was recovering from nasal surgery. During both breaks, Theora hooked up with Marion Meyers again, which Snook didn't mind. It seemed, however, that Theora had hoped to trigger some kind of jealous reaction from Snook. She wasn't as laid-back as she seemed to Meyers. Theora ruffled at the mention of Mrs. Snook and became more demanding, insisting she and Snook meet twice a week instead of once. As her demands increased, their relationship soured. What began as a frivolity was becoming more of an obligation. Their meetings sometimes devolved into fights. Four days before Theora's death, Snook was golfing with friends when the outing was interrupted by an angry Theora appearing at the fifth hole. Snook pleaded with her to keep her voice down, but she screamed that she wanted him to leave with her and would not relent until he did.

The night Theora died, she'd taken a break from her job and had been—as the cabbie had relayed—driven around looking for Snook. She finally spotted his blue Ford coupe and flagged him down. The two drove to the gun range for an assignation. Snook planned to end the affair, though he was struggling with how to do it. He figured an upcoming trip to Lebanon, Ohio, to visit his mother would provide enough distance to do the job, but he said that when Theora learned that Helen and the baby were going on the trip, she grew furious. She demanded he cancel the trip, but he refused.

"Damn you! I'll kill your wife and your baby! I'll kill you, too!" she spat, per Snook's retelling. Then she picked up her purse, which is where he knew she sometimes kept her handgun.

Snook said he was sure she was about to shoot him, so he reflexively grabbed a ball-peen hammer from a toolbox inside his car and bashed her in the head. She was stunned and screamed, "Damn you!" again. She tried to burst from the car and slam the door on Snook, but she managed to slam her own hand in the door instead. Bleeding now from the head and her hand, she reached for a handkerchief from her purse and staggered from the car. Snook slid across the seat and followed her, bashing her again and again in the head. Somehow, she was still alive, groaning in a heap on the grass. Snook told the reporters that while he was mad enough to kill her, he didn't want her to suffer, and her pitiful moans were too much to bear. He took out a pocketknife and calmly sliced her neck, making sure that he cut both her jugular vein and carotid artery to ensure a quick death.

After that, Snook said he grabbed Theora's purse and searched it—but found no gun. He'd killed her thinking she was going for a gun that she didn't even have on her that day.

While Helen Snook reported hearing the family's screen door open around 9:30 p.m.—a noise she assumed indicated that her husband had arrived home—the sound likely came from wind or other rustling, because Snook was still in his car driving away from the scene of the crime at that time. He didn't get home until 11:00 p.m. He washed his weapons of Theora's blood, and then cooked a hamburger. Helen came downstairs to check on him, and because it was dark in the kitchen, didn't notice his bloodstained clothes. The day after the slaying, Snook got his car cleaned, and he also cleared out belongings from the so-called love nest. Later, just as he mentioned to his wife that he vaguely knew the young woman whose death was reported in the newspaper that day, the police knocked on his door. Despite his best efforts to conceal his involvement, investigators had connected Snook to Theora within twenty-four hours of her murder. Once taken in for questioning, Snook was never again a free man.

Top reporters from the nation's biggest newspapers and wire services descended on Columbus for what they labeled the "Trial of the Century."[19] Snook never denied that he killed Theora, but he did expound on his motive for jurors. He said that once he and Theora arrived at the gun range, they had clumsy, unsatisfying sex in the car, after which Theora chastised Snook and berated his abilities. She also, according to Snook, performed an act on him with her mouth during which she used more force and teeth than he preferred. He was in intense pain when he swung that hammer to stop her, he said. This testimony was deemed unfit for print but was still alluded to in newspaper coverage of the day, helping to ensure that lines of spectators

Investigators search Snook's blue Ford coupe for blood stains, 1929.

Legal Legacy

The trial against James Snook was groundbreaking on several fronts, among them:

- Jurors decided to hold a well-respected man—an Olympic gold medalist, no less—accountable for killing a woman whose sexual escapades were risqué enough that journalists censored witness testimony on the grounds of decency.
- The manner in which prosecutors obtained Snook's confession—which included beatings said to have left red welts on Snook's face—sparked discussion about whether police or prosecutors should be allowed to physically beat witnesses to elicit incriminating statements, even if those confessions seem to stand up to subsequent scrutiny.
- Critics also questioned prosecutors' refusal to let Snook meet with his lawyer, which at the time wasn't a codified right for state charges.

clamored every day to find seats in the courtroom for the trial's three-week duration. It deviated in a key way from reporters' accounts a month earlier: Snook said he had no memory whatsoever of slitting Theora's throat. This, too, was what he had told police in his official confession: After beating Theora with the hammer outside of the car, he said his memory faltered. He remembered only sitting on the passenger-side running board of his car and calling out to Theora.

"I just called to her," Snook testified. "I can't tell what words I said, but I just said, 'Come on,' or 'Let's go,' or something like that. I can't remember the words, but I made some expression to her." When Theora didn't answer, fear set in. Snook said he took her purse, then tossed it from his car as he drove back home. It was clear from the prosecutors' questions on cross-examination that they found this explanation absurd.[20]

It would seem the jury did as well. The ten men and two women who had sat for weeks listening to testimony took less than half an hour to find Snook guilty. He was sentenced to death by execution. It was a swift conviction that underscored a shift in America's perspective on the agency of women. Though Theora was maligned in the press–portrayed as a vixen who'd lured a prominent man with her feminine wiles–her killer wasn't absolved.

Three months after the verdict–which had come just two months after Theora's death–Snook's appeal was rejected. The justices criticized investigators for how they elicited his confession, but they also said the circumstantial evidence would have still led to his conviction. On February 28, 1930, eight months after killing Theora, Snook spent his last day alive with his wife. He ate fried chicken, lamb chops, mashed potatoes, and ice cream, washed down with coffee, as his last meal.

"There was no restraint," said a minister who'd dined with the couple. "We might all have been at a picnic."[21]

At 7:10 p.m., Snook was strapped into Ohio's electric chair, where he was pronounced dead four minutes later.[22] His name had been so tarnished that when his remains were buried, his wife simply had "James Howard" engraved on his tombstone.[23]

Part 2

SOCIETAL SHIFTERS

FIRE ESCAPE.

6

How the Shirtwaist Factory Fire Changed Industry Standards

(1911)

Hundreds of people gathered at the base of the burning building in New York City's Greenwich Village to gawk skyward at flames and smoke pouring from the eighth, ninth, and tenth floors. Dozens of people trapped inside, pressed against the windows some eighty feet above the asphalt below, screamed in terror: "Fire! Get help!"

It was a horrifying and surreal scene to those gathered on the street, who could see that the flames behind the trapped masses were steadily growing. The people looking down knew there was no way out, so instead of burning alive they chose to jump. Most went alone, but some held hands. In one case, a man picked up three of the women near him, one by one, and held them "deliberately" through the open window in a sort of dancer's position before he them let go. William Gunn Shepherd, a reporter from United Press International who was on the scene, wrote, "They were as unresisting as if he were helping them onto a streetcar instead of into eternity."[1] The last of the three women was his sweetheart, so they embraced and kissed goodbye before she dropped, and after her broken body lay at rest on the sidewalk, the man jumped to join her.

The date was March 25, 1911. The workplace fire would ultimately kill 146 people and injure nearly eighty more, making it the deadliest industrial disaster ever in the city, as well as one of the worst in US history. The fire would also lead to manslaughter charges against the company's bosses and spark nearly three dozen new laws and statutes regulating labor. More than that, the blaze pitted bosses against workers in a way that had never been

OPPOSITE: Typical work conditions of the victims of the Triangle Shirtwaist Factory fire are seen in this photo of garment factory workers, c. 1910.

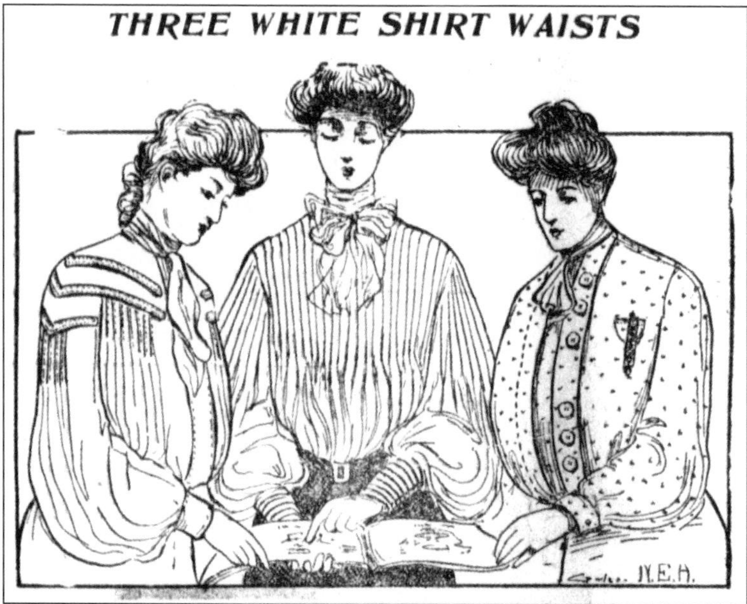

Three "spring shirt waists" are depicted in this illustration accompanying a fashion review in the *Tacoma Times*, April 20, 1904.

seen in America before, forever changing that dynamic after decades of growing tension fueled by innovation and immigration.

The company at the center of the disaster was the Triangle Waist Company, a thriving apparel firm that focused on producing a type of cotton women's blouse known as a "shirtwaist." As commonplace as the blouse is nowadays, they were revolutionary at the turn of the twentieth century, in part because they came on the heels of Singer Company's 1889 invention of the first practical electric sewing machine. By 1905, those machines were inexpensive enough to be in wide usage, which radically changed the clothing industry. Instead of laboring over handmade garb, women could buy readymade clothes for their families.

The shirtwaist, specifically, was a button-down design modeled after menswear that had emerged in the 1860s as an alternative to bodice-and-skirt ensembles. Thanks to electric sewing machines, these shirtwaists could be mass produced and sold for reasonable prices, meaning that most women could afford to buy one. Because of this, it became more difficult to gauge a woman's social status based on her clothing alone. At the same time, women were starting to work outside of the home more often—and many felt most comfortable tackling jobs they were familiar with, so while fewer women were hand-sewing the basics at home, plenty got jobs doing that work at factories. The Triangle Company employed hundreds of young immigrants, many of whom were women.

They generally weren't paid well. Many companies like Triangle set up shop in deplorable conditions, and as there were few regulations at the time, the workers' only recourse was to quit. Sometimes the work was done by women crammed into rooms of tenements—rundown, overcrowded buildings housing multiple families that had become ubiquitous to deal with the huge influx of immigrants combined with a massive housing shortage. These workshops were "fraught with grave danger to the health and morale of the community," said John Story, a New York State factory inspector in a story headlined "Abolish Sweatshops, Pleads Inspector Story," that ran on October 4, 1900, in the *Brooklyn Daily Eagle*.[2] He said that clothing companies operating out of tenements were "well known to be labor in its most poorly compensated form" and described diseases that had been spread by selling clothes contaminated with germs originating inside the cramped, unsanitary quarters.

These makeshift, sweatshop garment factories were housed in dank rooms, many of which didn't even have windows to the outdoors. The air was stale and dusty. Fires were commonplace. The workers were paid miserable wages. The oversight was so lacking that often workers would receive their pay only to realize it was a fraction of the amount expected; bosses were free to dock them for thread used or sewing-machine maintenance. Without legal recourse, the workers largely swallowed the lousy pay and horrid conditions because they desperately needed the work.

Triangle Waist Company wasn't a sweatshop, however. In fact, the two men who owned the company—Isaac Harris and Max Blanck—had themselves worked in awful conditions and vowed to do better by their own workers after they saved enough money to launch a company. Instead of operating out of a cheap tenement room, they took over three whole floors of lower Manhattan's Asch Building, named after its original owner, Joseph J. Asch. When it was built in 1900–1901 on Washington Place, the iron-and-steel structure had been heralded for its fireproof rooms. Sweatshops might burn easily, but this was a state-of-the-art building. As such, it attracted several garment makers as tenants. The Triangle factory had started out small but gradually grew until it employed more than five hundred workers, mostly Italian and Jewish immigrant women and girls, although some men worked there, too. The most prized job was as a cutter, which—not surprisingly in this era before women could even vote—was given to men. The job was to slice through stacks of cloth using electric blades. Those fabric fragments would then be pieced into a shirt. A good cutter kept wasted cloth to a bare minimum; the less cloth he wasted, the more profits the company retained.

Blanck and Harris had both been born in Russia before immigrating to the United States in the 1890s. They were in their twenties when they met in New York City, where they both worked for meager pay in the garment industry for about a decade. Harris's strength was as a garment maker, while Blanck's forte was business sense. As such, Harris figured out what equipment to buy and how to most efficiently make shirts, while Blanck served as the company's salesman. They proved to be formidable partners, selling shirts that cost about $3 at the time (about $94 in 2022 terms) in a venture that earned them the nickname the "Shirtwaist Kings."[3] Their personal fortunes grew so that they could upgrade from modest apartments to lavish brownstones overlooking the Hudson River. Each employed several household servants and arrived to work in chauffeured cars. By 1908, the factory was clearing $1 million a year. Still, competition was fierce, so holding onto their royalty status grew tougher by the week.[4] Just on the island of Manhattan, more than five hundred blouse manufacturers worked to dethrone the pair by cramming more workers into tighter quarters churning out shirts at half the cost.[5] To make sure as much profit was retained as possible, Triangle bosses kept a tight rein on workers. They were fined for mistakes and forced to work twelve-hour days—often including weekends. Despite this, working at Triangle was a coveted gig because the factory was more modern than most. It had high ceilings and natural light due to its huge windows, and the layout allowed for more air circulation. Still, conditions remained grueling, and production demands routinely led to women sewing straight through their fingers, which was not only painful but costly. Accidents were commonplace, and workers who got hurt typically found themselves replaced. The government imposed few regulations, instead adopting a laissez-faire attitude that reasoned that restrictions placed on business owners would translate to less growth in the economy.

Harris laid out the Triangle workspace to get as many sewing machines onto each floor as possible, while also minimizing conversation among the workers. As intended, this maximized production. Triangle had started operating from the Asch Building's ninth floor, then expanded to the eighth, and by 1911, the executives were situated on the tenth floor. But the growth wasn't painless. As they watched their bosses grow wealthier, the workers grew more resentful as the company's success only seemed to translate to tighter quarters and heftier demands. To make ends meet, mothers recruited their daughters to sew alongside them. It was not uncommon to find a girl as young as fourteen years old at a sewing machine. The garment workers began to grumble—and then to organize. The International Ladies' Garment Workers' Union had started in 1900 and, after years of trying myriad methods, had determined that going on strike was the best path for change. On September 26, 1909, that's what Triangle workers did. Strikers walked off the job, demanding higher wages. They also wanted their weekly hours capped at fifty-four, limiting them to six, nine-hour days per week, instead of the approximately seventy hours a week that workers had been toiling.

Max Blanck and Isaac Harris, owners of the Triangle Waist Company, c. 1908.

Harris and Blanck tried to nip these demands in the bud, going so far as to send hired goons to beat a Ukranian-born union organizer named Clara Lemlich. Still healing from six broken ribs, Clara gave a brief-but-historic speech before a gathering of thousands of laborers at New York City's Cooper Union on November 22, 1909. After a series of mealy-mouthed, ineffective, droning lectures by labor leaders, Lemich told the crowd: "I have listened to all the speakers. I have no further patience for talk. I am one of those who suffers from the abuses described here, and I move that we go on a general strike."[6] This was followed by cheers, stamps, and screams for five minutes, followed by a unanimous vote to strike. It was dubbed the Uprising of the Twenty Thousand. The Triangle workers had already been on strike for more than a month at this point, which was costing the company thousands of dollars, but Harris and Blanck had hung tough since they figured it was only a matter of time before their workers grew so desperate that they came crawling back to the factory. With the widespread uprising, however, the workers were fortified by thousands of other strikers. Faced with a showdown, the bosses turned up the heat. New York City and State were at this time controlled by a Democratic political organization known as Tammany Hall, which had aligned itself with the working class—though it ultimately would go down in history for its extensive corruption. (It's worth noting that Daniel Sickles, the man acquitted of killing Philip Barton Keys [see chapter 3], was a product of Tammany Hall[7] and accused of questionable business practices.) Tammany had formed in the late seventeenth century and peaked after the Civil War, but still clung to significant power in the early- to mid-twentieth century. It was the kind of power that could determine who would grace the ballot for Democrats. Tammany allies were placed in key positions throughout the city, as well as in state offices. People who managed to keep Tammany coffers full and deliver neighborhoods to Tammany candidates on Election Day might be rewarded with city contracts or government jobs. They were clever in their marketing to voters, too, first by presenting themselves as protectors of the working class. They also wooed average Joes and Janes by providing free picnics and sightseeing trips to curry support.

Tammany leaders made sure that they had allies on the police force, and those who supported the organization had a tendency to climb quickly up the ranks. The police chief was often on the payroll, too. Harris and Blanck knew Tammany had the power to push through legislation that could hurt their bottom line, so they greased that wheel, bribing police in hopes of keeping the workers down. Sometimes a hired goon would start a fight, beat a picketer bloody, and then police would come along and arrest the picketer rather than the goon. One striker after another wound their way through the court system, often facing judges who were on Tammany's payroll. As demoralizing as it must have been, the workers didn't give up. Like Clara

Women picketing during the New York Shirt Waist Strike, also known as the Uprising of the 20,000, February 1910.

Lemlich, they kept fighting, even with broken bones. After enough of these incidents were reported in the press, public opinion began to sway in favor of the workers. To combat the bad PR, Harris and Blanck started hiring female sex workers to pummel the strikers instead of burly men, but that didn't stem the tide. Public sympathy kept going the strikers' way, eventually drawing support from high-society women like Anne Tracy Morgan, daughter of the famously powerful financier J. P. Morgan. Having Morgan in their corner proved invaluable to the strikers, helping raise both awareness and money to help cushion lost wages and allowing the strike to continue into February 1910. Finally, the strike ended with many of the workers' demands being met—such as better pay and shorter hours. Workplace safety hadn't been touted as a priority, though events would unfold a year later that would prove it should have been.[8]

After the strike, workers at Triangle went back their sewing machines, though there was inevitably leftover tension and hostility that lingered from the ordeal, and the focus was still on maximizing productivity. Even the building's communication system was set up to keep chatter among workers to a minimum. Someone with a concern on the eighth or ninth floors could only call executives on the tenth; they had no way to reach their fellow workers on the neighboring floor. To even further curtail any chitchat, employees recently had been instructed to use a newly installed telautograph, which was a precursor to the fax machine. The device allowed the transmission of one person's handwriting to a distant point over a two-wire circuit. Again, though, the two worker floors couldn't speak to each other, each could get a message to the executives by pressing a button to sound an alarm that a message was incoming, and then writing a message on a sheet of paper that would appear simultaneously on another sheet on the tenth floor.

The bosses' primary focus was on curbing wasted time because it cut into production, which in turn cut into profits. Additionally, whether it was true or fueled by paranoia, Blanck and Harris became convinced that workers were routinely stealing materials from the shop. To combat the supposed problem, they kept one of each floor's two exits locked every day at quitting time so that workers would be forced to leave through a single door, where their bags were searched by nightwatchmen looking for pilfered blouses or bits of lace. Blanck would later acknowledge that even at its worst, theft by employees was minimal, costing the company about $25 in total[9]—representing less than .001 percent of the company's $1 million yearly profits. Regardless, every night at the end of the shift, the employees—mostly women—would grab their coats and purses and line up to be searched before exiting a door that led to Greene Street. (The door leading to Washington Place was the one typically locked every night, while the remaining streets that hugged the block-long building—Waverly Place and Washington Square East—had no exits.) Because fire-safety laws weren't widespread yet, the doors on these exits swung inward.

Saturday, March 25, 1911, began as a typical workday. Thanks to the strike a year earlier, staffing was a tad lighter than it would have been on a weekday, but not by much. Those who opted not to work—usually for religious reasons—weren't paid, so those who were willing to toil on the Sabbath for eight hours were spread among the three Triangle floors of the Asch building. Despite the widespread lack of safety precautions, there were a few rules that were supposed to help mitigate fire risk. For example, Harris and Blanck had taken to having pails of water available on each floor to help douse any early embers. Also, no one was supposed to smoke on the factory floor; blouses hung from one end to the other on wires stretched above. Each workstation had boxes filled with cloth scraps, and cans of machine oil were stored around the floor.[10] But cutters—the men tasked with saving as much fabric as possible—were so prized that bosses often bent the rules to keep them happy, even if that meant looking the other way as the cutters smoked cigars or cigarettes next to piles of thin, gauzy, highly flammable fabric—which is what apparently happened just before the day's 4:45 p.m. quitting time. No one knows which cutter it was or if he flicked a match or a cigarette, but the first flame was seen at 4:40 p.m. on the eighth floor.

Because of the usually cramped conditions at these factories, fires weren't uncommon. They often happened in the slower season before business hours when the businesses were empty. Even with Triangle being housed in the supposedly fireproof Asch building, the company routinely had fires in off-hours.[11] Insurance companies had grown suspicious that some of these factory fires had been set on purpose to pad the accounts in lean months, but at least with Triangle, nothing had ever been proven. Regardless of the cause of Triangle's previous fires, however, the one that started this Saturday did not seem intentionally set. Harris and Blanck were not only present when the blaze began, but they had family members there that day, including a teenage daughter who was just visiting. A manager named Samuel Bernstein was Blanck's brother-in-law and the cousin of Harris's wife. Working on the eighth floor, he was one of the first to spot trouble and grabbed pail after pail of water, each of which proved utterly useless. While his intentions were no doubt to save lives, his attempts to battle the blaze in those first few crucial minutes likely did the opposite. The efforts were in vain, and the fire spread incredibly quickly.

While Bernstein wasted precious minutes with pails of water, other workers tried to call for help. Dinah Lipschitz, who worked at a desk in a back corner, was tallying wages for the day when she realized the situation was growing dire. She turned to the new telautograph, signaled that a message was incoming, and scrawled "FIRE!" onto the pad.[12] Two floors up, a cousin of Bernstein's, Mary Alter, had spent the day typing up bills and helping to staff the switchboard. She noticed the alert that a message from

ABOVE: The twisted remains of the faulty fire escape at the back of the Triangle factory, photographed after the fire.

OPPOSITE: Firefighters on the scene at the Triangle factory fire. Their equipment was unable to reach the fire on the top floor of the building, and their ladders only reached the sixth floor.

another floor was coming, but no message followed. She assumed workers were toying with the new device as they lined up to leave for the day and thought nothing of it.[13] It took about two minutes before Dinah on the eighth floor realized that no response was coming from Mary on the tenth. Dinah grabbed the phone and called instead. By the time Mary answered, the eighth floor was in a panic, making it tough to decipher Dinah's words over the screams in the background. After a few beats, she heard the word "fire!" and dropped the phone to get the executives to safety. Dinah had no way of reaching anyone on the ninth floor. She had to trust that Mary would relay the message to the workers sandwiched between them.[14]

People on the eighth floor began trying to rush downstairs. People on the tenth floor went up instead. Once they reached the roof, they were spotted by students in a classroom in the neighboring New York University Law School building. The students sprang from their seats to help—extending ladders over the divide to serve as makeshift planks—helping around fifty people escape.[15] The two hundred or so workers on the ninth floor had no idea of what was happening until the floor below them was engulfed. They'd never even had a fire drill. The Washington Place door was locked, so the workers began stampeding toward the other door, which swung inward. As the mass of people reached the door, they pushed it closed, making it impossible for anyone to get out. Some were crushed to death before the fire even reached them. Others remembered that there was a fire escape, so they pivoted to use it. Though better designs were in other buildings, the Asch building's fire escape was flimsy and barely eighteen inches wide. The connecting drop ladders were never fully installed. Packed with panicked people, the fire escape tore away from the wall, plunging more than two dozen workers to their deaths down the air shaft. Meanwhile, the Greene Street stairwell was in flames, leaving only the elevators as a possible exit route. Only a dozen people could fit per trip, and time was running out.

"It was Bedlam," said the son of Rose Rosenfeld, an Austrian immigrant who instinctively thought of her bosses. Rose realized that if anyone was going to survive this, it would be them, so she picked up a skirt, wrapped it around her head and ran through the flames and to the tenth floor. Seeing the place emptied, she instinctively kept climbing up, onto the roof, where she was helped across to a neighboring roof. She and a few workers who'd followed her survived. Those who stayed, or who tried to go down instead of up, perished.[16]

As terror tore through the ninth floor, curious observers gathered at the ground level. It had been a beautiful spring Saturday, so Washington Square Park had been crowded with picnickers who first saw smoke, and then flames. They stood beneath the open windows and screamed for the workers to wait, that help was coming—and firefighters did arrive within minutes. But even within that short window of time, the place had devolved into an inferno. Making matters worse was the fact that fire truck ladders could only reach up to the sixth floor. Firefighters did have nets in which people could attempt to jump, but they had been known to work for people jumping six or fewer stories—and even that was under ideal conditions. These women were jumping from nine stories up off the ground. Still, some tried for the nets. Their bodies ripped through the material as though it were tissue paper. Only one woman survived the initial jump from that height, and while firefighters at first thought she that she might survive, they could see that she was badly injured—she sadly died within hours from internal bleeding. They packed away the nets, worried that their presence might falsely suggest to some in the windows above that they stood a chance if they jumped. With no nets to aim for, one worker decided to jump toward the ladder that stopped three floors beneath her. She, too, perished. Her coworkers could see that they were doomed.

Some died of smoke inhalation; some burned to death. But many chose instead to open the windows and step onto the ledge—and out into oblivion. William Gunn Shepherd happened to be near the scene when the fire started, and in a wire story, he wrote[17]:

> **I learned a new sound, a more horrible sound than description can picture. It was the thud of a speeding, living body on a stone sidewalk. Thud-dead. Thud-dead. Thud-dead. Thud-dead. Sixty-two thud-deads. I call them that, because the sound and the thought of death came to me each time, at the same instant. There was plenty of chance to watch them as they came down. The height was eighty feet.**

Shepherd described the onlookers begging the women not to jump. "Stay there!" they screamed. He wrote:

> **I even watched one girl falling. Waving her arms, trying to keep her body upright until the very instant she struck the sidewalk, she was trying to balance herself. Then came the thud—then a silent, unmoving pile of clothing and twisted, broken limbs.**

It's from Shepherd's reporting that we know of the man who helped two women jump before he helped his lover out the window, followed by himself. Shepherd wrote of the man:

> **His coat fluttered upward; the air filled his trouser legs; I could see that he wore tan shoes and hose. His hat remained on his head. Thud—dead! Thud—dead! They went into eternity together. I saw his face before they covered it; could see in it that this was a real man. He had done his best.**

The fire lasted less than half an hour. In that time, 146 people died—123 women and 23 men. The youngest victim was a 14-year-old girl. The 62 who died on the sidewalks were somewhat identifiable, but not so the dozens more who'd been charred beyond recognition. In hopes of identifying the dead, their remains were lined up on a pier along the East River. Family members filed by, looking for something about the corpses that would betray their identities. One girl recognized her mother's corpse by the hair on her head that hadn't burned away. The girl had styled her mother that day, and while she couldn't make out the features of the corpse's face, she knew it was her mother by the braid in her hair.[18] Ultimately, all but seven bodies were identified. Those seven were buried on April 5, 1911, in a mass funeral.

That same day, a massive protest march wound its way down Fifth Avenue in Manhattan, drawing an estimated 350,000 onlookers. Their grief and horror upon learning of the fire days earlier had quickly turned to outrage. The descriptive story by William Gunn Shepherd helped fuel the protest, especially because of the way he ended the piece. "These girls were all shirt waist makers," he wrote. "As I looked at the heap of dead bodies I remembered their great strike of last year, in which these girls demanded more sanitary work rooms and more safety precautions in shops."

Charles Seymour Whitman was a progressive man serving as New York County district attorney, though his ambitions aimed much higher. Someday, he hoped to move into the governor's mansion. He was astute enough to realize that the public would demand that someone be blamed for the conflagration at the Triangle factory. Early criticism questioned why firefighters hadn't come armed with axes to smash down the doors that had been locked, while the fire chief pointed fingers instead at the city's building department for allowing such tall buildings in the first place.[19] After an investigation, Whitman decided the Triangle's owners were to blame. He filed manslaughter charges against Harris and Blanck—charges that hinged on whether the two had ordered the Washington Place doors to be locked in their efforts to thwart theft. Several surviving workers testified that that indeed had been the standard practice, but the two men hired one of the city's best defense lawyers, Max D. Steuer, who put on what David Von Drehle, author of *Triangle: The Fire That Changed America* (2003), described as a "brilliant defense."

"His cross examination of the key witness is still taught in some law schools," Von Drehle said.[20]

He undermined survivors' memories of the day and painted the panic on the ninth floor as more at fault for the deaths than the locked door. Harris and Blanck were acquitted of criminal charges. As they left the courthouse, a brother of one of the fire's victims accosted them, screaming that they

were murderers before collapsing in the street and being rushed to the hospital. He wasn't alone in his outrage. Those immersed in the labor movement were determined to make sure the deaths at least led to change, so they pushed and protested. Their efforts were fueled by the paltry settlement eventually accepted by families of the victims, who were given just $75 apiece.[21] Tammany Hall, which had just a year earlier been helping to keep the workers down, had seen some turnover in leadership, and with that, the organization seemed to have a change of heart. An investigating commission—the Factory Investigation Commission—cochaired by Tammany politician Al Smith—who would later become New York governor and the Democratic candidate for president in 1928—conducted one of the most

Family members of the victims walk by rows of open coffins at the 26th Street Pier morgue, attempting to identify victims of the Triangle fire.

extensive investigations in state history. More than four hundred witnesses testified, creating some 7,000 pages of transcripts that outlined routine abuse by business owners at the expense of workers. Profits were paramount; safety was rarely a consideration. This led to the passage of dozens of new workplace safety laws in New York that would serve as models for laws in other states, and eventually the federal government.[22]

These laws started with fire-safety protocols, such as requiring automatic sprinklers in high-rise buildings and mandatory fire drills in large shops. Doors couldn't be locked, and they had to swing outward rather than inward. But the outrage sparked by this disaster fueled more than fire laws. The tragedy brought to light the routine dehumanization of workers. Regulations were adopted requiring improved eating and bathroom facilities and restricting the number of hours women and children could legally work. Even the federal minimum wage, which wasn't adopted until 1938, can be tied directly to the Triangle fire. That's because Frances Perkins, who was labor secretary under President Franklin D. Roosevelt in the 1930s and spearheaded the cause, had witnessed the fire in person.[23] She'd been among the hundreds who gathered streetside and gazed in horror at the crush of people frantically clawing at the windows. She'd watched the thud-dead of dozens of workers, and, as was true for so many witnesses that day, she vowed to do what she could to keep businesses from forcing others into the same fate.

Legal Legacy

The Triangle fire was a turning point in American workplace safety, not just because of its death toll, but because of the subsequent investigation that outlined workers' efforts to improve their working conditions in the years leading up to the fire. Among the impacts:

- Pressured by activists, New York governor John Alden Dix created the Factory Investigating Commission three months after the blaze. The FIC examined nearly 3,000 factories in dozens of industries and enacted several dozen occupational safety laws, covering fire safety and factory inspections, sanitation and employment rules for women and children, and more.
- The FIC led to the formation of an Industrial Commission in New York, to which Triangle fire witness Frances Perkins was appointed in 1919. In 1933, Perkins became the first woman to serve in a presidential cabinet, as the US Secretary of Labor.

7

The Radium Girls' Fight for Workplace Safety

(1917–1920s)

Amelia Maggia had been feeling rotten for months. It began with a terrible toothache, which her dentist treated in the most straightforward way possible: he pulled the tooth. But the hole left behind by the extraction refused to heal, and the pain didn't go away. Amelia was in agony, and she was embarrassed as well, with a festering ulcer in her mouth that oozed pus. Then the pain began to spread, first from her tooth to her jaw, and then to completely unrelated parts of her body. Her hips began to ache, followed by her feet. The twenty-four-year-old woman began walking with a limp.

None of this made any sense to Mollie, as her friends called her. She'd always been energetic and lively, landing her first job as a teenager and becoming financially independent enough that she moved out of her family's home and into an all-female boarding house—not a common feat for a young woman at the time. In May of that year, she visited surgeon Joseph Knef in hope that he might be able to achieve what had eluded the other doctors and stop her horrific pain. Knef took a look inside of Mollie's mouth and gently touched her face. Her jawbone snapped in his hand. Horrified, Dr. Knef removed the bone fragment—not by conducting any sort of surgery, but by simply pulling it from her mouth with his fingers.[1]

Within six months, in September 1922, Mollie was dead at twenty-five. While Knef was sure she was poisoned, this case would prove to be far more complex than your average homicide. For Mollie was just one of dozens of employees who would ultimately die from exposure to a mysterious killer unleashed by greedy companies that lied to protect their profits. The case that took years of lawsuits and court hearings to unfold not only made headlines nationwide but would forever change how America protects its workers.

Mollie's story began about five years earlier, which is when she and two of her sisters—Albina and Quinta—were hired to work for one of the most talked-about companies in town: the United States Radium Corp. It wasn't a glamorous job by any stretch. It was, in fact, fairly tedious work, but it was still one of the most sought-after gigs in the small town of Orange, New Jersey. Its pay was commensurate with that of skilled labor at the time, yet most of the people landing the jobs were teenagers who hadn't even graduated high school yet. The job entailed painting numerals on watch dials with a paint that glowed in the dark, for watches to be used by the US Army. The paint was invented by Dr. Sabin Arnold von Sochocky, a Ukraine-born American citizen who was cofounder of the corporation. He marketed his paint—a mix of radium and zinc sulfide—with the trade name Undark.[2] Today, such paint is made with phosphors like silver-activated zinc sulfide or strontium aluminate, which is generally considered safe so long as you don't eat it. When the Maggia girls were hired, however, the paint got its luminescent quality by being mixed with a somewhat newly discovered substance called radium.

A 1921 magazine ad for Undark, a product of the Radium Luminous Material Corporation.

Physicists Marie and Pierre Curie had discovered radium in 1898; they extracted it from uraninite ore they had been studying in their research on radiation. Marie especially was captivated by the silvery-white element that in sufficient quantities glowed an ethereal blue. She referred to the element as "my beautiful radium"[3] and put granules of the stuff in vials that she would show off as "fairy lights."[4] Soon, scientists discovered that when exposed to radium, cancer cells shrank faster than healthy cells, meaning that this discovery showed promise in fighting one of humanity's cruelest diseases. The medical community became hopeful that radium heralded a panacea for all of life's ills: arthritis, hypertension, schizophrenia, renal failure, fatigue, constipation, gout, low libido. Consumer companies caught wind of the potential and saw dollar signs. Radium was added to creams, candies, and rejuvenating powders and lotions. The energy drink Radithor was introduced in the 1920s and marketed first toward arthritis sufferers, as evidenced by newspaper ads of the era.[5] "It puts the sunshine into your blood stream," promised one such ad that labeled the stuff "the new weapon of curative science."[6]

People seeking energy and vitality could soak in irradiated water at health spas. Manufacturers sold radium-lined jugs for $200 and encouraged people to drink six to eight glasses of water from that jug daily. All of this was separate from one of the peripheral uses of radium, which was to make things glow in the dark. For the most part, that use was just for fun. There were glow-in-the-dark necklaces and neckties, for example. But during World War I, the ability to see objects in the dark proved practical, too. The military used glow-in the-dark paint on airplane controls, ship panels, compasses, and watch dials. After the war ended, the demand for the latter product didn't wane. It was useful to be able to quickly tell the time in the dark. Companies using the luminescent paint began popping up in cities nationwide, many hiring large groups of young women to work as so-called "radium girls."

"They were kind of suited to this work because if you think of the tiny, tiny numbers on watches, some of them were only a millimeter in width," said Kate Moore, author of *The Radium Girls: The Dark Story of America's*

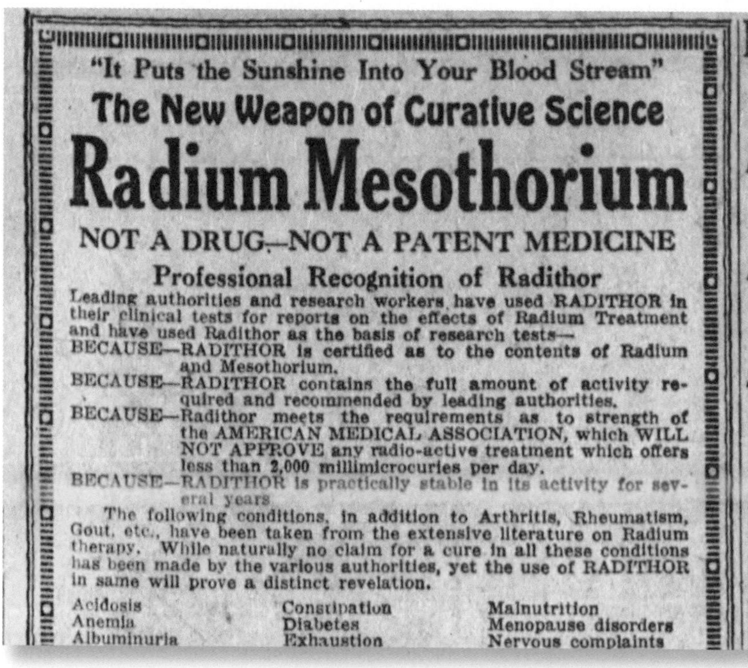

"It Puts the Sunshine Into Your Blood Stream"
The New Weapon of Curative Science
Radium Mesothorium
NOT A DRUG—NOT A PATENT MEDICINE
Professional Recognition of Radithor
Leading authorities and research workers have used RADITHOR in their clinical tests for reports on the effects of Radium Treatment and have used Radithor as the basis of research tests—
BECAUSE—RADITHOR is certified as to the contents of Radium and Mesothorium.
BECAUSE—RADITHOR contains the full amount of activity required and recommended by leading authorities.
BECAUSE—Radithor meets the requirements as to strength of the AMERICAN MEDICAL ASSOCIATION, which WILL NOT APPROVE any radio-active treatment which offers less than 2,000 millimicrocuries per day.
BECAUSE—RADITHOR is practically stable in its activity for several years
The following conditions, in addition to Arthritis, Rheumatism, Gout, etc., have been taken from the extensive literature on Radium therapy. While naturally no claim for a cure in all these conditions has been made by the various authorities, yet the use of RADITHOR in same will prove a distinct revelation.
Acidosis
Anemia
Albuminuria
Constipation
Diabetes
Exhaustion
Malnutrition
Menopause disorders
Nervous complaints

This newspaper ad from 1928 for Radium Mesothorium, the touted ingredient in the energy drink called Radithor, promised to cure everything from arthritis and diabetes to constipation and insomnia.

Shining Women (2017). "The small hands of these young teenage women were particularly suited to this job."[7] Their delicate hands were aided by very fine camel-hair brushes, but even still, the individual hairs of the brush could get unruly, threatening to smear the paint outside of the intended area. As Moore wrote: "The smallest pocket watch they painted measured only three-and-a-half centimeters across its face, meaning the tiniest element for painting was a single millimeter in width."[8] To keep the brushes as tightly tapered as possible, the workers were trained in lip pointing. This is a technique that anyone who's ever threaded a needle for sewing might recognize; it's often used to ensure the thread doesn't fray as it goes into the tiny needle eye. The workers would put the brush to their lips, then dip the brush in the irradiated paint, and then paint the tiny little numbers on the watches and clocks. Some initially questioned if they should wash the brushes before lip pointing again, but they were assured by company managers that the paint was perfectly safe. After all, it was made from the same element being added to countless other products and touted as a cure-all.

Marie Becker not only had misgivings her first day on the job, but so did her mother. When Marie came home from training at the Radium Dial Company in Ottawa, Illinois, both were unsettled by the idea of Marie putting that paint in her mouth day in and day out as she painted the dials. But Marie ended up keeping the job for two key reasons: first, she was assured by her employers that the paint was safe—it would in fact "put pink cheeks on you"[9]—and second, the pay. Marie would later recall that she was hired at $17.50 a week—a huge pay increase over her previous job at a five-and-dime store, where she'd made about $5 a week.[10] She felt blessed, and others felt envious. The women would walk home from work at night literally glowing like otherworldly beings. Some loved it so much, they'd skip showering, especially if they had a party to attend. Dial painting was a coveted job, so the tell-tale glow was a bit of silent showboating. At the end of the workday, knowing that whatever was left in their jars would be wasted, the girls would sometimes play with the stuff, painting their fingernails or painting mustaches on their faces. Marie recalled a group of girls painting parts of their faces, then going into a dark room, where they could only see the painted parts. "All you see is the radium," Marie said. "You're looking at eyebrows and mustaches and teeth."[11]

Radium Girls at work in a factory of the United States Radium Corp., c. 1922.

When Mollie Maggia died in December 1922, it wasn't clear at first what had caused her mysterious illness. The ailment had eaten away at her bones and infected her blood.[12] Her colleague Helen Quinlan died next, six months later, in June 1923. Next was Irene Rudolph. Then Catherine O'Donnell. Then Hazel Kuser. By 1927, dozens of women had died horrible, painful deaths. Sarah Maillefer was among them.[13]

Born Sarah Carlough, she'd been a rarity at the company, having been hired at twenty-eight—making her one of the oldest "girls" hired for the gig. A few years later, she started feeling achy and rundown, but she figured that was simply because she'd reached her thirties. With age comes fatigue. Still, it concerned her when she started needing a cane to walk. By the late spring of 1925, she'd dropped a shocking amount of weight and would bruise at the slightest touch. Her younger sister, Marguerite, was sick, too, and in the hospital under the care of Dr. Harrison Martland. Martland had studied at the College of Physicians and Surgeons in New York and also served as chief pathologist at the Newark City Hospital, where he ran his own laboratory. The first time he'd paid attention to the illness that was felling dial painters was because it had killed someone far higher profile: Dr. Edwin Leman, chief chemist of the United States Radium Corporation. Leman's death had initially been blamed on anemia, but Martland was called in to conduct an autopsy because the death, on June 5, 1925[14], had been so swift after the onset of symptoms. That led Martland to Marguerite, who, in turn, led him to Sarah Maillefer. By this point, Martland suspected radiation poisoning, but the only way doctors knew how to test for the disease was after death, by essentially cremating the body and testing the ashes for radioactive substances. With Sarah still alive—and now so ill that she had been admitted as a patient herself—he was able to devise a breath test he could administer antemortem instead. It wasn't easy for Sarah to muster the lung strength for the test, but she fought through it. The test proved that, even though Sarah had stopped working at the dial factory years earlier, she still exhaled radium with every breath. Though she'd been in better shape than her sister when she met Martland, Sarah deteriorated quickly. The breath test was conducted on June 16, 1925; she died two days later[15] of symptoms that Martland told reporters looked an awful lot like the ones that had plagued Dr. Leman.

"The circumstances of the two deaths were so similar that I decided upon a careful inquiry," he said.[16] "If my suspicions are correct, this poisoning is so insidious and sometimes takes so long to manifest itself that I think it possible it has been going on for a long time throughout the country without being discovered."[17]

Sarah was the first of the radium girls to be autopsied. Martland found radium everywhere—her bones, her blood, her organs. The highest concentrations were where she felt the most pain—her legs and jaw. Radium had even worn away her left leg so that it was four centimeters shorter than her right, causing her limp. Marguerite, realizing that she was only months away from the same fate, became a plaintiff in the first lawsuit against a radium-paint company. Others would follow. It would be through depositions and testimony related to those lawsuits that the world would come to learn that the creator of the paint had known from the start that it might be dangerous. That knowledge came courtesy of a worker named Grace Fryer, who'd begun working at the United States Radium Corporation on April 10, 1917, just four days after the United States declared war on Germany and formally entered World War I.[18] Sometime in 1918, Dr. von Sochocky had passed through the plant while Grace painted away, lip-pointing her brush and dipping it into the irradiated paint as usual.

"Do not do that," von Sochocky said as Grace put the brush between her lips. "You will get sick."[19]

The comment jumped out at Grace enough that she went to talk with Anna Rooney, the forewoman. "She told me there was nothing to it," Grace would later recall. "She told me it was not harmful."[20]

During court testimony, Dr. von Sochocky would downplay his warning to Grace, saying that he merely worried that the practice of lip pointing was unsanitary, but in the end, no amount of spin could change the truth: von Sochocky himself would die of radiation poisoning in 1928.[21] His demise came just months after his company settled a lawsuit with Grace and other coworkers, including the still-surviving Maggia sisters. The settlement—for $10,000 cash, medical attendance, and a life pension of $600 annually for each plantiff—fell far short of the $1.25 million they'd initially demanded, but they were sick and dying and desperate for help in covering their mounting medical bills. Something was better than nothing, after all, and most of the girls had little education and were from lower-class families. Many of their illnesses and deaths had been written off as diseases common among the poor, with syphilis a frequent scapegoat. This falsehood was reinforced by the fact that the illnesses didn't all present in the same way across the various victims. The trouble usually began in the girls' mouths, but not always. Some girls were hit with sudden fatigue. Others felt like the bones in their feet or shoulders were brittle and achy.

> "THE HEALTH OF THE EMPLOYEES OF THE RADIUM DIAL COMPANY IS ALWAYS FOREMOST IN THE MINDS OF ITS OFFICIALS."

Despite the variations in symptoms, newspaper reporters of the day pushed back on the industry's insistence that all the illnesses were unconnected. Each woman who died sparked another headline. The media coverage was bad enough that the industry took pains to combat it. On June 7, 1928, the Ottawa plant began running an advertisement in local newspapers that insisted radium poisoning didn't exist. The company had hired well-known doctors and technical experts to conduct physical and medical exams on employees, and "nothing even approaching such symptoms or conditions has ever been found by these men. On the contrary, they have commented on the high standard of health and appearance of our employees." The last line of the ad read: "The health of the employees of the Radium Dial Company is always foremost in the minds of its officials."[22]

Yet, five months later, the *New York Times* pulled no punches when reporting on von Sochocky's death, topping it with the headline: "RADIUM PAINT TAKES ITS INVENTOR'S LIFE."[23]

Though that happened in 1928, it would be nearly another decade before the matter had worked its way through the American court system. The evidence was again complicated by the fact that the girls had been exposed to varying levels of radiation that affected them in unpredictable ways. Additionally, not everyone exposed to radium suffered immediate or consistent symptoms. Myriad factors seemed to determine which girls were affected and how—while some, apparently graced with resilient genes—experienced no ill effects at all. Once concerns were raised that radium might have played a role in workers' illnesses, company officials could easily point to anecdotal cases in which an employee had toiled for months with the substance and yet remained alive and well. Even so, some workers got married and opted not to continue working, while others changed jobs.[24]

Still others trusted what their bosses told them and kept their jobs, even if they, themselves, had been unwell. Catherine Wolfe Donohue, at Radium Dial, fell into that last category. She'd fallen ill in the 1920s and wondered if radium was to blame, but the bosses' assurances had calmed her fears. By the late 1920s, she was having fainting spells and walking with a pronounced limp. In 1931, she was called into her boss's office and fired. The executives said she was making other workers uncomfortable. It wasn't a good look for the company to have her limping around in front of the other girls.[25]

Meanwhile, someone else's ill health made headlines. This time it was a well-known golf champion named Eben Byers, who had been a huge proponent of radium products—especially of the energy tonic Radithor (see page 89). Byers, the scion of an industrialist, was prescribed the patented medicine in 1927 for pain in his arm and began taking several doses a day. At first, as he reportedly told the Federal Trade Commission just months before his death, he was impressed with Radithor and consumed thousands of bottles.[26] By 1930, the effects had worn off, so he stopped taking it. Soon after, he began suffering from headaches and lost weight. His teeth fell out. His lawyer told the Federal Trade Commission that all that remained of Byers' upper jaw were two front teeth; the rest had been removed, as had most of his lower jaw. His bone tissue was disintegrating, and holes had formed in his skull. "Medical science can hold out no hope for him," said FTC Chairman W. E. Humphrey. "His is a slow, torturous, certain death."[27] When Byers died at age fifty-one on March 31, 1932, it brought an end to radium products,

though many who made money off those sales still denied radium was to blame. Dr. C. C. Moyar of Pittsburgh, who'd initially prescribed Radithor to Byers, said that his death was caused by gout, which in turn caused by a "serious blood disease and accentuated by the use of alcohol."[28]

The Eben story worried Catherine, but she had a life to lead. In 1933, she gave birth to a little boy named Tommy, followed the next year by a girl named Mary Jane. Both of the children seemed generally healthy, though when Mary Jane reached age two, she weighed only ten pounds. On Easter Sunday in 1937, Catherine Donohue's priest came by to give her communion—a kind gesture because she was too weak to go to church—and as she received the symbol of Christ's body, part of her jawbone broke through the flesh inside of her mouth. She decided it was time to sue.[29]

While Catherine's suit wasn't the first filed, it ended up being the case that finally seemed to make a difference. Marie Becker—who now went by her married name of Rossiter—took the reins of the case as its de facto leader because Donohue was far too weak. She and a small group of women reached out to reporters, who wrote heartbreaking stories about their plights with big headlines. "RADIUM DEATH ON RAMPAGE!" read one in the *Chicago Daily Times*. The stories were picked up nationwide,[30] and they had the desired effect of allowing them to recruit a lawyer willing to take on this case against an incredibly powerful company. His name was Leonard Grossman, an Atlanta man who'd been born in 1891, had been an early supporter of the suffragette movement, and was friends with legendary attorney Clarence Darrow.[31] With Catherine as the lead plaintiff, five Ottawa women sued Radium Dial to cover their medical and dental bills and for their lost wages. The company fought feverishly, delaying the proceedings as often as they could, which had the added weight of being more than just burdensome: The women were dying, and it seemed the company was intentionally dragging things out in hopes they'd die before the case was resolved.

Catherine, who weighed just over sixty pounds at this point, was fading the fastest. She had to keep a tissue pressed to her mouth so that pus wouldn't dribble down her face. Her case had caught the attention of US Secretary of Labor Frances Perkins—the first woman to ever serve in a presidential cabinet. Perkins had been about thirty when she witnessed the Triangle Shirtwaist Factory fire in 1911. Now, she was in a position of power and ordered an investigation into the radium girls' strange sickness.

When the first day of testimony finally came, Catherine was too sick to go, but she insisted on attending anyway. Her husband and friends carried her into the courtroom. A doctor took the stand and was asked a blunt question: Is Catherine Donohue's condition fatal? The doctor reluctantly gave a blunt reply: "Her life expectancy is a matter of months."[32] This might have been obvious to people who'd known Catherine, but it was the first time she'd been told that her life expectancy was just a few months. She fainted in the courtroom, then began screaming hysterically when she was revived.[33]

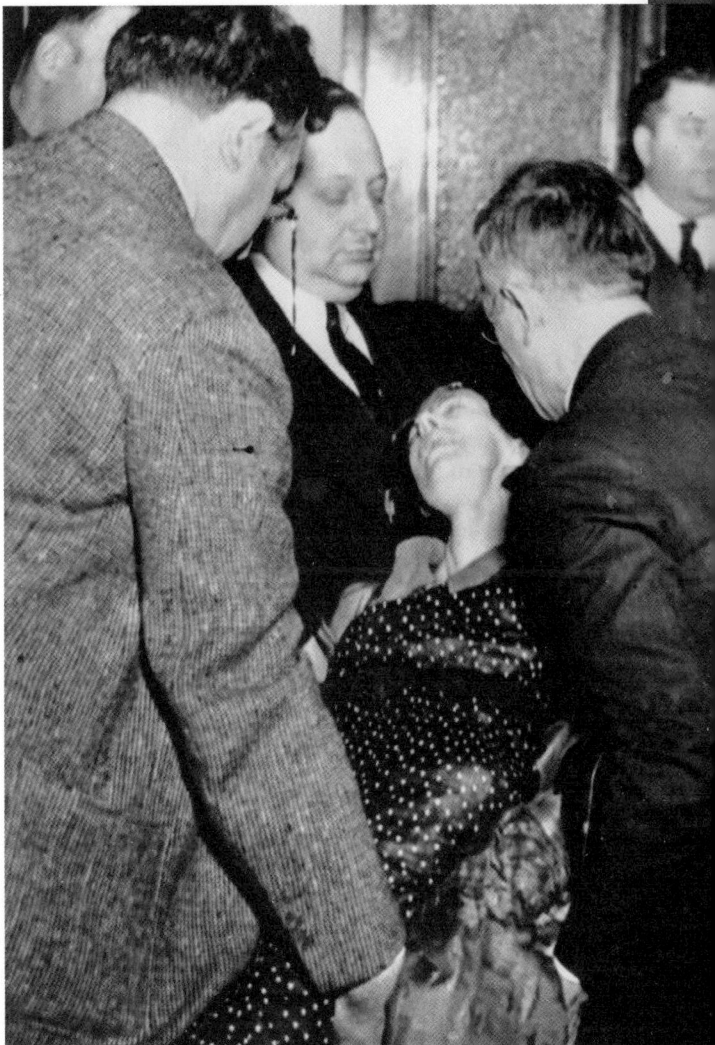

Catherine Wolf Donahue being carried from an Illinois Industrial Commission hearing in Ottawa, Illinois, after fainting, February 11, 1938; she had just heard a doctor testify that her life expectancy was only several months.

Catherine was removed from the courtroom and taken to an office where she was laid on a desk to recover. On the date of the next hearing, she was too weak to travel, so Grossman spearheaded efforts to take the courthouse to her. The judge, the witnesses, and the plaintiffs traveled to Catherine's home, where she gave testimony as she lay on the couch in her living room. Though she was weak, she pushed through, she said, because her fight wasn't about her. It was to ensure her husband and two children weren't saddled with overwhelming medical debt, and it was also for her friends. "I may not live to enjoy the money myself, but perhaps it will come in time for the other girls," she said. Some if those women weren't showing symptoms yet, but everyone knew that they could at any moment. Others were in early stages of sickness with no idea as to how many months or years of suffering might await them.[34]

Donohue and her co-plaintiffs won the lawsuit. In the fictionalized movie version of the tale, *Radium Girls* (2018), this was a convenient stopping point, but in reality, the ending wasn't so straightforward. Radium Dial appealed the ruling, so the sick women had to wait for a ruling on the appeal. When it was denied, Catherine told reporters she was relieved. But then the company appealed once more, on July 26, 1938; Catherine died the next day. The company lost that appeal as well, and then appealed again. In the end, they lost the case eight times, with it finally being put to rest in 1939 when the US Supreme Court declined to hear it, in turn upholding the lower court's decision[35]—eleven years after Radium Dial had run paid ads promising that they valued their workers' health far more than any profits.

At the time, Secretary Perkins said that the fight for workers' rights would continue. Though no one ever faced any criminal charges for the deaths of the women, in the wake of their lawsuits, the US government passed stricter laws protecting workers, especially those regarding occupational diseases. But the women's legacy goes beyond the law books: Scientists were also able to use the data from the women to determine what the long-term effects of nuclear fallout might be, which in turn prompted President John F. Kennedy to advocate for nuclear test bans—ultimately resulting in the Nuclear Test Ban Treaty of 1963. The data gathered continues to inform our handling of radioactive material to this day.

"The radium girls were incredibly important in science," *Radium Girls*' author Kate Moore said in an interview.[36] "They left us an enormous legacy in terms of understanding radioactivity and how it affects humans."

One of the last known radium girls died in 2015; luckily, she only worked in a factory in Waterbury, Connecticut for a few days[37]. Even those who survived, however, did so with a cloud over their heads. They knew that at any point in their lives there was a chance of developing a latent sarcoma—bone cancer—so fast-growing that they could be dead within months. Those whose bodies absorbed radiation knew they would never be free of it. Their bones still glow in their graves to this day.

Legal Legacy

While workplace safety laws existed prior to the radium workers' ordeal, the scope was so narrow that often companies could essentially act with impunity. The impact of these cases took decades to unfold (some manufacturers used radium paint until the early 1970s), but among them:

- Statutes of limitations were lengthened because the women's illnesses sometimes took years to manifest.
- Workers' compensation was created to address income shortages caused by unsafe work environments.
- Businesses are no longer permitted to knowingly hide from workers that they're handling dangerous chemicals.
- Eventually, the small changes enacted in these cases' wake helped lead to the Occupational Safety and Health Administration (OSHA) in 1971.

8

The Bath Massacre: America's Deadliest School Attack

(1928)

In the small Michigan town of Bath, children awoke the morning of May 18, 1927, with an extra jolt of excitement. It was the last day of school before summer break, and while a lot has changed in America over the past century, one thing that's remained constant is kids' love of their school-free summers.

Bath was near Lansing, the state's capital, and was largely rural, with a large farming population. The previous generation of children had been taught in a one-room schoolhouse that seemed sufficient considering that most expected to grow up and take over the family farm. That thinking had recently shifted, however. Priorities had changed in the wake of the Great War and the influenza epidemic of 1918, which, combined, had wiped out nearly 70 million people worldwide.[1] From the National Archives and Records Administration:

> **The plague did not discriminate. It was rampant in urban and rural areas, from the densely populated East coast to the remotest parts of Alaska. Young adults, usually unaffected by these types of infectious diseases, were among the hardest hit groups along with the elderly and young children. The flu afflicted over 25 percent of the US population. In one year, the average life expectancy in the United States dropped by 12 years.[2]**

Then, just as now, parents wanted what was best for their children, and in the wake of such heart-wrenching decimation, a new emphasis was placed on giving children a good education in the hope of helping them secure the brightest futures possible. Testing had consistently shown that urban students had the edge in this arena because of their bigger, better-funded schools. Rural kids had schooling, but because their homesteads sprawled over acres, the tendency was to have a smattering of one-room schoolhouses throughout an area so that every child in town had a school within about a mile's walk from their home. It wasn't an ideal setup, as there typically would be one teacher for all grades and subjects. It was no wonder that a single teacher spanning several grades produced students who tested poorly compared to students attending schools with multiple, grade-specific teachers.

The idea to beef up schools in farm towns and make them as effective as schools in the city had gripped much of the country. It hit Bath in 1922, when the town unveiled its state-of-the-art Bath Consolidated School. The facility had two wings to house all the community's schoolchildren in one location. Multiple teachers were hired to teach the various grades and subjects. No longer would a teenager be sitting in a classroom alongside his first-grade sibling. Instead, he'd be challenged by kids his own age and by teachers whose attention could be more focused, and whose areas of expertise, more honed.

There were drawbacks to this change, however, one of which had to do with proximity. The town was far too sprawling for the centralized school to be situated less than a mile from every kid in town, so newly hired school officials unveiled a solution: a busing system. Every morning, kids would be picked up from their homes and hauled to school, then brought back at day's end. Meanwhile, the additional teachers required oversight, so the district hired a superintendent named Emory Huyck, a lifelong Michigan resident who landed the gig just as he graduated Michigan State Agricultural College in 1922 at age twenty-seven.

Huyck—who, by all accounts, was an intelligent, enthusiastic young man who planned to make the school cutting edge—managed to meet all the standards required to get Bath Consolidated officially accredited, which was no easy feat for a new school with an inexperienced leader. Huyck was so respected that after his first year in Bath, the school board voted to extend his contract and give him a hefty annual raise.

All of this cost money. To foot the bill after the school was first built, Bath residents were charged about $12 per thousand dollars valuation—meaning that a home worth $10,000 had to pay $120 per year for the school. Four years later, in 1926, that property tax had climbed to $20 per thousand dollars valuation.[3] Then, as now, taxes weren't incredibly popular, but most residents in Bath were so impressed with—and proud of—the community's fancy new school that they were willing to pay without notable complaint.

Of course, that wasn't true for everyone. Andrew Kehoe was one of the most vocal opponents of the school and, more pointedly, of the taxes he had to pay to build the thing. "I'm being taxed into the poorhouse," he reportedly told a neighbor. "My assessments don't leave me enough to live on."[4]

Kehoe had been born in Tecumseh, Michigan—a rural town near Ann Arbor, home to the University of Michigan since it moved there from Detroit in 1837.[5] Andrew's parents were Mary and Philip, the latter of whom had emigrated from Ireland with his own father at about age eight. Philip Kehoe was considered the epitome of the immigrant success story, praised as a valuable citizen who served as drain commissioner of his hometown. He was also a devout Catholic. After his first wife—the mother of his two oldest children—died, Philip married Mary McGovern in 1864. With her, he'd have nine more children, of whom Andrew was the oldest, born on February 1, 1872.[6]

"I'M BEING TAXED INTO THE POORHOUSE. MY ASSESSMENTS DON'T LEAVE ME ENOUGH TO LIVE ON."

It seems Andrew grew up in an interesting household—one traditional enough that two of Philip's eight daughters became nuns, but also progressive enough that another daughter graduated the Detroit College of Law in 1909 to become one of only two hundred female lawyers in the entire country.[7] She was even a founding member of the Women Lawyers Association of Michigan—unquestionably a pioneer at the end of the nineteenth century. Andrew was a bright boy with an affinity toward all things mechanical and electrical. He was especially suited to this era of innovation, which saw the unveiling of the electric fan, the diesel engine, and the vacuum cleaner. Andrew was himself a tinkerer. He would fashion gadgets that made life on the farm a little bit easier. A neighbor described his family's Tecumseh farm as one big laboratory for Andrew, who excelled in physics class and studied electrical engineering.

In 1890, when Andrew turned eighteen, his mother, Mary, died at the age of fifty-five after a long illness. After his mother's death, he stayed on the farm and worked alongside his father until 1898, which is when Philip married a third time to a younger woman named Frances. She was forty to

Philip's sixty-five—so closer in age by eleven years to Andrew than to Andrew's father. How Andrew felt about Frances isn't clear, but census data shows that he moved away from the family farm after the marriage. In 1900, he was listed as a boarder in Ann Arbor with the occupation "dairyman." He would later claim that, around this time, he got a degree from the State Agriculture College of Michigan (present-day Michigan State University) in East Lansing, but there aren't records to back up the assertion.

By 1910, as Andrew was nearing forty himself, he moved back to his father's farm, living with Philip, Frances, and Irene, Andrew's far younger half-sister. She'd been born in 1902.

In 1911, tragedy struck the farm, courtesy of another turn-of-the-century invention. Gas stoves were all the rage, marketed as must-have appliances for housewives especially. Before this innovation, farm wives had to wake early in the morning to start a wood fire that would slowly grow hot enough to make breakfast for their husbands before the men went to work the fields. The gas stove made life much easier because it heated food far more quickly, saving people time and energy. But there was a trade-off to the convenience.

"If you read the papers at the time, there were all these terrible accidents," said historian Harold Schechter, author of *Maniac: The Bath School Disaster and the Birth of the Modern Mass Killer* (2021).[8]

Lighting these early gas stoves often caused explosions, many of which were fatal. Frances fell victim to such an explosion one morning as she put a match to her stove. Andrew was the first to hear her screams. He told authorities that he ran to the kitchen to see what was wrong. His nine-year-old sister Irene followed, finding her mother engulfed in flames. The little girl helped douse the blaze, but Frances's wounds were grave. She lingered in agony for hours, moaning beneath a cloak of charred skin. She was in such pain that when she finally died, it was a relief to her family.[9]

Less than a year later, Andrew married for the first time. His path to marriage was a bit odd—waiting until age forty to marry wasn't typical for a man back then. What was even less common, however, was the fact that his wife was thirty-seven, past her child-bearing years and that this, too, was her first wedding. Many of her contemporaries would have assumed she'd remain a spinster for life, but Ellen Agnes Price—called "Nellie" by her friends—seemed an ideal match for Andrew. Her uncle had been a successful businessman and farmer, and he'd also served as a Lansing city councilman, chief of police, and superintendent of public works. Nellie's father worked on her uncle's farm in Bath. Her mother died when she was young, leaving her to fill the role of woman of the house as she took over child-rearing duties for her siblings.

It's unclear where Nellie and Andrew met, though some reports suggest they'd crossed paths at the State Agricultural College. That seems unlikely, however, because the school would later say they didn't have a record of either Andrew or Nellie attending there—although as an adult, Andrew would haughtily tell people he was a college graduate. It's worth noting, too, that on the 1910 US Census, Andrew's parents reported that they'd attended school, but there is no mention of whether Andrew did.

Regardless of where they met, Nellie and Andrew settled at first on the forty-acre Kehoe farm in Tecumseh. A few years into the marriage, however, Nellie's rich uncle died, leaving behind an eighty-acre farm in Bath. Andrew thought the property was ideal, with its huge barn, chicken coop, and three-story home, but Nellie didn't inherit the land outright. It was part of her uncle's estate, which was managed by his widow, brother, and family attorney. That trio had no interest in giving the property to Andrew and Nellie, but they were willing to sell it to the couple. The farm was valued at $12,000. Andrew sold the Kehoe farm and paid half of the new farm's value up front. He arranged to pay the remaining $6,000 in monthly installments of $360.[10] Essentially, he had a mortgage, but rather than paying a bank, he paid Nellie's relatives. He was confident he'd own the land outright after a few solid farming seasons, about which he had reason to feel optimistic because the economy was booming in the 1910s. World War I had been traumatizing and brutal, but it had also been a godsend for American farmers, who made big bucks exporting crops to war-torn Europe.

Once Andrew and Nellie moved in, they made an impression on their neighbors. Nellie at times hosted the Ladies' Friday Afternoon Club at the farm and arranged card games with other couples. Andrew, with his flair for mechanics, was often sought out by neighbors who needed help repairing appliances and farming equipment. Though Andrew had a reputation for always being willing to lend a hand, he also was known as an eccentric grump at times, too. One neighbor reported that Andrew had beaten a horse to death, while another neighbor said he'd gotten so upset at her dog for burying a bone on his property that he'd shot the pooch.[11] He was regularly seen on his farm in business suits, instead of dirty overalls like everyone else. "He would hurry home to wash up if his hands got too greasy and was known to change his shirt in the middle of the day if he noticed a stain or smudge of dirt," Schechter wrote in *Maniac*.[12]

Andrew also was known for his condescension, regularly touting his supposed college degree and sneering at people he deemed less intelligent than he. When he spoke up about an issue, he expected people to listen. Come the 1920s, the issue he was most concerned with was the new consolidated school, the construction of which voters had approved over his objections. This wasn't the first time Andrew had shown distaste for public underwriting of a community construction project. Back in Tecumseh, shortly after his marriage, he had refused to chip in for the local church to erect a new building. It caused such tension that he quit going to the church altogether. In Bath, his disdain for the school project was two-pronged: he didn't see why he had to pay more taxes to pay for children to be educated when he was a childless man, and he was struggling financially. While the economy had been great for farmers in the 1910s, the 1920s were another story. After the Great War ended, farmland in Europe was restored and American farmers saw demand for their crops plummet. Corn dropped more than 60 percent, from $1.30 per bushel to just 47 cents, between 1919 and 1920.[13] Farm income dropped an from an estimated $14.5 billion in 1919 to $8.1 billion in 1921.[14]

Not only that, but the land on the Bath farm wasn't as fertile as Andrew had hoped. He and Nellie stopped paying the $360-a-month mortgage they'd arranged with Nellie's relatives. Her family was understanding, so the couple didn't risk foreclosure. Yet Nellie's family did want to be paid and routinely asked for updates on future payments. This made Andrew hate the fancy new school even more. He tried to alleviate his personal burden by getting the property's value reduced, thus lowering his tax bill, but was unsuccessful. He had better luck deciding he wanted a seat on the school board. After he won the post in 1924, his peers named him treasurer. They figured the role suited such a miserly fellow.

With cost cutting in mind, he managed some wins while in the post. He successfully lobbied to slash by $60 the salary of the school janitor—a one-armed man who wasn't known for his efficiency on the job.[15] When the janitor—and then the school principal and superintendent to boot—had trouble ridding the school of a swarm of bees that had infested the place, Andrew Kehoe stepped in and got it done. As Schechter wrote: "Exactly how he managed to accomplish the task is unknown, but—in the words of (biographer Monty) Ellsworth—'that was the last of the bees.'"[16] This impressed Kehoe's colleagues so much that they agreed to make him an unofficial handyman at the school. He set up a work area in the basement and had unlimited access to the building, coming and going as he pleased. Kehoe also convinced the board to have contracts filled via competitive bidding—a move designed to curtail the nepotism that was rampant in the district.

Andrew Kehoe at home in Bath, Michigan, c. 1920.

But he also lost plenty of times, often being the sole dissenting vote, which not only left him bitter but gave him the reputation of being difficult and contentious. That he and Emory Huyck were constantly butting heads didn't help. Kehoe didn't like that Huyck routinely attended the school board meetings. The penny pincher found the habit invasive and thought that Huyck's presence was swaying other board members to go along with the superintendent's seemingly never-ending stream of expenditure requests—requests that, in fairness, weren't unexpected coming from a superintendent trying to ensure his district was among the best in the state. Andrew had no such goal, however, and to him, every dollar spent on students was a dollar wasted. He tried to get Huyck banned from attending the board meetings, but he was overruled.

The year after Andrew Kehoe joined the school board, the elected clerk of Bath Township suddenly died. Maude Milliman had been married to school board member Albert Detluff, whose primary occupation was village blacksmith-turned-auto repairman (allowing him to weather the country's transition from horse-drawn to horseless carriages). Despite his crankiness, Kehoe had proven himself good with budgets, so when Milliman died of heart disease, he was asked to fill out the rest of her term. He was thrilled. With that role, in addition to his school board post, he felt he was finally being afforded the influence over the town that he deserved.[17] Milliman's term was set to expire the following year, so Kehoe began lobbying to keep the job straight away. He assumed he was a shoo-in as an incumbent, but it seemed his abrasive style rubbed many the wrong way. The next spring, his party nominated someone else as its candidate at their caucus. Humiliated, Kehoe shifted gears, and a year later ran for justice of the peace. He lost that race, too.[18]

In between the two failed election bids, Kehoe's wife, Nellie, began suffering from debilitating health symptoms—including rapid weight loss, incapacitating headaches, and coughing spells. She worried it might be tuberculosis, the infectious lung disease that had killed her mother. The condition led to a "string of hospitalizations that would prove to be both an emotional and financial burden to her husband."[19] Whatever hope the Kehoes might have had to catch up on their mortgage payments vanished alongside Andrew's political dreams.

By fall 1925, the couple hadn't paid on the property in four years. Nor did they have an automobile. One night, Andrew called on his neighbor, Job Sleight, to drive him about fifty miles south to Jackson, Michigan, to pick up a product called pyrotol, a new type of inexpensive explosive developed by the government from surplus smokeless powder and sodium nitrate left over after the war.[20] Farmers were eligible to buy up to 1,000 pounds of pyrotol, which was meant to help them clear their fields of boulders and tree stumps. The government charged $7.90 per 100 pounds of pyrotol, which was enough to blast a solid acre of tree stumps from a field.[21]

It made sense to a neighbor like Sleight that Kehoe would want pyrotol. Ever since his wife had taken ill, their property had fallen into disarray. The fields were overgrown and neglected. Andrew seemed to be keeping up fine with his school board work—and, in fact, was seen regularly visiting his workshop in the school's basement—but it seemed something had to give, and that something had been the farm. Sleight helped Kehoe haul five hundred pounds of pyrotol home and figured he'd soon hear a tell-tale ka-boom indicating that the overgrowth had been dealt with, but months passed with no explosion.

In May 1927, a teacher called Kehoe about having a group of schoolkids visit his farm, as had been done in years past. Despite the stress he clearly was under, Kehoe enthusiastically agreed—though he suggested a change to the teacher's request. She had asked to bring the children on Thursday,

May 19, which was the day after the last day of the school year. Andrew said two days earlier—on Tuesday, May 17, the school year's penultimate day—would work better. The teacher happily agreed to the tweak with no inkling of the sinister reason behind Andrew's request.

The day after the field trip, most of the older students who filed into the Bath Consolidated School were there to take the year's final examinations. This excluded the school's graduating seniors, whose fifteen members had taken their finals the previous week. They were expected to return Thursday for their graduation ceremony. Some underclassmen were exempt from finals, too, thanks to the good grades they'd maintained all year. A handful of other students missed the day for more mundane reasons, including Irene Dunham, who'd woken up with a sore throat and been granted a sick day by her mother. Still, about 250 students were in the school building as the final day of the school year started. Those in the lowest grades geared up for a gimme day of reading, goofing off, and inconsequential busy work.

At approximately 8:20 a.m., board member Albert Detloff—whose wife's death had briefly allowed Andrew Kehoe to serve as city clerk—spotted Kehoe out in front of the post office sitting in his recently purchased Ford truck. Detloff was headed to the school to summon a repairman for a malfunctioning water pipe and invited Kehoe to join him. Kehoe did, but seemed preoccupied, repeatedly checking his pocket watch for the time. In the few minutes it took for Detloff to chat with the school janitor, Kehoe disappeared. Nonplussed, Detloff headed back to his shop.[22] Soon after, an alarm clock hidden nearby ticked 8:45 a.m. Suddenly, an alarming crash echoed throughout the school, one that everyone present both heard and felt. The school's roof seemed to detach from the building as the ceiling rattled and plaster rained from above. Classrooms on the second floor collapsed onto students seated in desks one floor below. The repairman who'd just arrived was thrown six inches into a wall, while the janitor who stood nearby him screamed, "For God's sake, what happened?"[23] Older children who'd gathered outside for a leisurely game of catch were knocked to the ground by the explosion, which drew their eyes to the school just as the roof caved in. The blast was powerful enough to shatter windows in nearby homes. Mable Ellsworth, who lived a half mile from the school, heard the awful ruckus and ran to "see the cloud of white dust come up from the school" as she heard the

The remains of the Kehoe farm the day after the explosion on May 18, 1927—only the chimney and a few walls were left standing. Kehoe had murdered his wife, Nellie, before exploding the entire property.

gut-wrenching screams of children. She called out to her husband, Monty, but his attention was elsewhere: He was looking the other direction at a cloud of smoke pouring out of the barn at the Kehoe farm.[24]

Neighbors rushed to the house, screaming for Andrew or Nellie to answer so they could be located and pulled from the flames. No one replied. The neighbors entered the house. The Ellsworths were among the few in town with the vantage point to realize both disasters were happening at once, but even so, they didn't consider that the two might be connected. That would have been unthinkable. Still hearing neither Andrew nor Nellie, the neighbors did what was common at the time: they began hauling furniture from the house in hopes of sparing the Kehoes' belongings. As they did so, they noticed a stack of pyrotol planted in the house. Quickly recognizing the danger, they rushed from the house just before it exploded. Next went the barn. The blasts knocked the Kehoes' would-be saviors onto the ground, where they looked helplessly back at the house, certain that Andrew and Nellie had died.

The remains of Kehoe's Ford in front of the Bath Consolidated School on May 19. After murdering his wife, destroying his farm and the school, and killing dozens of people, Kehoe detonated his own dynamite-and-shrapnel-filled car in front of the school, killing himself and several others.

"People had no clue what was going on," said Arnie Bernstein, author of *Bath Massacre: America's First School Bombing* (2009). "It seemed like the end of the world."[25]

Across town, Andrew Kehoe pulled up to the Bath Consolidated School in his newly bought Ford truck. About three dozen schoolchildren were already dead, but Andrew wasn't done. He'd loaded the back with pyrotol and nails to serve as shrapnel. Wild eyed, he motioned for his perceived nemesis, superintendent Huyck, to come talk. Huyck, still trying to wrap his head around the devastation surrounding him, obliged. Just as he approached the truck, Kehoe flipped a switch that ignited the pyrotol, taking out both men instantaneously. The shrapnel also killed another child who'd been unscathed in the original explosion, plus two more adults who happened to be close by.

While Irene Babcock had stayed home with a sore throat, her brother and sister had gone to class that day. Irene and her mother jumped into their car and raced to the school to see what the "awful boom" was, only to encounter the horrifying sight of body parts dangling from the trees overhead. (Irene's siblings luckily survived.)[26]

"It was just a hellish, heartbreaking scene," Schechter said. "You had, first of all, the kids who were killed immediately, but then there were a lot of kids who were buried under all this rubble, who were shouting for help. You had all these parents, frantically, with their bare hands, struggling to uncover all this concrete and stone to reach their kids."[27]

As the parents' hands became raw and bloody, they uncovered one body after another. The corpses were carried to a nearby hill and arranged so that hysterical parents could find their children. They wailed as they clutched the unmoving bodies. In one case, all three children in a single family were among the dead. No one in Bath was removed from the devastation, however, because the school had served nearly 300 students. All told, forty-three people were killed on May 18 by the school explosions, including Kehoe and thirty-seven children—more than 10 percent of the school body. Everyone had a friend or a neighbor or a sibling who'd gone off to school that morning never to return.

Townspeople and family members search for survivors of the Bath School disaster trapped under the debris, May 18, 1927.

Another some fifty-eight people were injured. Some of those injuries plagued the survivors for the rest of their lives. One little girl was so badly hurt that she was hospitalized for three months. She died during a surgery meant to remove a fragment of the shrapnel that had lodged in her body. Like those killed instantly, she never made it home.

People searching the Kehoes' farm the day after the devastation finally found the body of Nellie, who'd been burned so badly that the mass representing her corpse was at first dismissed as just more debris. After an examination, they concluded that Kehoe had bashed in his wife's skull, killing her, before loading her body unceremoniously onto a hog cart and leaving her there to die.

"It was this apocalyptic act," Schechter said. "He was going to end not only his own life, but as much of the world as he could. So he murdered his wife, set the property on fire. He stripped bark from young trees to kill the trees. He wired his horses' legs together so they couldn't escape the conflagration in the barn."[28]

He'd also left behind a message, found wired to a fence hugging his property. It was in stenciled letters—a premeditated message that he had to have deliberately designed. It read: CRIMINALS ARE MADE, NOT BORN. Nature versus nurture had been a hotly debated subject at the time, in the wake of Darwin's theory of evolution, and it seemed Kehoe wanted to take a side. His message was to convey that a good man could be driven to do terrible things if pushed hard enough. In truth, the message mostly served as a final twist of the knife to the people left behind to bury their children. His message was simple: You made me do this. It's your fault that I killed your children. Their deaths are on your hands.

The residents of Bath refused to let Kehoe destroy their town. Heartbroken and traumatized, they raised money to rebuild the school, thanks in large part to a personal donation from Michigan senator James Couzens. The new school, renamed after Couzens, was dedicated in 1928, where it stood for nearly fifty years before being demolished. Today, that land is home to a small park dedicated to the bombing victims. At the heart of the park, still stands the original cupola of the school built more than one hundred years ago—a school that Andrew Kehoe once desperately and sadistically tried to destroy.

Legal Legacy

The Bath massacre was disturbingly unique: a first-of-its-kind attack on innocent youths. As such, the aftermath centered more on the recovery of the survivors, the rebuilding of the school, and the psychology of the perpetrator than on specific legal reforms.

- A somber two-day hearing soon after the explosion determined that to all outward appearances Kehoe had been legally sane when he committed the acts, though in subsequent newspaper reports, he'd often be referred to as a "maniac."[29]
- Newspaper disaster coverage spurred a nationwide outpouring of sympathy. While occasional stories ran marking the massacre's anniversary, Kehoe's name largely disappeared from the news, except for rare mentions comparing his crime to others deemed similarly baffling.[30] That changed in 1999, when newspapers across the country resurrected the horrifying tale after an attack at a high school in Columbine, Colorado.[31]

9

The Legacy of Kitty Genovese's Lonely Murder

(1964)

When a twenty-eight-year-old woman was viciously stabbed to death outside of her New York apartment in 1964, it wasn't huge news. Murders happened in the Empire City every day—the year ultimately saw 636 murders, in fact[1]—many of which were never reported on beyond a brief in the local paper.

But the details surrounding this particular murder caught the attention of the metropolitan editor of the *New York Times*, resulting in a story that ran on the Grey Lady's front page of March 27, 1964, with an explosive headline: "37 WHO SAW MURDER DIDN'T CALL THE POLICE; APATHY AT STABBING OF QUEENS WOMAN SHOCKS INSPECTOR."

With that headline, the murder of Kitty Genovese not only became nationwide news, but it became synonymous with apathy, serving as proof that our world was a heartless and selfish place where an innocent woman's cries for help were literally ignored by people who couldn't be bothered to get involved.

Decades later, details would surface that showed this initial take wasn't 100 percent right, but it still nailed the basic truth of Kitty's murder: that she had screamed and screamed for help while a man—a stranger who'd stalked her as prey—stabbed her repeatedly, attempted to rape her, and finally killed her. Regardless of whether Kitty's neighbors in Kew Gardens were truly as apathetic as the *New York Times* reported, her death not only helped create the 911 system in America, but it also became a symbol of the responsibility we have as members of a society to help each other in times of danger.

Kitty's story began on July 7, 1935, in Brooklyn, New York. She was the first of five children born to Vincent and Rachel Genovese. Named Catherine Susan but nicknamed "Kitty," she grew up an attractive chatterbox. The year

Kitty graduated her all-girls Catholic high school, she was named "Class Cutup" for her goofy sense of humor.[2]

The Genovese family lived in New York City until Kitty's high school graduation, after which her parents decided to move away because they'd decided the city had become too violent. Kitty was legally an adult, however, and she loved New York, so she opted to stay behind while her parents and four siblings settled down in New Canaan, Connecticut. For the next ten years, Kitty came home most weekends, sometimes with a friend in tow, and was still close with her family despite living across state lines. In a documentary he helped make as an adult, Bill Genovese—Kitty's younger brother, who was just six when he left New York with his parents—said that Kitty was a parent and friend rolled into one. She seemed worldly and knowledgeable.

"The best part was talking late into the night," Bill said. "Kitty seemed to know about everything. I was a curious kid and asked a lot of questions. Kitty always took the time to answer."[3]

As Kitty entered her post–high school life, she worked odd jobs to pay the bills—secretary, waitress, hostess. She briefly married her high school sweetheart, an army officer-turned-engineer who was a few years older. Finally, Kitty found a job that she genuinely liked: working in a bar. She liked the environment, first, but she also found that she had a knack for keeping things organized, which helped her climb the ladder quickly at Ev's 11th Hour in Hollis, Queens, where she became a bar manager. She worked hard and earned decent money, bringing in about $750 a month, about $7,300 today. Her hefty salary wasn't the only reason her male colleagues called her "one of the boys," however. Her personal life had bearing on that, too.

"Katie was part of the thriving underground gay scene in New York City," explained Kevin Cook, author of *Kitty Genovese: The Murder, the Bystanders, the Crime that Changed America* (2014).[4]

She lived with a woman named Mary Ann Zielonko.[5] Though Kitty introduced Mary Ann as just a friend to her family, the two were actually partners. They'd met at a bar several years prior and quickly fell in love. Even in Greenwich Village, this was a dangerous time to be gay. The Stonewall riots—a series of protests sparked by a police raid of the Village's Stonewall Inn—were still five years off. But while the couple didn't hold hands in public, they were a typical young couple in most ways: they worked days and

Kitty Genovese shown tending bar, likely at Ev's 11th Hour in Hollis, Queens, c. 1963.

spent nights together. One time they argued and, to make up for it, Kitty bought Mary Ann a puppy they named Andrew. Sometimes they'd barhop and hit the clubs, but they also had separate sets of friends and did things on their own.

"We just hit it off," Mary Ann told the *Chicago Tribune* in 2004. "We meshed. I'm very quiet, and she talked a lot. We both had struggles with our sexuality, as did many people back then. We had a quick bond."[6]

The night of March 13, 1964, Mary Ann had spent the evening bowling with friends before coming home and going to sleep. It wasn't unusual for Kitty to hang out at Ev's bar until closing time or later, even if she weren't working that night. This night, a Friday, she'd worked until 6:00 p.m., then gone out to dinner with a guy friend. They returned to the bar together about midnight, though her friend left soon afterward. Kitty stayed at Ev's until 3:00 a.m., and then she drove her little red Fiat sports car the seven miles that separated home from work. All of this was routine for Kitty. Though she loved the city and was much less fearful of it than her parents, she still took precautions walking from her car to her apartment late at night. There was a back path that was a tad faster than the front one, but she stuck with the streetside route because it was better lit.

Kitty had no way of knowing it when she parked her car, but she was being followed. Someone had spotted her driving and discreetly parked when she did. As she began walking toward the front of her building, she noticed a man was behind her. She started to run. He ran, too. She was about half a block from her front door when the man caught up with her outside of a darkened bookstore. He plunged a knife into her back at least twice. Kitty let out a scream so loud and bloodcurdling that it awoke one neighbor from a dead sleep. She yelled, "Oh, my God, he stabbed me! Please help me! Please help me!" Someone else, a man, opened a window and began screaming to leave the girl alone. The culprit ran away, ducking back to his car to move it out of the brightness of the streetlight, but he kept watching Kitty. He saw that she was badly injured and that no one had come to physically help her.

Kitty managed to get up and stagger to her feet, trying to make it to the rear of the building, where the apartment entrances were located.[7] She pulled on one door handle after another until one finally flung open. She dragged herself into the vestibule and was likely summoning strength and regrouping before moving on, for while she was injured, her wounds weren't yet mortal. After about ten minutes, her attacker decided to come back and finish the job. He changed from a stocking cap to a brimmed hat and went after her. A bone-handled knife in his hand, he found her again and resumed his attack. He heard a door creak open from down the hall. He made eye contact with a neighbor named Carl Ross, who could have stepped out to help but decided instead to shut his door. Ross would later tell police he didn't want to get involved. Kitty's attacker stabbed again and again, and then orgasmed on top of her body as she lay dying.[8]

Throughout the whole attack, Mary Ann—Kitty's roommate and girlfriend—was asleep in their apartment. Finally, she awoke to a knock at

A March 1964 news photograph of the walkway behind Austin Street in Kew Gardens, Queens, where Kitty Genovese was murdered that month.

the door. Police officers asked about her roommate and told her there had been an attack. Mary Ann was whisked to the morgue, where she was led to a gurney that had been covered in a white sheet. Mary Ann saw her lover's lifeless face and muttered an identification, but she was still in such shock that when investigators told her it was time to leave the morgue, she shook her head and refused. In a later interview, Mary Ann recalled telling them that she was waiting for Kitty, and did not want to leave her. "No," she had said, "Kitty's coming with us.[9]

In the initial news coverage, Kitty was demoted from a bar manager to a barmaid. A story in the *New York Daily News* read:

> **Catherine (Kitty) Genovese, 5 feet 1 and 105 pounds, was stabbed eight times in the chest and abdomen and four times in the back and she had three cuts on her hands—probably inflicted as she tried to**

> **fight off her attacker near her apartment in an alleyway at 82-70 Austin St., at Lefferts Blvd., Kew Gardens. Late yesterday, police said the 30 detectives assigned to the case had not come up with any clues or a possible motive for the savage murder.[10]**

The black-and-white photo of Kitty that ran in newspapers nationwide in March 1964.

The story didn't receive much attention until more than a week later, when A. M. Rosenthal, a respected journalist at the *New York Times* (and later, executive editor of the paper), happened to have lunch with the city's police commissioner, Michael J. Murphy. Rosenthal had been appointed the paper's metropolitan editor after ten years of reporting abroad, and figured that off-the-record lunches with city bigwigs might help him find his footing.[11] At lunch with the commissioner, Rosenthal asked about an arrest that had made headlines a couple of days prior. A man named Winston Moseley had been picked up for robbing a house, and he'd confessed to the recent murder of Barbara Kralik, a fifteen-year-old Queens girl who'd been stabbed in 1963 in her own bedroom while her family slept. The confession confused police because another man, eighteen-year-old Alvin Mitchell, had also confessed to killing Kralik, though he quickly recanted that confession, saying he made it under threat by police. Rosenthal asked Commissioner Murphy about the strange double confessions, but Murphy shrugged off the question. If Rosenthal wanted a real story, Murphy said, he should look at the Kew Gardens stabbing. Murphy explained that thirty-seven people heard her screams and did nothing to stop the attack while it was happening. The thirty-eighth person to hear her finally called police, but the call was too late to save her life. The commissioner said, "I've been in this business a long time, but this beats everything."[12]

Rosenthal assigned the story to reporter Martin Gansburg, who knocked on neighbors' doors and examined police logs before writing a story that began: "For more than half an hour, 38 respectable, law-abiding citizens in Queens watched a killer stalk and stab a woman in three separate attacks in Kew Gardens."[13] The story quoted several neighbors saying they heard the screams, they peered out their windows, but they didn't call police. The response to the story was seismic. Soon, Kitty's photo—a black-and-white image in which her hair is tousled and her expression serene—ran in newspapers nationwide. People who heard her story demanded

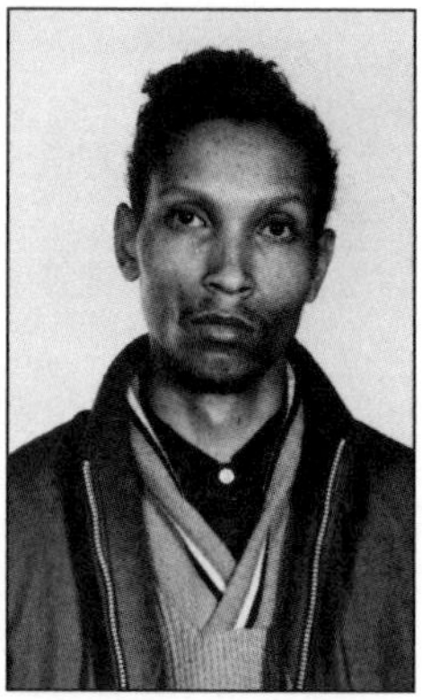

A March 1964 NYPD booking photo of Winston Moseley, taken after he had been arrested for robbing a house.

answers: How could we as a society have become so cold and complacent that we'd turn our backs on a woman screaming for help?

There were no suspects in the case for weeks. Even neighbors who said they'd seen more than they wanted to admit still hadn't seen enough of Kitty's attacker to describe him beyond broad strokes. Moseley, who initially had been picked up just for robbery, shared enough in common with the general descriptions of the suspect that police began to wonder if he might have been involved. He was about the same build and height as the slayer, and he drove the same kind of car—a late-model, light-domestic compact car.

Asked about a murder, Moseley quickly confessed to the Barbara Kralik killing—and then kept confessing. He claimed he'd been involved in three separate slayings, of which Kitty's was his most recent. He'd also killed a twenty-four-year-old woman named Annie Mae Johnson, he said, and provided details about her death that even the coroner had initially missed: Moseley said he'd shot Annie Mae, but the coroner had ruled that she'd been stabbed to death by something thin, like an ice pick. When Moseley said he shot her, the police—who were already dubious about his Kralik confession—dismissed the confession as proof he was an attention-seeking nut who wanted to take credit for other people's kills. But the coroner took another look at Annie Mae's case and realized he'd missed the bullets. She *had* been shot to death after all. Despite this development, police still refused to believe that they might have solicited a false confession in Kralik's case. Their initial suspect, Alvin Mitchell, ultimately spent nearly thirteen years in prison for the crime, despite Moseley having testified in a trial that he alone was responsible for the teen's death.[14]

As for Kitty's murder, Moseley relayed the details in a detached and clinical manner. He said he had left his wife and two children at home that night because he had an urge to kill a woman, any woman, and it so happened that Kitty caught his eye. He couldn't explain why he'd done it, beyond being driven by a compulsive urge. He thought his attack had been interrupted when someone screamed for him to stop, but when he saw no one had come to actually help Kitty, he felt compelled to continue. He told a judge: "I'd not finished what I set out to do."[15]

In the documentary he helped make about his sister's death, Bill Genovese reflected on learning about Kitty's last moments. The family felt such guilt, he said, learning that she'd died alone. It hurt so much to think about that they stopped talking about Kitty altogether. They couldn't reminisce in their happy memories because they were so haunted by her horrified, lonely end.[16]

Moseley pleaded not guilty by reason of insanity. He tried to bolster the sense of his own mental instability with an odd aside about the night he killed Kitty. He told the court that after he was done killing and assaulting her, he returned to his vehicle and happened to notice that a man in a running car had fallen asleep at a red light. Moseley got out of his car, tapped the other car's window and helpfully suggested that the snoozing driver head home. Moseley's court-appointed attorney, Sidney Sparrow, argued: Does that really sound like something a sane man would do? The jury, comprised of eleven men and one woman, decided it might be odd, but it wasn't insane. They took just forty-five minutes to find him guilty. He was sentenced to die in the electric chair, though that would be commuted two years later after the New York Court of Appeals ruled that jurors in the sentencing phase of the trial should have been allowed to hear more evidence related to Moseley's mental health.[17]

In the decades after Kitty's death, her surviving family has found a little comfort in learning that she wasn't, in fact, completely ignored and alone when she died. Affidavits have since been gathered indicating that at least one man–Samuel Hoffman, whose actions were witnessed by his son, Samuel–reportedly called police and described a woman staggering on the sidewalk after the first attack. No officer responded. Another important detail in Kitty's tale is that a friend reached her and held her as she died. Sophia Farrar got a phone call from a neighbor that Kitty was hurt, and Sophia rushed to Kitty's side, cradled her friend, and told her, "Help is on the way." Farrar could feel blood oozing from the wounds in Kitty's back and though her words were true–help *was* coming–she knew it wouldn't come in time. She comforted Kitty until her last breath.

Winston Moseley eventually adopted the belief that his murder of Kitty Genovese bettered society. He tried to argue his way out of prison eighteen times, saying as much to members of the parole boards charged with deciding his fate.[18] He never swayed them. Moseley died behind bars in 2016 at the age of eighty-one.[19]

Legal Legacy

While not all the original reporting about Kitty's killing has held up over the decades, the impact of her death is undisputed.

- Social psychologists began studying the so-called bystander effect—which became so entwined with Kitty's case that it is sometimes called the Genovese effect. Some studies found that people were less likely to help a victim the more witnesses there were—although other studies contradicted these findings, citing many variables.
- Reporting on these studies sparked articles, discussion, and even more studies, leading to more states adopting Good Samaritan laws.
- At the time of the attack, 9-1-1 didn't exist. Some cities had systems in place to dispatch officers quickly to emergencies, but procedures varied from one city to the next. Kitty's case served as the spark to implement a nationwide emergency telephone system, starting in 1968.

10

The Mass Hysteria of the Satanic Panic

(1980s)

Judy Johnson had been dealt a rough hand in recent years. The mother of two boys watched her marriage crumble as her husband of thirteen years left her for another woman. Far worse, her oldest son was dying of cancer. To outsiders, he might have looked as though he were leading a normal life, but doctors had told Judy that thirteen-year-old Mark had inoperable, terminal brain cancer.

By May 12, 1983, Judy was so overwhelmed that she reportedly did what most parents would consider inconceivable: She packed a lunch for her three-year-old son Mitchell and dropped him off in front of a preschool—without telling anyone. She not only hadn't enrolled him, but she hadn't even contacted anyone at McMartin Preschool to make sure he'd be taken care of. She simply left Mitchell out front with the hope that the reputed workers in the school would take him in for the day.[1]

Lucky for her, they did. Not only that, but, after reaching Judy—who'd at least had sense enough to leave her phone number with her son—they forgave her very bizarre behavior and said that while they didn't have room for Mitchell to enroll at McMartin right away, they would let him start school there in the summer. It was a generous offer from the school, which had been founded some thirty years prior—an offer that would ultimately lead to a criminal case that would prove to not only be among the longest and most expensive in American history, but one that would be wrapped up in an era now referred to as Satanic Panic.

The school had been founded in the 1950s by Virginia McMartin,[2] a woman with a stellar reputation in Manhattan Beach, California, who earned the city's equivalent of woman of the year in 1977. After the school launched, it grew into a family business. Virginia's daughter, Peggy McMartin-Buckey,

An early 1980s' photograph of the McMartin Preschool in Manhattan Beach, California.

began working there, followed by Peggy's children, named Peggy Ann and Ray Buckey.[3] Nonfamily members worked there as well, and by the 1970s, McMartin was considered a prestigious school, where some teachers had worked for more than a dozen years. Situated at the corner of Walnut Avenue and Manhattan Beach Boulevard, the Los Angeles County preschool was housed in an L-shaped structure that had big bay windows and a stucco exterior.[4] It looked like a typical preschool, with children's toys littering the yard and a chain-link fence surrounding the property to both keep children away from passing traffic and to keep trespassers away

It was outside of that fence that Judy Johnson left three-year-old Mitchell, which naturally worried the McMartin staff. A child that young could bolt into traffic or be nabbed by a stranger. By that point, Virginia McMartin was seventy-six years old and no longer charged with the school's day-to-day operations. Her daughter, Peggy, did that instead. Peggy's children both worked as teachers, the newest of which was Ray. He was the kind of kid who graduated high school with no real ambition in mind. He'd dropped out of college twice and spent much of his time hanging out at the beach, which he managed to do because he lived rent-free in an apartment owned by his parents.[5] His dream wasn't to work with preschool children, but the job was available and he needed work, so he joined the family business, only to quickly discover that he actually liked the job. He related to kids better than adults. Plus, he was the only male teacher there, and the representation seemed to matter, especially to some of the young boys.

When Judy Johnson's son Mitchell was accepted to the school in August, he was placed in Ray's class. Soon after, Judy reported that Mitchell began having outbursts.[6] He would awaken from nightmares screaming in his sleep. Sometimes he would hide under his bed, which Judy believed happened more often when a man was around. Judy also said she noticed angry red marks on Mitchell's bottom that caused her to panic. She had thought it odd that Ray was teaching at the preschool. Who was this college dropout, and what had he done to earn easy access to vulnerable children? On August 12, 1983, Judy called the Manhattan Beach Police Department with concerns and was patched through to Detective Joan Hoag, an eleven-year veteran. Hoag, who'd started working with the department at age twenty-two, was known as a tough-talking, old-school cop assigned to investigate sexual abuse allegations.

Hoag listened as Judy spelled out her suspicions, which she said Mitchell had confirmed himself: Ray Buckey had been molesting her son, she said. Hoag knew this was a potential bombshell. McMartin had such a good reputation in the community that residents would be absolutely rocked if they heard this allegation. The detective wanted everything to be handled carefully, so she told Judy to take her son to a specialist straight away. Judy followed the instructions and took Mitchell for an examination with a UCLA doctor, who found that Mitchell's anus was lax and surrounded by a rash, which could indeed point to molestation. Buckey was briefly arrested, but there wasn't enough evidence to charge him.

Judy Johnson, who believed her son had been assaulted, was furious, as was Hoag, who believed Buckey was guilty. Still, the two women only had some circumstantial evidence about the condition of the boy's bottom, plus the toddler's own disjointed story. To try to determine if anyone else had stories pointing to Ray being an abuser, Police Chief Harry Kuhlmeyer Jr. sent out a letter to the homes of all McMartin students. The letter began: "Dear Parent: This department is conducting a criminal investigation involving child molestation. Ray Buckey, an employee of Virginia McMartin's Preschool, was arrested September 7, 1983, by this Department."[7]

The letter wasn't just sent to current McMartin parents, however. It was also sent to families whose now-older children had already graduated from the preschool—kids whose tenure didn't even overlap with Ray Buckey's employment. Investigators' thinking was that because Ray's mother and grandmother were the main business runners, he might have had access to the place long before he officially worked there. The letter went on to request that parents talk to their children and ask if anyone had been subjected to abuse or witnessed any.

"Our investigation indicates that possible criminal acts include: oral sex, fondling of genitals, buttock or chest area, and sodomy, possibly committed under the pretense of 'taking the child's temperature.' Also photos may have been taken of children without their clothing. Any information from your child regarding having ever observed Ray Buckey to leave a classroom alone with a child during any nap period, or if they have ever observed Ray Buckey tie up a child, is important."[8]

After requesting that parents keep word of the investigation private because of the "emotional effect it would have on our community," the letter assured in all capital letters:

> THERE IS NO EVIDENCE TO INDICATE THAT THE MANAGEMENT OF VIRGINIA MCMARTIN'S PRESCHOOL HAD ANY KNOWLEDGE OF THIS SITUATION AND NO DETRIMENTAL INFORMATION CONCERNING THE OPERATION OF THE SCHOOL HAS BEEN DISCOVERED DURING THIS INVESTIGATION. ALSO, NO OTHER EMPLOYEE OF THE PRESCHOOL IS UNDER INVESTIGATION FOR ANY CRIMINAL ACT.[9]

Of course, the notion that parents would keep quiet about the investigation proved laughable. The allegations outlined were so shocking, so reprehensible, that the news spread like wildfire. Rattled parents sat down with their children and began asking them questions. The children seemed just as shocked. Nothing like that happened, they said. But the parents pressed: *Are you sure? You seemed a little hesitant. You fidgeted a bit. Are you absolutely positive?* Some of the kids got defensive and quit answering the questions. Their parents worried that they were shutting down because of the trauma they had endured. The parents asked again and again. Their persistence was eventually rewarded. One child after another finally agreed: Yes, Ray

Buckey hurt me, he hurt my friends, and he threatened me not to tell. Soon, authorities believed at least sixty children had been victimized, and that the ultimate number was likely even higher.

Buckey was at home, sitting with his family, when a news story aired on KABC-TV Channel 7 unveiling the allegations not only to its viewers, but to the rest of the country. "In a case which has been described as one of the most bizarre and shocking ever to involve young children, the district attorney has a team of six investigating the allegations of more than sixty young children that they were sexually assaulted, photographed, and terrorized into silence while in the care of a prestigious preschool in Manhattan Beach."[10]

Award-winning investigative reporter Wayne Satz reported that not only had children been molested, but that they'd been forced to appear in pornographic films and made to watch teachers torture and slay animals as part of elaborate Satanic rituals.[11] The report seemed timed to kick off a sweeps period, during which Nielsen tracked audience habits, which would in turn help determine advertising rates for the coming months. Satz denied that the sweeps played a role in his timing, but there was no question that was effective programming.[12] Parents flooded the police department with one allegation after another. The pool of alleged abusers began to expand. Detective Hoag arranged for all of the children to be interviewed at the Children's Institute International, a Los Angeles–based nonprofit providing trauma services to children.[13] Because therapy and abuse was in the organization's wheelhouse, it seemed a good fit for experts there to handle the interviews of children. The director, Kathleen "Kee" MacFarlane, was especially passionate about child abuse issues and had learned after years of experience and heart-wrenching interviews that children were typically reluctant to talk about abuse they endured. This made sense to MacFarlane, who reasoned that many adults have difficulty handling trauma, so it seemed logical that children might have an even harder time. With this in mind, MacFarlane developed an interview technique in which she employed puppets to communicate with the children—the thinking being that it would be easier for children to tell scary secrets to a harmless-looking puppet rather than an adult authority figure.[14] The children were also provided puppets, so that if they had been sworn to secrecy by their abuser, they could rationalize that they weren't breaking that promise by sharing the secret. It was the puppet talking, after all.

"I'm not the only puppet lady in this case," MacFarlane once told reporters, explaining that she worked with a co-therapist and pediatrician who also used the puppets, "even in the medical exam."[15]

The problem with these puppets was that they didn't simply ask the children to tell the truth. Videos of, and transcripts from, the puppets' supposed interviews with children showed that their questions were incredibly leading, and children who didn't remember abuse were often berated. For example, in one interview MacFarlane's puppet was talking to another puppet named Mr. Alligator. Mr. Alligator was controlled by a little boy from whom MacFarlane was trying to get information. Through the puppet, MacFarlane asked about a game that other children had talked about called Naked Movie Star. "Do you remember that game, Mr. Alligator, or is your memory too bad?" her puppet asked. The phrasing straight away suggested what answer MacFarlane wanted, but still, the boy said through Mr. Alligator that, no, he didn't remember the game. MacFarlane's puppet sounded disappointed. "Oh, Mr. Alligator," it chided. Then the boy said there was a children's rhyme that included the phrase "naked movie star." It went: "What you see is what you are. You're a naked movie star."[16]

MacFarlane's puppet rewarded the boy with praise. "You know what, Mr. Alligator? That means you're smart 'cause that's the same song the other kids knew and that's how we really know you're smarter than you look. So you better not play dumb, Mr. Alligator." The flattery didn't last long, however, because when asked if he remember someone peeking in a window while he and other children played Naked Movie Star, the boy said he didn't know anything more about the phrase than the sing-songy rhyme. "What good are you?" MacFarlane's puppet said. "You must be dumb."[17] Eventually, the boy did remember. He remembered the game, he remembered kids being photographed in the nude by adults, and he remembered other details first suggested by MacFarlane's puppet. The interviews conducted by her assistants were much the same. Dr. Astrid Heger told a little girl, "I don't want to hear anymore nos."[18]

One boy named Kyle Sapp would later recall these puppet-led interviews to a reporter with the *Los Angeles Times*. As he wrote in 2005:

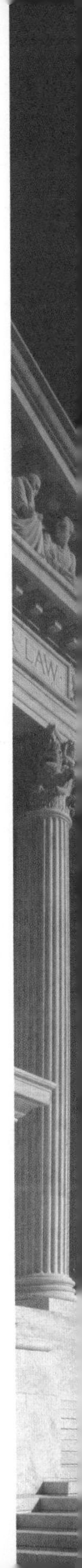

> **I remember them asking extremely uncomfortable questions about whether Ray touched me and about all the teachers and what they did. I remember telling them nothing happened to me. I remember them almost giggling and laughing, saying, "Oh, we know these things happened to you. Why don't you go ahead and tell us? Use these dolls if you're scared." Anytime I would give them an answer that they didn't like, they would ask again and encourage me to give them the answer they were looking for. It was really obvious what they wanted.[19]**

When he finally relented, they told him how smart he was and how much he was helping other kids who were being hurt but weren't as smart and brave as he was being.

He said the lie ate at him, though. At some point, he tried to come clean with his mom. He described crying hysterically on his bed with his mother begging him to tell her what was wrong. "You won't believe me," he said. She promised that she would. Finally, he said: "Nothing happened. Nothing ever happened to me at that school."

She didn't believe him.[20] Like many parents, she instead chose to believe only the awful parts of what their children had told them. Parents were mortified and guilt-ridden that they'd been sending their innocent children off to be abused day after day at the McMartin school. MacFarlane assured them that they couldn't have known, that children are conditioned to block out such trauma until the truth was pulled from them by a trained expert. MacFarlane at the time was working with a nationally recognized physician named Roland Summit, who published an article titled "Child Sexual Abuse Accommodation Syndrome," which argued that children could not detail false allegations of sex abuse.[21] According to Summit, children had neither the imaginations nor the maliciousness required to make up sex abuse allegations about innocent people. The article posited that abused children acted in certain ways so they could learn to survive with the abuse. Summit laid it out in five stages: secrecy; helplessness; entrapment and accommodation; delayed disclosure; and, lastly, retraction.[22]

A saying took hold in Manhattan Beach: *Believe the children.* The parents did—until the kids retracted, because that was supposedly an expected part of their trauma. Plenty of children who eventually had agreed in interviews with MacFarlane or others that they had been molested recanted those allegations, but the recantations were ignored as proof that the abuse indeed occurred. Soon, Raymond Buckey was arrested again—alongside his mother, sister, and seventy-six-year-old grandmother, Virginia McMartin. Three nonfamilial teachers also were arrested: Mary Ann Jackson, Betty Raidor and Babette Spitler. NBC news anchor Tom Brokaw reported: "In what may become one of the biggest child molestation cases ever on record, seven nursery schoolteachers were arraigned today on more than one hundred counts of child molestation."[23]

Lawyer Danny Davis was hired as Ray Buckey's defense attorney for a preliminary hearing that began in fall 1984. Davis decided to drag out the proceedings as long as possible—a strategic move meant to provide time for the fury to subside and cooler heads to prevail. Davis later explained that his foot-dragging was inspired by his studies of social contagion in sixteenth-century Europe, which suggested that enraged people will "grab, enslave,

Virginia McMartin at a preliminary hearing of the McMartin Preschool molestation case in Los Angeles, August 18, 1984.

and kill a scapegoat" and then "look back with shameful retrospect." Instead of allowing that to happen to his clients, Davis instead filed every motion and demanded every delay he could, eventually making the preliminary hearing "the longest in the history of American jurisprudence."[24]

His efforts worked. Preliminary hearings are typically a few weeks at most—many are done in a day—but the McMartin preliminary hearing dragged on for twenty months. By the time the hearing wrapped in 1986, charges against five of the seven McMartin defendants were dismissed. Only Ray and his mother, Peggy McMartin Buckey, remained defendants after the hearing finished.

Meanwhile, allegations of abuse spread far beyond the McMartin school. The tally reached more than 100, then 1,000, then 1,400, most in the Manhattan Beach area. "That's a third of the school system in the city of Manhattan Beach," one parent said. "We have eight preschools closed here. This is the child molestation capital of the world."[25]

The allegations that spread were becoming more and more bizarre. Some daycare workers were accused of forcing children to eat pies made of excrement and stabbing them in the genitals with forks and knives. Prosecutors pursued charges in these cases even though no corroborating evidence existed; the children's tales were all the evidence they needed. One couple who ran a daycare center in Texas was accused in 1991 of slicing a student's dog with a chainsaw and taking the child, a little girl, to a cemetery where she saw a person dressed like a policeman throw another person into a hole, after which one of the daycare owners shot the person and cut the body into pieces. They were accused of forcing kids to drink blood-laced Kool-Aid, and to have videotaped sex with adults. The couple was convicted entirely on the statements of preschoolers, whose tales were obtained using puppets and coercive language, just as had been used in the McMartin case. (That couple, Fran and Dan Keller of Texas, spent twenty-two years in prison before being released in 2013 and eventually declared "factually innocent." The two were awarded more than $3.4 million for their wrongful convictions.[26])

The trial against Raymond Buckey and his mother was complicated by the death of Judy Johnson, the mother whose allegations sparked the initial investigation. Johnson died just before she was set to give testimony in the case, prompting conspiracy theories that she'd been killed to silence her. In

Peggy McMartin Buckey and her son, Ray Buckey, listen to the opening statements for their trial, Los Angeles, July 13, 1987.

truth, she'd struggled with mental health issues and alcoholism, facts that had been withheld from defense lawyers. She'd come to Detective Hoag with increasingly bizarre allegations that she claimed her son Mitchell had made—that his eyes had been poked, that he'd been forced to assault goats, that he'd been made to drink concoctions of urine and blood.[27] As outlandish as these claims sounded, respectable news organizations were reporting similar allegations at face value, lending Johnson's stories credibility.

What wasn't reported, however, was that Johnson had had a mental breakdown, her children had been removed from her home and sent to live with her brother, and she had been diagnosed with paranoid schizophrenia. She had been drinking heavily and ignoring symptoms of a stomach ulcer that was tearing her insides apart. Johnson was found in her home on December 19, 1986, dead from liver disease. [28] Her son Mitchell never took the stand, but nine alleged victims—whose stories Mitchell's had helped inspire—did testify.

MacFarlane, the puppeteer, said more would have testified but many were afraid for their lives. Those who did told tales about having been ushered through underground tunnels beneath the school and flown on private planes to participate in Satanic rituals in Palm Springs. But no one could locate the supposed plane or find flight information substantiating the claim. Nor could anyone find proof of the described underground tunnels. The jury noticed,

Legal Legacy

The McMartin Preschool investigation led to changes in how experts approached children to discuss concerns about abuse, especially in situations where those allegations could be used in court.

- Subsequent studies, some citing the McMartin case, were conducted on issues of false memory, particularly the notion that they could be implanted in impressionable brains via leading questions.
- The interview techniques used in the case are regularly cited in newspapers and textbooks as examples of how not to talk to children about suspected abuse,[33] while research has led to new psychiatric protocols and practices.

Raymond Buckey displays a copy of the *Los Angeles Times* with the headline "A Mistrial for Buckey" as he leaves Los Angeles Criminal Courts Building after his acquittal, July 27, 1990.

and on January 18, 1990, Peggy McMartin Buckey was acquitted of all charges. Her son was acquitted of fifty-two charges, but the jury couldn't reach a consensus on the remaining thirteen charges. The prosecutor retried him on six of those counts, but the second trial again ended in a hung jury on July 27, 1990, after which prosecutors gave up. It wasn't ideal for Ray, who wanted an outright acquittal, but he at least got to move forward with his life.[29]

In the end, the case lasted seven years and cost $15 million, making it one of the longest and most expensive cases in the history of the US legal system—one that resulted in zero convictions.[30] In the aftermath, Virginia McMartin and her granddaughter, Peggy Ann Buckey—the two women who did not face trial—unsuccessfully sued Kee MacFarlane and the Children's Institute International for violating their civil rights. The suit also alleged that MacFarlane leaked information to Wayne Satz, the investigative reporter who broke the story, with whom the suit alleged MacFarland was having an intimate relationship.[31] Peggy McMartin Buckey—Ray's mother—also filed a $1 million civil rights suit against Manhattan Beach and media members, which also failed. The only suit the family won was a slander lawsuit against a parent, for which they were each awarded a single dollar.[32]

Part 3

CIVIL RIGHTS CATALYSTS

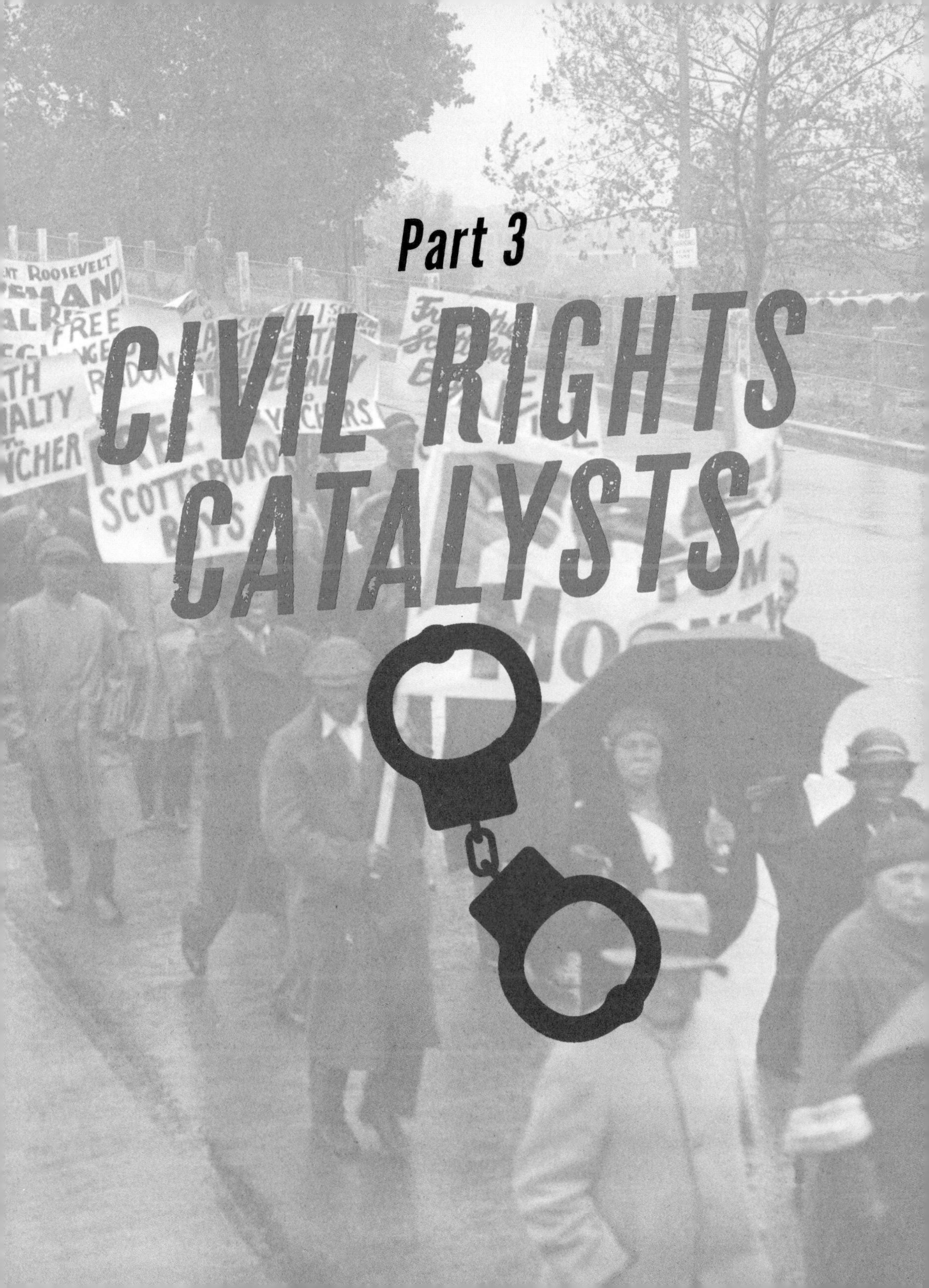

ONE WAY STREET
WARRINGTON

11

Delphine LaLaurie's Horrific Torture Chamber

(1834)

When smoke began to billow from a New Orleans home on April 10, 1834, neighbors sprang into action, reaching the scene and barreling their way inside the house to save whomever, and whatever of value, they could. This was a typical reaction to a burning building at the time. New Orleans wouldn't get its first steam pump engines and fire hydrants for a few more decades—and the first paid fire department would not be in service until 1891[1]—so blazes were battled by volunteers with buckets of water. As neighborly as the effort sounds, it was largely self-serving: Fires left unchecked threatened to burn down more than a single house. They could take out entire neighborhoods in a flash.

Not only that, but this particular fire was burning a house with a questionable reputation. Rumors had been rampant for years about the couple who owned it. They owned enslaved people, which in and of itself wasn't controversial—Louisiana was a slave-holding state—but the woman whose house was on fire was rumored to be especially vicious to the humans she owned. Mutterings had made the rounds about an upstairs room serving as a makeshift prison.

The neighbors who had arrived pushed their way inside and quickly encountered verification of the rumors. In the kitchen, they found an enslaved woman in chains, unable to free herself. The bruising on her skin suggested she'd been horrifically beaten. After she was brought to safety outside, her saviors returned to the house, determined to see if anyone else was impeded

OPPOSITE: A 1937 photograph of the building that stands on the site of the original LaLaurie mansion on Royal Street in New Orleans. It was built in 1838, four years after the LaLaurie mansion was destroyed.

from leaving on their own accord. They ran from room to room, opening one door after another, in search of anyone needing help. Some hauled expensive furniture outside as they were able, but most stayed focused on the unspoken mission: saving lives. Finally, they reached the apartment they'd heard about and flung open the door. Inside were seven people so emaciated and badly tortured that, though alive, they barely looked human anymore.

The victims were carried from the home and laid nearby, beneath the outdoor arches that surrounded the city hall building, the Cabildo. The sight of these humans—bones broken, ribs protruding, ancient wounds healed in unnatural ways—was so unsettling that townspeople demanded justice. Instead, Madame Delphine LaLaurie got away. By the time the townsfolk realized she'd managed to escape, they were so enraged that they took their fury out on her home, leaving it in ruins. So outraged were people that the case made headlines far beyond New Orleans, reaching even Great Britain and France, and served as a catalyst for the abolitionist movement.

The case also ensured that a woman who'd been born Delphine Macarty on March 19, 1787, would forever be labeled one of the cruelest, most depraved women in American history.

Delphine was born to parents Louis Bartélémy and Marie-Jeanne in New Orleans. The union was Marie-Jeanne's second. Her first husband had died, leaving her a childless widow. With Louis, she had two children—first a boy who shared his father's name, then Delphine, whose first marriage at age thirteen caused quite a scandal.

"It seems like it was a shotgun wedding," said historian Carolyn Morrow Long, author of *Madame Lalaurie: Mistress of the Haunted House* (2012), during an interview. "One assumes that she was pregnant, but there was never any baby."[2]

Long posits that it's possible Delphine was impregnated out of wedlock, prompting the quick marriage—she cites some letters in which Delphine's husband worries about saving the reputation of the girl's family—but perhaps Delphine miscarried the baby or gave birth to one who didn't live long. Infant mortality rates were abysmal in 1800. Regardless, Delphine's new husband was a prominent man, a Spaniard who'd been sent to work in America by King Charles IV of Spain. Don Ramón de Lopez y Ángulo was a high-ranking royal officer who had left Spain with his wife, a woman named

Borja who he considered his soulmate. The overseas trip was so grueling, however, that Borja fell sick and died en route, breaking Ramón's heart. It doesn't seem likely that love had much to do with him ending up in the arms of a teenager soon after his arrival to the New World, but whatever led him to Delphine, he seemed determined to stand by her. His position as an officer meant that he was supposed to get permission from the king before marrying, but communication was slow back then and the couple seemed in a rush, so Ramón smooth-talked an officiant into performing the ceremony in June 1800. Still, he faced a series of consequences—first a demotion and then threat of exile. He battled this indignity for years, resulting in his pardon by late 1804, after which he was appointed Spanish consul to New Orleans under the American administration. But the new job ultimately led to Ramón early death, as Long wrote:

> **As he was proceeding to his new post on the American ship *Ulysses* from Bordeaux, the vessel ran upon a sandbar and capsized near Havana. A despatch from Havana dated January 11, 1805, reported that López y Ángulo had died "as a result of the running aground of the ship." He may have drowned, he may have sustained injuries that resulted in his death or, as one historian has suggested, he may have died of heart failure from the shock. The Widow López desired "to preserve the corpse in salt so that she could give it a holy burial."[3]**

When this happened, Delphine was heavily pregnant. She gave birth soon afterward in a Havana hospital to a daughter she named in part after her late husband's first wife. The little girl was called Borja. Now widowed, Delphine remarried a Frenchman named Jean Blanque, an attorney, land speculator, and smuggler. The couple had four children before Jean died in 1816, deeply in debt. This could have ruined a widowed mother of five, but a few subsequent tragedies ironically kept her from going broke. First, Delphine's mother died, leaving Delphine and her brother a sum of money and land, followed by her father, whose death left Delphine the quite comfortable owner of a plantation. In addition to inheriting property and money, she also had at least ten enslaved persons to cook, keep house, watch the children, tend the yard, and run the plantation.

An undated portrait of Delphine LaLaurie.

This gave her time to pursue a new romance when the opportunity arose. One of Delphine's daughters was born with a back deformity, likely scoliosis. While searching for someone to treat the issue, Delphine met a younger man who'd sailed from France with dreams of establishing a medical practice in New Orleans. At this point, Delphine was nearing forty, while the man who caught her eye was just twenty-five. Louis LaLaurie specialized in treating deformities of the spine by using intricate contraptions to elongate people's spines in hopes of setting them straight. The treatments could be quite painful, but they were considered cutting-edge. References to the "young hunchback lady Madamoiselle Blanque" are made in letters from Louis's father in France sent to his son in New Orleans. LaLaurie's father references Delphine in some of his letters, too, though it's apparent he didn't have a clear vision of how his son's relationship with the patient's mother would unfold. "His father is saying, 'Get your act together, marry a rich woman, make your name as a doctor and come home and live in your home village and return to the family,'" Long noted.[4] "So of course, Papa is imagining a young girl, not this widow who is old enough to be (Louis's) mother."

Details that explain how the relationship blossomed are lacking, but regardless, Delphine learned she was pregnant with Louis's child; after she gave birth, Louis left her for five months. There's no record of why he left or where he went, but upon his return, Louis married Delphine. Their relationship was an unusual one, especially for the era. While it was common for husbands to be older than wives—both of Delphine's previous husbands were about twice her age—it was odd for a bride to be older than her groom. Additionally, the couple entered a prenuptial agreement when they married, which wasn't common at the time. Louis's mother had died not long after he moved to New Orleans, and because of that, he'd inherited a bit of land in France, which he signed over to his father to manage. Otherwise, Louis was quite poor. Per the prenuptial agreement, he stayed poor in marriage. Delphine retained control of her land, her houses, and her enslaved people.[5]

Up until this marriage, there's no evidence that Delphine was suspected of mistreating the people in her household. It's possible that rumors predated the first surviving documentation, which came in 1828, but it's also possible no one had paid her much attention until she'd inspired gossip with her unusual marriage. It could be, too, that she didn't start abusing the people in her house until after she and Louis married, though that seems the least likely of the scenarios. Someone who unleashes the cruelty that Delphine was later documented to have perpetrated is likely to have been cruel for some time.

Whatever the case, the first records came via letters that are now stored in the Historic New Orleans Collection. The correspondences were written by Jean Boze, who was the business manager of a nearby plantation. Less than a year after Delphine and Louis married, Boze wrote a letter about the two keeping an unhappy household. "They fight, they separate, and then return to each other, which would make one believe that someday they will abandon each other completely," wrote Boze, who added that Delphine was also investigated several times for being cruel to her slaves. Backing up this assertion was a note Long found "tucked away in an unrelated civil suit before the Parish Court." The note indicates that Delphine paid a prominent attorney, John Randolph Grymes, $300 for "defending the prosecution of the State against her in the Criminal Court." While the note doesn't spell out what charges had been lodged against Delphine, Boze wrote soon after that Delphine had been brought before the court for "the barbarous treatment of her slaves." She was not convicted, however, because, per Boze, no one was willing to testify that they had actually seen her deliver the beatings.[6]

Louisiana has a complicated history, having been settled in the early 1700s and then switching back and forth between French and Spanish rule. The United States bought the land from France in the Louisiana Purchase of 1803, which ultimately led to the territory becoming a state in 1812. Louisiana's history with slavery is equally complex. While slavery was legal in the region, the importation of slaves was outlawed in 1796. That was largely in response to worries that the slave population would revolt because enslaved people had come to outnumber the white population. In December of 1800, however, Delphine's first husband—Ramon López y Ángulo—issued a proclamation permitting the importation of captives from Africa—over government officials' objections, which cited recent uprisings in Louisiana, Saint-Domingue, and elsewhere in the Caribbean.[7]

As such, the law in Louisiana allowed landowners to buy and sell other human beings. The law even allowed so-called owners to abuse the people

they bought by lashing them as punishment for things such as trying to flee or even just talking back. But there were limits to how much punishment was legally allowed. Excessive mistreatment was frowned upon—mostly to protect slaves as assets. There are a smattering of slave-cruelty cases in court records from the era, though it seems charges were reserved for instances of exceptional brutality. Lashing a slave for trying to run away was not egregious enough to warrant charges. In fact, fears of revolts were so rampant that such punishments were expected. Delphine's family knew those fears well: One of her uncles was killed in 1771 by two men he'd enslaved.[8]

New Orleans also had been near the biggest slave revolt in American history—the German Coast Uprising of 1811, in three parishes just west of the city. Forty-five people in that revolt were sentenced to death, their heads placed on poles alongside the river levee as a warning to others. It wasn't as much of a deterrent as some had hoped, as New Orleans' Slave Jail House was regularly filled with runaways.[9] Slave owners would place ads when someone would flee—some 12,000 of which ran in newspapers nationwide between 1800 and 1860[10]—and offer a reward for the enslaved person's return. Delphine ran several such ads, including one Long found searching for a "negro man" described as "about 30, of a stout make, not above 5 feet 3 inches . . . of a very black complexion speaking English well enough and a Creole of the country."

While the ad didn't name the man who'd fled Delphine's home, it likely was her coachman Bastien, who was rumored to be one of her favorites. Bastien is believed to have provided intel on the other enslaved people in the house, letting Delphine know if someone was sneaking extra portions of dinner or plotting to flee. He's also believed to have played an important role on the day the LaLaurie's home caught on fire.[11]

The home wasn't the riverside plantation Delphine had inherited from her father, but rather a house she and Louis had built around 1831 at Royal and Hospital streets. Once construction was finished, the couple threw lavish parties and other fashionable affairs attended by the elite. Delphine presented herself as a high-class, proper lady. She was polite and kind to the guests who came to dine at her mansion, and she was known to put on a show to convey that she treated her enslaved servants well, too. She'd hand one of them a half-finished glass of wine and encourage them to finish it, saying, "It'll do you good."[12]

That behavior didn't quiet the rumors about how she abused enslaved people in her home, however. According to a book written in 1889 by George Washington Cable titled *Strange True Stories of Louisiana*, the next notable claim came when a neighbor saw a young girl, who looked to be about eight years old, tearing through the mansion's yard with Delphine following her, whip in hand. The girl ran through the house and raced up the stairs to flee. With Delphine still chasing her, the girl made it to the roof, from which she fell to her death. Descriptions circulated of Delphine carrying the girl's broken body across the property, which prompted a police investigation. Authorities searched the property and found nine slaves in terrible shape. In a move that they surely viewed as heroic, they rounded up those nine people and led them away from Delphine—but, according to Cable, the people were simply sold again. Some had even been bought by family members of Delphine, who had them returned to her mansion under cover of night. Cable wrote: "All Madame LaLaurie ever suffered for this part of her hideous misdeeds was a fine."[13]

"ALL MADAME LALAURIE EVER SUFFERED FOR THIS PART OF HER HIDEOUS MISDEEDS WAS A FINE."

It's unclear if Louis took part in the abuse his wife unleashed on their servants. What *is* clear is that the couple's relationship was strained from the beginning, and moving into the extravagant new home did nothing to calm matters. A year after the move, Delphine took steps to end the marriage by applying for a separation. At the time, it wasn't easy to uncouple legally. Today, Louisiana law allows parties to divorce each other for no reason at all once they have lived apart between six months and a year, depending on whether they had children together.[14] In 1832, the time of Delphine's filing, however, that wasn't the case. A husband could claim separation if his wife were having an affair, but a woman's bar was higher. The husband had to move his lover into the shared home for that to be justification enough. Delphine's separation request cited ill treatment, saying that Louis "went so far as to not only ill treat her, but even to beat and wound her in the most outrageous and cruel manner."[15] She testified that Louis had moved from their shared home to rural Plaquemines Parish. Still, the two weren't rid of each other. Louis's signature routinely appeared next to Delphine's when she bought real estate or enslaved people, though she was described as a "wife separated" in such business transactions.[16]

Louis returned to the Royal Street mansion on April 10, 1834, for reasons unknown, but records show he was there when the air above the home began to fill with soot and smoke. The fire began in the kitchen, but back then, wealthy Southern homeowners often located their kitchens in semidetached or completely detached buildings, to avoid extra heat, smells, and smoke in the main house and help prevent fires; also to segregate enslaved kitchen workers.[17] The LaLaurie kitchen was in a detached building that abutted the main residence at a right angle. As the fire began, neighbors flooded the streets, arriving by the dozens to attempt to extinguish the blaze. When it became clear that the flames would likely spread from the kitchen annex to the main building, those neighbors started hauling out the expensive furniture, draperies, jewels, and other belongings they found inside. Delphine supposedly helped direct this traffic, yelling commands like, "This way! Take this—go, now, and hurry back, if you please!" As some headed toward a door that she hadn't directed them to, she supposedly waved them off. "That is only the servants' quarters," she spat.[18]

But some of the neighbors insisted on finding the servants. Judge Jacques François Canonge, who lived across the street from the LaLauries, asked if they were housed in the service wing. Delphine said not to worry about them, so the judge turned to Louis instead. According to newspaper reports, Louis shot back that the judge should mind his own business, do as Delphine said, and focus on saving the valuables.[19] Judge Canonge did not oblige. He and other prominent residents broke down doors trying to find the enslaved people inside. Finally, they found a locked apartment on an upper floor. From a newspaper account:

> **The most appalling spectacle met their eyes—seven slaves more or less horribly mutilated, were seen suspended by the neck, with their limbs apparently stretched and torn from one extremity to the other. Language is powerless and inadequate to give a proper conception of the horror which a scene like this must have inspired. . . . These slaves were the property of the demon, in the shape of a woman, whom we mentioned in the beginning of this article. They had been confined by her for several months in the situation from which they had thus providentially been rescued and had been merely kept in**

> **existence to prolong their sufferings and to make them taste all that the most refined cruelty could inflict.**[20]

The seven victims were carried from the house and laid beneath the arches of the Cabildo, an ornate building that had served as the seat of government during the Spanish colonial period, and now served as city hall. One woman, estimated to be at least sixty years old, couldn't move on her own. Another man was described as having "a large hole in his head: his body from head to foot was covered with scars and filled with worms."[21] Armand Saillard, French consul to New Orleans, was among some three thousand people who filed through to see the victims. He wrote in a report that he saw "dislocated heads, legs torn by the chains, [and] bodies streaked [with blood] from head to foot from whiplashes and sharp instruments."[22]

While putting the victims on display seems cruel, it served a purpose: townsfolk saw with their own eyes the condition of the people pulled from the mansion, making it impossible for them to pretend that the allegations were exaggerated. And those who didn't see for themselves read about it in the local newspapers, whose accounts were republished across the globe. Even though some of the news accounts carried differing details—one newspaper reported that bodies had been found buried in Delphine's yard, for example, while a competitor reported that wasn't true—the condition of the victims was consistent. Judge Canonge and others were described as rushing to feed the emaciated victims. Two of the seven reportedly didn't survive the day, with the rest ultimately ending up "pensioners of the city."[23]

Days later, a mob of New Orleans residents screaming for justice surrounded the LaLaurie mansion while Delphine hid inside with her children and Louis. Delphine's coachman—the servant she supposedly treated well, though he had run away at least once before—suggested a simple plan: he said that the family should behave like nothing was wrong. He would pull the coach up to the house and they would climb aboard as though they were simply leaving to go for a short ride on a normal day. The ruse worked. It wasn't until after the coach was out of sight that the angry mob realized that Delphine had fled, which enraged the mob further They began destroying the mansion, smashing every piece of furniture they could find, tearing down the draperies, even attacking the stone façade. Several more days passed, and a newspaper reported that the destruction was still continuing: "At the time of writing this, the fury of the mob remained still unabated and threatens the total demolition of the entire edifice," read a *New Orleans Bee* story reprinted in the *New York Evening Post*.[24]

Delphine settled some business matters and then traveled to Mobile, Alabama, and from there, to New York City, where she and Louis were recognized. As word spread that they were the infamous LaLauries, onlookers hurled insults at them. They decided to head to France aboard the ship *Poland*. The American poet William Cullen Bryant happened to be on the same ship. He wrote in his journal on June 24, 1834, that Delphine was there, describing her as a "pretty-looking French woman" known to be the same who "committed such horrible cruelties upon her slaves last winter in New Orleans." She "was now returning with her husband to his . . . native country," wrote Bryant, who also noted that Delphine was frequently in tears because other ladies aboard the ship were mean to her.[25]

An illustration of the sacking of the LaLaurie mansion in April 1934, from a book by Paul M. Hollister titled *Famous Colonial Houses* (1921).

Delphine lived the rest of her life in France. Louis never divorced her, but he did eventually abandon her, resettling in Havana. At some point, Delphine wrote a letter to one of her sons, who had stayed behind in the States. In the correspondence, she contemplated returning to New Orleans, but the son was insistent that shouldn't happen. The LaLaurie mansion, which had been utterly demolished, was rebuilt a few years later (see photograph on page 132). Originally a two-story building, the reconstruction included a third floor that still exists today. Even though the house isn't really the same structure the LaLauries once owned, it's still referred to by locals as the Haunted House. At one point, it was divided into low-rent apartments. At another, it served as an all-girls school. No matter its incarnation, for nearly two hundred years, people have reported paranormal activity there—sounds of phantom footsteps, eerie green lights of unknown origin,[26] and scratches and bruises of mysterious nature.[27] Newspapers began regaling readers with stories of strange occurrences as early as 1883. "Of course the place is haunted," read one piece in the *Carolina Watchman*.[28] In 1892, the *Times-Picayune* wrote: "Strange stories began to be whispered about the old place, stories of ghosts and evil spirits, of strange lights and unearthly noises."[29] Neighbors reportedly found themselves started by "seeing the doors swing open untouched by human hands, and close violently, and the windows were seen to rise up and fall again without a soul being near."[30] Rather than those rumors fading into obscurity, they continue still today as ghost-hunting tourists and so-called paranormal investigators are drawn to the place, lured by its horrifying history.

In all, twenty enslaved people are documented to have died in Delphine's care—eight before her marriage to Louis, and twelve between 1831 and 1833. Almost all of those whose deaths were documented were women and children.[31]

Legal Legacy

The public display of Delphine LaLaurie's cruelty toward the people discovered in her home helped to change public discourse about the barbarity of slavery and fueled the abolitionist movement.

- In her 1838 memoir *Retrospect of Western Travel*, English reformer Harriet Martineau wrote that while Delphine was atypically vicious, her actions were "a revelation of what may happen in a slave-holding country, and can happen nowhere else."[32]
- The conditions uncovered in the LaLaurie home were described in numerous articles printed by abolitionist newspapers mailed to households nationwide.[33] Those publications are credited with galvanizing the anti-slavery movement, turning Northern sentiment against slavery, and fueling abolitionists' "unapologetic fight for freedom."[34]

12

The Slaying of Marie Smith, and the Black Man Nearly Lynched for It

(1910)

Peter and Nora Smith had left behind the tenements of Brooklyn, New York, in 1909 in search of a better life—a safer one—along the shore in Asbury Park, New Jersey. The couple had recently lost their youngest child at eighteen months, leaving them with two older ones—ten-year-old Marie and five-year-old Thomas.

A year after the move, the Smiths were pregnant again and looking forward to expanding their family in Asbury Park, a quaint burg with a year-round population of about twelve thousand people. The city had been founded in the 1870s by a fervent Methodist named James A. Bradley, whose visions of a moral utopia led him to outlaw alcohol at its inception, more than forty years before the entire nation would attempt the so-called Noble Experiment on a much wider scale. Had teetotalers used Asbury Park as a case study, they might have saved themselves some trouble because Bradley's efforts to ban alcohol failed entirely.

"The irony is it was never really dry," said Alex Tresniowski, author of *The Rope* (2021). "It certainly was prohibited, but they had beer being sold out. You had to go into a pharmacy and ask for 'seafoam,' and that would be beer. And there was another code for ale or whiskey. There were people in carts going up and down streets, and James Bradley would sometimes go out into the streets and chase them down himself and say, 'Get outta here!' but you could get booze anywhere."[1]

Bradley had developed the town as a Christian resort community meant to draw thousands of God-fearing visitors to its hotels, parks, and boardwalks, but he soon realized that he needed thousands of workers to run the place—hotel hands, resort employees, city workers, and such. The pay for such gigs wasn't great, so those jobs drew people Bradley deemed as less-than-desirables in his intended utopia. As such, crime was sometimes a problem, though it paled in comparison to the Smiths' previous homestead. In Asbury Park, the Smiths didn't hesitate to let their children walk to school every day. Marie, as the older of the two, even came home at lunchtime every school day so she could fetch a meal for her father and drop it off at his work before returning to school to finish out her day.

That's what she was expected to do November 9, 1910, a Wednesday. Instead, what unfolded was a tragic and bizarre criminal case that not only launched the career of one of history's most revered detectives, but also helped solidify the role of a fledgling civil rights group known as the National Association for the Advancement of Colored People.

The day started like any other in the Smith household, except that Peter noticed his little girl was even more chipper than usual. Marie was a small girl—many who saw her assumed she was closer to seven years old than ten—and striking in appearance, with pretty dark-blonde hair and delicate features. After breakfast that morning, Marie kissed her mother goodbye and took her little brother's hand. The two walked to the school building at the corner of Third Avenue and Pine Street, where Marie swung by Thomas's kindergarten class to drop him off first. Nothing seemed amiss that morning until after the 10:30 a.m. dismissal, which was when Marie was expected to rush home and grab lunch for her father.[2] At first, Nora wasn't worried when she didn't appear. She figured that Marie's schoolteacher must have held the class over for some reason. After school ended, however, Nora began to sense something was terribly wrong. She went to the schoolyard and watched as the children streamed from the building. Soon, she spotted Thomas, but her firstborn never appeared.

Fourth Avenue in Asbury Park, New Jersey, several blocks from where Marie's school was located, photographed in c. 1905.

Nora alerted the police, who initially assured her that Marie would turn up quickly. Asbury Park was too small for any real danger, they said. After all, dozens of kids from their neighborhood walked the near-mile route to and from school every single day without incident. Search parties were formed involving police, school officials, and Marie's classmates, who scoured the area near the school, as well as the path Marie was known to have walked. At first, they turned up nothing. Marie's parents worried all night. Nora couldn't sleep at all, alternating between pacing and weeping.[3]

A cub reporter with the *Asbury Park Press*—a newspaper founded by Bradley a few decades prior[4]—developed an interest in the case and decided to start investigating. Alvin Cliver followed up on one of Nora's agonized thoughts: she thought maybe Marie missed her old home in Brooklyn and had found a way to travel back there. Cliver called the Smiths' relatives in New York, but no one had seen or heard from the girl. Cliver shifted gears and began searching for Marie himself. As he traced Marie's last known steps, he ran into a local Black tradesman named Thomas Williams.

Williams was known around town as an affable guy who'd come to New Jersey by way of Lynchburg, Virginia, where he'd been an amateur prizefighter who went by the nickname Black Diamond.[5] He was about forty-five years old and six feet tall with broad shoulders and a taste for liquor[6]—which, luckily for him, was no longer banned in Asbury Park by 1910. Williams had a few convictions under his belt for crimes like theft and public drunkenness, but he was generally considered a pleasant man whom townsfolk would tap for itinerant handyman work—painting houses or cutting down trees, for example. One of the people in town who hired him regularly for odd jobs was Delia Jackson, Nora Smith's aunt. Nora knew him well enough that she sent him on occasional errands to buy her beer.

Williams lived in a rented room of a boarding house. Because he walked where he needed to go around town, most residents at least knew who he was. One little boy told his mom a story about Williams spotting him with a toad. Williams had asked the boy what he was planning to do with the toad, and the boy replied that he meant to kill it. Williams said, no, don't do that. The boy asked why. "Because that would be cruel," Williams said. The boy pondered a minute and then decided to let the toad hop away.[7] That's the Williams most people in Asbury Park knew—a guy soft-hearted enough to preach empathy for a toad. When he encountered Cliver searching for little Marie Smith, he volunteered to help. As they roamed the area, Cliver began to get suspicious. Maybe Williams was a bit too eager to help find this girl. Cliver started asking questions: *Where were you when Marie went missing?* Williams answered that he'd been in the barroom at Griffin's Wanamassa Hotel, where he could be found most mornings, and that others had seen him there. Cliver wasn't sure he believed him. Still, with no leads on Marie's whereabouts, there wasn't much anyone could do.

Police attempted to retrace her last known steps by searching along the ten-minute route Marie walked every day going to and from school and interviewing anyone who recalled seeing her along that path. They located witnesses who could place the girl at various spots along the way after the 10:30 a.m. lunch dismissal. A schoolmate named Albert Foster said he remembered trailing Marie as she speedily walked up Third Avenue wearing her brown coat and skating cap. Albert had an eye on Marie until she turned onto Whitesville Road, at which point Albert ran inside his own house. He noticed Marie dart past a floral shop owned by neighborhood crank Max Kruschka. There, Albert said that Marie hesitated a moment, then recrossed the street as though doubling back to the florist. After that Albert lost sight.

"FROM THAT MOMENT, MARIE SMITH DISAPPEARED AS COMPLETELY AS THOUGH THE EARTH HAD OPENED AND SWALLOWED HER."

From there, a woman named Emma Davison spotted Marie, still at the intersection of Third and Whitesville. Davison told police she'd noticed Marie walking in her direction because the girl was singing as she walked, which caught her attention. Before Marie reached her, Davison turned and went down Whitesville just before Marie turned in the same direction, a few paces behind her. Suddenly, a fox terrier bolted from Kruschka's flower shop and began chasing and barking at Davison, who swatted the dog away. Just as Albert had seen, Davison noticed Marie had gotten close to her house, but then doubled back. Unlike Albert, Davison thought she saw why: A man was standing in the florist's yard, and he'd called out. Davison couldn't hear what he said, so she didn't know if he'd called for the dog or for Marie, but either way, Marie had turned back and started walking toward him. As an *Asbury Park Press* story later reported: "From that moment, Marie Smith disappeared as completely as though the earth had opened and swallowed her."[8]

With no new developments in days, Cliver told police his suspicions about Thomas Williams, who agreed they should chat with the handyman if

only to rule him out. Trouble was, they couldn't find him. Two witnesses came forward to tell police they remembered seeing Williams the day Marie disappeared. The two, John C. Conover and William Taylor, told police they were sitting on an embankment on Ridge Avenue when they saw Williams leave Griffin's barroom at about 10:30 a.m. The direction he was walking could have put him near the intersection where Davison said she last saw Marie.

Police Chief William H. Smith (no relation to the missing girl's family) wanted answers and found it suspicious that Williams was nowhere to be found to provide any. Peter Smith, Marie's father, grew desperate as well, chasing down every rumor, no matter how far-fetched—and early tips went in myriad directions. On Saturday, November 12, one newspaper reported that Marie might have been kidnapped by "gypsies."[9] The same day, another paper reported that a lake was being dragged for the girl's body.[10] Lead after lead led nowhere. Finally, on Sunday, a man named William Benson made a horrible discovery not three hundred feet from Kruschka's flower shop. He'd walked into some nearby woods and spotted what looked to be a bundle of rags. As he stepped closer, he realized it was the little girl everyone had been searching for desperately over the previous five dive days. "There seemed to have been no effort at concealment," a news story reported. "The wind had strewn fallen leaves until their color so matched the brown of the child's dress and her brown hair that as she lay face downward she was nearly indistinguishable from her shroud." Searchers had walked by her time and again in the days since her disappearance, but she simply blended in with her surroundings. "Chance discovered the body, as chance had hidden it."[11]

Once Benson recognized that the bundle he'd spotted was human, the corpse was turned over, revealing injuries that suggested she'd fought violently for her life. Marie's skirt was raised, her body exposed, and the pretty blue ribbon she'd put in her hair that morning had been tied around her neck. She'd also been bashed in the head with such force that her skull was cracked in two places. A headline on the front page of the *Baltimore Sun* the next morning read: "CHILD SLAIN BY FIEND." It began:

> **The maltreated body of little Marie Smith, a schoolgirl of 10, who had been missing since last Wednesday, was found at dusk today in a clump of woods not far from her home.**

> Some instinct seemed to warn her mother of how the search had ended, for, although an effort was made to shield her from the truth, she rushed from the home and took in the full horror of the fact before she could be withheld.
>
> Fainting, and half in convulsions, she was carried into the house, and there is grave fear that she will die and with her the life she was soon to have brought into the world.[12]

That same story concluded that Marie had been killed by a Black man and included an inflammatory subhead that read: "TOO MANY NEGROS." It lamented that the hotels and other resort businesses were drawing Black people looking for jobs. "They come from New York and other large cities to work in the hotels in summer and remain here throughout the winter in such numbers that all cannot find work and many resort to crime."[13]

Thomas Williams was found just as word spread that he was allegedly guilty. As Williams arrived, a crowd of men and women gathered around police headquarters, screaming for his lynching. "Several men moved toward the negro and he trembled with fear," the story went on, "but the policemen having him in charge were reinforced and while the threatening crowd was driven back with uplifted clubs, the negro was literally thrown through the door of police headquarters."[14]

Chief Smith took his duty to thwart vigilante justice seriously. He and his subordinate officers tried to calm the crowd by explaining that Williams, in fact, had provided a substantial alibi for the day of the murder, but the mob thought it was lip service meant to placate their cries for immediate justice. Lynchings were common enough in 1910 that the story of Asbury Park residents demanding one in Marie's case ran alongside another piece on the front page of the *Sun* titled "LYNCHING FEARED IN GEORGIA; NEGRO MURDERER CAUGHT AND POLICE ARE BUSY."[15] The lynching of Black people in America peaked in the year 1892, with 161 reported lynchings; yet in 1910 there were still sixty-seven tallied by year's end.[16] Though they were more common in Southern states, New Jersey's record wasn't spotless. In 1886, a man known as Mingo Jack was lynched after being falsely accused of raping a white woman. As members of the mob encroached on the jail harboring

Williams that first night, some chanted, "Mingo Jack, Mingo Jack". Chief Smith, wanting to ensure Williams was spared the same fate, sneaked him out of Monmouth County overnight and had him held about fifteen miles away in the town of Freehold. There he stayed, day after day, as investigators tried to find physical evidence to crack the case.

Helping on that front was Randolph Miller, Peter Smith's boss at the Flavell rendering plant in town.[17] Peter's job was to collect little bits of bone and grease from butchers, which would then be turned into soap at Miller's plant.[18] Miller had a daughter near Marie's age and said he couldn't imagine the anguish her parents were enduring. He also thought well of Peter, whom he considered a good employee and an honest man.[19] He wanted to help in any way he could, which at first meant joining the search parties and offering a reward for Marie's safe return. Once her body was discovered, Miller suggested that police hire an outside detective agency to find her killer. Though he was friendly with Cliver, he wasn't as convinced of Williams's guilt as was the reporter—whose news stories about the case unfailingly presented Williams as the killer. Asbury Park's police department was inexperienced in murder investigations, and using outside detective agencies was common at the time. The Greater New York Detective Agency, headquartered in Manhattan's Greenwich Village, was hired by the local prosecutor, John Applegate Jr., five days after Marie's body was found.[20] Unlike Miller, however, Applegate was sure of Williams's guilt, and it's perhaps not surprising that the two detectives he hired immediately agreed. B. F. Johnson and George W. Cunningham interviewed Williams in jail, as well as speaking to Max Kruschka—who owned the floral shop where Marie had last been seen—and his employee, Frank Heidemann. Kruschka and his wife had each been away on separate trips when Marie disappeared, and both had alibi witnesses corroborating their whereabouts. Heidemann, on the other hand, had been working alone at the nursery, and was even identified by Davison as the man she'd seen in Kruschka's yard when Marie double-backed toward it. But Heidemann said that while he remembered spotting Davison, he hadn't seen a little girl. He wasn't very fond of children, he explained, and, besides, she would have been short and easy to miss in a yard lined with hedges. Not an hour after Marie's disappearance, Heidemann had eaten lunch with Marie's great aunt, Mrs. Jackson. The notion that he would dine with a family member after viciously attacking the girl seemed barbaric—more in line with something a Black man would do than an employed German immigrant.

When they interviewed Williams, Johnson and Cunningham jarred him awake at 2:00 a.m. with a lie that someone had implicated him in the crime. Williams insisted it wasn't true. "I swear by all my hope for the future that I did not kill this poor little girl," he said. "I knew her and liked her. . . . I would like to go out and help find the man who killed her. I am only a poor Black man that earned my living by chopping wood and doing odd work. My past record don't show that I could be guilty of this crime. I wasn't near the place where Marie was killed at the time of the murder."[21]

The detectives didn't believe him. One told a reporter: "Just so positive am I that the negro Thomas Williams is the murderer of Marie Smith that if he declared in the gallows that he was innocent of this crime, I would still believe him guilty."[22] Their belief was bolstered when an axe was found in the lake about three hundred yards from where Marie's body had been discovered. A news story said: "The police believe it to be the weapon used by the slayer as it had been in the water but a short time. . . . The finding of the axe, the officers believe, will strengthen the case against 'Black Diamond' Williams now in the county jail."[23]

Randolph Miller still wasn't convinced. He insisted that an independent detective was needed—one whose investigation started with as clean a slate as possible—and so he helped front the money[24] to hire a man named Raymond Campbell Schindler, a top investigator with the Burns Detective Agency.[25] Schindler had started his career as a salesman and unexpectedly made the switch to private detective work after the San Francisco earthquake of 1906,[26] when he found a job purportedly documenting the extent of the damage done. After he started the gig, he realized his job hadn't been as a documentarian, but rather as a detective for an insurance company trying to make sure it squirmed out of paying as many home-policy claims as possible. Schindler realized that not only was he good at the job, but he liked it, after which he joined the agency founded by William Burns and became a manager. Still, despite being considered one of the agency's best, he'd never investigated a murder case before.

"He had a lot on his shoulders here," said Peter Lucia, historian and author of the book *Murder at Asbury Park* (2017), in an interview.[27]

"I KNEW HER AND LIKED HER. . . . I WOULD LIKE TO GO OUT AND HELP FIND THE MAN WHO KILLED HER. . . . I WASN'T NEAR THE PLACE WHERE MARIE WAS KILLED AT THE TIME OF THE MURDER."

It seems that pressure convinced Schindler he needed help. He brought fellow agent Charles Scholl with him to Asbury Park, who joined him in ignoring the work already done by local investigators and starting completely from scratch.[28] After a couple of rounds of interviews, they narrowed the field of viable suspects to two: Thomas Williams and Frank Heidemann. Prosecutor Applegate was still firmly of the belief that Williams was guilty,[29] and he presented an inquest meant to finally lay the matter to rest and officially declare Marie's death a murder, while also hopefully pinpointing which of the two suspects would be charged. As forcefully as Applegate argued his case against Williams, however, the jury didn't declare him the killer. Rather, they vaguely determined the culprit was "persons unknown."[30]

Schindler knew the physical evidence in the case was lacking, so he decided that his best bet was to secure a confession from the killer. First, he sent a stooge into Williams's jail to chat him up, hoping that Williams might share some details of the crime with someone presented as a fellow inmate. Not only did Williams not share any new information, but he asked if the fellow inmate's lawyer might be willing to represent him, too. Schindler went to the jail pretending to be that lawyer, interviewed Williams himself and walked away more certain than ever that Williams was not the killer. Meanwhile, Schindler caught Heidemann in some fibs. For starters, Heidemann claimed he'd only recently come to the country, but Schindler had done enough homework to know he'd been in the country for four years, living in New York before answering a "help wanted" ad posted by Kruschka in a newspaper. Also, Schindler asked Heidemann about any girlfriends, and Heidemann acted like he had no interest in women at all—which didn't quite jibe with the fact that he had risqué photos hanging in his rented room. Then there was the way Heidemann's lower lip trembled when Schindler talked about Marie's battered little body. And finally, there was a damning allegation made by a different neighborhood girl named Grace. Grace—who, at age seven, was about the age Marie looked to be—said that Heidemann tried to lure her to his place for candy, making a point to tell her not to bring her brothers along. He'd done that just days before the murder.

Certain that Heidemann was hiding something, Schindler began playing mind games. He sent a colleague to pester Kruschka's dog at night by throwing rocks. At about 1:00 a.m. every morning for nine days, the colleague threw stones at the dog, wrote reporter Ira Wolfert in a 1936 retrospective. Wolfert added: "The dog, leashed to a trolley and unable to get at his tormenter, howled mournfully."[31] The dog would bark, waking up the house night after night. While Kruschka and others were able to eventually sleep through the dog's noise, Heidemann seemed unable to ignore it, turning on the light and pacing in his room—which Schindler took to mean he had a guilty conscience. After a few days, Heidemann disappeared from Asbury Park, which is what Schindler had hoped would happen. Once Heidemann settled into a boarding house in New York, Schindler sent a new, carefully selected detective after him. Carl Neumeister had been born in Germany, like Heidemann, which Schindler thought might help the two bond. Plus, Neumeister had years of experience and, Schindler wrote, was "one of the best qualified experts in the business."[32]

Following strict orders not to be the first to engage Heidemann in conversation, Neumeister began visiting a German restaurant that Heidemann frequented. One morning, Heidemann noticed Neumeister reading a German-language newspaper and began chatting him up. The two quickly became friends—or, at least, that's how it seemed to Heidemann.[33]

Neumeister pretended he was in New York awaiting a lawyer to finalize an inheritance he was to receive, so he offered to pay for many of Heidemann's expenses. Pretty soon, the two were living together in a rented boardinghouse room, where Neumeister quickly learned of Heidemann's fondness for young girls. Neumeister also pretended to be a criminal, figuring that if Heidemann had killed little Marie Smith, he'd be more likely to confess to a fellow killer than to a perfect angel. So Neumeister talked of heists he pulled and people he killed, and then even staged a fake murder with the help of an actor for Heidemann to witness. One night, while Heidemann and Neumeister were riding through a snow-covered park, an actor stepped out of the darkness and asked for a light. Neumeister gave him one but also gave him some lip, prompting a fake scuffle, during which Neumeister pulled out a gun loaded with blanks and shot the guy. Heidemann, thinking he'd just watched his new friend kill a man, was worried the two would get caught, so he and Neumeister began talking of fleeing together.[34]

Schindler, who'd been getting regular, detailed reports from his "rope," or sting artist, Neumeister, decided to up the pressure a bit. Schindler

managed to get three fake news stories published—two naming Heidemann as a suspect on the run in Marie's death, and another about the dead stranger in the snow. After seeing the articles, Heidemann was frantic to leave town. Neumeister pretended to have another partner, however, who threw a wrench into things. The phantom partner supposedly was worried about Neumeister's new friend, insisting that they had to ditch Heidemann because he wasn't a criminal like they were and, as such, he could rat them out at any minute. Heidemann eventually met someone pretending to be this mob-boss-type figure, who was portrayed by Schindler's own brother, and Heidemann was desperate to convince his two new buddies that he wasn't a threat to them, so he confessed: "I am far from being an angel. I may have done something similar to what you did in Yonkers."[35]

Neumeister played it cool but alerted Schindler as soon as he could. He also teased out as much detail from Heidemann as possible, then arranged for Schindler to be in a room next to theirs when he convinced Heidemann to tell the story again. Schindler had his ear pressed to the shared wall and furiously took notes.

Meanwhile, Williams still languished in jail. The Asbury Park police and prosecutor were still so sure of Williams's guilt that they needed first-hand convincing, so Neumeister managed to get Heidemann to tell the story of Marie's death a third time. This time, Randolph Miller—Marie's father's boss, the one who'd suggested hiring Schindler in the first place—was listening. After months of dogged legwork, Schindler and his crew got Heidemann to confess not just once or twice, but eleven times.

Heidemann saw his buddy Neumeister walk into his holding cell with Detective Schindler and suddenly realized he'd been duped. He fell into a blubbering heap and didn't even try to fight the charges. He confessed again, in writing, and was convicted of first-degree murder.[36] He explained that he'd spotted Marie the morning she disappeared as she was walking home. He called over to her and asked if she'd like to bring some plant cuttings home to her father, and Marie said she did. So Heidemann led the little girl, who was so trusting that she held his hand, into the woods. He sexually assaulted her as she sobbed. When he was finished, he tied her skating cap and blue hair ribbon around her throat to strangle her, but then switched gears. He reached into his pocket, grabbed a hammer he'd been using for

OPPOSITE: A detail from the front page of the *Asbury Park Evening Press* of April 19, 1911. Frank Heidemann had been sentenced to death the day before, and was then taken to Trenton to await his execution on May 23.

work and smashed her skull in two blows. He left her body in the woods, where falling leaves made her brown coat blend in well enough with her surroundings that she was overlooked by search parties for four long days.[37]

Schindler was heralded as a real-life Sherlock Holmes for devising the ingenious plan to have Carl Neumeister pose as Heidemann's friend for more than two months before managing to get a confession. (Until the end of his life, Schindler retained his status as "the world's greatest detective."[38]) The case against Williams, meanwhile, had drawn the attention of the newly formed NAACP and ultimately went down in its annals as the third case the agency ever adopted. Here was yet another example in post–Reconstruction America of a Black man accused of a crime—and nearly lynched for it by a mob of white people unwilling to see the case brought to trial. After the NAACP's lawyers demanded that prosecutors either release Williams or charge him, Williams was finally freed. He lived out the rest of his years in anonymity, while his case helped solidify the NAACP's footing. Today, it remains one of America's largest and most enduring civil rights organizations.

"I DESERVE TO DIE," DECLARES HEIDEMANN ON WAY TO TRENTON

"I Was Given a Fair Trial and Have No Fault to Find. I Was Treated Even Better Than I Should Have Been," Wails Young Murderer.

SPED TO STATE PRISON IN AN AUTOMOBILE

Utterly Collapses When Sentence Is Pronounced---Makes Gifts to Warden Cashion and Kruschkas, Herbert Receiving Signet Ring With Initials "G. L." For "Good Luck."

"I was given a fair trial and have no fault to find. I was treated even better than I should have been. I am sorry for what I did, but that can't help me now. The verdict was fair and the fate I am to meet is no more than I deserve. I have no feeling against anyone. The fault is entirely my own, and I must bear the consequences."

Sentenced late yesterday afternoon by Justice Willard P. Voorhees to be electrocuted during the week of May 22 for the murder of Marie Simth, the 10-year-old schoolgirl, in this city

FRANK E. HEIDEMANN

Legal Legacy

In addition to this case's role in the formation of the NAACP, the investigatory tactics used would inform police work for decades to come. Specifically:

- The tireless shoe-leather detective work that secured Frank Heidemann's multiple confessions was both celebrated and used to illustrate why investigators should keep their minds open, despite feeling certain they'd solved a case without solid evidence.
- Reporters at the time heralded Raymond Schindler's approach, describing his "remarkable instances of deduction and scientific tracking."[39] However, some of Schindler's tactics would be side-eyed by current standards, including faking a murder and planting articles in newspapers in hopes of inspiring a confession from a suspect.

13

How the FBI Helped End the Osage Nation Murders

(1910s–1930s)

Mollie Burkhart couldn't stay mad at her sister, Anna Brown, for long, though she'd been awfully upset on May 21, 1921, when Anna had arrived for a little gathering at Mollie's house in Gray Horse, Oklahoma, completely drunk. It wasn't the first time Anna had over-imbibed. Anna was the type of woman who kept whiskey in a flask and offered it to others, despite Prohibition having outlawed alcohol the year prior. She was thirty-six years old, recently divorced, extremely wealthy, and a fan of partying.

According to journalist and author David Grann—who wrote the Edgar Award–winning book about the Osage murders called *Killers of the Flower Moon* (2017)—Anna wasn't a pleasant drunk, either. "She was drinking and quarreling," a servant told authorities. Anna argued with her sister, her mother, and even with other guests in attendance. "They had an awful time with Anna, and I was afraid."[1]

As embarrassed as Mollie had been by Anna's antics that day, they still made up before day's end. Mollie washed her sister's clothes, fed her some food to counter the alcohol in her system, and made sure she was sufficiently sober before seeing her off. Anna left with Bryan Burkhart, the brother of Mollie's husband, Ernest. The two were friendly—in the biblical sense on occasion; although earlier that day Anna had drunkenly threatened to kill Bryan if he dated anyone else, they were in a platonic phase of their relationship. Later, Bryan told Mollie that he'd dropped off her sister at her house before he headed out to catch a show.[2]

A few days passed with no word from Anna, and Mollie began to worry. She sent Ernest to check Anna's house. It was locked up, and a servant who lived next door said she hadn't seen Anna in days. That was concerning enough, but reports were spreading through town that another man was also missing. Charles Whitehorn was a well-liked thirty-one-year-old married man who'd last been seen May 14, a week before Anna's last sighting. Still, this was an era in which traveling was becoming commonplace thanks to consumer automobiles[3]—both Anna and Charles, as members of the wealthy Native American tribe called the Osage Nation, were rich enough to own their own cars—but communication was spotty. About one-third of the nation's homes had telephones installed,[4] but phones weren't so ubiquitous that people expected to hear from loved ones every single day, especially not loved ones prone to travel. And Anna loved to flit from town to town, especially nearby boomtowns that catered to oil workers.

With no word from Anna, Mollie's distress grew steadily by the day. Then, on May 27, an oil worker spotted something in hillside brush as crews drilled about a mile north of the town of Pawhuska, Oklahoma. When the worker got closer, he realized he was looking at a badly decomposed corpse. About the same time, some thirty miles away in Fairfax, hunters stumbled across another body. This one was bloated and black, faceup in a ravine. Though this corpse was also badly decomposed, it was fresh enough for onlookers to at least surmise that it belonged to a Native American woman. That was as specific as they could get, however. Even when Anna's two surviving sisters, Mollie and Rita, came to the ravine to see if it was her, they could only be sure based on the gold fillings in the corpse's mouth and the clothes it wore. They had found Anna; the other corpse was identified by a letter found in a pocket as Charles Whitehorn.

While these weren't the first mysterious deaths in the Osage Nation, they were the ones that served as harbingers of awful things to come, revealing a horrifying conspiracy in which white people aimed to steal money from Nation members—a conspiracy that, when exposed, not only changed federal laws but helped birth the Federal Bureau of Investigations.

It's hard to know exactly who the first victim was in the Osage murders because many of the deaths had been quickly explained away as accidents by officials in charge. Key evidence had been destroyed before the wider plot was uncovered, thwarting subsequent investigation attempts. What's easier to parse is the backstory: as the nineteenth century drew to a close, the Osage Nation had grown tired of being forced by white settlers to leave one swath of land after another. They'd most recently been run out of Kansas,

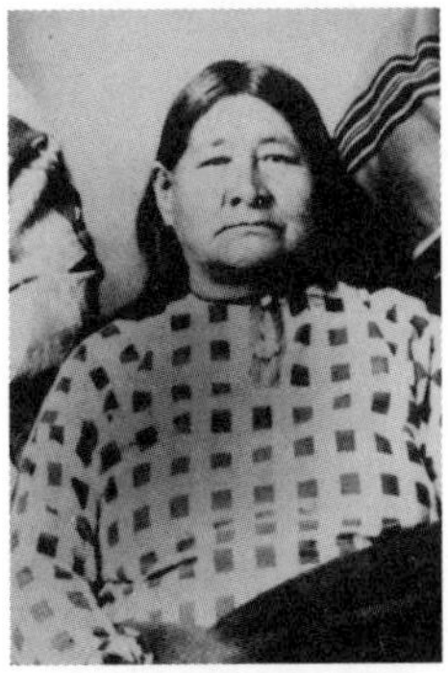

A portrait of Mollie Burkhart, 1926, top, and undated photographs of Anna Burkhart and Charles Whitehorn, who were both discovered murdered in Oklahoma in May 1921.

uprooted because the federal government decided it wanted to make Kansas a state. After that, the Osage relocated south to an area of rough terrain in what would later become Oklahoma. The land was inhospitable to farming and while it was unlikely to be overrun by settlers, the move caused the tribe great hardship. But then something happened: the Osage discovered oil.

The federal government surely would have attempted to relocate the tribe again had this land been allocated by treaty, but it wasn't. The Nation had bought the land themselves—1.5 million acres of it—to ensure that they would remain the rightful owners. Their original plan had been for the tribe to own the acreage as a collective, but the federal government mounted a campaign to divvy up the lots when talk turned to making Oklahoma a state instead of a territory. The Osage agreed to allot the surface rights—the above-ground land—but they insisted that the tribe would retain the mineral rights—meaning the Osage would own everything beneath the surface of the land, no matter how the homesteads above might be partioned.[5] The agreement with lawmakers said the mineral rights—also known as the headrights—could never be sold.[6] They could only be inherited. This set the stage for Oklahoma to become a state in 1907.

The feds weren't terribly worried when oil was initially found on the property. At first, the profits were in the $100 range, which was split among tribe members. But then the profits climbed to the thousands, and then to the tens of thousands. By 1923, the Osage people split some $30 million annually—which translates to approximately $520 million today.[7] At that time, there were about two thousand tribe members, meaning that each member was allotted $15,000 annually in an era when the average American yearly salary was less than $3,500.[8] The Osage allotments were the equivalent of about $262,000 in 2023, making its members the wealthiest people per capita in the world. Reporters often parachuted in to regale readers with stories about the "red millionaires:"

> **A good while ago the Osages were segregated on tribal lands of dubious value in what was then the Indian Territory, by the white man, who had separated them and the other tribes from their rather extensive original holdings. By and by oil was discovered on the Indians' lands, which in spite of the Indians' indifference to affluence, is**

> **rapidly making millionaires of all of them. . . . The Osage is guileless, but he knows a thing or two and one of them is that if the white brother had known all that oil was under Oklahoma the noble red man would have been sent somewhere else. So the Osage just laughs and laughs. The white man does not laugh with him.[9]**

"People were jealous that they had all this money and who were they to spend it?" said Jennifer Penland, an indigenous scholar and professor at Shepherd University in West Virginia.[10] The coverage reflected the prevailing sentiment toward the tribe, Penland said: "They couldn't speak English. They weren't white. They didn't deserve it." That condescension reached the federal government, officials of which decided that the Osage couldn't possibly know how to manage this vast wealth—never mind that they'd managed money well enough even before the oil was struck to buy their own land. Indigenous people were viewed as childlike, even subhuman.

"It went so far that members of the US Congress passed this legislation requiring that many Osage have these white guardians, these businessmen, these bankers, these politicians, to manage the fortunes," said author David Grann. "This system was not abstractly racist. It was literally racist. It was based on the quantum of Osage blood, so if you were a full-blooded Osage, you were deemed 'incompetent,' and you were given one of these guardians."[11]

The guardians—pronounced locally as *gar-deens*—were tasked with giving the Osage their royalty checks each quarter and advising them on how to spend the money wisely. Guardians were only required to dole out $1,000 a quarter, even when headright earnings were three times that. It was up to the guardians to keep track of the rest—and there was little oversight if someone's accounting practices were rather lax. Some guardians were assigned multiple Osage. Grann, in his research, found one who'd been assigned a full dozen, giving them access to outright fortunes.

Grann also noticed something else in his research: Sometimes, several clients assigned to the same guardian would all die within a short time span. On the surface, this might not have struck anyone as potentially nefarious because the guardians themselves weren't in line to inherit headrights. Only family members could. That was how, in fact, Anna Brown got to be so wealthy. She'd been one of four daughters born to mother Lizzie Q and

father Ne-kah-e-se-y. (Her father had been dubbed "Jimmy" by a local trader, which had stuck. Mollie's name was borne in similar fashion: She'd been Wah-kon-tah-he-um-pah until being renamed by a white trader.[12]) Jimmy died around 1895, leaving Lizzie his headright. The couple's four daughters—Minnie, Mollie, Anna, and Rita—retained their own headrights.

Each girl grew up and eventually married. In 1918, Minnie, who was married to a man named William Smith, fell ill. It was an odd illness that seemed to sap her energy and strength from within, causing her to waste away. Despite the family's ability to pay for good doctors, the cause was never identified and Minnie died. Though Smith hadn't been a model husband, he seemed genuinely grief-stricken. He'd become part of the family, so much so that a few months after Minnie's death, he married her sister, Rita. Still, Mollie couldn't help but feel suspicious that Smith somehow had played a role in the mysterious death. Mollie raised her concerns to her uncle-in-law, William K. Hale, who served as a surrogate father to Ernest and Bryan. After Minnie's death had been ruled natural, Hale agreed that the circumstances seemed suspect, but without any evidence, there was nothing they could do.[13]

Hale had been born and raised in Greenville, Texas,[14] and came from humble roots. At eighteen, he left Texas for the southwest Oklahoma territory, working for a year on a ranch in the Comanche reservation, after which he returned to Texas, where he worked for the next five years saving his earnings. He put about $100 into the Greenville National Bank, which grew enough that he was eventually able to start buying and selling cattle, making Hale "his first real money," according to a news story in February 1926.[15] At age twenty-eight, he packed up and moved to Osage County around the turn of the century, lured by the oil and all the opportunity that oil promised. He didn't come from money—his roots were pretty humble, in fact—but he was ambitious and chatty and could win over a crowd with jokes and rope tricks. He invested in businesses all over town—a bank, a general store, a funeral home. His investments made him rich. He owned one house in the town of Fairfax and another in the countryside, plus five thousand acres of grazing land.[16] He leased another forty-five thousand acres from Osage landowners and was known to be generous to tribe members, buying townsfolk impromptu gifts like brand-new suits akin to the ones he wore every single day. He visited the sick and elderly and even bought ponies for Osage children.[17] By the time Minnie died, Hale had accumulated so much wealth and power that he became known as the King of the Osage Hills.[18]

Three years after Minnie's death, Mollie again was turning to her uncle-in-law with questions. Local authorities at first had dismissed Anna's death as accidental alcohol poisoning,[19] but then the undertaker found a bullet hole in the back of her skull. As much trouble as Anna was known to get herself in, she was beloved in the community. The news that she'd been brutally murdered was devastating, prompting her guardian, Ben Mason, to offer a $2,000 reward.[20] People from all over came to pay their respects at her funeral. While early reports suggested that she might have been killed in a robbery, the newspapers also made a point to reference her estranged husband, Oda Brown, a white man from Ponca City.[21]

William K. Hale, the so-called "King of the Osage Hills," photographed in 1926.

Hale offered his heartfelt condolences and assured Mollie that officials would thoroughly investigate. To improve their odds, he even hired a private detective named Pike to assist the investigation.[22] It briefly seemed as though authorities had cracked the case when an imprisoned forger said he had been paid $8,000 by Anna's ex-husband to kill her, but within days, that confession proved to be bogus.[23] Weeks passed with no further news.

Two months after the bodies were discovered, Mollie realized with horror that her mother was sick with what seemed to be the same wasting disease that had killed Minnie in 1918. Granted, her mother was elderly and had now lost her husband and two of her four children, so it seemed feasible that grief had weakened her. Mollie tried to save her by any means she could. When western doctors failed, she turned to Osage medicine men and kept vigil herself. Despite Mollie's efforts, Lizzie died in July,[24] leaving just Mollie and Rita remaining in a family that had originally numbered six. Rita and Mollie were in fine health, but the deaths were far from over.

William Stepson was a handsome and popular Osage steer-roping champion and World War I veteran[25] who, at twenty-nine years old, seemed to be in stellar health. His mother-in-law later told investigators that Stepson had spent February 28, 1922, at home, until a phone call drew him into town at about 6:00 p.m. When he returned later that night, a neighbor found him on his porch, seemingly blackout drunk. A couple of men helped Stepson get back to his own house, where his mother-in-law checked on him through the night. When she went to rouse him in the morning, he was dead. At first, alcohol poisoning was suspected, but a coroner's inquest didn't find evidence of booze in his system. The cause of death was ruled unknown.[26]

Bernard McBride, affectionately called Barney by most, was a rich, retired oil operator. McBride—a white man considered an ally by the Osage—saw the bodies adding up and was outraged they weren't being properly investigated. He had been married to a Muscogee woman who'd died some eighteen years earlier and had raised his late wife's daughter as his own. The sixty-year-old traveled to Washington, DC, to talk to lawmakers in the hope of convincing them to take the Osage deaths more seriously. Soon after he had arrived in DC, a *Sioux City Journal* headline ran: "WEALTHY OIL MAN FOUND SLAIN, HIS BODY SLASHED WITH SCORE KNIFE WOUNDS."[27] McBride's best friend and stepdaughter told reporters that he had no known enemies, so the only motive they could imagine for killing him was robbery.[28] They didn't know, however, his reason for the trip—he'd told his stepdaughter only that he planned to go fishing—nor were they aware that when McBride checked into a rooming house in the district, a note was waiting for him. It read: "Be careful."[29]

McBride's murder was a turning point. Not only was he a rich white man, but he hadn't shared his whereabouts with most people. It appeared someone—possibly more than one person, in fact—had shadowed McBride from Oklahoma to stop him from talking with federal authorities. Ironically, his death probably got the feds' attention better than any speech would have. Still, more murders followed. Within a few months' time, Joe "Yellowhorse" Bates and "Big Annie" Sanford both died, Bates from unknown "natural" causes and Sanford from "slow poisoning."[30] In February 1923, Henry Roan disappeared. He'd supposedly argued with his wife and driven away from his home, never to return. Roan—who's alternately described as

Mollie's first husband and/or her cousin—was spotted sitting upright behind the wheel of his car two days later. Clearly, something was wrong; the car was at the bottom of a rocky swale. A deputy sheriff and town marshal went to investigate the report called in by a couple of hunters and assumed at first that they'd find a drunkard in the car. Instead, they found Roan had been shot in the back of the head. "I seen he had been murdered," the deputy later said.[31]

An undated photograph of Henry Roan.

William Hale was one of the first people told about Roan's death, because the two had been close. "We were good friends and he sought my aid when in trouble," said Hale, explaining that because Roan was a full-blooded Osage, his financial allowance was curbed so much that he often asked Hale to advance him cash.[32] Roan had borrowed a few dollars from Hale just days before his death—he'd learned his wife was having an affair and wanted to get a drink. Hale admonished him but lent Roan the money anyway. Hale said he hadn't heard from him since.

Just days after Roan's death, an explosion in the middle of the night rocked Osage County. Mollie had been asleep, but the blast jolted her awake. She rushed to her window to spy its cause and saw that her sister Rita's house had been demolished. Rita and her housekeeper, Nettie Brookshire, were killed instantly. Rita's husband, William Smith—the one who'd previously been married to Minnie—was pulled from the rubble barely alive. He'd been mortally wounded, just as much a target as his wife in this latest crime. Before he died of his injuries, he told authorities he had just two enemies who would have reason to kill him: William Hale and Ernest Burkhart.[33]

Smith said that Hale had once gotten him drunk and forced him to sign a check for $8,000. Once Smith's wits returned, he flew into a rage. He hadn't owed Hale the money and found Hale's method of obtaining it suspicious at best—and downright criminal at worst. The next day, Smith had tried to stop payment on the check, but Hale was the kind of man who managed to get a banker to cash it for him at 11:00 p.m. the night before. After sharing his suspicions, Smith succumbed to his injuries.[34] The aspersions he'd cast on Hale gave people pause, especially when they considered Hale's relationship with Roan, the man found dead just days before. Hale and Roan had been good friends, and Hale didn't seem poised to gain anything by these Osage deaths. But then, months later after Smith's allegations, Hale filed a lawsuit.

He said he was owed $25,000 on a life insurance policy he'd taken out on Roan.[35] He'd made all the payments on the policy and was miffed that Capitol Life Insurance and Roan's estate executor were denying him payment.

Suddenly, it became clear that Hale stood to benefit from Roan's death—and while he wouldn't benefit directly from the deaths of Rita and Bill Smith, his nephew Ernest would. Mollie Burkhart was the only remaining member of her family, and she'd inherited the headrights of her father, mother, and three sisters. Suspicion was building, but the Osage didn't know whom they could trust.

"In addition to local law enforcement, you had doctors that were also not trustworthy," said Tara Damron of White Hair Memorial, an Osage learning center.[36] "You had medical examiners, you had coroners. It went all the way up to the top."

Bernard McBride had tried to involve federal authorities, and while his death did pique interest, it didn't spark much immediate action. A federal law enforcement bureau had started decades earlier as a clearinghouse to try to track known criminals, then shifted its focus after the 1901 assassination of President William McKinley to tracking domestic anarchists. Renamed the Bureau of Investigation (BOI), its focus shifted again around 1908 to target prostitution and sex trafficking, though it was also often used to prosecute "immoral" premarital, extramarital, and interracial relationships (encapsulated as federal law in the 1910 Mann Act).[37] The bureau's jurisdiction had always been quite limited; murder had never been in its purview. That said, one of the jurisdictions it could claim was over American Indian reservations, which is how the Osage deaths fell to the BOI—and why it became one of their first major homicide cases in the early stages of J. Edgar Hoover's nearly half-century career.[38]

Hoover at first fumbled the case. He pulled an outlaw named Blackie Thompson out of prison with the idea he would work for the bureau as an informant by weaseling his way into the Osage community and reporting back. Instead, Thompson robbed a bank and killed a police officer. Hoover wanted to dump the case after that, but he was only twenty-nine and new to the job. He worried that dropping the case would cost him politically, so he instead handed over the reins to a long-time agent named Tom White. White, standing six-foot-four, had worked as a Texas Ranger earlier in his career, and he was a rough-and-tumble lawman compared to Hoover, who instructed his agents to wear jackets and ties.[39]

But Hoover's ideal G-men just weren't the types of men who'd be able to infiltrate Osage County. White recruited a different sort of crew with an array of skill sets. Some posed as businessmen, some cattlemen, and one—John Wren—was even Native American, apparently the first indigenous person to serve as an FBI agent.[40]

Before long, this crew developed a theory that centered on William Hale. They believed Hale was manipulating his nephew Ernest, who was known as being weak willed. Every time someone in Mollie Burkhart's family died, she inherited control of more money—control she shared with her husband. While the feds were trying to figure out how to prove their theory was true, more victims died. Henry Grammer, who was thought to have incriminating evidence against Hale, died June 14, 1923, in a car

J. Edgar Hoover in 1924, as director of the Bureau of Investigation, the forerunner of the FBI.

accident. Grammer had once been a world champion roper who appeared in a 1910 Tom Mix movie called *Ranch Life in the Great Southwest*.[41]

Around the same time, a man named George Bigheart fell sick. As he was treated in an Oklahoma City hospital, Bigheart called his friend and lawyer William W. Vaughan, who lived some 140 miles away in Pawhuska. Vaughan agreed to come to Bigheart's side, but before he left, Vaughan ominously left instructions for his wife to follow if anything happened to him while he was away. He told her he had stored some important documents that would lead her to his killer. She must have been terrified, but if she lodged any objections to her husband's travels, he didn't heed them. The father of ten boarded a train and met Bigheart at the hospital. All things considered, the meeting went well. Bigheart had been able to hand over more documents to Vaughan—ones that he believed would prove he'd been poisoned, and by whom. The documents were damning enough that Vaughan called the sheriff back home and said he was bringing back evidence to prove someone guilty of murder.[42]

After staying with Bigheart for several hours, he boarded a train back to Pawhuska. The next morning, Bigheart died and Vaughan disappeared. It would be thirty-six hours before a search party would discover the lawyer's body near railroad tracks. He'd been viciously beaten, stripped naked, and tossed from the train. The documents Bigheart had given him were gone. Brokenhearted, Vaughan's wife, Rosa, went to retrieve the documents he'd told her about—but they, too, had disappeared.[43]

As convinced as they were that Hale was at the center of these deaths, White and his crew of federal undercover agents couldn't move prematurely. They continued living in Osage County as though they were just regular residents, but they were slowly and steadily gathering bits and pieces of information for White to flesh out. They felt a renewed sense of urgency when, in 1925, Mollie Burkhart started getting sick. Eight years after she'd married Ernest, she was the last in her family, save for the two children she'd had with her husband, who would assume control of the entire family's fortune. The G-men were certain that Ernest and his brother, Bryan, were pawns in a diabolical scheme hatched by their uncle, William Hale.

It just so happened that another man was equally certain: Bert Lawson.[44] Lawson, who in late 1925 was in prison on a burglary conviction, said he wanted to "make a clean breast" of what he knew. He told agents Tom White and Frank Smith that he had worked for William Smith a few years prior but left the post when he discovered Smith was having an affair with Lawson's wife. The matter left Lawson unmoored as his marriage collapsed. Knowing this, Ernest Burkhart approached him and suggested he blow up Smith's home with Smith's family inside. Lawson declined, but later found himself in a bind, both legally and financially, after he was arrested in connection with a fisherman's death. Hale, who, as a reserve deputy sheriff, was allowed easy access to the jail, visited him there and said, you know, you need money and I have a job I want done. Lawson relented. Hale snuck him out of his cell one night so he could blow up the Smiths' home for $5,000. After sneaking Lawson back into his cell, Hale warned, "If you ever cheep this to anybody, we will kill you."[45]

While this breakthrough in the case warranted a "congratulations" to White from Hoover, the agent in charge wanted corroboration.[46] Ernest's reputation as being weak willed proved useful in the feds' quest to learn the truth. He was the first to crack, followed by Bryan, about their role in Anna Brown's death[47]—and that confession eventually led to the unraveling of a vast criminal conspiracy years in the making. They said Hale had arranged the slayings of some two dozen Osage. He had encouraged Ernest to marry Mollie, and then he, Ernest, Bryan, and others methodically killed off members of Mollie's family, plus people who might know something about their evil plot. Henry Grammer, for example, had apparently solicited hitmen on Hale's behalf, so his car accident had been orchestrated to keep him quiet.

"These murder schemes were essentially inheritance schemes, and it's one of the things that made these crimes so deeply sinister," Grann said. "They involve these intimate levels of betrayal. They involve people marrying into families, sometimes having children with an Osage, while systematically plotting to murder them and sometimes their children as well, so that they could then inherit those headrights."[48]

"THESE MURDER SCHEMES WERE ESSENTIALLY INHERITANCE SCHEMES, AND IT'S ONE OF THE THINGS THAT MADE THESE CRIMES SO DEEPLY SINISTER."

Through the Burkhart brothers' confessions, the FBI was able to relay to Mollie what had happened to her sister Anna. After leaving Mollie's house, Anna had gotten in a car with Bryan, who'd offered to drive her home. Instead, he'd plied her with more alcohol and, with a bootlegger named Kelsie Morrison, lured her to a canyon that would become her murder site.

Morrison's wife at the time saw Anna Brown in a car with the two men. Soon after, another bootlegger named Matt Williams, who'd gone to the canyon to deliver whiskey, heard a woman's scream, followed by a gunshot. He then saw Bryan and Kelsie walk from the direction of the scream. As if that weren't incriminating enough, Williams said the two then told him they'd just "laid out" an Indian woman. Neither Morrison's wife nor Williams came forward immediately because both assumed they'd be killed if they did. All the slayings went down similarly, though the cast of killers sometimes rotated. In Henry Roan's case, the killers were Hale and a Fairfax cowboy and farmer named John Ramsey. Hale likely never would have been suspected had he not filed the lawsuit to get Roan's $25,000 life insurance policy.[49]

Ramsey and Hale were charged at the federal level, and—after years of the case being dragged out thanks to motions challenging the jurisdiction, as well as one hung jury and a conviction that was set aside on appeal—they eventually were convicted in 1929 after Ernest agreed to testify against his uncle. All three men were sentenced to life in prison, though none remained behind bars nearly as long as that. Bryan Burkhart got off the easiest because, after one attempt at convicting him ended with a deadlocked jury, the feds granted him immunity in exchange for testifying against Morrison.[50] Hale and Ramsey were paroled in 1947, having served less than twenty years. Hale died a free man in 1962. His nephew Ernest, who surely had testified against Hale in hopes of securing a lesser sentence, actually spent far more time behind bars than the mastermind of the murders. Ernest was released in 1959. That disparity in sentencing was significantly softened in 1966, when the Oklahoma governor inexplicably pardoned Ernest altogether. Mollie, meanwhile, divorced Ernest in 1927 and remarried a man named John Cobb, with whom she'd been living since Ernest's arrest.[51]

Despite there being an estimated two dozen victims in the overall scheme, Roan's death was the only one taken to trial.

"It is still such a personal, horrible story because we still suffer from [it] today . . . we still have so many murders that were unsolved," Tara Damron said.[52] "So many suspicious deaths and headrights have been taken from us. Our land has been taken from us. And these people—these murderers—they get royalty checks every quarter."

Legal Legacy

The sheer scope of the "Osage murder conspiracy," as newspapers dubbed it,[53] shocked the nation and sparked new laws.

- In 1925, the federal government barred anyone who was not at least half Osage from inheriting headrights from a member of the tribe.[54]
- In 1934, the courts also ended the system of guardianship, which had swindled the Osage out of millions of dollars.[55]
- In 2000, the Osage filed a lawsuit against the US Department of the Interior, alleging federal mismanagement of their trust assets. In 2011, the government settled with the Osage for $380 million—at the time, the largest trust settlement with one tribe in US history.[56]

14

The Legacy of the Scottsboro Boys (1931–2013)

Officials in Stevenson, Alabama, were outraged when they learned that there had been trouble between two groups of stowaways who'd snuck aboard a Southern Railroad freight train on March 25, 1931. Normally in this type of situation, the outrage would have been directed at both sides—hopping onto trains without paying was illegal, after all—but this scenario featured mitigating circumstances that translated to more sympathy for one side than the other.

Put simply, one of the groups was comprised of white teens; the other, of Black. The white group had rushed to Stevenson officials complaining that they'd been viciously attacked by the Black group, who they claimed overpowered them with guns and knives. Some of the white teens, bruised and covered in dust, said they'd been physically thrown from the moving train by the Black teens. The sympathetic townsfolk hearing the tale were so incensed that they organized a posse, some of whom showed up armed with guns and ropes, ready not just for a fight, but for a lynching. Once the posse reached the train at its next stop in Paint Rock, Alabama, the vigilantes inspected the cars to flush out the culprits. Soon, they found the group of African Americans they were looking for, plus a few young white men—though, upon closer inspection, two of those white men were actually white women dressed as men in overalls. And those women said the violence aboard the train hadn't stopped after the white boys had been booted.

After roping the Black teens together, the posse forced the group of nine onto the back of a truck and drove them from Paint Rock to Scottsboro, the seat of Jackson County, where they were placed in a stifling hot cell inside the town's two-story jail. A crowd of white people began gathering outside the cell's window. As the hours passed and the crowd grew, so did their cries for Sheriff M. L. Wann to bring the prisoners outside. Though the sheriff had

been aggressive in rounding up the teens from the train, he wasn't keen to have them lynched on his watch, so when the mob grew impatient and started toward the door, he issued a stern warning.

"If you come in here, I will blow your brains out," he said, pulling out his gun. "Get away from here."[1]

Most of the crowd dissipated, but those who remained stayed fervent enough that Wann called the governor and asked for National Guard troops to be sent to Scottsboro. Governor Benjamin Meek Miller obliged. The next morning, the jailed youths learned why the crowd had been so bloodthirsty. Even with racial tensions as high as they were at that time in Alabama, it had seemed an outsized reaction for a nonfatal skirmish between two sets of teens. The cloud of confusion dissipated when Sheriff Wann walked in with the two women who'd been dressed in men's attire aboard the train and asked each to point out which of the Black teens had raped them. The women—twenty-three-year-old Victoria Price and seventeen-year-old Ruby Bates—assessed the men. Price pointed out six of them as her assailants. The sheriff then turned to Bates to name hers, but Bates didn't speak. A guard spoke on her behalf, reasoning that if six of the nine captured had assaulted Price, it was only logical to assume that the remaining three had assaulted Bates. The group of prisoners suddenly realized the gravity of their situation. Evening newspapers the night prior had already labeled them fiends who'd committed a "revolting crime."[2] Even if they survived the threats of lynching, they faced the death penalty if convicted by the state. The fight that would unfold would become one of the country's most infamous and divisive, involving multiple trials and court hearings, as well as two rulings from the Supreme Court of the United States. The case—or, more accurately, the *cases*—would drag on from start to resolution for more than eighty years.

How the story began was pretty typical for the time, which was about one and a half years after the massive stock market collapse that launched the Great Depression. Unemployment jumped 5 percent from 1929 to 1930, and by the time the "Scottsboro boys"—as they were quickly dubbed by the press—had been arrested in 1931, the rate had climbed past 15 percent and was showing no signs of slowing its ascent. It would eventually peak at 25 percent—a quarter of the country unemployed.[3] With jobs disappearing across the United States, it was tough enough for skilled adults to find work, let alone inexperienced teenagers. Parents struggled to feed their families, so many teens old enough to travel threw a few necessities into a bindle, tied the bindle to a stick, and left home to fend for themselves. They'd find work shoveling coal or shucking corn or picking fruit, and when the seasons changed or that job otherwise dried up, they'd hop on a freight train and head someplace new.[4]

Riding the rails wasn't the safest way to get from town to town, but it was cost-effective and generally reliable. Freight riders would find an empty car to huddle in if they were lucky. If they weren't, they'd end up on top of the train or even beneath a car. In the Scottsboro case, a Black eighteen-year-old named Haywood Patterson was hanging onto the side of the train when a group of white men scrambled across the top of the train looking for an empty car. One of the white men stepped on Patterson's hand, nearly knocking him off. That, Patterson would later say, is what launched the confrontation.

"We was just minding our own business when one of them said, 'This is a white man's train. . . . All you nigger bastards unload,'" Patterson later recalled. "But we weren't going nowhere, so there was a fight. We got the best of it and threw them off."[5]

Patterson didn't know most of the Black males who fought alongside him, a group that ranged in age from 13 to 20. They bonded simply over the racist name-calling of the white crew. They were: Andy Wright, 19; Andy's brother Leroy ("Roy"), 13; Eugene Williams, 13; Clarence Norris, 19; Ozie Powell, 15; Willie Roberson, 16; Olen Montgomery, 17; and, as the only one aged out of his teens, 20-year-old Charles Weems. While two were brothers, only four in total had ever crossed paths before. For the most part, these were nine strangers who banded together as they crossed through Alabama—whose state constitution, which was adopted just thirty years prior at a convention, announced its intention to "establish white supremacy in this State."[6]

It's fair to assume that law enforcement officials were predisposed to believe the white crew when they claimed the Black crew had instigated the scuffle, as well as the allegations leveled by the two young white women at the center of the controversary. Victoria Price and Ruby Bates had hopped the train for the same reason as the boys and young men: they were looking

for work. Price grew up poor in Huntsville, Alabama, where she got her first job at age ten as a spinner in a cotton mill. Price's mother worked at the same mill but was injured, leaving Price the pair's sole income earner. In the 1920s, she'd earned about $2 a day, but the market crash had slashed her daily pay down to $1.20 by 1931. To supplement her meager wages, Price—who by this time had been married three times—sometimes engaged in sex work. Price had had sex with a man on the train who wasn't her husband, and because of that, she risked being charged with a federal crime because she had violated the 1910 Mann Act (see page 164), which prohibited women from crossing state lines "for the purpose of prostitution or debauchery, or for any other immoral purpose."[7]

As soon as she was discovered dressed as a man on the train, she risked facing charges, but by reporting that she and her friend Ruby Bates had been assaulted on that train, the risk disappeared. For her part, Bates had never been as forthcoming as Price. Not only had she failed to initially identify any of the Scottsboro boys as having assaulted her, but she wrote a letter to a male friend that insisting they'd never touched her. The morning after police learned of the letter, officers had Ruby recant it, claiming that she'd written it while "so drunk she did not know what she was doing."[8] Even so, she'd also seemed reluctant to testify against them when the trial against the nine men began on April 6—just fifteen days after the alleged incident. The defendants had been assigned Milo Moody as their court-appointed attorney. He was a notoriously forgetful sixty-nine-year-old who hadn't defended a case in years. Worried that Moody wasn't up to the task of defending their sons, the boys' families scraped together $50 to hire a lawyer, although the paltry sum only got them Stephen Roddy, a Tennessee real-estate attorney unfamiliar with Alabama criminal law. A prosecutor later described Roddy as staggering into the courtroom at his first hearing, so drunk that he could barely walk. Moody stayed on as his assistant. Carol Anderson, chair of African American studies at Emory University described the duo this way: "One of your attorneys is senile, looking for butterflies; the other one is drunk, seeing butterflies.[9]

A legal dream team, they were not.

Judge Alfred Hawkins made it clear he wanted to be done with these defendants as quickly as possible. He split the nine into three groups with

Victoria Price at the Morgan County Courthouse in Decatur, Alabama, during preliminary proceedings of the Scottsboro trial, April 1933.

three separate juries, but their trials were to be back-to-back in a single day. Hawkins didn't even want a break in between the trials.[10] Though this was all at a breakneck speed, word had spread rapidly enough that thousands of people came to town, traveling from hundreds of miles away. It was clear that the trial was about much more than assault. To one side, it was about maintaining white supremacy and protecting the virtue of white women. To the other side, it was about the system being manipulated in a notoriously racist state to railroad innocent Black men.[11]

The prosecution's star witnesses were the two accusing women, both of whom took the stand, repeating the tale they had already told a *Chattanooga Times* correspondent. Price, described as "blonde and with a faraway look in her eyes," was the most forceful and accusatory, identifying the

defendants as her attackers and providing more detail about the alleged assault with each question posed.[12]

"When the train was going real fast, a whole bunch of Negroes suddenly jumped into the gondola, two of them shooting pistols and the others waving knives. . . . I started to jump, but a Negro grabbed my leg and threw me down into the car. Another punched me in the mouth."[13]

Bates, by comparison, said very little, acknowledging only that she lived with her mother and two younger brothers in Huntsville.

"Victoria . . . did the talking for the two, Ruby merely nodding her head once in a while," reported the *Times*.[14]

Price named Patterson as the first man who'd assaulted her and said that during the vicious and repeated attacks, she was beaten with fists and

The Scottsboro trial also set off protests in Washington, DC, and New York. Here, thousands of demonstrators march in Washington, DC, on May 8, 1933.

smashed in the head with a gun. She also claimed a knife had been held to her throat and her back had been sliced by jagged rocks on the floor of the train.[15]

"Those Negroes have ruined me and Ruby forever," Price said.[16]

Two doctors who'd examined the women within ninety minutes of the alleged attack, however, could only say that they determined the women had recently had sex based on recovered sperm—it was nonmotile—but they recounted no physical injuries corroborating a sustained, violent assault.[17]

Moody and Roddy barely asked any questions of the prosecution's witnesses. When it was their turn to put on a defense, the only witnesses they called to the stand were the defendants themselves. The all-white, all-male jury in the first trial reached its guilty verdict as the jury in the second trial was hearing testimony. That second jury heard the crowd outside the courthouse celebrate upon receiving word that the defendants in the first trial were convicted. Such was the stage set for the rest of the day. In the end, eight of the nine defendants were convicted and sentenced to death. The ninth was one of the two thirteen-year-olds, whose jury couldn't decide whether he should be sentenced to life in prison or to death, so that trial ended with a hung jury. Everyone else was set to die in the electric chair.

As the defendants readied for their executions, they learned they'd found some allies. The NAACP had been following the case in the media, but at first were not yet certain of the boys' innocence. By the time they tried to become involved in the boys' defense, the Communist Party USA had already committed their resources, via their International Labor Defense (ILD) organization.[18]

The Communist Party USA had formed in 1919 after splintering from the Socialist Party of America, following the 1917 Russian Revolution. The CPUSA was public-relations savvy, aiming to build alliances by taking up a number of causes, with racial equality being one of the biggest. The Communists were eager to adopt the Scottsboro case as one of their highest-profile cases to date. If the ILD hadn't gotten the boys better lawyers for their appeals, eight of the nine defendants likely would've been executed as scheduled. Instead, they recruited a criminal defense attorney from New York named Samuel Leibowitz, who himself was not a Communist—he was a registered Democrat—but was a solid attorney who'd never lost a murder trial.[19]

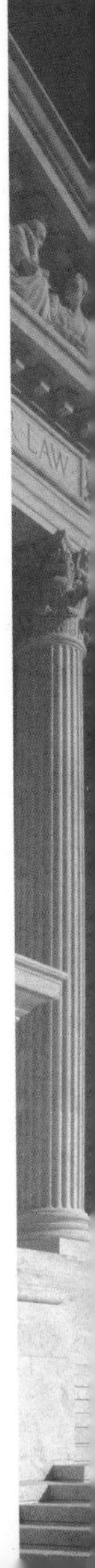

The defendants in the Scottsboro trial and their lawyer, Samuel Leibowitz, at a Decatur jail, March 1933. Standing, left to right: Olen Montgomery, Clarence Norris, Willie Roberson (front), Andrew Wright (partially obscured), Ozie Powell, Eugene Williams, Charley Weems, and Roy Wright. Haywood Patterson is seated next to Leibowitz.

"What happens now that they've got a real legal team is that they began to construct the train and found out that many of the Scottsboro boys weren't even in the same car as the women," said Professor Anderson.[20] "So how can a rape happen if the guys aren't in that car?"

Leibowitz attacked the case from every angle he could. One appeal he filed was based on the juries' lack of diversity because, despite there being three trials, not one juror on any of the separate panels was Black. Leibowitz fought to see Jackson County's list of potential jurors and found there were no Black people on it at all—which didn't make sense in the wake of the 13th, 14th, and 15th Amendments, which determined that slavery was unconstitutional, that if you were born or naturalized in the United States you were officially a US citizen and as such were to be afforded equal protection under the law, and that citizens had the right to vote regardless of race, color, or previous condition of servitude. While Alabama and some other states, mostly Southern, chipped away at Black people's ability to vote (and therefore serve on juries) by instituting poll taxes and literacy tests, there was no legal justification for an entire county to have *zero* Black jurors. Leibowitz argued all the way to the Supreme Court, which eventually sided with him and ordered that the Scottsboro defendants had to be retried.

Alabama did so reluctantly, but Ruby Bates had disappeared in the interim. Prosecutors had wanted her to testify again alongside Victoria Price, but they couldn't locate her after the first trials. Just as the defense was preparing to rest its case in Haywood Patterson's retrial, Bates suddenly surfaced in the courtroom on April 6, 1933. Like the court watchers who murmured in disbelief, Judge James Horton was taken aback by her arrival but allowed her to testify. Bates said that neither she nor Victoria had ever been assaulted and that Price had insisted she lie.[21]

What really happened, she said, was that she and Price met up with two men—Jack Tiller and Lester Carter—who were being released from jail. Bates and Carter split off into a couple, as did Price and Tiller. Both couples had sex and spent the next day and night together. Carter and the two women decided to hop a train to Chattanooga, but Tiller wasn't keen, so he stayed behind. The threesome picked up another man, Orville Gilley, tried in vain to find some work, spent the night in what was called "Hobo Swamp" near the train tracks, then decided to head back toward Huntsville the next morning. The four hopped another train and, after a while, noticed that in the next train car over from them, a group of white guys and Black guys had started fighting. Carter and Gilley, the two boys they'd met, jumped over to help. The Black men had tossed or shooed off most of the whites but kept Gilley from jumping off because they worried that they were going too fast by then and he might get hurt. As such, Gilley supposedly witnessed the attacks—in fact, police told reporters he'd been asked to participate but declined—and yet Gilley was never called to testify.

Bates said the reason she'd lied in the first trial was to make her testimony match Price's. "I told it just like Victoria did because she said we might have to stay in jail if we did not frame up a story after crossing a state line

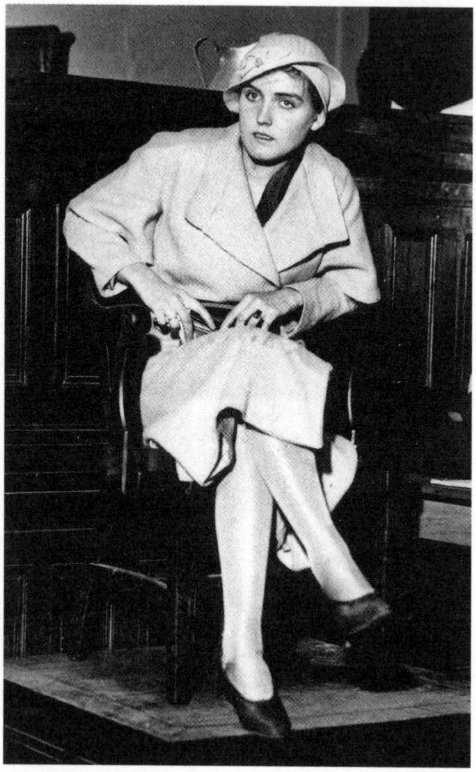

Ruby Bates, testifying during the Scottsboro trial in April 1933 that Victoria Price had insisted she lie about the assault.

with men," she said.[22] After the first trial, she'd felt such torment about the role she'd played in convicting the defendants that she confided in a New York pastor named Harry Emerson Fosdick. She'd come in for a private confessional because she was "disturbed in her conscience about her testimony," Fosdick told an Associated Press reporter.[23]

"I, as a clergyman, advised her to tell the truth," Fosdick said. "She promised me she would go back to the second trial and do so."[24]

Each retrial ended the same, however: time and again, jurors sided with Price's version of events. The verdicts dripped with racism, though not only against the Black defendants. One of the prosecutors, Wade Wright, weaponized Leibowitz's Judaism, too, urging jurors to "show them that Alabama justice cannot be bought and sold with Jew money from New York."[25]

Leibowitz couldn't hide his fury. Upon his return to New York on April 11, he angrily referred to the jurors as "bigots, whose mouths are slits in their faces, whose eyes pop out at you like a frog's, whose chins drip tobacco juice, bewhiskered and filthy."[26] He declared that the defendants never stood a chance in Alabama, not even at the state's Supreme Court level. "One of the justices, Thomas Edmund Knight, is the father of the prosecutor, Thomas Edmund Knight Jr.," he explained. "So the defense counsel has to argue against the prosecutor before the prosecutor's father."[27]

Through the course of the state battles, Leibowitz came to respect one judge—Judge James E. Horton, who gave a powerful, dramatic speech setting aside one of the verdicts and ordering a new trial. He pointed out that the doctors who'd examined the alleged victims found no injuries, and that most of the white men who had tussled with the defendants weren't called to testify and the one who was—Lester Carter—actually corroborated Bates's recantation.[28] But Horton's stance cost him his next election, and the judge who replaced him on the case was far less sympathetic. Bates's recantation eventually resulted in charges against four of the nine—Roberson, Montgomery, Williams, and Leroy Wright—being dropped in 1937, but the remaining five faced retrial yet again, and all five were convicted.[29] Thanks in part to Judge Horton's documented concerns, public sentiment on the national level was in the defendants' favor—so much so that when one, Haywood Patterson, managed to escape Alabama's chain gang in 1948 and was located in Michigan, that state refused to extradite him back to Alabama.

"Think about this: A state refusing to extradite a convicted felon back to Alabama because Michigan said, 'This is wrong. This is just wrong,'" Professor Anderson said.[30]

Though not one of the Scottsboro defendants was ever acquitted in trial at the state level, some subsequent prosecutors began questioning Price's version of things. The men's death sentences were commuted, and their time significantly shortened. Alabama slowly and quietly began paroling the convicted men: Weems in 1943, Powell in 1946, and Wright twice—in 1943, and after fleeing parole, returning, and being imprisoned again, in 1950.[31] This was a stark about-face for Haywood Patterson especially, who'd been sentenced to die four times.[32]

The Supreme Court leveled two precedent-setting rulings: in 1935, the court ruled in *Norris v. Alabama* that the Scottsboro boys were denied a fair trial because of the systematic exclusion of Blacks on Jackson County jury rolls. Earlier, in 1932, the Supreme Court had ruled, in *Powell v. Alabama*, that denying a defendant competent counsel was a violation of due process (although the case then was remanded back to the Alabama courts, albeit to a different county). Both of those rulings had huge implications for the rest of the country and were cited time and again in other cases by other judges and lawyers.[33]

While each of the convicted defendants eventually was officially pardoned by the Alabama Board of Pardons and Paroles, it was a long time coming and, in fact, posthumous for three of the four.[34] While Clarence Norris was pardoned and declared not guilty in 1976 (thirteen years before his death of Alzheimer's disease), pardons for Haywood Patterson, Charlie Weems, and Andy Wright didn't come until an activist named Sheila Washington lobbied for them in 2013—eighty-two years after their ill-fated train ride through Alabama.[35]

Legal Legacy

The Scottsboro case "marked the first stirrings of the civil rights movement,"[36] united disparate organizations, and ultimately led to important Supreme Court rulings. Among the aftershocks:

- The ACLU dispatched journalist Hollace Ransdell to Alabama and Tennessee to investigate; she produced a report that challenged the rape allegations and became the basis for subsequent appeals.[37] Ultimately, the ACLU, the NAACP, and the ILD all joined in the defense.
- The appeals led to the 1932 Supreme Court decision in *Powell v. Alabama*, which held that defendants in capital cases were guaranteed under the 14th Amendment to have adequate, competent legal representation, as well as enough time to prepare a defense.[38]
- In 1935, SCOTUS again ruled on a Scottsboro case, finding in *Norris v. Alabama* that the intentional exclusion of Blacks from jury pools was unlawful.[39]

15

The Galvanizing Murder of Emmett Till

(1955)

The family, gathered in a modest house on a stretch of country road in Money, Mississippi, had heard rumblings that something bad might be afoot. There had been ominous warnings from others in the neighborhood that "this thing" wasn't over yet. Sure enough, on August 28, 1955, two men drove up to the house in the early morning hours ready for trouble. Moses Wright heard a voice at the door.[1]

"He just said, 'This is Mr. Bryant. I want to talk with you and the boy,'" recalled Wright, who happened to be great-uncle of the "boy" in question. "When I opened the door, there was a man standing with a pistol in one hand and flashlight in the other."[2]

Wright and his wife pleaded with the men to leave. The Wrights had two sons asleep in the house, as well as the fourteen-year-old nephew being sought, but it was clear by their gun and their firm voices that these men weren't looking to talk things out. They walked toward the sleeping children until they found the one they were looking for—the out-of-towner, the kid visiting from Chicago, the one who they said had the audacity to talk smart to one of the men's wives. They wanted Emmett Till, and the brutality they would unleash on him would galvanize the civil rights movement in America thanks to the efforts of his mother, Mamie.

There was little in Mamie's upbringing that foreshadowed the role she would later play in US history. She'd been born in Mississippi on November 23, 1921, to Nash and Alma Carthan, Black sharecroppers. Six months earlier, the Greenwood District—a vibrant stretch of Tulsa, Oklahoma, known as Black Wall Street—had been brutally demolished by white rioters. In what became known as the Tulsa Massacre, the mob killed, looted, and burned. Some 300 people died over a two-day span; another 800 were injured, and 9,000 people were left without homes.[3] Two years earlier, there had been a rash of race riots in dozens of cities across the country in the so-called Red Summer of 1919. Segregation was rampant—either by law, mostly in the South, or by practice. But since slavery had been abolished in 1865, there had been some progress. Black people could own a house and a business. Sharecropping was a meager step above slavery, though, so Nash set off for Chicago to find work. Argo Corn Products on the city's southwest side had built a new $5 million plant in 1910 and was a huge employer, where workers made things like corn starch and cooking oil.[4] Nash got a job there and, after settling in, sent for his wife and daughter to move to the North with him.

"Chicago was a land of promise," Mamie would later say in a documentary.[5] "And they thought that milk and honey was everywhere. And so it was a lot of excitement leaving the South, leaving the cotton fields. You could hold your head up in Chicago."

By 1930, the family had settled in a house in Summit on 63rd Place, which they shared with Nash's brother and sister-in-law. According to that year's census data, the Carthan home was worth $25, while homes owned by white people nearby were listed as being worth in the $4,000 to $5,000 range.[6] Mamie's parents wanted to provide her a safe home, a good education, and the chance to make something of herself. This remained their focus even as the couple's marriage faltered, leading to their divorce when Mamie was about thirteen. While many parents of the era planned on marrying their daughters off, Alma Carthan wanted hers to become a scholar, so Mamie was intentionally sheltered. Dating was forbidden. The approach seemed to work: Mamie was one of the first Black students to graduate from her high school in Summit, and she graduated at the top of her class. Afterward, she became one of the first Black women in town to hold a civil service job.

At age eighteen, Mamie met a brash boxer from Missouri named Louis Till. Alma did not condone the relationship, so Mamie dutifully broke up with Louis, but he proved to be persistent. When Louis learned Mamie was on a date with another man, he showed up to fight for her. Mamie was touched by the gesture; her mother's misgivings be damned. In 1940, she and Louis married. A year later, on July 25, they had their only child, a son they named Emmett Louis. Emmett's birth hadn't been easy. He was a breech baby, which, Mamie later said, caused her enormous physical pain.

But she said the tough delivery was offset by the easygoing nature of her baby, whom she nicknamed “Bobo.” “He was the happiest baby in the world,” Mamie said. “I mean, you didn’t have to hold him and rock him and pet him. If you gave him that bottle, you made sure he was dry, you could put him in his bed, and he would lie and kick and coo for hours.”[7]

As Mamie’s mother had worried, Louis Till wasn’t an ideal husband. Mamie learned he was cheating on her while Emmett was still a baby. He was also violent. When Mamie left him, he choked her to unconsciousness. She got a restraining order, which he repeatedly violated. Eventually, a judge gave him a choice: either serve time in prison or join the US Army. In 1943, Till chose the army, two years after which Mamie learned by telegram that he was dead. He’d been executed by the US government for “willful misconduct.” Mamie found it curious that his death came in July, two months after the war had ended in Italy, where he was killed, but details on the execution were scant. Mamie later received a few of her estranged husband’s belongings, including a signet ring with the initials L. T. Left a widow, Mamie relied on her mother to help raise little Emmett, making him feel more like a sibling than a son.

When Emmett was young, he contracted polio at age six, about eight years before a vaccine was developed that would eradicate it. Mamie and her mother were devastated.

“Polio was the worst thing that could happen to you back then,” Mamie later said. “It didn’t kill you, but it could take your life away from you just the same.”[8]

The illness can damage motor neurons within the spinal cord and brainstem. In Emmett’s case, it left him with a persistent stutter that he couldn’t shake as he got older. It didn’t seem to bother him, however. In fact, nothing seemed to faze Emmett. He was a jokester who loved being the center of attention. He would shoot off fireworks within Chicago’s city limits, even though he wasn’t supposed to, and while he’d occasionally get reprimanded for saying something smart or breaking the rules, he was always forgiven because it was clear he wasn’t being mean-spirited. He was just silly, simply aiming for laughs. He especially loved to make his mom, Mamie, laugh.

The year after Louis’s death, Mamie remarried one of his army buddies, twenty-eight-year-old Lemorse Mallory. The marriage soon ended in divorce and was such an insignificance in Mamie’s life that she didn’t even mention it in her 2003 memoir, *Death of Innocence*.[9] Another short-lived union followed in 1951 with a man named Pink Bradley.[10] A few years into that marriage, Mamie learned he was seeing other women, so she piled his clothes onto the lawn and filed for divorce. By 1953, Mamie was raising Emmett alone. She'd gotten a job at the Social Security Administration, and Emmett, then a preteen, did his part by keeping the house clean and regularly cooking dinner for the two of them. For a while, their only regular company was their dog, Mike, though around 1954, Mamie met and fell for a barber named Gene Mobley. Emmett liked him, too.

Emmett Till with his mother, Mamie, c. 1953.

Christmas of that year was a big one for the family. Mamie gave Emmett a new suit, while Gene added a hat, tie, and coat. They took photos of Emmett in that garb, one of which would later be used in countless publications worldwide to show how handsome he had been before he was pulled from his great-uncle's house in the middle of the night by a man with a pistol and a flashlight.

Emmett traveled to Mississippi because he'd learned that one of his cousins, sixteen-year-old Wheeler Parker, was planning to travel there to visit relatives. That was pretty common for families who had moved in what became known as the Great Migration—the period from the 1910s to the 1970s in which 6 million African Americans moved out of the South to other parts of the country. Families who'd moved away often sent their children back to visit relatives during the summer months.

At this point in history, Mississippi was fighting hard against integration. *Brown v. Board of Education*, the landmark case that led to the Supreme Court ruling declaring racial segregation in public schools unconstitutional, was in 1954, but many Mississippi schools wouldn't be integrated for nearly two decades after that ruling. In fact, a federal judge as late as 2016 ordered one district in the Mississippi Delta to finally desegregate its middle and high schools.[11] In the mid-1950s, racial segregation was the norm. Mixed use of drinking fountains, restrooms, and even building entrances was forbidden.

Jim Crow laws were rampant and went far beyond separate water fountains and seating sections. In Mississippi, it wasn't only illegal for a white person to marry someone with one-eighth or more "Negro blood," but it was illegal to publish or circulate written material promoting the acceptance of interracial marriage. Mississippi didn't repeal its 1890 constitutional ban on interracial marriage until 1987, and that was by a slim margin.[12] On top of the codified rules of the era, there were plenty of unwritten ones, too—ones that, if violated, could lead to vigilante "justice" by way of lynching, and Mississippi was the state with the highest number of lynchings recorded.[13]

Mamie was worried about Emmett's safety on the trip. In later interviews, she would talk about how foreign the idea of racism was to her as a child, and how that sheltered view was passed along to her son. It's not that they never experienced racism, but Illinois was far more progressive than Mississippi. Efforts to segregate Chicago after a 1919 race riot failed, with the Governor's Commission on Race Relations declaring that segregation was "illegal, impracticable and would not solve, but would accentuate, the race problem and postpone its just and orderly solution by the process of adjustment."[14] There were racists, of course, who would discourage Black patrons by treating them rudely, overcharging them, or ignoring them,[15] but outright prejudice was routinely challenged in court, and, though progress was slow, it was somewhat measurable. The South might as well have been another country altogether. Following these unspoken rules was literally a life-or-death matter for Black people in Mississippi, which is why some of Emmett's extended family worried so much about him visiting Money, Mississippi.

But Emmett really wanted to go, and Mamie thought it'd be good for him to see family in another part of the country. She had a heart-to-heart talk with him before he left, trying to impress upon him just how different things were going to be there. Mamie told her son bluntly: "Don't start up any conversations with white people. Only talk if you're spoken to." She drilled into him that his only responses should be "yes, sir" and "no, sir." "Don't just say 'yes' and 'no' or 'naw.' ... If you're walking down the street and a white woman is walking toward you, step off the sidewalk, lower your head. Don't look her in the eye."[16]

Emmett assured her he would stay out of trouble.

On August 21, 1955, during cotton-harvest season, Emmett and Parker arrived in Money to stay with their great-uncle, Moses "Mose" Wright, a sharecropper. Parker would later remember that he and Emmett just played around in the fields while their other cousins worked. He recalled it being "a wonderful time."[17] It didn't last long, however. Three days after arriving, Emmett and his cousins stopped by a store called Bryant's Grocery & Meat Market. The store was owned by Roy and Carolyn Bryant, a white couple, whose customers were largely Black workers from nearby cotton plantations. Carolyn, who was twenty-one at the time, worked behind the counter. Parker went in first and bought some candy, after which Emmett stepped inside. Emmett asked for ten cents worth of bubble gum.

Simeon Wright, one of Emmett's other cousins, had been sent inside the store in part to make sure Emmett didn't say anything out of line. According to him, Emmett didn't.

"We didn't have any conversation with Mrs. Bryant," Wright later said.[18] "We left together."

Carolyn came out of the store and headed to her parked car.

"And as she was going to her car, that's when Emmett whistled at her," Wright said.[19]

People who knew Emmett knew he'd meant no harm. He was a fun-loving, goofball of a boy who had probably whistled to make his cousins laugh, maybe to even make the woman laugh—if it indeed was even directed at Carolyn, which some people doubted. One of Emmett's uncles told reporters that when Emmett's stutter got him stuck on a word, he would whistle to help himself get through it.[20] Mamie would later explain that she'd taught him to do that, to "whistle when he got stuck on a word like 'bubble gum.'"[21] Regardless of the reason for the whistle, it was the kind of behavior that they'd been worried about from Emmett. Carolyn Bryant didn't laugh. She looked so stern as she headed to her car that the boys thought she aimed to retrieve a gun.

"No one knew that he was going to whistle, and when he did, he scared everybody," Wright said. "And when he saw our reaction, then he got scared."[22]

The panicked kids piled into their car and fled, but as they sped down a gravel road, they noticed a car was tailing them. They figured they were being chased, so they pulled to the side of the road and started running until they reached a cotton field. Some of them tripped in the field, but their panic relaxed when they noticed the car that had been tailing them had driven past. Emmett begged the cousins not to tell Mose that he had, in fact, behaved in the type of way he'd been warned not to. They all agreed and went on home. A girl named Ruth Crawford approached the boys soon after and warned them that they were going to hear more about what had happened at Bryant's store, but three days passed without incident. Emmett and his cousins had been given quite a fright, but it seemed the incident had passed.[23]

And then Roy Bryant and his half-brother, J. W. Milam, knocked on the Wrights' door in the middle of the night brandishing a .45-caliber handgun. Milam asked Emmett if he was the boy they sought, to which Emmett said, "Yeah." The man replied: "You say 'yeah' again and I'll blow your head off."[24] The men began to lead Emmett outside. Mose heard the men ask a woman in the car waiting for them if they had the correct boy, and he said that he heard her reply yes, they did. After that, Emmett was forced into the car. Mose alerted the local sheriff, who visited Bryant and Milam to follow up. The men agreed that they had grabbed Emmett in the middle of the night, but they said when they asked Carolyn Bryant if he was the one who had whistled at her, she'd said no, so they released him. When the sheriff said Emmett hadn't returned, they said they had no idea what had happened to him.[25]

The first headlines about the case were confined mostly to Mississippi because it was at that point a local story about a missing teenager. The next day, the story spread a bit because it became clear that Emmett had been kidnapped for doing something as benign as whistling at a woman. The day after that, the missing teen still hadn't surfaced, and his story made national news. Speaking to reporters, Leflore County Sheriff George W. Smith said that where Emmett had gone was the "$64 question."[26] He added: "I'm kinda scared there's been foul play."[27]

Roy Bryant and J. W. Milam were arrested on suspicion of kidnapping on August 29. They maintained they had no idea what happened to Emmett Till. Two days later, Emmett's mangled body was found in the early morning hours by a seventeen-year-old boy fishing in the Tallahatchie River, near a spot called Pecan Point.[28] Robert Hodges was inspecting his trotline when he noticed a pair of human legs poking through the water's surface. The teen returned home and told his father what he'd seen, and his father in turn alerted authorities in Tallahatchie County, including its notoriously racist sheriff, H. C. Strider. The condition of the discovered corpse was so horrifying that he couldn't immediately be identified. Strider insisted that it couldn't be the missing child Emmett Till because the body was that of an adult man, not a teenage boy. Moses Wright saw the corpse and though he couldn't make out his great-nephew's facial features, he was able to identify him via the signet ring found with the body. The ring sported the initials L. T. It had been Emmett's father's ring, which Mamie had passed on to her son.

Strider told reporters that he was sure the whole murder story had been concocted to make Mississippi look bad. In reality, he insisted, Emmett was likely alive and well, living with relatives in Detroit. Yet Strider knew that the condition of the body would cause an uproar, so he tried to arrange an immediate burial, which Mamie fought to prevent. Though the corpse looked nothing like the broad-grinned boy she loved—in fact, she'd later say it barely looked human at all—she knew it was her son. Swollen and bloated, he had been dead for days with a 125-pound cotton-gin blower tied to his neck in an effort to sink him to the river's bottom. He'd been beaten so viciously that all but two of his teeth were knocked from his head. One eye had been knocked from its socket and was resting on its cheek. It appeared he'd been choked by the way his tongue bulged from his mouth. He also had been shot through the head.[29]

Pallbearers carry Emmett Till's casket out of Roberts Temple Church of God in Christ in Chicago on September 3, 1955.

The all-white male jury during the trial of Roy Bryant and his half-brother, J. W. Milam, September 21, 1955.

After Mamie had her son's body transported to Illinois, she decided that people needed to see what had happened to him. She insisted that he be put in a box beneath glass—to keep people from both touching and smelling him—and displayed at his funeral.[30] In an enormous, unprecedented display of grief and solidarity, some fifty thousand people turned out for Emmett's service.

As outrage grew over what had been done to this teenager, the Bryants began to amend the story of Emmett's supposed transgressions. At first it was reported that Emmett had whistled at a white lady, which is what his cousins maintained in the subsequent decades. But as the days passed, the story changed to suggest that Emmett had actually insulted Carolyn Bryant. By the time she took the stand at her husband's murder trial, the tale would be that Emmett had put his hands on her. The teen with a pronounced stutter somehow said: "What's the matter, baby? Can't you take it? You needn't be afraid of me." After that, she said he boasted that he'd been "with white women before."[31]

Roy Bryant and J. W. Milam had initially been arrested and charged with kidnapping, but that changed after Emmett's body was discovered; they were then charged with murder. The state appointed a special prosecutor to handle the case. Five weeks after Emmett's death, an all-white, all-male jury heard the case against Bryant and Milam. They heard testimony from Willie Reed, a young Black farmhand,, who said he saw four white men and two or three Black men carry Emmet into a plantation barn. After an hour's deliberation, the jury acquitted Bryant and Milam of murder on September 23, 1955. "I'm just glad it's over with," Roy Bryant told a reporter after the verdict. Mrs. Bryant added that she felt "fine."[32]

Left to right: J. W. Milam and his wife, Juanita, and Carolyn and Roy Bryant, after their acquittal on September 25, 1955. Not long after the trial, the pair admitted to murdering Till in an interview with a *Look* magazine reporter, showing no remorse.

Mamie was horrified by the verdict. "What I saw was a shame before God and man, and the way the jury chose to believe the ridiculous stories of the defense attorneys," she said.[33]

The acquittal was nationally divisive; a month later, there were reports that Mississippi senators James Eastland and John C. Stennis had allegedly helped "reporters force the army to release" the story that Emmett's father had been executed by the US Army,[34] which the Tills knew, though they hadn't known the details as to why. The telegram Mamie had received said only that he'd displayed "willful misconduct." It turned out, however, that Louis Till had been accused along with another Black soldier of raping two women and killing another. He had denied it but was found guilty and hanged. This allowed some to argue that Emmett had been ready to follow in his father's footsteps—though some have speculated that Louis's trial had been racially motivated as well.[35] In November, a month after the story about Emmett's father made headlines, a grand jury was asked to weigh whether Bryant and Milam should be tried for kidnapping—a crime to which they had already admitted to two separate sheriffs. The jury declined to indict them.[36]

Two months after that, Bryant and Milam sold their story to *Look* magazine for $4,000. Through that story, they confessed outright to killing Emmett Till. They'd intended to whip him and scare him, they said, but he didn't react the way they thought he should. He was defiant, they said. (People who knew Emmett say this wasn't likely. He had been compliant when kidnapped, after all.) Whatever their reasoning, the men beat Emmett brutally, and then they shot him. That night, they burned his clothes and complained that his shoes took a long time to incinerate.[37]

After confessing the crime, Bryant and Milam found they were shunned by many of the people who'd previously supported them—people who apparently had bought their story that they had nabbed Emmett and let him go unharmed. At one point, Bryant told an interviewer that Emmett Till ruined his life. Unlike Emmett, however, they both lived their lives; Milam died of cancer in 1980 at age sixty-one, and Bryant in 1994 at age sixty-three.

In the decades after Emmett's death, his case from time to time has been resurrected, most recently in 2017, after the release of the book *The Blood of Emmett Till* by historian Timothy B. Tyson. The book quoted Carolyn Bryant as saying she made up some of the allegations against Emmett on the stand—specifically that he hadn't merely whistled at her, but that he'd grabbed her hand and made an advance.[38] On December 13, 2021, the US Department of Justice officially closed the case again without filing any new charges, though witnesses have come forward saying Milam and Bryant weren't alone when they killed Emmett.

"We have good reason to believe that anywhere between four or possibly as many as seven people—a literal gang of adult men—murdered a child, and/or witnessed or participated to some extent or another in the torture and murder and brutalization of this child," said Benjamin Saulsberry of the Emmett Till Interpretive Center in Sumner, Mississippi.[39]

As of this writing, Carolyn Bryant is in her late eighties, remarried, and still living in the South, now under the surname Donham. Media outlets in 2022 obtained drafts of a memoir she had written, in which she reportedly lied when claiming that Emmett had physically accosted her and made sexual advances. Although a grand jury in Leflore County, Mississippi, declined in August of 2022 to indict Carolyn, Emmett's surviving relatives continue to say that as long as someone is alive to prosecute, they want justice.[40]

Mamie Till married Gene Mobley, the boyfriend who had bought Emmett his wide-brimmed hat, and she spent the rest of her life telling her son's story, making sure his name was never forgotten. She died on January 6, 2003.

Legal Legacy

Mamie Till's decision to put her son's mutilated body on display galvanized the civil rights movement and brought nationwide attention to racial violence and injustice in the South. Among other impacts:

- Black Americans who grew up in the 1950s as civil rights advocates often called themselves "the Emmett Till generation"—including Georgia-born John Lewis, who was 15 when Emmett was killed and would go on to serve for 33 years in Congress.[41]
- The case inspired New York City Council president Abe Stark to call on Congress to pass a federal law against lynching in 1955,[42] though it was not until 2022 before the Emmett Till Antilynching Act, introduced by Rep. Bobby L. Rush (D-IL), was finally adopted.[43]
- In 2020, the Emmett Till Cold Case Investigations and Prosecution Program was launched by the US Bureau of Justice Assistance to provide support in the investigation and prosecution of cold case murders associated with civil rights violations.[44]

Part 4

FORENSIC ADVANCES

16

How an Orthopedic Shoe Felled Criminal Genius Edward Rulloff

(1845)

Edward Rulloff had a problem. He needed to get rid of the wooden chest he had just filled, but it was so heavy that he could barely lift it, much less carry it anywhere. He turned to a neighbor, hoping for a little help.[1]

The neighbor agreed and loaned Rulloff a horse and carriage and even helped him load that one hundred-plus-pound chest. To satisfy the neighbor's curiosity, Rulloff explained that his wife's uncle had come and picked up his wife and infant daughter to take them on a trip, but the trunk had been in the uncle's carriage, and it had to be left behind to make room for the passengers.[2] Rulloff wanted to follow the others to reunite the chest with its owner, but he didn't have his own horse and carriage. Hence, the request for help.

After the chest was loaded, the two men said goodbye and, a few hours after that, Rulloff returned the carriage, thanking his neighbor.

It would be six full weeks before people began to realize that ever since that day, no one had seen Rulloff's wife and infant daughter. The relative he'd mentioned to his neighbor never surfaced, and Rulloff himself had told different stories to others who asked after his family. People in Ithaca, New York, where Rulloff worked as a botanical doctor, started to get suspicious, but Rulloff was brilliant, with a brain size that would literally set records. While he proved to be one of the country's smartest and most slippery criminals, he also was one of the first in history to be felled by a new type of shoe-leather detective work that's still used to solve crimes to this day.

OPPOSITE: A c. 1860 stereograph frame of the town of Ithaca, New York, overlooking Cayuga Lake, where Edward Rulloff is believed to have disposed of the bodies of his wife and daughter.

Rulloff was born John Edward Howard Rulofson in 1819, a year after his parents' marriage,[3] to a farming family in New Brunswick, Canada.[4] His father, William, was a hard-working farmer but—as was customary at the time—content to leave the child-rearing entirely to his wife, Priscilla. Priscilla's focus was on providing the best education possible for her children, which was unusual at a time when schools in Canada were still scarce.[5] Priscilla was "incredibly smart and very well read and encouraged all of her sons to be well read," said Kate Winkler Dawson, a journalism professor, author, and podcaster at the University of Texas in Austin who studied Rulloff for her book *All That Is Wicked* (2022).[6]

Rulloff was one of three boys growing up in a stable but unaffluent family. When Rulloff was eight, the family's circumstances became more difficult because Rulloff's father died, leaving his mother a widow. Rulloff's uncle took over the family's finances and gave Priscilla something of a stipend, until she remarried in 1831.[7]

Priscilla raised Rulloff and his two brothers to be bookworms. "She was a woman of more than ordinary intellect," Rulloff would later tell a journalist named Edward Hamilton, "and I presume that whatever genius for study that any of us boys ever had, we inherited from her."[8]

By focusing on education, she helped her boys rise above their social status. Rulloff loved reading anything he could get his hands on and was particularly enamored with the study of language. He soon became a self-taught polyglot, learning to speak at least seven languages,[9] including French, Greek, Latin, and German.[10]

But Rulloff was also a troublemaker. He set fires and stole things.[11] He was smart enough to talk his way out of trouble for some of his antics, but not all of them. By the time he graduated from his elite school, he had an impressive rap sheet that wasn't mirrored by his brothers and confounded his mother. There was just something in Rulloff's makeup that seemed different.

Rulloff's dream was to become an academic, Dawson explained in an interview. He went to his uncle and told him he would like to be an academic, so needed tuition money to go to university, but his uncle said no. "He was a big believer in having a solid blue-collar background," Dawson noted. "He said Edward could be a printer or a farmer. They were better trades as far as his uncle was concerned, which sent Edward into a tailspin."[12]

With college out of reach, Rulloff began leaning into his worst impulses. He got by with working odd jobs and committing petty theft, small crimes that he continued to get away with—mostly—because he didn't seem like a criminal to most people. In truth, he was actually quite sloppy, so, good image or not, he got busted a few times before he moved from Canada to New York in 1842.[13]

An engraved frontispiece portrait of Edward Rulloff from an 1871 book titled *The Man of Two Lives!*, by Edward Crapsey.

Within months of his arrival, Rulloff met a boat master and farmer who regularly hired desperate men looking for work. Rulloff stood out because he was clearly better educated than most. He also gave himself an exotic edge by pretending to be not from Canada, but from Germany. Because he spoke fluent German, he could convincingly feign a German accent.

Rulloff seemed smart and reliable, plus he had a wide chest to boot, so Henry Schutt, the boat master and member of a prominent local family, invited him to work on his family's farm in Dryden, New York, about thirteen miles northeast of Ithaca in Tompkins County. Rulloff met Henry's parents, John and Hannah, as well as Henry's siblings. He wasn't embraced entirely by the family, but he did impress the crew. Rulloff did plenty of hard labor on the farm, but it was soon clear that he really was more of an academic than a farmer, so Henry helped Rulloff open a school. Local students signed up to take classes from him.[14]

Among his students was Harriet, one of Henry's teenage sisters, described as striking with pale skin and hazel eyes. She was both flirtatious and naive, a compelling combination. Plenty of men had shown interest in her, and her father, John, would've signed off on many of those men, but not Rulloff. Ironically, Rulloff's supposed German roots didn't impress John. Even though the Schutts's ancestors hailed from the Netherlands and, like Rulloff, had risen from humble beginnings, they held Rulloff's social class and immigrant status against him. John wanted his daughter to marry an American. Also, the longer he knew Rulloff, the less stable he seemed to be. He had an ego that could be off-putting, plus a worrisome jealous streak. When Harriet returned Rulloff's interest, he became possessive and manipulative. John tried to keep Rulloff away from his daughter, but to no avail. She'd fallen in love. The two were married in December 1843, which predictably did nothing to curb Rulloff's jealousy.[15] "Unfortunately, from the wedding day, there was a cousin who Harriet was close with, a man named

Dr. Henry Bull, who apparently was very good looking and a successful physician," Dawson said. "Edward claimed that he and Harriet were having an affair."[16]

Rulloff tried to get Harriet's older brother William to banish Dr. Bull from the family's farm and functions, but William refused. This infuriated Rulloff, who quietly stored away that anger. Rulloff's jealousy was noteworthy even by nineteenth-century standards, as evidenced by newspaper reports of the time. According to one story, Rulloff repeatedly accused Harriet of "improper intimacy with Dr. Bull." He supposedly got so enraged that he sometimes beat her.[17]

Rulloff confided in William his suspicions about Harriet and Dr. Bull's relationship. William would later recall that Rulloff "thought Dr. Bull and his wife had had intercourse together" and that he should leave Harriett. William heard these complaints so often that he eventually told Rulloff he was "tired of hearing about these troubles," and asked him to stay away if he couldn't steer clear of the subject.[18]

William wasn't the only one concerned with Rulloff's behavior. One of his sisters, Jane Schutt, said that within months of the couple's marriage she witnessed physical abuse. Harriet had been pounding pepper for a meal, but Rulloff complained she wasn't pounding it finely enough. "He snatched the pestle and hit her on the forehead; she carried the mark for some days," Jane said.[19]

It still can be challenging for women to leave abusive relationships today, but in the nineteenth century it was extremely difficult. Wives weren't so much equals in a marriage as much as they were property. And Rulloff had been clever. Soon after they married, he moved her ten miles away to Lansing, where he had gotten a teaching job.[20] For a woman in the 1840s, moving even just ten miles was akin to moving to the other side of the state, especially for Harriet, as Rulloff didn't have a carriage. He had effectively isolated her from her family.

The more time passed, the more Harriet's family came to rue the day Rulloff entered their lives. Then Harriet learned she was pregnant.

Meanwhile, Rulloff struggled at first to find his footing professionally. It seems teaching kids wasn't fulfilling enough, so he dabbled in law and studied alternative medicine, which had been pioneered earlier in the century by a self-taught herbalist and botanist named Samuel Thomson, who believed all illness resulted from cold. Thomson used herbs that helped create internal heat, like cayenne, or that were emetic, like lobelia. Botanical physicians eschewed the traditional treatments of the time such as bloodletting and calomel (mercury chloride) and used herbs and roots instead. With diseases like dysentery and cholera, patients had as good a chance of survival by being treated with leeches as they did with lobelia.[21]

Just as he'd done when he was a bachelor, Rulloff bounced around from job to job. In the winter of 1844, he worked as a drug clerk in Ithaca for a few months.[22] He and Harriet lived in a boarding house during that time, but Harriet missed her family and returned to her father's house at some point. While her parents were probably thrilled to have her back, the return was short-lived, and the wedge between Rulloff and his in-laws continued to grow.

Harriet's brother Ephraim once found his sister sobbing after Rulloff apparently beat her and gave a stern ultimatum: either stop mistreating her or leave. "I said to him his conduct was very strange," Ephraim later testified. "He finally concluded to stay."[23]

Dawson described the incident as "pretty extraordinary, because in the 1800s, once you married a woman, she was essentially your property and the families didn't step in. The Schutt brothers just hated him so much that they felt compelled to say, 'We will take her off your hands. We have had enough.' And Edward promised he was going to be better—which of course he wasn't."

Harriet gave birth to a baby daughter on April 12, 1845.[24] She and her family hoped that fatherhood would temper him in ways that marriage hadn't. The baby was named Priscilla, after Rulloff's mother.

Despite their dislike of Rulloff, the Schutt family still respected him, more or less—or at least respected his brain. In June 1845, Harriet's older brother William begged him to use his botanical medicine to try to save his dying wife and newborn daughter.[25] The two were sick with some kind of bacterial infection, and they were quickly becoming listless. Rulloff agreed to travel from Lansing to Ithaca to treat his in-laws, but on the ride over, he reportedly made it clear to his mother-in-law, Hannah, that he really didn't care if William's wife lived or died. Hannah later said: "It was wholly indifferent to him whether she got well. William had misused him about Dr. Bull, and that thing would yet mount to the shedding of blood."[26] Hannah should

have seen this comment as a red flag, but Rulloff was so prone to being melodramatic that she wrote it off as theatrics. He might be a bastard, but she had no reason to think he was a killer.

Rulloff failed to heal William's wife and daughter. First, the days-old daughter died after Rulloff's examination. Then the mother passed away. William was, of course, grief-stricken, but not upset with Rulloff. Even Hannah, who had heard Rulloff express his indifference, thought he had done all he could. After all, it wasn't uncommon in the nineteenth century for a mother and infant to die in childbirth, and the two had been failing before Rulloff arrived. Asking his brother-in-law to try to save the two had been a desperate gambit at best.[27]

Besides, Rulloff wasn't an actual doctor. He dabbled in fringe botanical medicine. His goal was still to land in academia, a dream that finally seemed within reach in June 1845 when he was offered a prestigious job as a principal at an all-boys' academy in Ohio.[28] The offer came a few weeks after the deaths of his wife's relatives. He announced the big news to Harriet and told her they'd be moving to Ohio.

"And she said absolutely not. I have zero interest in going anywhere with you, and if you're going to go, then I'm not going with you," Dawson told me.[29]

This sparked a huge fight, and while it's impossible to know exactly what happened next, most historians believe that Rulloff killed his wife and daughter that night. The next day, he asked his neighbor to borrow a horse and carriage to haul a heavy chest that happened to be large enough to contain two bodies. As Rulloff drove off, he "gaily bade his neighbors goodbye, and drove down the dusty turnpike, whistling softly as the horse moved along."[30] Rulloff later said he traveled to Cayuga Lake, took the chest on a boat out to the middle of the lake, and emptied it there. Some consider Rulloff an unreliable narrator, which fueled belief that the bodies had actually been sold to the Geneva Medical College,[31] a common practice in mid-nineteenth century New England.[32] Whatever the truth, his wife and daughter were never heard from again. Afterward, he traveled to his brother-in-law William's house for breakfast.

Rulloff was sweaty, red-faced, and nervous, but the Schutts had no reason to be suspicious—though he did do something odd. William Schutt had given his sister a gold ring as a gift once, and Harriet wore that ring every day. But this day, at breakfast, Rulloff pulled out the gold ring from his vest pocket and handed it to William, saying, you probably want this. William, confused, said, no, give it back to Harriet.[33]

After breakfast, Rulloff returned the horse and carriage to his neighbor, who noted that Rulloff still had the chest, but now it was light enough for him to carry it on his own.[34]

This illustration, captioned "He attempted to take the child away from her," depicts Priscilla Rulloff struggling with her husband, Edward, as he attempts to snatch their baby daughter. It is from a published trial report printed in 1871 titled *Life, Trial, and Execution of Edward H. Ruloff: Perpetrator of Eight Murders, Numerous Burglaries . . .*

When Harriet's family asked where she and baby Priscilla were, Rulloff said they were "between the lakes," a phrase locals used to describe visiting small towns that dotted the lands between the region's Great Lakes. Harriet's friends asked after her, too, but Rulloff was inconsistent in his replies. According to a newspaper account, he told one that she was between the lakes, another that she was in Pennsylvania, and others that she was in Madison, Ohio. The story read: "Being pressed in the matter, he wrote a letter to her, directed to the latter place."[35] In the letter, he asked her to write her friends and let them know that she was okay. Such assurances never arrived.

After six weeks of Rulloff's prevarications, two of Harriet's brothers—Ephraim and William—could take it no longer, and they insisted Rulloff bring them to her. Rulloff tried to appease them by leading them to the Ohio town where he now claimed his wife and daughter supposedly were. He managed to ditch the brothers along the way, but they stayed the course and arrived in the town and began asking around. No one had seen any new woman with a newborn child. Exceptionally dogged, Ephraim caught up with Rulloff hiding out on a steamship in Cleveland filled with German immigrants, and he summoned a police officer to handcuff him. Aboard a steamer headed back to New York to bring Rulloff to prison, he offered his captors a deal: he suggested that the brothers let him jump into the sea and drown, as the alternative was surely for him to return to New York and be hanged. Ephraim scoffed, saying he believed Rulloff was too much of a coward to do it, which proved accurate. Instead, Ephraim contented himself to trust in the rule of law and wanted to see Rulloff face trial for what the family was now certain was the murder of his wife and baby.[36]

But the legal system in America was still evolving in the 1840s. There had never been a case tried without a body, because the thinking—based on precedent set in Great Britain by seventeenth-century barrister Sir Matthew Hale—was no body, no crime.[37]

The Schutts tried to shore up the case by searching for the remains of Harriet and Priscilla in Cayuga Lake. They spent $10,000 to drag the lake to no avail.[38]

Still, Rulloff went on trial for murder and served as his own lawyer—a move that was considered as ill-advised then as it is today. Rulloff didn't win the case, but he didn't exactly lose it, either. Because there was no corpse and, thus, no cause of death and no proof of homicide, he wasn't convicted of murder, but of kidnapping.[39] He was sentenced to ten years, during which he kept busy. He wrote an appeal challenging his conviction and began formulating a theory on language that he was sure would revolutionize the world.

"He bought books and papers, he read, and this is where he came up with this theory of language that was really pivotal in his life," Dawson said. "It's what drove him."[40]

Rulloff's theoretical writings in prison earned him money that he managed to save. The Schutts, meanwhile, stewed. They were furious with the sentence he'd gotten, and they had public opinion on their side. Rulloff, as newspaper fodder, was loathed by most readers. He had a charming side that could win some folks over in person, but he did not translate well in print at all.

As Rulloff's sentence neared its end, the Schutts worked to convince the prosecutor to level new charges against him. They couldn't charge him with Harriet's murder again because of double jeopardy rules, but the first trial hadn't included charges related to Priscilla, the baby. The family tried convincing the prosecutor to charge Rulloff with murder in that case instead.

Meanwhile, this suspected killer and convicted kidnapper was an oddity in prison. Officials were used to criminals. They'd even seen a few murderers. But they'd never seen anyone like Rulloff. He could switch personalities on a dime. Officials decided it would be a waste for them not to tap into Rulloff's smarts, so the adults in town entrusted him to tutor their children. Not only did local law enforcement sign off on this, but it took part. One of Rulloff's pupils was a young man named Al Jarvis, who was the undersheriff's son. Rulloff seduced Jarvis intellectually–and then did the same to Jarvis's mother, Jane.[41] They were both so smitten with him that they broke him out of prison. From this point, it became his life's mission to get his theory about the origin of human language out into the world. It eventually took the form of a manuscript called *Method in the Formation of Language*.

"He believed there was a pattern to human language . . . and because of this pattern, you could teach a Frenchman Italian almost instantly," Dawson said. "Now, there is no pattern in that way. It's not real, but it was enough of a hoax to convince people, and for Edward to convince himself."[42]

Rulloff, now a fugitive, took on an alias and a new persona—James Nelson.[43] He schemed his way into getting a temporary position teaching languages at Allegheny College in Meadville, Pennsylvania. There were no full-time openings, but Rulloff convinced Allegheny's president, Reverend John Barker, to write him a letter of recommendation for a job at the University of North Carolina at Chapel Hill; in the letter Barker described Rulloff as "one of the best linguists I have ever met."[44]

Rulloff got a formal offer and was about to head to North Carolina when he received letters from Jane and Al Jarvis at a post office box he used in Meadville (he had kept them apprised of his whereabouts). Al Jarvis informed Rulloff that he and his mother were now penniless after being kicked out of their home for their role in freeing him from prison. Jarvis even threatened his former teacher by saying that if Rulloff didn't help them, the teen would find him and slit his throat.[45]

"He was without friends or money," Rulloff later explained to a reporter named Hamilton Freeman, "and the letter concluded by saying: 'I helped you once, and now I want you to help me.'"[46]

Probably sensing that his new identity wasn't as foolproof as he'd hoped, Rulloff bailed on the North Carolina job and robbed a jewelry store instead. He got caught but managed to talk his way out of it. Then he landed in New York City, where he got by as a burglar. Al Jarvis—now a petty criminal as well—became his partner. Jarvis, in turn, connected Rulloff with another convict named William Dexter.

Even as the trio lived the lives of thieves, Rulloff still tried to get his theory of language accepted. He was certain that his findings were brilliant and that he would revolutionize the field of philology. Using yet another alias—this one a supposed Oxford graduate[47]—he wrote the fledgling American Philological Association and announced that he'd be offering his book for sale for the bargain-basement price of half a million dollars. No one bit.[48]

In the late summer of 1870, Jarvis, Dexter, and Rulloff decided to rob a dry goods store in Binghamton, New York. On August 18, they broke into an establishment called Halbert Bros, where two store clerks were sleeping in a room above the store. They managed to catch one of the burglars, whose cries for help lured his accomplices to his aid. Frederick Merrick (or Mirick), one of the two clerks, fired his gun but missed. The burglars returned fire, hitting Merrick in the head and killing him instantly.[49]

The trio ran and apparently jumped into the Chenango River, aiming to swim across to safety, but they weren't all able swimmers. The waterlogged bodies of Dexter and Jarvis were found floating in the river the next day.[50] After police fished the burglars' corpses from the river, the clerk who'd survived the shootout identified them as the men who'd shot at him the night before—but he also said that there had been a third accomplice as well.

At the scene of the crime, police had found a crucial clue. Somehow during the scuffle at the dry goods store, Rulloff lost his shoes, and it just so happened that his left foot was deformed in a specific way and his shoe was modified to accommodate it. After a shoeless Rulloff was spotted wandering around town, he was arrested. Jurors were presented with the shoe and decided that if the shoe fit, they couldn't acquit. Rulloff was found guilty of Merrick's murder and sentenced to death.[51]

He appealed the sentencing, while some people argued on his behalf that it'd be a shame to kill someone with a brain like his, but, despite a few delays, the sentence ultimately stood. On May 18, 1871, Rulloff walked to the gallows, where a noose was tied around his neck. His neck didn't break, so it took fifteen agonizing minutes for him to choke to death.

A news story of the events read:

> **He died as he had lived: impudent, blasphemous, hypocritical, profane and intolerably vile. In his last moments he spurned the proffers of instruction and consolation from the Scriptures. . . . He died, almost literally with horrid oaths upon his tongue and infamous curses on his lips. A consummate mountebank in literature as in all else, he carried out his unblushing effrontery to the last, pretending to be affected with profound regret for the huge and irreparable loss the world must experience by his death, before the completion of his marvel of a book on language.[52]**

"HE DIED AS HE HAD LIVED: IMPUDENT, BLASPHEMOUS, HYPOCRITICAL, PROFANE AND INTOLERABLY VILE."

Rulloff probably would've taken some comfort in knowing that the thing he valued most about himself would be preserved. His head was cut off and his brain examined, which turned out to be quite a bit larger than average. Apparently, Rulloff had been right: His brain was important, though not quite in the way he thought it was.

"There was a belief among white, elite neurologists that the men who had the most intelligence—the most morals, particularly—would have the biggest brains," Dawson said, "so when they crack open this degenerate's skull and see how big his brain is, it doesn't look like there's a major abnormality. There's no tumor, there's no nothing that points to why he would have done all of this. . . . It was very controversial at the time."[53]

These findings were made by an anatomist at Cornell University named Burt Green Wilder, who bought Rulloff's brain to study it[54]—making Rulloff's one of the first brains purchased for the first brain collection in America.[55] By comparing the brains of different people, Wilder learned some important truths—namely that, contrary to popular assumptions at the time, white men do not have bigger brains than women and people of color. Wilder had the literal brains to prove it. He compared Rulloff's brain with the brain of a mixed-race woman, the brain of an elite white philosopher, and the brain of someone with diagnosed mental illness. Wilder showed that structurally, they were largely identical. He was the first person of note to publicly say that the brains of people of color were in no way inferior. The Wilder Brain Collection is still housed at Cornell, a century and a half later, albeit there are only some seventy specimens that remain, out of more than six hundred.[56]

Rulloff has a special place in the collection, as his is the largest—and the only one that belonged to a serial killer.

Legal Legacy

Rulloff's case impacted the legal and scientific communities for myriad reasons. Among them:

- Previously, few questioned the "no body, no crime" precedent that had been passed down by Great Britain.[57]
- Rulloff's intelligence inspired some experts to testify on his behalf that he should not be executed because he was a unique specimen among criminals. Academic Richard Mather, who interviewed Rulloff in prison in 1871, argued that he was "worthy of further study."[58]
- Alienists of the day had long assumed criminality to be a sign of inferior intelligence—a belief that Rulloff's obvious smarts bucked. Not only did experts argue that this made a convicted murderer worth saving in an era in which hangings were standard sentences, but it also sparked culture's ongoing fascination with "genius" killers.

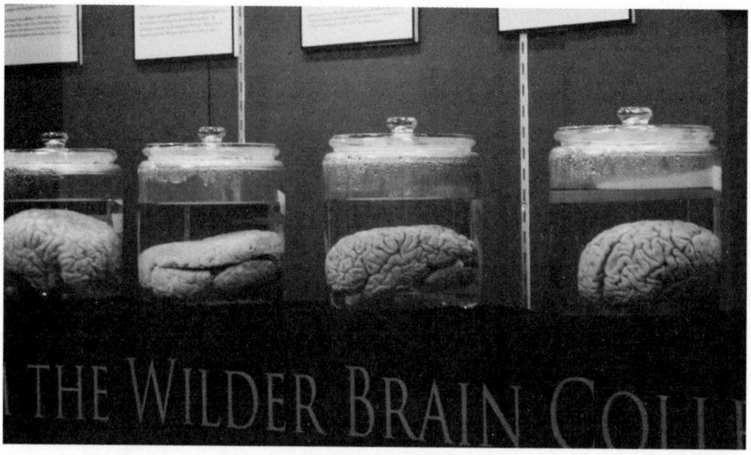

Brains on view at the Wilder Brain Collection exhibit at Cornell University. Edward Rulloff's brain is second from left.

17

The Beheading of Pearl Bryan

(1896)

One morning, a teenage farmhand was snipping dead branches off an apple tree when he spotted something odd on the ground below and went to investigate. Seventeen-year-old Johnny Hewling climbed down to discover a grisly sight: a pregnant woman's decapitated body.[1]

Hewling worked on a piece of land in Fort Thomas, Kentucky, in Campbell County—about five miles southeast of Cincinnati—owned by a farmer named James Locke. The Locke farm was in an odd, triangular shape that featured a steep hill covered with heavy underbrush. The headless body was discovered on the hill, down a bit from an old dirt road. This was in 1896, and horse-drawn carriages were the most common mode of transport. When the police arrived, they found the body lying on its stomach in a pool of blood, with arms outstretched. It appeared she had defensive wounds on her hands, suggesting she'd put up a fight against a sharp instrument—which the police assumed was the same sharp instrument used to separate her head from her body. While forensic science was still rudimentary, it had come along enough for investigators to feel comfortable determining that the woman had been killed where her body was found—and likely alive at the point of her decapitation.[2] The copious blood made for a gruesome scene.

Determining the victim's identity promised straight away to be a challenge. The body was clothed, but there was nothing distinctive about the dress. Given the location of the body near Newport, Kentucky—which once had the dubious reputation as America's first Sin City, before Las Vegas usurped the title—investigators initially assumed the woman must have been a sex worker. But then a shoe merchant noticed her shoes. He had no way of knowing that his observation would not only lead to the victim's identity, but it would unravel a complicated and shocking case that would enthrall the entire nation and lead two men to the gallows.

An illustration of L. D. Poock, a shoe dealer from Newport, Kentucky, who helped track down Pearl Bryan's identity. The portrait was included in a book Poock wrote about the case, called *Headless, Yet Identified: A Story of the Solution of the Pearl Bryan, or Fort Thomas Mystery, through Shoes* (1897).

"There was a shoe dealer named [L. D.] Poock in Newport when the body was found, and he noticed that her feet were exceptionally small," said Andrew Young, a writer and historian who wrote a book about the case called *Unwanted: A Murder Mystery of the Gilded Age* (2016).[3]

Poock looked at the victim's shoes after the body was transported to a Newport funeral home and noted that they were leather around the foot, topped with cloth. The merchant determined from a stamp inside the shoes that they came from a store called Louis & Hayes in Greencastle, Indiana.[4] Poock investigated further and found out that a lot of a dozen shoes had been made in Portsmouth, Ohio, and that the entire lot had been sold to Louis & Hayes, who in turn had sold nine pairs.[5] The store kept good records, so police began tracking down the buyers of each pair. They tracked the first eight, then reached the ninth pair, and found that they had been bought by a woman named Pearl Bryan in November 1895. They tried to find Pearl—quietly, because they didn't want to rumors to spread that she'd been found dead near Cincinnati—and learned she came from a good home and had left town a few days prior to visit family friends in Indianapolis. Interestingly, the shoes on the feet of the dead girl were a size 3 (the average women's shoe size at the time was around 3.5 to 4).[6] Pearl Bryan wore size 3 shoes.

Meanwhile, the gruesome discovery of a headless body made headlines far beyond Cincinnati, reaching all the way to Greencastle, about 150 miles away. Pearl's family read about the horrific crime, and something about the description of the corpse was even more unsettling. The body was described as having thin, seamstress-like hands with a small wart on one of the thumbs. Pearl sewed and had such a wart.[7] But she was supposed to be in Indianapolis, so they kept calm while sending a telegram to friends in Indiana's capital city. The calm broke when the friends replied that Pearl wasn't there and never had been.

While the pieces were falling together at Pearl's home, a friend of Pearl's second cousin was figuring things out, too. A. W. Early worked for Western Union in Greencastle and had an interesting relationship with a man named Will Wood, who happened to be related to Pearl Bryan.[8] The two men were close, so much so that Wood let Early read his correspondence, some of which was to and from Bryan. Early had read that Bryan was in love with a man in Cincinnati and that she'd become pregnant. He'd read that her lover had invited her to Cincinnati. He'd also read the family's Indianapolis-bound query of Pearl's whereabouts and the reply saying, no, Pearl was not in Indy.[9] With all this knowledge, Early went to the police and shared everything he knew. In one letter, Early told police, Bryan's lover asked Wood for help dealing with the trouble caused by him and Bryan having been "too intimate."

"He quoted recipes calculated to prevent evil results of their indiscretion, and asked Wood to get them and give them to Pearl. . . . These drugs did not have the desired effect."[10]

Pearl was the youngest daughter of a farmer in Greencastle. The family was well off, and Pearl taught Sunday school. Her home was described in one newspaper story as a rambling white mansion with green shutters, set back from the road behind a clump of pine trees.[11] Pearl had attended public school, graduating from Greencastle's high school in 1892.[12] She was said to be very pretty, with an oval face and blonde hair.[13] She was a sweet and sunny farmgirl who didn't really have close friends. She seemed to be too quiet and reserved to deeply connect with others, though as she got older, she drew more male attention. The newspaper states: "As a virtuous young woman, her reputation was never impugned until this flood of scandal."[14]

Back at the Locke farm, word had spread of the farmhand's horrific discovery, which drew all the townsfolk out as though on a grisly field trip. James Locke didn't want a horde of people trampling his land so he told Hewling, the farmhand, to amend his story of where he'd found the body and move it a bit up the hill, closer to the road, so people wouldn't be tromping on so much of Locke's land. This had the inadvertent benefit of better preserving the crime scene. Bloodhounds were brought in to try to track the scent. The dogs led detectives to the Covington Reservoir in Fort Thomas, which authorities then had drained in hopes of finding Pearl's head. It wasn't there.[15]

A coroner performed Pearl's autopsy and learned that Pearl had been five months pregnant, and that her fetus had likely been alive until Pearl died. The autopsy also found cocaine in her system.

When a pregnant woman is found dead, police tend to look for the baby's father first. That was just as true in 1896—especially for a case involving an unwed Sunday-school teacher. And finding that man didn't take them

long. It turned out that Pearl had been introduced by her second cousin, Will Wood, to an attractive, steely-eyed man named Scott Jackson about three years before her death. Scott came from a respectable family. His father was a well-known captain of a merchant vessel, while his mother volunteered at her church.[16] Scott's dad died when he was still young, though, causing him and his mother to move around. Eventually, Scott landed at a dental school in Indiana, and his mother moved to Greencastle. Scott moved to Cincinnati to continue his dental training, but he would travel back to Greencastle to visit his mother fairly regularly.[17]

He and Pearl became friendly, and they would meet up whenever Scott was back in town. At first, "friendly" just meant friendly, but sometime in 1895, it started to take on a more euphemistic meaning. After one of Scott's visits, Pearl made a "discovery," about which she confided in her cousin Will, and apparently no one else. She had no intention of keeping it a secret from the baby's father, however. She told Scott she was pregnant, in response to which he invited her to visit him in Cincinnati.

Will told police that he had explained to Pearl Scott's plan for a doctor and chemist to perform an "operation" to save the family from shame—news that, Will said, Pearl embraced. "I never saw her so happy in my life," Will later told officials. But it would seem that Pearl had understood that conversation differently. She arrived at the city's Central Union Station on January 28, 1896, a Tuesday night.[18]

It's not totally clear what happened once she got to Cincinnati, but witnesses over the next couple of days helped to at least provide pieces of the puzzle, even if they didn't all fit together perfectly. It seemed that when Scott Jackson suggested the family should be spared the shame her pregnancy would bring, they both agreed that would be best, but they didn't quite agree on how to do it. Pearl thought Scott was going to marry her. Scott, age twenty-eight to Pearl's twenty-two, apparently meant for Pearl to have the abortion and then move on with her life—without him.

Scott enlisted a friend he'd met at dental school named Alonzo Walling to help with the situation. Alonzo and Scott were seen several times with Pearl in various parts of the city, as police learned from witnesses. At one point soon after Pearl's arrival, the trio was spotted at Fourth and Elm arguing loudly. Workers at a business there said they overheard the men talking

This illustration from Poock's book *Headless, Yet Identified* shows Pearl Bryan getting into the coach with Scott Jackson and Alonzo Walling.

to Pearl about an abortion, but Pearl angrily shouted that she'd go back to Greencastle the next day, tell her brother what was happening, and he would see to it that "wrong was righted."[19] But Pearl didn't take the train out of town the next day. Instead, she stayed in Cincinnati and joined Scott and Alonzo that night at a tavern at Fourth and Plum. They started arguing again, and a porter said he saw one of the men putting something into Pearl's sarsaparilla. Later, a Black coachman or hack driver—the nineteenth-century equivalent of a cabdriver—said he picked up the trio in his hack at Fourth and Plum Streets in the evening. One man sat out front next to the driver. The other man sat in the carriage with a woman who was either very ill or drugged. She was moaning and in obvious pain. The men told the coachman to drive across the Ohio River into Kentucky, entering Newport at York Street. They gave him turn-by-turn directions, ultimately leading him to the Locke farm. The girl's steady moans became much louder, and she started crying, too. The coachman got scared. When the trio finally got out—the two men supporting the weight of the drugged or sick girl—the driver hightailed it away (see page 213). Pearl was never seen alive again.

The day her body was found, Alonzo and Scott had gone back to the tavern at Fourth and Plum and asked the bartender to hold onto a valise for them. The bartender noticed the bag was heavy and asked if it carried a bowling ball. The men didn't answer. Scott retrieved the bag the next night, then later brought it to a barber in town for safekeeping, though the valise was empty.[20]

Police were certain that these witness descriptions were pieces of a sinister puzzle coming together. They believed that Scott wanted Pearl dead because she refused to get an abortion and threatened to tell her family about her pregnancy and Scott's dereliction of fatherly duty. But the

investigators' suspicions were not enough. They needed to figure out how he did it, how he got Alonzo to help, and what they did with the victim's head.

Alonzo Walling and Scott Jackson were about as different in their personalities as two men can be. Scott was charming and outgoing, definitely a leader. He had an undeniable charisma that made him popular with young women.

"He was kind of a philanderer," said Andrew Young. "He was a party boy, and I think it's pretty obvious that he did not want to be tied down to Pearl, and he did not want to have a child."[21]

Scott had also been in his share of trouble. Before he enrolled in dental school, he worked in New Jersey opening mail in search of checks sent to the Pennsylvania Railroad. His job was to collect the checks, add them up, and deposit them into the railroad's accounts. His boss figured they had better use for that money, so he and Scott devised a scheme to steal some of the checks and split the money, most of which they spent at saloons and betting on horses. This was no petty theft, even by modern standards. They pocketed some $23,000[22]—the equivalent of more than $800,000 nowadays. Both Scott and his boss were arrested and charged, but the first trial ended in a hung jury. For the second trial, prosecutors had Scott testify against his boss in exchange for the charges being dropped against him. Scott did so, the boss was convicted, and Scott was set free. It was soon after that he enrolled in the Indianapolis dental school.[23]

Alonzo was far less outgoing. He was a few inches taller than Scott but carried himself as though he were much smaller. His father had died when he was three, leaving his mom with three young boys to raise. When Alonzo was old enough to work, he got hired in a glass factory to help support the family, while his mother put money aside for him to enroll in dental school.[24] It was there that he met Scott, though they didn't become friends at first. That happened later, when they happened to cross paths again in Cincinnati.

To people who had the opportunity to talk with both men, it seemed pretty evident that Alonzo was the follower and Scott, the leader. The two occasionally got into trouble for frequenting sex workers, but beyond that, they weren't known to be too extreme. Just two guys with a fairly common dynamic: one outgoing and popular with women, the other shy and less sure of himself.

At first, both men denied having killed Pearl, but it didn't take long for gathered evidence to suggest otherwise. A Cincinnati druggist named H. C. Uhlen told investigators he'd sold Scott seventeen grams of cocaine a few days before Pearl's body was found—a noteworthy admission, because cocaine indeed was found in Pearl's system.[25] (At the time, cocaine was sold at pharmacies without a prescription.) Additionally, the clothes Scott and Alonzo wore the night Pearl died were located in various spots—Scott's coat in a sewer, Alonzo's trousers in a locker at the Cincinnati dental college, which was near downtown—and every item found appeared to be spattered with blood.[26] The valise that Scott had asked a barber to hold onto the day Pearl's body was found—the bag that, when previously handed to a barkeep, felt like it might contain a bowling ball—was identified as Pearl's valise. Inside of it were blonde hairs and clots of blood.[27] Dirt found on the men's clothing looked the same as the dirt found on Locke's farm.

All of this was damning, but more evidence came four days after Pearl's murder, when Scott wrote Will a letter that ended up being read during his trial. In the letter, Scott told Wood to tell Pearl's family that she was tired of Indianapolis and had moved away to Chicago. He wrote, "Get that letter off without a second's delay—and burn this at once. . . . Be careful what you write me."[28] Police intercepted this letter and arrested Will as an accomplice to the murder, but he was soon freed. Another suspected accomplice was arrested soon after: a woman named Laura, or "Lulu," Hollingsworth (sometimes also called May),[29] who had stepped forward saying she had information about Pearl's last days.[30] She told investigators that one afternoon she had spotted Pearl at Cincinnati's Central Union Station. Lulu was boarding a train there, and Pearl had just arrived. Lulu said the encounter was at about 4:00 p.m. in the afternoon, and that during their talk, Pearl told her all about her pregnancy and the nerves accompanying it. Lulu said she gave Pearl a prescription to help her out of her condition, and that Pearl actually used that prescription to kill herself—a bold and interesting claim in a case in which the victim was beheaded. Lulu offered no explanation for how the woman's head disappeared after the supposed suicide.[31] Police deduced that Lulu was smitten with Scott, and they arrested her on suspicion of aiding in the murder. A day later, she was released after authorities felt satisfied she had nothing to do with it and had only inserted herself in the case in hopes of clearing Scott of suspicion.

"GET THAT LETTER OFF WITHOUT A SECOND'S DELAY—AND BURN THIS AT ONCE. . . . BE CAREFUL WHAT YOU WRITE ME."

4 THE INDIANAPOLIS SUNDAY STAR, MARCH 7, 1937.

MYSTERY IN PEARL BRYAN MURDER STILL UNSOLVED

Forty Years Ago Two Depraved Dental Students Paid Supreme Penalty on Kentucky Gallows for Crime—Concealing Forever Disposal of Indiana Girl's Head

By FRANK ROLANDELLI JR.

FORTY years ago this month two men paid with their lives for having murdered Pearl Bryan, Sunday school teacher and member of a prominent Greencastle (Ind.) family . . .

An *Indianapolis Sunday Star* article of March 7, 1937, looking back on the case; it featured photographs of Pearl Bryan (top), Scott Jackson (left), and Alonzo Walling (right), as well as an aerial map of the crime scene and the gallows where Jackson and Walling were executed.

Lulu managed to linger over the case like a sickly fog, however. At one point, she told police she had performed an abortion on Pearl the night before Pearl died. She said a hotel room had been rented, but Pearl refused to enter it. Instead, she permitted Lulu to perform the abortion on a stairway along Kentucky Avenue. At another point, without suggesting she herself had performed the abortion, Lulu said Pearl had undergone one and accidentally died because of it. Trouble was, according to the coroner, there'd been no abortion or even an apparent attempt. As described in an article in the *Chicago Chronicle* on February 12, 1896: "Two careful post-mortem examinations absolutely preclude abortion, natural or attempted, as well as death by poisoning. . . . The knife cuts on the poor girl's hand were made while struggling for life with her murderers, and the pool of blood where she lay set at rest the theory she was first killed by anesthetics and then taken out and beheaded."[32]

While Lulu's ramblings didn't shed much light, a station watchman was able to offer some info police considered valuable. Pat Kinney said he saw Alonzo and Pearl at the depot's waiting room on the afternoon of the murder.[33] Pearl was sobbing, he said. Alonzo seemed to be attempting to calm her. It was clearly a tough job, because Pearl cried bitterly for two or three hours, Kinney said. In the end, Alonzo's efforts apparently worked because the two walked out of the station at about 4:10 p.m. It would end up being Pearl's last day alive.

That final day seemed pretty normal to people who knew Scott and Alonzo. Aside from the lengthy detour to the train station, they kept their schedules pretty much the same as usual. They both went to class at the dental school that day, which was a Thursday. A porter named Allen Johnson ran into Alonzo and Scott later that night at the saloon,[34] and Pearl was with them. Johnson was used to seeing Scott with women, but this particular woman stood out because she was "not of the class that generally visited the saloon."[35] At one point, Pearl left the table and stayed in the ladies' room for about fifteen minutes. Scott asked the saloon owner, a man named Dave Wallingford, to borrow two dollars, and Wallingford obliged.[36]

Scott, Alonzo, and Pearl ate dinner. Scott ordered a whiskey for himself and a sarsaparilla for Pearl. He took the small vial of cocaine he'd bought at the pharmacy and emptied its contents into Pearl's beverage. He failed to be discreet about it. Pearl didn't notice, but the porter friend did and said he was willing to testify to it, despite being offered money by Scott's defense lawyer not to take the stand. The Black coachman also surfaced. His memories of the night Pearl died were vivid because he was highly uncomfortable with an ailing white woman moaning in his cab.[37]

"He was in fear that he could get blamed for it if something went wrong," Young told me, "so in his testimony, he said he pulled over in front of the distillery and wanted them to get out because he was scared, but they refused and told him to keep going. So he did, he went a couple miles farther, and he ended up in what is now the city of Fort Thomas."[38]

The driver was so unnerved that when he was told to stop, he started running. As he ran, he said he heard the woman scream once and then go silent. He was so scared that he kept running and left his horse and buggy behind.[39]

Police were certain Alonzo and Scott were responsible for Pearl's death and beheading, and they were confident they had enough evidence to convince a jury. But what they really wanted was Pearl's head. It was important to her family since they wanted to bury her whole. To that end, they made some truly bizarre choices. For example, they brought Scott and Alonzo to

the undertaker's office to see Pearl's body, where awaiting them were Pearl's sister, one of her brothers, and several police officials. Authorities hoped that seeing the headless corpse and hearing the family members sob and grieve might weigh on the men's consciences and loosen their tongues. Edward Black, the undertaker, later said the effort failed. "Jackson acted as if completely heartless," Black said. "He lowered his eyes when brought in the presence of the body. I could not discover one bit of evidence in his manner of any feeling."[40] Black thought Alonzo was a bit nervous, and neither man seemed able to meet Pearl's brother's gaze.

Police Chief Phil Deitsch wasn't content with just showing the men the body, though. He interrogated them, right then and there. They coolly agreed that the corpse appeared to be Pearl, but they insisted they had no idea what had happened to her. Pearl's sister fell to her knees, begging that they tell her where to find her sister's head. Neither answered.

Because this story was of such a high profile, reporters covering it were relentless. A *Cincinnati Enquirer* reporter named Edward Anthony went searching for Pearl's head in a sewer close to the death site. He didn't find the head, but he did find Scott Jackson's coat. It had been wrapped in a newspaper and was covered in blood. This reporter also misrepresented himself as an investigator to Alonzo. The published story read: "An *Enquirer* reporter was lucky enough to get into the cell room at the Central Station at 11:30 last night, and he went at once to Walling's cell." Anthony told Alonzo that it would be better for him to tell the truth. Alonzo, thinking he was speaking to an investigator being particularly nice to him, said: "You have treated me right, and I am going to tell you all I know about this affair." He told Anthony that Scott had been planning to kill Pearl since January, but plans had changed a few times in the interim. Originally, Scott planned to drug her with cocaine, then give her a fatal dose of arsenic mixed with cocaine. But then Alonzo heard him asking a doctor what method was the best way to kill a woman, and the doctor said an injection of hydrocyanic acid would kill a person before the needle could be drawn out. The acid is also called prussic acid because it was originally chemically isolated from Prussian blue pigment. A doctor told reporters that the acid was the deadliest poison known. "One drop will kill," he said. Alonzo said Scott found some of the acid but still tried the cocaine first. When it didn't work quickly enough, he apparently injected Pearl with the acid to hasten her death.[41]

Though officials believed that Scott and Alonzo were co-conspirators, the men had separate trials. The first, against Scott, came in April 1896, just three months after Pearl's death. To convince jurors that the body indeed belonged to Pearl, Pearl's sister identified her clothes and shoes. Jurors got to see the items up close, including her bloody dress and stained underwear. Both Pearl's sister and mother said they'd met Scott Jackson several times. They'd trusted him. Pearl often went on buggy rides with Scott. Fred Bryan—the older brother Pearl had threatened Scott with—removed any lingering doubt about the slain woman's identity when he pulled a key from his pocket and slipped it into a lock on the valise. The key fit, the lock clicked open. The valise, he explained, had actually been his first, as he had bought it five years earlier in Indianapolis. He never could have imagined it would one day carry his sister's head.[42]

The circumstantial evidence in the case wasn't as airtight as it would surely be today—they found blood, for example, but back then there was no way to test for blood type, much less DNA—so officials worked to put the bits and pieces together to form as solid a case as possible. Not only did the Cincinnati druggist testify that Scott had bought cocaine shortly before Pearl's death, but another witness testified about a strange conversation he'd heard regarding the drug. A doctor had met Scott through the dental school about six months before the murder. Ten days before Pearl's body was discovered, that doctor walked by a room where Alonzo and Scott were talking, and Scott beckoned him to come in. Scott said that he and Alonzo disagreed about something, and they were hoping the doctor might know the answer to the question they were pondering. They asked if one grain of cocaine diluted in a gram of water would have the same effect on someone ingesting it as a grain would if it was in one-half gram of water. Scott said he thought the effect would be the same on the cocaine consumer; Alonzo disagreed. The doctor, thinking it was just an oddball hypothetical conversation, said he thought the effects would be the same and went on his way.[43]

Also, there were the letters sent from Scott to Will Wood, the second cousin, that certainly suggested sinister plans. The letters were deemed by the judge to be vulgar, so he excused women from the courtroom before the jury heard their contents. As a wire story read: "These letters are too coarse and indecent to be printed."[44] One sentence read: "If you have let a chance go

by, I'll give you hell." Another read: "If you have grown chicken-hearted, you ought to be shot."

The evidence pointed to Scott having made plans, and Alonzo perhaps tagging along for the ride. The two were roommates, and Alonzo had supposedly performed several abortions for women in the past. Asked on the stand if he believed Scott when he prattled about his plans to murder Pearl, Alonzo said no. He didn't think the comments were "in earnest" and seemed certain that if Pearl's "condition" was remedied,[45] Scott would quit talking about doing something drastic to the young woman. Still, Alonzo maintained he hadn't played any role in Pearl's death. He'd simply been recruited to assist with the abortion, he said.[46]

In the end, separate juries convicted each man. Both were sentenced to death. The crime was so heinous and had enraged so many that the county sheriff worried about a lynching. In fact, soon after Scott and Alonzo were sentenced, crowds had surrounded the Newport jail where the two were being held; amid the commotion six inmates broke out, but Scott and Alonzo stayed put. They seemed to figure that if they busted out, they'd likely be handing themselves over to a lynch mob.[47]

The date of the hanging was March 20, 1897, fourteen months after the slaying. At the last minute—literally, because the hanging was scheduled for 9:00 a.m., and this happened just as the march to the scaffold began—Scott offered a confession that cleared Alonzo. He "wept like a child as he cried out that Walling was not guilty," a wire story said.[48] This move bought the men some time. The hanging was delayed for a few hours as the Kentucky governor William O'Connell Bradley conferred with the circuit court judge Charles Helm, who thought Scott's confession was a stalling tactic. Helm was tasked with getting Scott to offer proof that Alonzo was innocent, but also to let Scott know that he would hang either way. Scott soon recanted and said "he could not say that Walling was innocent."[49] The dual hanging was back on.

OPPOSITE: The crowd at the hanging of Jackson and Walling on March 20, 1897, in Newport, Kentucky; it was the last legal hanging in Campbell County.

The two men had separate traps beneath them but just one lever controlled the traps. Around 11:41 a.m., the lever was pulled, the traps opened, and the men violently dropped. Their necks did not break, newspaper coverage says. Rather, the men died slowly and painfully, writhing at the ends of their ropes until they suffocated. It was the last legal hanging in Campbell County.

des after Pearl's death, her gruesome fate continued to infuri-nate. Will Wood, Pearl's second cousin—who'd been briefly possible accomplice in her death—had a cloud of suspicion him for the rest of his life. People thought him responsible not lucing Pearl and Scott, but for encouraging Pearl to visit Scott. rly, the Western Union worker whose tip to police helped solve his job and had to move.[50] While he was initially praised as a ging forth information leading to Pearl's killers, people turned se they decided that, having read all the pertinent correspon-Pearl's death, he should have known something was afoot but vene or alert anyone. Maybe if he'd done something, the angry soned, Pearl never would have gone to Cincinnati.[51] Early's aim a $500 reward for assisting in the case were ultimately only key player in the case whose reputation was never at risk store owner named Poock, who spotted the shoes on the feet nd ultimately ensured she didn't die in anonymity.

Legal Legacy

The murder of Pearl Bryan would go down in history as one of the most-covered homicides in the media. Aside from the sensational elements of the case, it remains noteworthy because:

- Shoe dealer Poock's tactic of helping identify the headless victim through her shoes earned him praise for his creative sleuthing and inspired other detectives to look for similar clues at crime scenes.[53]
- The headlines surrounding Poock's assistance in the case prompted others looking for answers in separate investigations to find outside experts and hire independent private eyes, a relatively new procedure in the era.
- Jackson's and Walling's deaths marked the last legal hanging in Campbell County, Kentucky.[54]

18

Leopold and Loeb: The Evidence that Felled Them

(1924)

The University of Michigan at Ann Arbor (UM) is home to one of the most beautiful college campuses in the country—with one of the best reputations. Arthur Miller studied there. So did Gilda Radner and Madonna[1] and a number of Nobel and Pulitzer Prize winners whose names aren't as well known but who are certainly very accomplished. When the University of Michigan recruits new students, those names come up pretty often.

But there's one alumnus the university doesn't seem to flaunt: In 1923, a seventeen-year-old boy named Richard Loeb graduated from UM as the college's youngest graduate in history.[2] This was a kid who was so smart, he'd graduated from high school at age fourteen. If he'd lived up to the potential he clearly must have had, maybe UM would have a building named after him. Instead, officials there largely act like he never existed because the year after graduation, Loeb and his best friend—another incredibly intelligent, promising young man named Nathan Leopold—became two of the most notorious criminals in the world.[3]Their case not only made headlines worldwide and inspired more crime stories than one can count, but it also brought to the national stage a legendary lawyer who fought to save the boys' lives.

Nathan and Richard both came from rich families living among Chicago's elite. The two, separated in age by seven months (Nathan was the older) met around 1920,[4] and found they both were "precocious intellectually," according to Paula Fass, a professor at the University of California, Berkeley and award-winning author of *Kidnapped: Child Abduction in America* (1997).[5]

Leopold wasn't a record breaker when he graduated from high school at fifteen, but he was nationally regarded as an expert ornithologist and was reportedly proficient in fifteen languages.[6] He graduated from college around the same time as his friend Loeb, though Leopold's alma mater was the University of Chicago.[7]

Both boys were raised in mansions by parents who were incredibly loose with their purse strings. If the children wanted something, they simply asked and their wish was granted. Case in point: There were 17 million people with car registrations out of a population of 114 million in 1924, yet both boys had access to cars.[8] Leopold's was a red Willys-Knight,[9] which newspapers at the time said typically cost between $1,400 and $2,200.[10] Adjusted for inflation, that's the equivalent of between $22,000 and $37,000 today.

Despite their many superficial overlaps, when the two first met, they didn't click right away. Their backgrounds might've been similar, but their personalities were anything but. Loeb was charming and quick to smile. People who knew him said he had the kind of charisma a camera just couldn't capture. Leopold, on the other hand, was standoffish. He had a closed, brooding air about him, accentuated by a near-unibrow that gave him a darker look.

Their upbringings weren't identical, either. Loeb was the son of wealthy lawyer Albert Henry Loeb, who had retired as vice president of Sears, Roebuck & Co.,[11] then a hugely successful mail-order catalog company. (The physical stores started appearing in 1925.)[12] Alfred and his wife, Anna, had four children. Richard Loeb was third in line. He'd been a somewhat sickly child, catching mumps and measles and whooping cough, which meant he was stuck indoors a lot.[13] When he was four, his family hired a governess named Emily Struthers, who would become an incredibly strong force in his life.[14] She caught on quickly that Loeb was inherently quite smart, so she pushed him academically. She tutored him herself, admonishing him when he wanted to go outside and play with other kids. She was mentally domineering and manipulative, feeding into his paranoia that he was the least liked of his parents' children.[15]

Loeb's means of escape was his imagination. He grew up pretending to be both lawman and criminal.[16] He supposedly invented hand signals that he'd flash to an imaginary gang while he walked around town. Sometimes he packaged his fantasies as bedtime stories that he'd tell his teddy bear.[17] By the time he was twelve, he was allowed to sit with the adults during dinner parties because he could handle mature conversation. At one of those dinners, he showed a business partner of his dad's a copy of *Richard's Magazine*, which Loeb had created and written, according to author John Theodore in the book *Evil Summer* (2007).[18] Loeb—called "Dickie" by his family and few friends—penned an editorial about how awful it was that so much money was spent on war and death. "Think if that amount of money was spent daily in the beautifying of the world," he wrote.[19] His father's friend was so impressed that he mailed the magazine to former president Theodore Roosevelt, who happened to be a friend. Roosevelt sent Dickie a handwritten note in May 1906 that read: "It does me good to see young men of your stamp growing up in this country."[20]

When Loeb graduated from the University of Michigan, his father was so proud of him that he built a miniature nine-hole golf course on their property at 5017 South Ellis Avenue in Chicago's Kenwood neighborhood. That land also had a tennis court.[21]

Leopold was similarly doted on by his parents, yet had a much harder time charming other adults in his life. He was a junior, named after his father, who'd been born in Michigan. Leopold Sr. had worked as president of the Manitou Steamship Co. before buying the Morris Paper Mill, where he earned a reputation as a union buster. He'd married a woman named Florence Foreman in 1892.[22] The couple had three children, of whom Nathan was the youngest, having succeeded brothers Mike and Sam. Leopold was gifted, a child prodigy even. Academics seemed to come more naturally to him than they did to Loeb, but so did arrogance. Unlike Loeb, he wasn't raised mostly by a governess. He apparently loved his mother, who called Nathan by the nickname "Babe." She died in 1921,[23] when Leopold was sixteen.

After Leopold graduated from the University of Chicago, he set his sights on law school and was already teaching ornithology. Everyone assumed he would have a brilliant career.

Loeb and Leopold eventually warmed up to each other, in part because they bonded over their shared fascination with crime—specifically committing crimes and getting away with it. Loeb had started solo and small, shoplifting here and there and setting small fires. Once he and Leopold joined forces, things went up a notch. That they were sexually attracted to each other only added fuel to the already volatile partnership. Both had had sex with girls, and both seemed pretty unimpressed by it. That was a tough thing to admit in the early 1900s, when being gay would cause a scandal for an affluent family.

An undated family photograph of young Bobby Franks.

Rumors began circulating that the two were sexually involved. Those rumors circled back to the boys' parents, who tried to split the pair up, but the two were like magnets of opposite poles. Soon, they were increasing the scope of their illegal adventures, though Leopold was getting impatient. On the way back from robbing Loeb's University of Michigan fraternity—a long drive that only netted them some $80 and a typewriter—Leopold complained that their escapades were too small-scale and their relationship too one-sided. Looking to appease him, Loeb got an idea: What if we raised the stakes?

That's when another young boy entered the story. Unlike Leopold and Loeb, Bobby Franks wasn't a loner. He came from a wealthy family, as they did, and also had a prominent father. Jacob Franks was a retired industrialist who'd once been president of the Rockford Watch Company and was respected in academic circles, having served as president of the Chicago Public Library. Jacob's wife was a woman named Flora, who gave birth to three children: a girl named Josephine and two boys, Robert and Jacob Jr.[24]

While Bobby wasn't a prodigy like Leopold and Loeb, he was very bright and had a promising future, according to Paul Durrica, the director of exhibitions at the Newberry Library in Chicago, who began giving walking tours of the case in 2008.[25] One of the spots on Durrica's tour has been the Franks' stately 10,000-square-foot home on South Ellis down the street from the Loeb mansion, which still stood as of this writing. Bobby, fourteen, was Loeb's second cousin; he and Loeb had even played tennis on Loeb's court.[26] This connection surely played a role in Bobby's choice to climb into a car with Leopold and Loeb on May 21, 1924, after the two pulled up alongside him as he walked home from school around 5:00 p.m.[27]

The next morning, the body of a teenage boy was discovered stuffed into a culvert beneath the Pennsylvania Railroad tracks at 118th Street. It'd been spotted by a man named Tony Minke, who saw something odd near Wolf Lake out of the corner of his eye as he walked to a watch repair shop.[28] It was a sight he'd never forget. The body was nude, the face and genitals deformed by acid. Minke found a policeman, and an inquest was underway.[29]

Investigators scoured the area around the culvert, where they found a wool sock and a pair of glasses.

Meanwhile, across town, a man who identified himself as George Johnson called Bobby's house and assured his mother that Bobby was safe and that a letter would arrive soon to explain everything.[30] At noon the next day, Jacob Franks received a typewritten ransom note, which began: "As you no doubt know by this time, your son has been kidnapped. Allow us to assure you that he is at present well and safe. You need fear no physical harm for him provided you live up carefully to the following instructions and such otherwise you will receive by future communications. Should you, however, disobey any of our instructions, even slightly, his death will be the penalty."[31] The kidnappers then said they wanted $10,000, a paltry sum for Jacob Franks, who was worth about $4 million at the time.[32]

Though the kidnappers had insisted that the police not be notified, Jacob Franks was no fool. He and his lawyer, Samuel Ettelson, notified the police straightaway, albeit discreetly. Franks was fully prepared to pay the ransom.[33] He had actually gathered the money as directed, in the denominations specified, and got a phone call that afternoon instructing him to hop in a cab that would be sent to him and go to a drugstore on 63rd Street, where he and the kidnappers would meet up. The money would be exchanged, thus saving Bobby's life. It probably sounded like a simple enough plan, but as willing as Franks was to follow the instructions, the experience was traumatizing, which made it hard for Franks to think clearly. He forgot the address he was supposed to go to, stalling his departure. One of the kidnappers soon called a drugstore at 1465 E. 63rd Street and asked for Mr. Franks. Percy van de Bogert, a druggist, answered, checked around and said, sorry, no Mr. Franks here. Ten minutes later, he did it again when the kidnapper called once more.[34]

Meanwhile, Franks was still at home, where the police had intercepted him and broken horrific news. A body had been found about 8:00 that morning in a culvert. It seemed to be a teenage boy's body. Jacob Frank's brother-in-law went to the morgue to see the body and called Jacob with the wrenching confirmation—it was Bobby.

Leopold and Loeb never expected Bobby Frank's remains to be found so quickly, but they thought they'd built in a fail-safe regardless. The acid

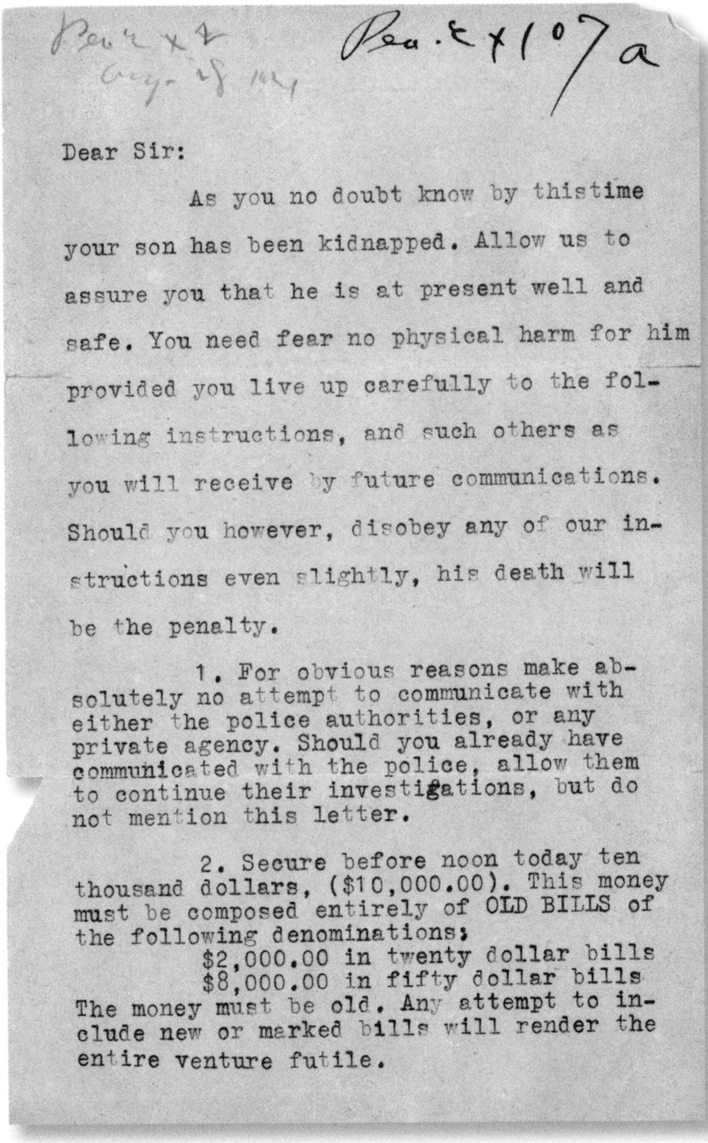

Peo. Ex 107a

Dear Sir:

As you no doubt know by thistime your son has been kidnapped. Allow us to assure you that he is at present well and safe. You need fear no physical harm for him provided you live up carefully to the following instructions, and such others as you will receive by future communications. Should you however, disobey any of our instructions even slightly, his death will be the penalty.

1. For obvious reasons make absolutely no attempt to communicate with either the police authorities, or any private agency. Should you already have communicated with the police, allow them to continue their investigations, but do not mention this letter.

2. Secure before noon today ten thousand dollars, ($10,000.00). This money must be composed entirely of OLD BILLS of the following denominations;
$2,000.00 in twenty dollar bills
$8,000.00 in fifty dollar bills
The money must be old. Any attempt to include new or marked bills will render the entire venture futile.

Ransom note mailed by the kidnappers to Jacob Franks, postmarked May 21, 1924.

applied to Bobby's face and genitals was supposed to conceal his identity enough to ensure that it would take police some time to identify the corpse. As it turned out, Leopold and Loeb weren't as smart as they thought they were, and everyone else wasn't as stupid—an irony, because the whole point of their crime was to prove that they were so brilliant that they could get away with murder.

This case is where the term "thrill kill" comes from. It's also generally recognized as the first clear-cut "affluenza" case.[35] Leopold and Loeb were so convinced that they could get away with murder that they hatched a plan on the way back from the frat house burglary the two committed in October 1923. Although Loeb later said that the two had taken "everything we could get our hands on,"[36] Leopold had found that caper underwhelming. He was upset because there was no way the theft of $80 and a typewriter would make it into the newspapers. Plus, he and Loeb had a sort of quid pro quo going that he often felt was one-sided. What precisely happened the day the teens approached Bobby will always be subject to debate because while the duo eventually confessed, their versions differed in a few key ways. Explained Durrica: "In Leopold's version, he's the person driving the car and Richard Loeb is in the backseat. In Loeb's confession, he's the person driving the car and Leopold is in the backseat."[37]

Only Leopold and Loeb knew for certain the way things went down, but most historians believe it happened like this: Loeb was the one hungry for thrills, so he often planned the crimes that the pair would commit. Loeb would entice Leopold to join him by promising sex afterward. Sometimes they'd run into obstacles, prompting Loeb to push off the plans, which meant delaying the sex. Other times, he'd engage in sex despite the planned caper not having been committed, but Loeb would be less than enthusiastic about the encounter. Loeb's standoffishness would disappoint Leopold, who wanted to do something that would forge a special, unbreakable bond between the two.

Their recent college graduation was also a factor. Leopold had been accepted to Harvard Law School, which he planned to start after spending the summer tooling around Europe. If they did something together that would forever bond them, the two could be sure that even if long periods of time passed in which they didn't see each other, they'd be connected by this deed, this caper, that only they knew about. They soon hatched a plan to kill someone. They would prove themselves the intellectual gods they believed themselves to be by committing the ultimate crime without getting caught. And it wouldn't weigh on their consciences because—as Friedrich Nietzsche believed (see page 231)—morality is arbitrary, so there would be nothing to feel guilty about.

To pull off the ruse, they created a fictional character named Morton Ballard, a traveling salesman from Peoria, Illinois.

"They would check out hotel rooms in his name, most often at the Morrison Hotel," Durrica said. Usually, Loeb would check in as Ballard, bring a suitcase full of books from the University of Chicago library to imply that "Ballard" would be intending to stay a while, and they would get in the habit of renting an automobile in Ballard's name. They even sent letters addressed to Ballard at the hotel.[38] That way, when they decided to ultimately commit the crime, they had a false identity in place that would allow them to rent a car and assemble other resources without garnering a lot of suspicion.

Their victim would be young—for maximum news coverage—they decided.[39] They would stage it as a kidnapping, knowing full well that they intended to kill their victim no matter the response to their ransom note. In fact, the note sent to Bobby Frank's father wasn't personalized because they'd written it in advance and weren't sure who their victim would be. That's how cold and calculated this plan was.

"We don't care who," Loeb would later explain in rambling confessions.[40] "Hey, why not my kid brother Tommy? We know his dad has money. Plenty of boys in Kenwood fit the bill."

They'd even done dry runs during the planning phase, which lasted seven months. The day they finally chose to do it, they had first cased a boys' school, where Loeb talked to one possible victim, a boy named John Levinson. They stalked Levinson as he went to play with friends, and Loeb even looked up the boy's last name in the phone book at a drugstore to get his mailing address, but eventually they lost the trail. It just so happened that they then encountered Bobby Franks walking home alone after school.[41]

After Bobby's body was found, the newspaper reporters were relentless. This was an era of morning and afternoon papers, of *Extra! Extra!* bulldog editions. That Bobby was from a prominent family with a rich father definitely played into the coverage. A front-page story in the *Chicago Daily Tribune* ran May 24, 1924, with a cartoon of the bad guy reading headlines and trembling because authorities were closing in. Inside the newspaper was a full page of one story after another: "Franks Inquest Awaits Report from Chemist." "Queries Race Theories Based on Boy Murder." "Kidnappers' Ransom Letter Shows Hand of Expert Letterer."[42] Those headlines were

precisely what Leopold and Loeb wanted. Loeb actually said later that he'd started to feel a little bad about what he'd done the night he did it, but when he saw the headlines, wow, what a thrill.

The theories that first day were all over the map: Chicago chief of detectives Michael Hughes told the *Tribune* that ransom really had been the motive. He said: "After a hard day's work on the Franks mystery, I am convinced tonight that it was a plain case of kidnapping for ransom, not a case of a victim of perverts." The coroner agreed.[43]

Others thought maybe little Bobby was killed because some kids were upset with how he had umpired a recent ball game.

Another theory was that Bobby was only targeted to inflict pain upon his father, who must have wronged someone.

Various suspects were considered. For example, because the ransom note had been written so headily, the principal and a few instructors at a local Harvard-connected college preparatory school were dragged in for questioning. Investigators thought maybe one of them had kidnapped the boy for money and things went bad. Detectives also considered that the killers might live in the neighborhood where Franks's body was found. It was not nearly as posh as Kenwood, where rich kids like Leopold and Loeb lived. The coroner even said: "I am having a check made on a disorderly house in that vicinity to get a roster of the patrons. If the killer is a degenerate, he may have frequented the house I have in mind."[44]

For all the theories, there weren't a lot of clues. The sock found near Bobby was his. And the coroner assumed the glasses were, too—but then Bobby's father set him straight. Bobby didn't wear glasses. And this is where the pieces all started falling together.

The frame on the pair of glasses discovered was ordinary. It was horn-rimmed and had round lenses, kind of like the ones the old silent film star Harold Lloyd wore. The prescription of the lenses was also common. But what wasn't common was the hinge connecting the arms to the rims. It had been patented and manufactured by a New York company with only one Chicago distributor: Almer Coe & Co.[45] Detectives went to that oculist and learned they'd sold just three pairs of glasses with that hinge. One belonged to a woman who still had hers, another belonged to a lawyer who was traveling in Europe at the time, and the third had been sold to Nathan Leopold.

Six months before the killing—so after they concocted the scheme, but before they'd started their dry runs—Leopold was getting headaches that he decided were probably from eyestrain. He went to an optometrist, got a prescription, ordered a pair of glasses, and wore them for a few weeks. The headaches went away, so Leopold mostly stopped wearing them. On the day of the kidnapping, he'd retrieved them to ensure he'd be able to spot potential prey from a distance.[46] They had slipped out of his pocket while he helped stuff Bobby into the culvert.

Leopold saw his glasses mentioned in the paper and knew right away they were his. He called Loeb and suggested that he should go to the police to claim them. He knew that area well, after all, because he genuinely had gone there to go birding before. He told Loeb they'd be easy to explain away. But he also told Loeb he didn't think they were traceable, what with such a common prescription and all, and Loeb advised him to keep his mouth shut. "Don't get mixed up in the case at all," Loeb said. "They might try some rough stuff on you. And besides, it might take you a hell of a while to talk your way out of it. You've got your exams coming up."[47]

This quote above comes from a memoir Leopold later wrote, *Life Plus 99 Years* (1958), and if it's accurate, it's pretty ironic. Because Loeb had already inserted himself into the case more than once. He visited the Franks home, talked to the father at the boy's inquest, helped detectives locate the drugstore from which the mysterious "Mr. Johnson" called, and urged police that they follow every clue to catch the "fiendish" slayer. He was absolutely certain that their plan had been flawless, so he could afford to interject himself into the case.

Because of the unique hinge, police were at Leopold's door within two days of Bobby's death. They weren't suspicious of him yet, but he didn't know that. They had asked around and heard he'd been birding in that area fairly often, so their thinking was that he might be able to tell them who else frequented the place. But when one of the officers asked Leopold whether he wore glasses, Leopold said, "No, sir, I don't."[48] That lie shattered everything. When officers called him on it, he

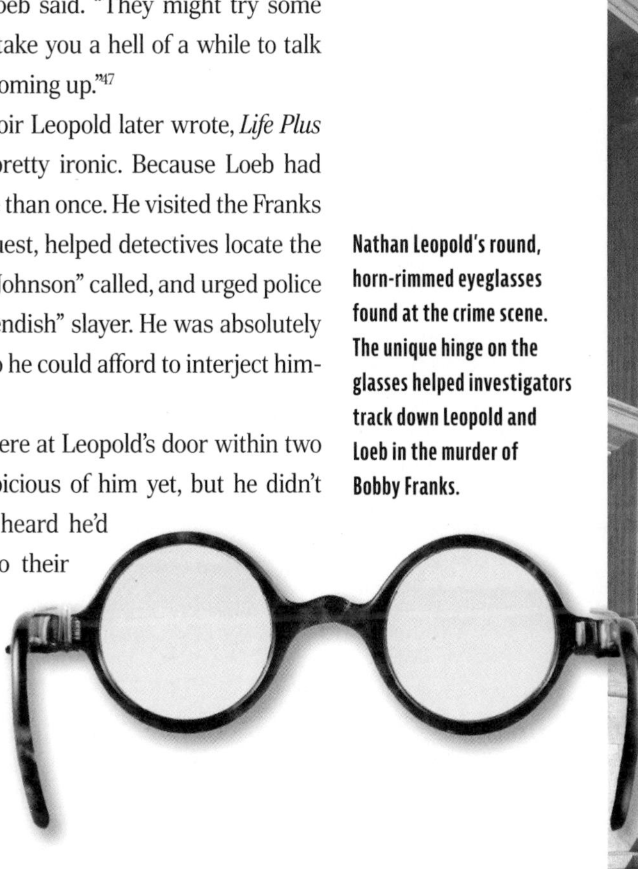

Nathan Leopold's round, horn-rimmed eyeglasses found at the crime scene. The unique hinge on the glasses helped investigators track down Leopold and Loeb in the murder of Bobby Franks.

changed his story quickly, and then offered an alibi for the day of the murder. The cover story he came up with included Loeb. He said that the two had met and picked up two girls the night of the murder. They partied a bit, then the girls had to go, but the boys didn't drive them all the way home. They dropped them off somewhere en route because the girls said they'd walk the rest of the way. They told the cops they didn't get the girls' last names. They weren't concerned with making the alibi particularly convincing because with no evidence to connect them to the crime, they figured they'd be fine.[49]

> "IT WAS A GAME THAT THEY HAD CONSTRUCTED, WHICH WAS IN SOME WAYS... AS IMPORTANT TO THEM AS THE ACTUAL MURDER ITSELF."

But their plan had been incredibly complex, requiring them to tool around town renting a car and hotel room under that Morton Ballard pseudonym, which they'd done to avoid suspicion—but the plan backfired. The more they were out and about, the more opportunity people had to see them. And they weren't strangers to the neighborhood. They chose their neighborhood on purpose because they wouldn't stand out to anyone when planning or doing the deed, but that also meant that people who spotted them didn't see a pair of average-looking guys whose faces they'd soon forget. They saw Babe and Dickie, as they were known.

"They were basing it all on this detective fiction that they had read," Paula Fass told me. "It was a game that they had constructed, which was in some ways . . . as important to them as the actual murder itself. It was all part of what they saw as a game, an elaborate, almost intellectual game."[50]

But the game hadn't gone as planned. Their intent was to kidnap their victim, take him somewhere secluded, and then Leopold and Loeb would each hold one end of a garrote to strangle him to death.[51] That way, they were both equally culpable, and their bond was ensured. They used ether on Bobby to incapacitate him, but it didn't knock him out. They bashed him in the head with the handle of a chisel to finish rendering him unconscious but that drew blood, which threatened to leave evidence in the car tying them to the crime. In a panic, one of the teens shoved a chloroform-soaked rag into Bobby's mouth and crammed his body into the trunk of the car.

When Leopold and Loeb reached their planned murder site, they opened the trunk and found Bobby had already died. He'd suffocated on the rag they'd jammed down his throat.

Their panic over Bobby's head wound bleeding was rendered ludicrous when analyzing the many blunders the teens made in committing their so-called perfect crime. So many people had witnessed various portions of the scheme. A Rent-a-Car employee recognized Leopold when shown a photo of the man who'd rented a car under the name Morton Ballard. A night watchman happened to notice an object thrown from a car as it sped by. He went to investigate and found the chisel, covered in blood. He'd gotten a decent look at the car and filed a police report before Bobby was even discovered. Another witness had been driving by the culvert that night and had spotted two men matching the duo's general descriptions—which wouldn't have meant much on its own, but it served to bolster the investigators' case once a theory had been developed.

The Leopolds' chauffeur saw them cleaning blood from the rental car and, having been told the stain was red wine, offered to help them. The boys declined. That chauffeur also said he was certain the family car had never left the garage that night. Ironically, that was the detail that helped seal their fate because the car in question was the same vehicle Leopold and Loeb had told police they'd been driving and partying in on the night of the murder. Their alibi was shredded.

The boys then decided that the smart thing to do would be to save their own hides. Each confessed, though both pinned the actual murder on the other. Their confessions went beyond words; the boys literally walked investigators through the crime by walking the physical paths they'd taken. The nation was shocked, but in Chicago especially, this crime was incomprehensible. The Loeb name was famous in the city. The family had a reputation as builders and leaders in philanthropy, charity, and educational movements. Loeb's uncle had been president of the board of education.

"It's a damned lie!" Loeb's friend Richard Rubel was quoted saying in the *Chicago Tribune*. "I'm Dick Loeb's best friend and he couldn't have done it!" The story—which, incidentally, was written by Maurine Watkins, who went on to pen the play *Chicago*, the basis for the famed musical—described Loeb's magnificent home with a garage stocked with a "limousine, sedan, coupe, [and] touring car," not to mention that golf course and tennis court. Rubel said: "Why, those boys could have had all the money in the world! Why should they do that?"[52]

Leopold's and Loeb's parents didn't believe it, either. Leopold's father called any suspicion cast upon his son "groundless," but nobly said the

family would endure the scrutiny "for the sake of justice and truth." "The affair will so easily straighten itself out," Loeb's mother told a reporter. "The idea of Nathan having anything to do with the Franks boy's death is too silly to discuss," added an older brother. "We know so well where he was that night, we know our brother so well, that we are in no way alarmed at his examination by police."[53]

That faith was undermined by the boys' own confessions, which were eventually detailed in an account by Richard Loeb published in 1925 in the *Journal of Criminal Law and Criminology*.[54] The article filled in most of the blanks, though it didn't do much to help people better understand the motive.

Just two months after Bobby's death, Leopold and Loeb were tried for murder and kidnapping. The trial lasted four weeks. Because the defendants weren't short on cash, they hired one of the greatest trial lawyers in American history: Clarence Darrow, who attended the University of Michigan decades before Loeb's stint there.[55] Darrow had started his career representing large corporations, which paid well but was unfulfilling. He then started representing unions instead. In 1896, he ran for the Senate but lost. After that, he moved on to criminal defense. He was convinced that too many lives had been ruined because suspects often had shoddy lawyers. He tried more than one hundred murder cases, losing only one, which helped him gain nationwide fame.[56]

But no case had ever drawn as much publicity as Leopold and Loeb's would. The common assumption was that Darrow would go for an insanity defense. After all, who in their right mind would set out to kill just to prove they could? But Darrow didn't think they were insane. He thought they were maladjusted, and that they got that way through no fault of their own.

Darrow laid out for the judge how the boys had been raised, how so much emphasis put on intellect caused them to be emotionally stunted—how, really, when you looked at the whole picture, this end result was basically inevitable. Darrow adamantly opposed the death penalty, and, in one of the most revered and studied closing arguments in history, he laid out over three days why he thought they should be spared.

That sounds like a lot of talking, and it surely was, but back then, there was no nightly news designed for minuscule attention spans. Newspapers weren't as stingy with their pages; they'd sometimes reprint whole speeches

Nathan Leopold, left, and Richard Loeb, right, meet with defense attorney Clarence Darrow, center, to discuss their defense, June 4, 1924.

verbatim. Darrow was an excellent orator, it was one of the things that made him famous, and people only knew he was an excellent orator because they read what he said.

Darrow argued: "I'm pleading for the future, not merely for these boys, but for all boys, for all the young I'm pleading, not for these two lives, but for life itself for a time when we could learn to overcome hatred with love, and we can learn that all life is worth saving."[57]

Darrow argued that Loeb's domineering nanny, Emily Struthers, had inadvertently robbed him of childhood friends. She dictated what he did, who he saw, and what he read. Loeb rebelled, as all kids do, but his way was to read detective magazines on the sly. He retreated into a world of fantasy because he had no other outlet. His parents weren't unloving. They did love him. That's why they gave him everything he asked for. But he needed boundaries and, more than anything, he needed guidance.

Leopold, on the other hand, was too smart for his own good. While Loeb was reading about cops and robbers and fantasizing about being the latter, Leopold was adopting an unhealthy view of life thanks to his readings of Friedrich Nietzsche. Darrow said: "Nietzsche held a contemptuous, scornful attitude to all those things which the young are taught as important in life; a fixing of new values which are not the values by which any normal child has ever yet been reared."[58] Loeb took the writings seriously. He became obsessed not just with the philosophy, but with proving himself what Nietzsche called an Übermensch—a superman. And being a superman meant suppressing normal human emotion and abiding by a moral code counter to that of society.

"Their legal team was very shrewd and trying to invert that perspective and make them not superheroes, which is how they presented themselves, but rather pathetic little boys who had never grown out of the traumas of their childhood," Fass said. "Darrow, in his summation to the judge, made it even deeper because he blamed it all on the reaction of American youth to the war."[59]

Clarence Darrow during his epic twelve-hour closing argument during the trial of Leopold and Loeb (both seated behind Darrow, center right)—one of the most famous arguments in US legal history, August 25, 1924.

This was just a few years after World War I, during which some 40 million people died, both civilian and military. Even though Leopold and Loeb weren't in the war, the effects of that trauma went beyond the people who saw it firsthand. It affected how people valued life and set their priorities and raised their kids.

Darrow's argument is full of eloquent and passionate quotes, such as: "For God's sake, are we crazy? In the face of history, of every line of philosophy, against the teaching of every religionist and seer and prophet the world has ever given us, we are still doing what our barbaric ancestors did when they came out of the caves and the woods."

Another: "Great wealth often curses all who touch it."

And another: "This world has been one long slaughterhouse from the beginning until today, and killing goes on and on and on, and will forever. Why not read something, why not study something, why not think instead of blindly shouting for death? Kill them. Will that prevent other senseless boys or other vicious men or vicious women from killing? No! It will simply call upon every weak-minded person to do as they have done."[60]

This case was not the one that Darrow lost. His skilled oration saved the boys' lives. After contemplating for two weeks, Judge John R. Caverly sentenced them to life in prison, plus ninety-nine years. He said he made his choice in part because of their ages, but he also wanted them spared to be studied.

Additionally, he thought being behind bars for the rest of their lives was a greater punishment than death. They were smart enough to know how things should have been—*would* have been, had they not screwed everything up.

The two both were moved to the Joliet Penitentiary. Prison officials at first tried to keep them apart, but they were still drawn to each other, and after several years, the officers just gave up. For the next ten years, they remained objects of fascination, averaging more than a headline a week in Illinois—including a series in 1927 related to another alleged kidnapping. The two were sued by a former Chicago taxicab driver named Charles Ream who accused them of kidnapping and mutilating him the November before Bobby's death.[61]

Those court hearings drew crowds of girls swarming to catch glimpses of Loeb, and as Ream tried to convince a court he was owed $100,000 for his pain and suffering, he and Leopold laughed. "I never saw this man until this trial was in progress. I never held him up, robbed him or harmed him in any way, or assisted in harming him."[62] The jury deliberated for twenty-four hours and took thirty ballots. They leaned toward not guilty 8–4. Though it seems likely in hindsight that their accuser was an opportunist, he was at least a persistent one. He planned to file another suit, but Leopold's and Loeb's families settled out of court to make him go away.[63]

Most of the headlines were far more mundane, though: when Loeb transferred jobs in prison, when they passed the five-year mark behind bars, when they celebrated their birthdays, it made headlines. In June 1925, when Loeb got deliriously sick with the measles at the same time Leopold was operated on for appendicitis, it was front-page news across the country.[64]

Then, in January 1936, Loeb's cellmate—a 23-year-old man named James Day convicted of grand larceny—slashed him with a razor.[65] Reports of the time variously describe the slashing as occurring near the prison dining hall or in the shower room.

Loeb staggered into the corridor, bleeding, before he collapsed. Prison physicians rushed to him, as did the warden. When they realized the severity of the wounds—he had been slashed nearly fifty-eight times—they allowed Leopold to be at Loeb's side. "I'm all right, Warden; I'll pull through," Loeb was reported to have whispered.[66] After the time of death was called, Leopold was left alone with the body. He washed away the blood caked on his friend.[67] An inquiry followed to determine how the slaying could have happened, which

Leopold wouldn't help. James Day said Loeb had been coming on to him and he got tired of it. Day was indicted for murder, but a trial jury believed his story of self-defense, and he was acquitted in June 1936.[68]

Richard Loeb was thirty years old when he died. All the potential that his parents and tutors had seen in him amounted to nothing more than family heartache and shame. He had been the youngest graduate in University of Michigan history. Leopold never quite recovered from Loeb's death. If he'd been certain at some point that the two of them were destined for greatness because of their supposed status as intellectuals, watching that greatness drain from his friend's body must have been a rude awakening. They were but mortal after all. Loeb's death hollowed him. He began to consider how Bobby's family must feel.[69]

When he appeared alone in newspaper photographs afterward, his demeanor was completely different. He wouldn't court the cameras, he didn't seem as smug, he actually expressed remorse. He forged friendships with clergy in prison, and he began praying. He prayed for Bobby Franks' soul, for his parents to find comfort, for himself to be forgiven. He did good deeds behind bars, teaching fellow inmates and even establishing a correspondence college at the penitentiary. After twenty years, he was eligible for parole. He was denied five times before finally being freed in 1958. Two years later, he told a journalist he was still deeply in love with Loeb.[70] The year after that, he moved to Puerto Rico, married a woman, and lived a quiet life until 1971, when he died an ordinary death of congestive heart failure.

Leopold in his cell at Stateville Penitentiary in Crest Hill, Illinois, July 1955, where he and Loeb had been transferred in the early 1930s—and where Loeb was killed by another inmate in 1971.

Legal Legacy

Few cases of the Jazz Age left the kind of multifaceted mark that the Leopold and Loeb investigation and trial did. Among the impacts:

- The discovery and identification of Leopold's glasses near Bobby Franks's body highlighted how sophisticated sleuthing was becoming—and how even seemingly brilliant criminals were no match for a keen-eyed detective.
- Legendary attorney Clarence Darrow was already a well-known figure by the time he represented Leopold and Loeb, but this case solidified him as one of the highest-profile criminal defense attorneys in American history. That, in turn, helped elevate the profile of the American Civil Liberties Union, of which Darrow was a leading member.
- Leopold and Loeb's case popularized the term "thrill kill" and planted the seeds for what's today referred to as the "affluenza defense."[71]

19

Nannie Doss: The Giggling Grandma

(1954)

When Samuel Doss went to the hospital with such searing abdominal pain that he was admitted immediately in September 1954, his attending physician was flummoxed. Sam had been healthy, with a seemingly iron stomach, but now he was doubled over in pain and suffering other bizarre symptoms that seemed to have come out of nowhere.

After a few weeks of touch and go, Sam slowly began to improve. His doctor wasn't sure what had triggered the confounding ailment but was relieved to see it fading. After all, Sam had survived unspeakable loss during his nearly sixty years alive and finally seemed poised for a beautiful second act. Just a few months before falling ill, the widower had remarried.

Sam's doctor was happy to send him home with his smiling new bride—and then horrified to learn that just days after he left the hospital on October 4, he'd fallen ill again and on October 6, died anyway.[1] The timing piqued suspicion, so the doctor nudged the local coroner to do a little digging. What he found led to authorities uncovering a string of untimely deaths all tied to the same giggling grandmother—a case that dramatically changed death investigations in the United States.

Sam had been born in 1895 in Arkansas[2] to parents George Doss and Nancy Mervina Keen. He was one of seven children—two girls and five boys—and around the time he reached adulthood, Sam joined millions of other young men in the United States by registering for the World War I draft. At that point, he listed his occupation as a farmer in Cabanal, Arkansas.[3] In January 1928, he married Winnie Artis Smith, a woman nine years his junior, in a small ceremony at her parents' house. The couple raised six children—two girls named Anna Lee and Wilma Jean, as well as four boys: Arnold, James, Willie, and Ernest.[4]

Sam and Winnie lived a relatively pleasant life, considering that most of their marriage was sandwiched between two world wars (although records suggest that Sam did not see action in either conflict). In 1942, when Sam registered for the World War II draft, he listed his occupation as self-employed farm tenant living in Oak Ridge, Oklahoma.[5] Winnie was a homemaker, and stayed home with the children. Sam did some moonlighting as a United Baptist minister, too.[6]

Around March 1945, the family moved from Oak Ridge into a farmhouse near a small town called Marble, Arkansas. On April 12, 1945, terrible news spread throughout the country: President Franklin D. Roosevelt, the first and only president to have ever been elected to four terms, had died suddenly of a cerebral hemorrhage. In a world before social media, word spread slowly, especially in rural parts of the country. The Doss children, oblivious to the news, ranged in age from three to sixteen. Tragically, that is as old as they ever got. The same day as FDR's death, the most destructive tornado in Madison County history tore through, killing ten people, destroying approximately one hundred buildings, and causing, as one news story described it, "inestimable damage" to homes, businesses, schools, and churches. Farmland and equipment weren't spared; nor were farm animals.[7]

When the *Madison County Record* wrote a story detailing the twister's path, it described what happened to the Doss property as the "most tragic scene of destruction and death ever known in Madison County." Sam Doss was at his brother's house in a nearby town, but Sam's wife and six kids were home. The newspaper wrote: "The house was picked up, tossed into a hollow nearby, and smashed into splinters. All outbuildings and the cellar were destroyed, and the canned fruit and all other supplies blown away. Not a thing could be salvaged about the place. The bodies of the mother and children were scattered promiscuously among the ruins."[8]

Sam Doss had simply gone to work one normal day and come home to find his family dead, and his house destroyed.

Sam relied on his faith to get him through the horrific loss. It took years before he reached a point at which he wanted to find companionship again. Back then, one way to meet was through a personal ad in the local newspaper. One of the earliest documented personal ads appeared in 1727 and was posted by Helen Morrison in the *Manchester Weekly Journal*. Society wasn't quite ready for such a thing, and, because of the ad, Morrison was committed to an asylum for a month. But someone must have thought Morrison was on to something because personal ads caught on by the early 1800s and were huge moneymakers for newspapers and local magazines. (In the early 2000s, as more people gained internet access and websites like Craigslist and Match took over, personal print ads began to disappear with all the other classified ads.)

It was through such an ad placed in 1953 that Sam Doss was introduced to a woman named Nancy Hazel, called "Nannie" by those who knew her. At least, Hazel was her maiden name. She'd also been Nannie Braggs, Nanny Harrelson, Nannie Lanning, and Nannie Morton. Sam likely didn't know she'd had quite that many surnames, though. Being the God-fearing man he was, he probably wouldn't have approved.

Nannie was a charming woman. At forty-seven years old, she was buxom and matronly with rosy cheeks, and she spoke in a cutesy, folksy way. She wore pearl necklaces and cat-eye glasses. Like Sam, she'd had some difficulties in her life. Nannie had been born in 1905 to Louisa and James Hazel.[9] Tori Rose, an attorney who studied this case at the University of Texas at Austin, said Nannie's upbringing had been both verbally and physically abusive. James was "incredibly controlling," Rose said. "He didn't let [Nannie or her sisters] go out or interact with men really at all."[10]

Nannie Doss in custody in November 1954, after her arrest (see page 239).

The children didn't go to school, either, but were instead expected to work on the family farm. Nannie never got beyond a fifth grade education.[11] Earlier than that, when Nannie was about seven, she endured a traumatic brain injury, she later told a reporter with *Life* magazine.[12] She and her family were taking a train ride to visit a relative when the train had to make an emergency stop, and Nannie's head slammed into the iron seat frame in front of her. She later said she suffered headaches and blackouts for the rest of her life.[13]

"She tried to attribute her behavior to that incident," Rose said. "There were never any brain scans, so we don't really know how damaging it was and there wasn't anyone to corroborate this incident, but it is something that she definitely tried to pin her behavior on later."[14]

Between her clouded thinking and her controlling, abusive father, Nannie took refuge in her mother's romance novels. The books fed into a fantasy life that often centered around a Prince Charming.[15] The men in her life were certainly nothing of the sort. By the time she was a teenager, she had reportedly been molested by a series of them.[16]

Sam had moved to Oklahoma from Arkansas about two years before he started writing letters to Nannie, whose name was on a Lonely Hearts Club mailing list, according to a summary by *The Oklahoman*.[17] Sam and Nannie hit it off, writing each other letters for eight months before marrying in Tulsa on July 13, 1954.[18] Barely two months had passed before Sam was taken to the hospital in terrible shape. That was in early September, and whatever was plaguing him was so bad that he wasn't released from the hospital until October 4. Nannie took him home. She gave him a cup of coffee. The pain came back, and Sam returned to the hospital. He died October 6 at age fifty-eight. Nannie told the nurses, "He was a good man."[19]

It turned out that Sam's doctor from his initial hospital stay had already suspected his patient's illness had been caused by poison. After the burial, a tip came into the Oklahoma State Crime Bureau suggesting an inquiry. Bureau head Ray Page and police homicide captain Harry Stege began to investigate. They learned that the brief marriage between Nannie and Sam had been strained.[20]

"Sam was a hardcore Fundamentalist, which meant he frowned upon some of Nannie's most beloved interests, like dancing and singing," Rose said.[21] Sam reportedly forbade Nannie from reading true detective magazines or her beloved romance novels. He also refused to let her have a radio or TV set. A later story in the *Corpus Christi Times* relayed: "Unless there was an evening church service, he made Nannie retire with him at 9:30 every night."[22]

Police decided to question her, though at first they were just going through the motions because of the tip. As officers asked Nannie questions about her husband, she seemed to answer them candidly, though her demeanor was a bit odd. She didn't seem to be in shock or mourning, as they expected. Rather, she smiled and giggled and kept insisting she knew nothing about Sam's death.

The cops asked for permission to perform an autopsy on Sam. Nannie agreed, saying she wanted them to perform an autopsy because whatever had killed her husband might kill somebody else too.

In the autopsy, the coroner found what he described as enough arsenic "to kill a horse."[23] At first, Nannie said she had no idea how arsenic got into her new husband's system. But, after some marathon interrogations, she finally came clean: Sam had been pretty "mean" to her. One night, she fixed him one of his favorite foods. "He sure did like prunes," she said. "I fixed a whole box, and he ate them all."[24] Those prunes had been liberally doused in rat poison, which contained arsenic.

That didn't kill him, though. It landed him in the hospital, where he fought for his life for a few weeks. She took him home, then served him a cup of coffee. That's the dose that did him in. Nannie quickly tried to cash in on a couple of insurance policies that she'd taken out on her new husband—so quickly, in fact, that Rose said it became clear to investigators that she was responsible for his death. She was arrested in the case, though something about her demeanor compelled investigators to keep digging. Nannie insisted they were wasting their time. She told police, "You can dig up all the graves in the country and you won't find any more on me."[25]

"YOU CAN DIG UP ALL THE GRAVES IN THE COUNTRY AND YOU WON'T FIND ANY MORE ON ME."

Bit by bit, they tracked the wildly winding route of Nannie's life, love and otherwise, and discovered a trail of untimely, unexplained deaths that spanned some thirty years. It began with Nannie's first marriage to a guy named Charlie Braggs,[26] who worked with her at a linen factory. She'd caught his eye when she was sixteen because she was a pretty girl and lots of fun. The two wed May 8, 1921, in Alabama's Calhoun County, and things went well at first. They had five children, one of whom died right after birth. The four who survived were all girls. A few years in, the couple's marriage started to suffer, and both parties were unfaithful to the other. Sometimes Nannie would up and leave with someone and Charlie would have to track her down to bring her home.

In 1927, the couple's two youngest daughters, a newborn named Zelmer and a one-year-old named Gertrude, died suddenly of suspected food

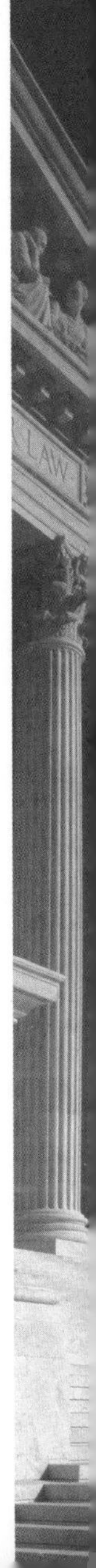

Nannie Doss poses with her daughter, Melvina Nodrick, and granddaughters Janice and Peggy, during her trial in Tulsa, Oklahoma, May 1955.

poisoning. Charlie wasn't sure the deaths were accidental. He'd left in the morning for work, and all had been fine in the house. When he came home, the girls were mortally ill. "Some of the neighbors said there was something funny about the way they died because they turned black so quick," he told a reporter.[27] Charlie said he left Nannie after the deaths because he was scared something would happen to him. The two divorced.

About a year later, in 1929, Nannie met and married Robert "Frank" Harrelson and brought her two surviving children—Melvina and Florine—with her to Jacksonville, Alabama, though at some point early in the marriage, Nannie abandoned Florine in an empty house, leaving her and Frank with only Melvina. Florine eventually reunited with her father, Charlie, and according to Rose, had a strained relationship with her mother—which could explain the absence of Florine in any of the news stories following Nannie's arrest. (Florine would die in 1957; her tombstone says simply "mother.")[28]

Frank, listed as a farm laborer in the 1940 census,[29] was apparently a romantic guy. He was a year younger than Nannie, just twenty-three when the two met, and liked to write her romantic poetry. Unfortunately, he was also an alcoholic whose proclivity to drink led to a criminal record. Though they stayed married for around sixteen years, it was a rocky union, during which Nannie's life seemed inexplicably marred by various tragedies. For example, in 1943, Melvina gave birth to her own child, a son she named Robert Lee. There's an oft-repeated story that suggests baby Robert, Nannie's grandson, died a few hours after birth, but that's not true. His obituary and death records show he was actually two years old when he died in Nannie's care. That was July 7, 1945.[30]

Two months after that, Frank, now thirty-nine, came home one night after partying, demanded sex, and then raped Nannie—or at least that's the story she later told. The next day, Frank mysteriously died a slow and painful death.

Two years later, Nannie met a North Carolina man named Arlie Jackson Lanning, who worked in the furniture business. The story is that she married him three days after meeting him, and soon after that, his elderly mother suddenly died. Even before that, Arlie had endured plenty of trauma: He appeared in the 1940 Census as an inmate in a North Carolina prison,[31] and in 1946 his first wife, Viola, died of cancer.[32] Looking for love once again, he placed a personal ad, and married Nannie a year later. Arlie was felled by what doctors believed was a heart attack in February 1952. He didn't die right after his supposed cardiac arrest. Rather, he languished in the hospital for three painful days before Nannie became a widow for the second time on February 16.[33]

By this point, she'd lost a number of loved ones under suspicious circumstances. In 1950, her sister, Dovie Frances Weaver, died, though doctors couldn't pin down exactly what had caused it. The year after Arlie's death, another of Nannie's sisters, Sula Bartlett, died as well.[34] The sisters were both in their early forties when they succumbed to a mysterious ailment. During this era, though many states had enacted autopsy protocols, authorities either needed a court order or permission from the dead person's family.

An unusual or suspicious death didn't automatically result in an investigation, as it does today.[35] Nannie was often a witness to these deaths, as well as the decedent's next of kin. She told coroners there was nothing suspicious about the deaths, and coroners apparently believed her, so autopsies typically weren't performed.

After her husband Arlie died, Nannie again returned to submitting advertisements to so-called Lonely Hearts columns. Through one, she met a Kansas man named Richard Lewis Morton, described as manager of a billiard academy in Emporia, Kansas.[36] Based on Morton's World War I draft registration, he was part Native American and had been married before with three children. It appears he and his first wife divorced, after which he remarried in 1928 to a woman who would remain his wife until her death in March 1952.[37] Newly widowed, Richard was sixty-nine to Nannie's forty-seven, and the two swapped letters for a few months. They married in October 1952.[38] Then poor Nannie faced another loss: Her mother, Louisa, died while Nannie was serving as her caretaker in North Carolina. The date was January 3, 1953.[39] Nannie turned to her new husband for emotional support.

Nannie and Richard shared several interests—notably, music and dancing. But Morton also showed a lot of interest in other women, which Nannie didn't like. The couple had just passed four months of marriage when, on May 19, 1953,[40] Richard drank a strong cup of coffee and died. Within months, Nannie was corresponding with Sam Doss, the widower whose death launched the investigation.

Nannie was arrested in late November 1954[41] and could have faced the death penalty for Doss's death alone. But police had more questions. Wanting to know just how deadly this adorable woman had been, they exhumed the bodies of her suspected victims one by one to test for arsenic. Each case seemed to have the same possible motive at its core: Nannie had been awarded at least a few hundred bucks in life insurance, plus, in the cases where the dead person was her husband, she'd been the beneficiary to his estate—with one exception. Arlie Lanning had actually left his estate to his sister, but then a strange thing happened: just as Nannie was moving away, Arlie's house burned down. The house had been insured and, as Arlie's spouse, Nannie was the beneficiary. Arlie's sister got nothing.

Each time a late husband was exhumed, newspapers splashed the inevitable findings in stories nationwide: Incredible levels of arsenic were found in each. It should be noted that dying of arsenic poisoning is a horrific way to die. Arsenic is a naturally occurring element found in food and soil, even in water and air, but in this case, "natural" doesn't mean "safe." Arsenic can make someone sick either from a single large dose or from small, repeated doses.[42] Acute poisoning causes symptoms like nausea, vomiting, burning of the mouth and throat, and severe abdominal pains. When the dose is large enough, arsenic can kill within just a few hours. Repeated, or chronic, exposure presents more subtly. The poisoned person might feel weak. They might get diarrhea or constipation. Their skin might get scaly or change color. Streaks might appear on their fingernails. The mind may get cloudy, and the body, anemic. Arsenic is recognized as a carcinogen today, and the Environmental Protection Agency and the Occupational Safety and Health Administration have both set limits on safe exposure levels.

Because arsenic is odorless and tasteless, it had been the perfect murder method for centuries, dating back to the Roman Empire. As a story on LiveScience.com says, "History is riddled with accounts of both royalty and commoners carrying out assassinations for personal gain" using arsenic.[43]

Arsenic use began to slow down after a British chemist named James Marsh developed a test in 1836 to detect even tiny amounts of arsenic in blood, urine, hair, and fingernails. By the time Nannie's loved ones began dying from arsenic poisoning, doctors knew well how to test for it. The problem was that they couldn't get an autopsy without Nannie's consent, so instead the deaths were attributed to other ailments, like heart attacks or food poisoning.

Now that the bodies were being tested, police were building a solid case against Nannie, though she at first denied all but Sam Doss's murder. Nannie was, initially, a reluctant witness. She even denied knowing Richard Morton, her fourth husband, until her interrogators showed her proof of five insurance policies, totalling $1,400, that named her as a beneficiary.

"Well, you got me trapped," Nannie said with a chuckle. "I guess I did know him."[44]

Newspapers that started running the wire stories about Nannie often ran her photo alongside the headlines. The first that made the rounds was a

The infamous photo of a smiling Nannie Doss being escorted into the county attorney's office by investigator Ross Billingsley for questioning in the death of her former husband, Sam, November 26, 1956.

picture of Nannie looking straight at the camera and smiling this huge, I'm-gonna-come-pinch-your-cheeks smile, while being escorted by county investigator Ross Billingsley for questioning. The next photo that circulated was Nannie, identified in the caption as Nannie Morton Lanning Doss (they forgot her first two surnames, Hazel/Hazle and Braggs). In the picture, she's smiling at the camera again, this time with a bit more subtlety, like a mother-in-law posing for a wedding portrait. Standing next to her is one of the homicide detectives who grilled her for two days straight. These photos of Grandma Nannie were so at odds with the stories running alongside them.

"She looks like someone that would bake cookies and then give them to neighborhood children," Rose said. "She does not look like someone you would expect to have killed four husbands, two children, and a grandchild."[45]

It was grueling work, but interrogators eventually got a confession to each husband's murder. Each time she admitted to one, she would claim that it was the only other one she had done and "my conscience is clear."[46] Then interrogators would press some more, and she'd cheerfully begin her next confession.

One wire story read:

> **Prolonged grilling of the smiling, talkative widow by relays of officers over the weekend produced signed statements from her admitting each husband's death. Calmly smoking a cigarette, she related in detail how she put the poison into the food and drink of her mates, each from a different state.**[47]

It was a slow, exhausting process for investigators. The interrogation sessions lasted hours on end. That said, Nannie wasn't the most unpleasant killer they'd ever encountered. At one point, she noted that investigators looked weary and said: "I feel awful bad about keeping you fellows up this way. I'm sorry to be so much trouble."[48]

As the confessions tumbled forth, so did Nannie's supposed motivation for each killing. It wasn't about money, she insisted. Frank Harrelson beat her, she said. With Arlie Lanning, she had been jealous because he was so popular with the ladies. Her reason for killing Richard Morton was similar. About him, she said: "I lost my head and blew up when I found out he had been running around with another woman and had bought some rings."[49] Sam Doss was mean to her, so she poisoned him twice.

After killing the men, she took care in choosing their epitaphs, according to a December 1954 wire story. On their tombstones, she had engraved messages like: "We will meet again," "Darling, how we miss thee," and "God be with you."[50]

Some of the men's families had suspicions about their sudden deaths. Arlie's family had alerted the coroner in Lexington, North Carolina, saying that they had suspected foul play, but the coroner didn't have enough evidence to exhume the body.[51] After the confessions, the evidence was plenty, and the family's suspicions were finally validated.

Ultimately, Nannie confessed to killing her husbands, but she did not confess to everything police suspected her of. She insisted she never killed a blood relative—or, as she worded it, "I never harmed any of my blood kin"—meaning she denied killing her mother, two sisters, two daughters, and her two-year-old grandson. Tulsa police commissioner John Henderson said: "When we started talking about her blood kins' death, her mood changed abruptly." He said the look of merriment quickly faded from her face and was replaced by one of depression.[52]

Authorities exhumed the relatives' bodies, and while the testing results weren't reported on each of the deceased, Nannie's mother was teeming with arsenic.[53] In all, Nannie was suspected of eleven murders, though she confessed to only four. The seven murders that she did not confess to committing are the aforementioned six relatives, whose deaths seem likely to have been by her hand,[54] and Arlie's eighty-five-year-old mother, whose death likely wasn't.

For a while, it appeared Nannie might be aiming to mount an insanity defense. Her court-appointed attorney told the judge who arraigned her that his client was "crazy." The descriptions of her that appeared in newspaper stories must have helped. She supposedly smiled and laughed while describing the agonizing deaths she inflicted. During her confessions, she paused to pretty herself up, then allowed television cameramen into the room to film while authorities continued asking her questions. She chuckled and gave folksy-sounding answers that, had they not been describing murder, might well have sounded charming. Her demeanor was like nothing anyone had seen before in a killer, and it earned her some of the most memorable monikers imaginable for a murderer. She was called the Giggling Granny, the Giggling Nanny, the Jolly Black Widow, the Lonely Hearts Killer. Psychiatrists observed her for ninety days at Eastern State Hospital in Vinita, Oklahoma, and said she was mentally defective. Nannie herself pointed to that childhood head injury she'd sustained, telling a jail matron that she began "thinking crooked" after that. "I don't understand those big legal words," she said after one hearing. "They said something about a mental checkup, and I guess I need one. Maybe those docs at the hospital will teach me to think straight."[55] In the end, a Tulsa County jury ruled she was sane.

As it turned out, Nannie didn't plead insanity. She pleaded guilty—and did so with a smile. She made it plain that she didn't feel remorse. "My conscience is still clear," she said.[56] It was also clear that she'd had no plans of stopping after killing Sam Doss. Before she'd poisoned Sam the first time, she'd already started a relationship with a North Carolina man named Coy Foust. After Nannie's face was plastered across newspapers nationwide, Coy pulled out two snapshots of Nannie he kept in his wallet. "I guess I'm the luckiest man in the world," he said, telling reporters that he and Nannie had dated for six months.[57] Nannie asked him to marry her several times, he said, but he declined. Whatever the reason—intuition maybe, or fear of commitment—it probably saved his life. He told reporters: "I had $2,500 worth of life insurance, and it looks like now they might have had to pay off on it if I had married her." Foust apparently wasn't the only new man in Nannie's life, either. Dairy farmer John Keel, another North Carolinian, said he'd been corresponding with Nannie since October—the same month Sam died—and Keel found himself falling for her. He found it especially endearing that she once sent him a cake. His thoughts had turned to marriage.

Nannie's guilty plea could have gotten her the death penalty in Oklahoma, but Judge Elmer Adams decided it would be a "poor precedent" to make her the first woman to receive the death penalty in Oklahoma, so he sentenced her to life instead.[58] Before long, though, Nannie was complaining about having been spared. Life was boring behind bars, she said. She was disappointed that her offers to work in the kitchen preparing food for fellow inmates had been rebuffed. She told reporters who interviewed her that she wished North Carolina or Kansas would charge her with one of the other murders so she might be sentenced to death and just get it over with. "Maybe they would give me the electric chair," she said, adding that she had "lost my desire to live."[59]

Nannie Doss's case was so bizarre—so counter to the typical image people have when envisioning a serial killer—that it quickly rose to national news. The early stories ran in dozens of states, many times on the front page. It helped that Nannie's victims spanned at least four separate states as well, allowing reporters in those areas to write localized versions. But the ramifications of her case went far beyond the sensational. It has a real place in forensics history.

The same year Nannie was arrested and pleaded guilty to murder, a movement swelled to reform the system that had let her get away with killing so many men undetected. For example, this is from a December 1954 story in the *Rocky Mount Telegram* out of North Carolina:

> **These ghastly and almost unbelievable revelations have touched off some interesting consequences in North Carolina. There have been renewed and proper demands for overdue reform of North Carolina's archaic coroner system. . . . As it is now, nearly anyone can be a coroner in North Carolina who can get elected regardless of qualifications.[60]**

Nannie Doss's case came to an official close ten years to the day after she was sentenced to life in prison for Sam's murder. She'd been sick with leukemia while held at a state penitentiary in McAlester, Oklahoma, and after being transferred to an Oklahoma City hospital for treatment, she succumbed on June 2, 1965. It was reportedly a much more serene death than she'd allowed any of her victims.

Legal Legacy

While controversy still surrounds the patchwork of US laws overseeing death examinations, the Nannie Doss case triggered a wave of changes.

- At the time of the murders, much of the country was on a coroner system headed by elected lay people. Autopsies were conducted only with family consent or by court order. Today, about half the country—including all but a handful of counties in North Carolina—has shifted to a medical examiner system, which requires board certification.[61]
- Oklahoma lawmakers passed what was commonly called the "Nannie Doss law," requiring a medical examination be conducted for any death that happened outside the presence of a physician.[62]
- The case also helped create the framework for the Model Postmortem Examinations Act of 1954, which promoted the shift from coroners to medical examiners and suggested that death investigation statutes should be "more uniform and modernized."[63]

20

Kirk Bloodsworth and America's First DNA Exoneration

(1984–93)

As soon as word spread that nine-year-old Dawn Hamilton had walked into the woods with a strange man, the search began. This is noteworthy because often in the 1980s, a child's disappearance was handled too cavalierly, too slowly. Police would tell anxious parents not to worry, that the kid would turn up. Take the case of Jonelle Matthews of Greeley, Colorado, for example. The twelve-year-old disappeared days before Christmas in 1984, but few newspapers ran her name, much less her photo, until March 1985, after her parents lobbied President Reagan for help in publicizing the case.[1] (Jonelle's remains were finally found in 2019, and a former Greeley resident named Steve Pankey was convicted in her murder.)[2]

But something about the circumstances surrounding Dawn's disappearance struck everyone as suspicious right away. Police arrived within minutes. Family members began scouring the area in and around the woods. A command post was set up to start organizing a search party.[3]

It was all for naught. Dawn had vanished around 11:00 a.m. on July 25, 1984.[4] That afternoon, a man in the woods found her jean shorts and underwear in a tree. Dawn's father found her still-warm body minutes later.

It was as shocking a crime as they come. This little girl hadn't just been killed. Her skull had been crushed. Shoe imprints showed that her killer had stepped on her little body. She'd been sexually assaulted and then violated further with a stick. The small community where this happened, about twenty miles northeast of Baltimore, Maryland, was outraged. *What kind of monster does that to an innocent child?* Everyone wanted justice. They worried that their kids weren't safe, but the police had a tough case ahead of them. There were witnesses who'd seen Dawn walk off with a man into the woods, but two of those witnesses were just children themselves. Dawn had been talking with two little boys, ages ten and seven, near a pond when she was approached by the man.[5]

The boys said the man asked Dawn what she was doing. She said she was looking for her friend Lisa. The man offered to help find Lisa in the woods, and off the two went.

The boys gave police a description of the man—about 6-foot-5, muscular, blond curly hair[6]—and a rendering created by a sketch artist did yield some tips, but the police weren't sure which to pursue, so they asked the FBI for help in creating a profile of the killer. Armed with that, they winnowed the pool of possibilities to just one: a man named Kirk Bloodsworth. Kirk was arrested, tried, and convicted. Authorities were relieved, and the community celebrated.[7] But there was a problem: Kirk was innocent, and his case would mark the first time in American history that DNA testing would reverse a murder conviction.

When Dawn was born in 1975 to Toni and Thomas Hamilton, her parents weren't in a good place in their lives. Toni was just seventeen.[8] Thomas worked odd jobs, mostly as an electrician, and the two weren't faring too well as a couple. Neither felt like they could handle a child.

Luckily for them—and for Dawn—there were other adults around with big hearts and open doors. Dawn was entrusted to a family friend, a woman named Casimira but nicknamed Mercy.[9] Born in 1934, she was in her forties when Dawn came into her life. Already a mother to four older children, Mercy Sponaugle had been born in the Philippines and would dote on Dawn no differently than she would her own children. In 1979, the little girl would be a ray of sunshine during a spell of unthinkable darkness for Mercy, who lost her own teenage daughter in a car accident in that year. The obituary for the teen says that the girl's nickname had been Angel.[10]

Mercy didn't outright adopt Dawn, though she was willing to, because Dawn's father, Thomas, was still involved in his daughter's life and would take Dawn with him during work stints. He and Mercy acted as though they were an amicably divorced couple sharing custody, and normally this arrangement worked out well. It just so happened, though, that a miscommunication on July 25, 1984, meant that Dawn wasn't where she was supposed to be that day.[11]

Mercy had enrolled Dawn in a Catholic summer camp near Annapolis. The idea was that starting July 16, Dawn would get time to play with other kids, swim in the river, and learn to canoe and sail.[12] Before camp, however, Dawn's dad Thomas had taken Dawn to Pennsylvania to see her grandparents. Mercy apparently thought she'd relayed the camp schedule clearly to Thomas, and she thought that he took Dawn to camp after the visit to the grandparents. Thomas, meanwhile, claimed he'd never been told about this camp. He was crashing at some friends' apartment through the summer, and while he went to work, his friend Elinor Helmick was watching Dawn and a few other kids.[13]

This is why Dawn was at an apartment in Fontana Village on the day she disappeared.

Dawn, headstrong and self-sufficient for a nine-year-old, was considered a leader in her Rosedale Elementary fourth grade class. Mercy called Dawn "Big Mama" because she acted like one, wrote Tim Junkin in his book *Bloodsworth* (2005). Dawn was confident and cheerful. She didn't have the most orthodox upbringing, but it had been stable enough that she was trusting of adults, even if they were strangers.

The day that Dawn disappeared, her father had gone to work at around six in the morning. He left her with Elinor, who was also watching her two kids—four-year-old Lisa and six-year-old Gary—as well as Elinor's sister's two children. Elinor made the kids breakfast, then told them to go outside to play. There was a field with a playground, though the kids weren't supposed to go into the nearby woods or adjacent pond. All five of the kids went outside around 10:30 a.m., though Dawn circled back soon after to report that two of the younger kids had gone into the woods. Elinor told Dawn to call them back, and the children who'd been temporarily out of sight quickly came home. But Dawn wasn't with them.

Elinor then went looking for her. She found two boys near the pond that her kids were supposed to avoid. The boys, ten-year-old Christian Shipley and six-year-old Jackie Poling, knew Dawn and told Elinor they had indeed seen her.[14] She had come up to them at Bethke Pond and asked for their help in finding her friend. The boys declined because they'd just caught a turtle and were far more interested in the reptile than in helping find a little girl in the woods. The boys relayed that someone else had stepped in to help Dawn, however. This was a man on the rise of the hill who'd been looking down at the scene. Hearing that Dawn was looking for her friend, Lisa, the man said, "Lisa and me is playing hide-and-seek. Let's go find her."[15] Dawn, seeming grateful, walked off with the man.

Elinor grew alarmed. She went to the woods and called for Dawn but got no answer. She went back to her apartment and called police at 11:49 a.m., barely an hour after shooing the kids outside in the first place. Then Elinor called Thomas at work to tell him she couldn't find his daughter.[16] Thomas, who had just begun his lunch break, told his boss what was happening and left work immediately.[17]

When Thomas arrived, he encountered a man in the woods named Richard Gray, who pointed up into the trees. Gray had found a pair of shorts and underpants.[18] Everyone knew at that point that Dawn was in terrible danger. Their fears were soon confirmed. Just past 2:00 p.m., Dawn's body was found.[19]

Police canvassed the area. Some had seen a man who at least vaguely aligned with the description the two boys at the pond had provided: a tall guy wearing shorts. Bits of description varied, though—like his precise hair color. Some said it was blond. Some said brown. The colors on his shirt changed from person to person, too. Of the two boys, the older one seemed more confident in the description he had provided to the police. That was Chris, the ten-year-old. He worked with a sketch artist who used preexisting templates to try to create a likeness resembling the man in Chris's memory.[20] Chris couldn't deviate from the templates, which frustrated his attempts to help the sketch artist get a proper likeness of the man he saw.[21] For example, Chris had a static set of eyes from which he could choose, but if he needed to customize a template—like by asking that the eyes be a bit more rounded or closer together—the artist waved him along. Making those kinds of changes would have required the police to hire a freelance artist, and the cops didn't want to take the time to do that. They felt a sense of urgency in the case, so they wanted to create the composite as quickly as possible so they could release it to the public and get this killer off the street.

Chris said he wasn't totally happy with the sketch he'd helped create, but it was deemed close enough and released anyway. It showed a white man with frizzy, tight curls, a broad nose, and a mustache. Based on the

telephone calls it sparked, it looked like a lot of men in the Baltimore area. People called saying things such as, hey, that kind of looks like my neighbor. Or my boss. Or my husband. Each tip should have been vetted, but not all of them were.

For example, one tip came in about a guy who'd been driving around the area passing out free ice cream to children. He was weird enough that parents began warning their kids to stay away from him, but he was never investigated. Another tip suggested that the sketch looked sort of like a man suspected of raping children in the area. He had, in fact, been accused of assaulting two girls just weeks before Dawn's attack.

Police jotted down the name, Kimberly Ruffner, but they never followed up.[22]

Kirk Bloodsworth had heard about the murder near Baltimore. The news was impossible to escape for anyone in Maryland, and Kirk had been bouncing between the Baltimore area and his hometown of Cambridge, about ninety miles southeast on the other side of the Chesapeake Bay.

Kirk came from a long line of watermen who worked the bay as fishermen, oystermen, crab scrapers, and trappers.[23] His ancestors had emigrated to the New World from the United Kingdom in the 1600s, and over the centuries since, it seemed as though the saltwater had seeped into their veins. Life on the bay was more a way of life than a way to make a living. As Junkin writes, Kirk had learned this from a young age. He started working the water with his father tonging oysters around age six. He'd started duck hunting even earlier. He routinely got muskrat traps from his folks for Christmas and had made a little business out of setting his traps before sunrise between January and March. Local businesses would pay $10 for black pelts and at least $7 for brown ones.[24]

He was a hard worker, but when he got exposed to the party lifestyle, he went hard at that, too.[25] He started drinking at sixteen and smoking pot at seventeen.[26] His parents enrolled him in a religious school from which he did graduate, but because it wasn't accredited, that didn't count for much. He didn't get a diploma for his efforts. After his pseudo-graduation, he joined the Marines, signing up for a four-year term beginning in the summer of 1977. He joined the track team as a discus thrower and was the All-Marine Discus Champion three years running. When he was competing, he was stationed in Spain. After his honorable discharge, he returned home to Cambridge, where he worked odd jobs, grew his ginger hair long, and made up for some partying he'd missed while a Marine.

One weekend in 1984, a buddy invited him to hang out in Baltimore. As Kirk later recalled it, the two went to a bar in Baltimore where Kirk was introduced to a woman named Wanda.

"She jumped into the car, looked at me and said, 'How are you doing?'" Kirk later said. "And I guess that was kind of the end of me. I mean, I was really enthralled with her right from the beginning."

Wanda Gardenier was ten years older than Kirk. She had two kids from a previous marriage who lived with their father in Pennsylvania. Kirk's parents weren't exactly fans, as this line in Junkin's book *Bloodsworth* puts it: "Kirk's parents disliked her at first and then came to despise her."[27]

Over his parents' objections, Kirk and Wanda got married in April 1984, just two months after first meeting. He later said he ignored two omens the day of his wedding. The first came when he was driving to the church and felt hunger pangs. He found a fortune cookie loose in the car to eat, and when he read the note inside of the cookie, his fortune advised him to turn around.[28]

"I SHOULD HAVE TURNED THE HELL AROUND."

"I should have turned the hell around," Kirk later said in a 2015 documentary titled *Bloodsworth: An Innocent Man*.

The second omen came during the ceremony. Kirk said Wanda was so stoned that he had to help steady her to keep her upright for the vows.[29]

With the vows exchanged, Wanda moved to Cambridge, but it was clear within weeks that she hated it there. The life that Kirk knew and loved on the waterfront wasn't a good fit for his new bride. Wanda wanted to go back to Baltimore, so she did, and Kirk followed her there. He'd seen how unhappy she was in his town, so he thought he'd try to do what he'd requested of her: uproot and move his whole life to make their marriage work. He figured he could find a job that he liked well enough in Baltimore, which was still a port city, so he hitchhiked there over the July 4 weekend. First, he found Wanda, and then he got a job. It wasn't an ideal setup. Wanda was living in a small two-bedroom row house with her half-sister and some friends. Adding Kirk to the mix made the already-cramped quarters even tighter. He hoped the situation would be temporary, so he got a job delivering furniture at an outlet

store called Harbor to Harbor. Kirk was the only one in the apartment with a normal day job. Most of the others were unemployed bikers prone to all-day partying.

It was a tough environment for a married couple. The two shared a pull-out couch in the living room, so they had no privacy. He didn't get much sleep because it was noisy and, on the rare occasions it was quiet, he was either worried or annoyed because that meant Wanda was out partying somewhere without him. Sometimes she wouldn't come home until dawn.

It was during this spell that Kirk heard news of the murdered girl. He and Wanda were watching the news together when the black-and-white composite sketch flashed on the screen. Wanda turned to Kirk and eyeballed him.

"I said, 'Why are you looking at me for it?' and she said, 'Well, it does look like you a little bit,'" Kirk would later say.[30]

Wanda was joking—she'd been with Kirk at the time of the murder and knew he wasn't culpable—but she wasn't alone in thinking that the sketch resembled him a little. The full description wasn't as similar. Kirk was just shy of 6 feet tall, not the 6-foot-5 estimate given by the child witnesses. His hair also wasn't blond, nor was his skin tan, as other witnesses had described the man near Bethke Pond. Kirk's Scottish heritage showed in his red hair and fair skin. Also, the suspect was supposedly tall and slim. Kirk was on the hefty side, weighing more than 200 pounds. Though Wanda and Kirk were already stressed as a couple and constantly bickering, she didn't actually think her new husband was possibly to blame. The day of the murder had been a Wednesday, Kirk's one day of the week that he had off from work, and the morning had stood out because it started with Wanda's half-sister's cat peeing on Kirk in his bed.[31] You don't forget a morning like that.

While police were still searching for the killer, Kirk and Wanda had their biggest fight to date.[32] Something clicked in him, and he decided his parents were right—though he was also humiliated at the realization. He went to his boss at Harbor to Harbor and said he felt too sick to work but needed his paycheck. He walked to a store to cash the check, then began hitchhiking home.[33] He wasn't in a rush to get there and face his parents, so he stayed the night in a motel. Along the way, he called Wanda's mom and said something about having done something bad—meaning leaving his job and his wife—and Wanda filed a missing person's report soon after.[34]

Around the same time, the FBI had been asked to help create a psychological profile of the crime and perpetrator. It posited that the killer had been dominated by women his whole life and his repressed rage had boiled over the morning of the attack. Dawn was chosen because she was vulnerable, an easy target, but she represented far more than just the little girl she was. She represented all women.

"The detectives had this profile done that said whoever was responsible for this crime may have had an argument with a woman—a domineering woman—in his life," said journalist Tony Pipitone,[35] who had worked in Baltimore as an investigative TV reporter. "They said whoever did this, according to this profile, grew up around the water because he was near the pond where these boys were fishing and had gone to this pond to some kind of refuge in a troubled time."[36]

"THE DETECTIVES HAD THIS PROFILE DONE THAT SAID WHOEVER WAS RESPONSIBLE FOR THIS CRIME MAY HAVE HAD AN ARGUMENT WITH A WOMAN—A DOMINEERING WOMAN—IN HIS LIFE."

Amid the slew of calls police fielded in the days after Dawn's murder was one logged as tip No. 286 that mentioned Kirk Bloodsworth.[37] It seemed Wanda wasn't the only person who'd sensed the composite sketch bore a resemblance to him, and three days after the killing—several days before Kirk hitchhiked home to Cambridge—his name went down on a list of people to check out. Soon after Kirk left town, a cop got around to calling Harbor to Harbor, Kirk's employer, to ask about him. The employee said he'd abruptly quit August 3, that he'd mostly kept to himself, didn't have a car, and walked to work. Investigators noticed that Wanda had filed a missing person's report, and they noted that this lined up with the psychological profile's prediction that the killer would be having problems with his wife, who had a noteworthy age difference.

When police reached Wanda to ask for more information, she told them that she assumed Kirk had returned home to Cambridge. Police pursued him there, where they found him at a friend's house. Kirk had tried to go home to his parents' first, but it so happened that his folks were on a short trip. As he crashed with friends, he spent the rest of his paycheck on pot. He was high, in fact, when a Cambridge cop approached him on August 7. Detective Mark Cottom knew Kirk from around town—not due to any previous arrests because Kirk had a clean record, but Cambridge was small enough and Kirk stood out enough that when Baltimore investigators asked for help tracking him down, it was no problem.[38]

Cottom thought Kirk seemed jittery, which he assumed meant that Kirk was nervous about being asked questions about a missing and murdered girl in Baltimore. In reality, Kirk had pot hidden in his shoe and was stoned when Cottom approached. The conversation was brief, but it turned out to be just a prelude to an ambush the next day. Police had decided to try to elicit some kind of tell-tale reaction from Kirk by buying shorts and underpants similar to the ones Dawn Hamilton had been wearing when she was killed. They put that, plus a cinder block picked up from the police station parking lot, in the center of a table in the interrogation room. They brought Kirk into the room and watched for a reaction. He gave none—which meant he passed this sort of makeshift test they were secretly giving him. They figured the killer would react strongly to the girl's clothes and the suspected murder weapon on the table. Kirk didn't react at all. Instead of it suggesting to investigators that he was innocent, they instead decided it must mean Kirk was a cold-hearted killer, too detached to even react to a murdered girl's clothes. The detectives swept the decoy evidence away and focused on asking Kirk about where he was July 25, the day Dawn was killed. Kirk repeatedly told them he had nothing to do with Dawn's death. Detectives, however, had already interviewed some people who'd relayed comments of Kirk's that they deemed suspicious. For example, they asked why Kirk had told someone he'd done something bad that would upset his wife, to which Kirk responded that he'd told her he'd soon buy Wanda her favorite dinner—a taco salad. Instead of getting her a taco salad, he had quit his job and left her. To police, this explanation was preposterous.[39]

It was clear to Kirk that the police didn't believe him, but it was just as clear they didn't have enough evidence to charge him with anything. He was sent back to his friend's house. Little did he know that witnesses were being shown his image in a photo lineup after he left. Though Bloodsworth was shorter, heavier, and had different-colored hair than the child witnesses had described, they nevertheless picked him out of the lineup as the man they had seen with Dawn near the pond.[40]

Kirk was arrested in the middle of the night. TV journalists had been alerted so images of a shirtless, disheveled Kirk being arrested and perp-walked in handcuffs played on the news. Several of the eyewitnesses, including ones who hadn't yet identified him in the photo lineup, saw him on the

news before they were asked to spot the man they'd seen the day of Dawn's death in an in-person lineup. This did not comport with proper witness-identification protocols, which would forbid letting a witness see a suspect in handcuffs on television before being asked to ID him. Even with multiple character and alibi witnesses in his corner—including an estranged wife who had no clear reason to cover for him—Kirk was convicted in less than three hours. When he returned to court for sentencing and got the death penalty, the courtroom erupted in applause. Transferred to his new home on death row, he was greeted by catcalls from other inmates promising to do to him what he'd done to little Dawn Hamilton. Kirk wasn't sure he'd survive to see his execution date.[41]

In 1986, Kirk's appellate lawyers managed to convince Maryland's highest court that his trial had been unfair, so his conviction was overturned.[42] Bloodsworth was tried a second time. This time, his hired attorney—as opposed to the appointed ones he'd used the first time around—ditched the character and alibi witnesses who'd apparently done Kirk no good the first time around and instead focused on highlighting an alternate suspect.[43]

Richard Gray had been the man who'd spotted Dawn's shorts and underpants in the brush near the spot her body was found soon after. Gray had struck a few people as odd, especially because he had a balled-up pair of girls' underpants in his truck at the time of Dawn's disappearance. His explanation was that he'd found them in the woods and had a habit of picking up items like that to use as rags, but Kirk's lawyer thought it was odd enough that it should be highlighted in trial. It didn't help dispel lawyer Leslie Stein's suspicions when he learned that Gray had been given a lie-detector test that he supposedly failed—but by then police had been adamant that Kirk was their suspect, so Gray wasn't further investigated.

Jurors weren't swayed by the theory Gray was the real killer, however. They still believed the eyewitnesses and were confused by the lack of alibi testimony, which Kirk's new lawyers hadn't bothered to present. With several witnesses testifying that Kirk was the man they'd seen at the murder scene the day of the killing, jurors assumed it meant that Kirk had no alibi when none was presented as rebuttal. The second jury took six hours to convict him. Kirk's sentence was left to Judge James T. Smith,[44] who wasn't as convinced by the evidence. Instead of sentencing Kirk to death again, he gave Kirk two consecutive life sentences, and he also put a box of peripheral evidence in the closet of his office for safekeeping. This box contained Dawn's shorts and underpants, among other things. Supposedly these items had no biological matter on them and, as such, they would likely have been tossed in the trash after the second conviction, but because Smith had doubts, he'd held onto them.[45]

Meanwhile, Kirk wrote letters from prison to presidents and governors and actors and activists. He read case law and stories about cutting-edge forensic science, specifically related to a burgeoning field of forensic science known as DNA testing.[46]

"It's not that scientists didn't know about DNA," said Dr. Ed Blake, who ran a private lab in northern California that had started conducting DNA tests for criminal justice purposes. "It's just that the technology for doing work in a forensic setting hadn't evolved to the point where that technology was useful."[47]

Kirk got a new lawyer named Bob Morin, whom he begged to have anything and everything tested for DNA.[48] Morin wasn't optimistic because the FBI had said no semen remained to be tested, but when he learned of the shorts and underpants that'd been spared by Judge Smith's misgivings, he sent them to Blake's lab. The lab found a small deposit of semen on the shorts—something the FBI had earlier missed. The lab was at the forefront of something called PCR testing: a technique—now well-known for its use in COVID-19 testing—that amplifies small quantities of DNA so that even tiny amounts could be successfully analyzed.

On April 27, 1993—nearly nine years after Dawn's murder—someone slipped Kirk a note in his cell that read: *Call your attorney. Urgent*.

Kirk called Morin, who was normally a mild-mannered attorney with a reserved demeanor. But Morin wasn't his usual calm self.

"He was screaming on the other end," Kirk later said. "'Kirk! You're innocent, man! You're innocent!'"[49]

Two months later, Kirk walked out of prison a free man. But being exonerated by DNA didn't mean that others accepted he was innocent. After he returned home, he sometimes found notes on his car calling him a child killer. The prosecutor's office stopped short of clearing him, too, saying instead that the evidence that had convicted him was undermined by the DNA testing. Kirk wanted his name cleared altogether, and when he learned there was a DNA database called CODIS that could compare DNA samples

Kirk Bloodsworth testifies in Washington, DC, on July 23, 1993, before the House Civil and Constitutional Rights subcommittee, which was holding hearings on innocent people on death row.

from crime scenes with swabs collected from felons, he called prosecutors and asked that the sample from Dawn's murder be submitted to it. They refused, saying that entering the sample into the system would cost too much money. Kirk offered to foot the bill, but the state declined, saying that it would be unethical for him, as the only suspect still, to pay the associated costs. Kirk was livid. He wanted his name officially cleared. He wanted to be able to speak about his case without the state casting doubt on his innocence every time he did so. Not only that, he also worried that the killer of this nine-year-old girl was still walking the streets.

It took ten years before the DNA was uploaded to CODIS, but once it was, it got a hit. Kirk was home when he got a phone call from prosecutor Ann Brobst, who'd been co-counsel against him in his first trial and lead counsel in his second. She'd publicly called him a killer and a monster. She told him that she had some news about the case and offered to meet him anywhere in Maryland to tell him in person. He chose a Burger King. There, Ann and a couple of detectives told him they'd gotten what's called a "cold hit" on the DNA in Dawn's case. It came back to a man named Kimberly Shay Ruffner. He'd been accused of assaulting two girls about two weeks before Dawn was killed, though he'd been released for lack of evidence. About a month after Dawn's death, he was arrested in another case and convicted of attempted rape and murder. He'd been in prison ever since.

Legal Legacy

If any criminal case proves the importance of self-advocacy, it's that of Kirk Bloodsworth. Despite being told time and again that there was not enough biological matter to test, he kept pushing his lawyers to pursue it. Because of that:

- Dr. Edward T. Blake, who had experience with a DNA technology known as PCR (polymerase chain reaction) in testing for paternity, used it for the first time in a criminal case. Those tests showed that Bloodsworth was not the person who had assaulted Dawn Hamilton before her death.
- Blake's findings were confirmed in 1993 by the FBI, leading to Bloodsworth's release.
- The profile found in the testing was uploaded to a DNA database, eventually identifying convicted sex offender Kimberly Ruffner as Dawn's killer. Ruffner pled guilty in 2004, and was sentenced to life in prison.[53]

The strangest part was, Kirk knew Ruffner—not from the real world, but from the penitentiary. Ruffner was in the same prison Kirk had been sent to the second time around—when he got life instead of death.

"He slept in the tier below me for several years and never said a word," Kirk said. "I gave him library books and lifted weights with him in the yard. He would never look at me, though, and I never put two and two together."[50]

Ruffner pleaded guilty to the crime in exchange for having the death sentence removed as a possible penalty. When he entered his plea, he said he committed the crime alone, high on the drug PCP. Kirk Bloodsworth had nothing to do with it, he said.[51]

Bloodsworth was awarded $300,000 in 1994 in restitution, but in 2021, Maryland passed a new law to determine what wrongfully convicted people should be paid after being exonerated. That provided him an additional $400,000 under a law that makes compensation for exonerees equal to the median household income for the time they wrongfully served in prison. It's named after Walter Lomax, who spent nearly forty years in prison for a murder he didn't commit. Lomax's conviction was overturned in 2014. As of this writing, Kimberly Ruffner remains in prison in Westover, Maryland.[52]

Kirk Bloodsworth shows pictures of the convicted murderer Kimberly Shay Ruffner during an interview in his apartment in Mount Rainier, Maryland, in September 2012—almost twenty years after his exoneration by DNA.

Part 5

UNSOLVED WITH IMPACT

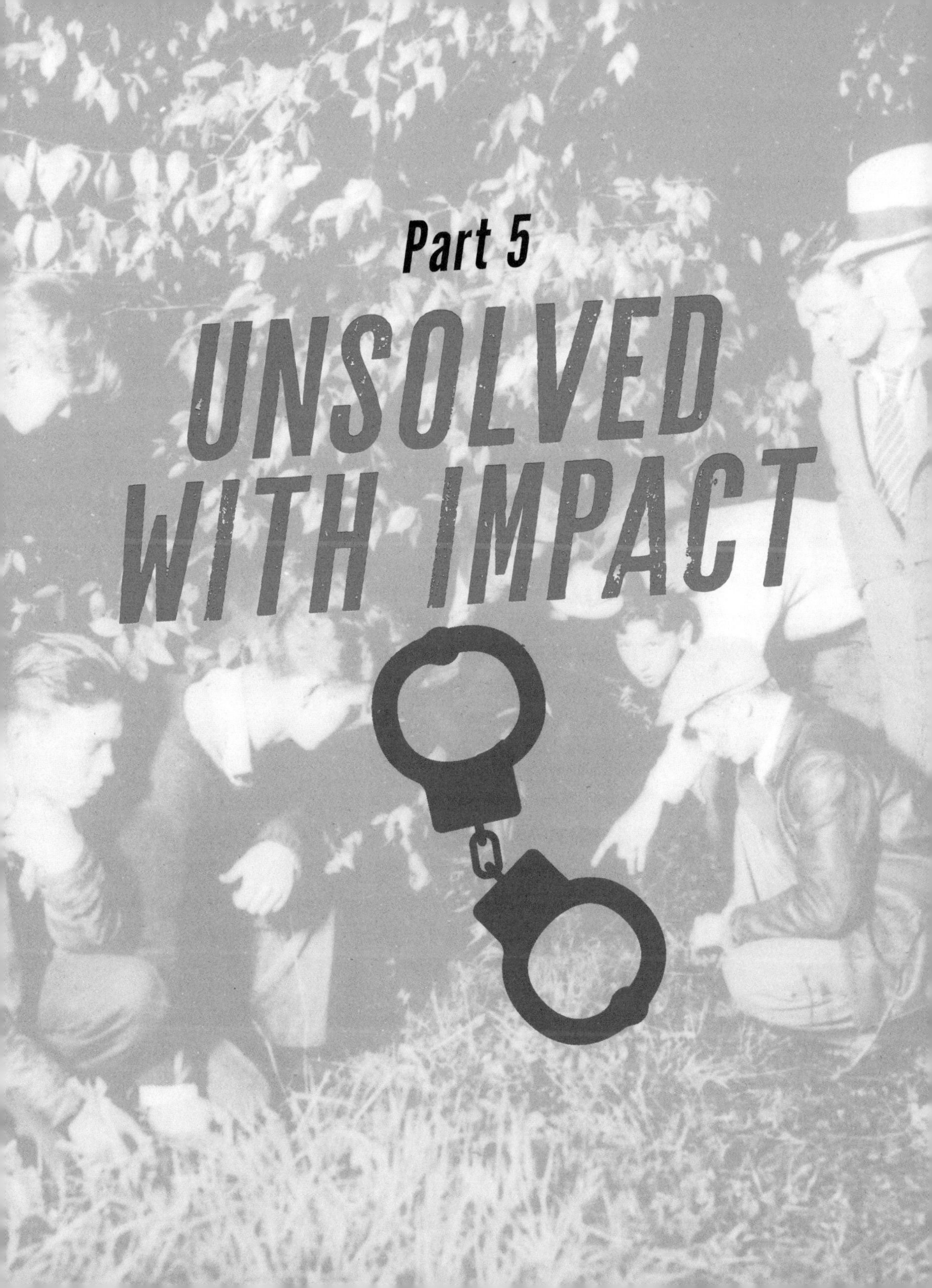

ABDUCTION OF CHARLIE BREWSTER ROSS.

On July 1st, 1874, at about four o'clock, P. M., Charlie Brewster, and Walter, the latter about six years old, sons of Christian K. Ross, were taken from the side-walk in front of their father's residence, on Washington Lane, Germantown, Pa., by two men in a buggy. Walter was carried about five miles, and there left upon the street; but of Charlie no subsequent clue has been obtained; it is earnestly solicited that every one, who shall receive this circular, make diligent inquiry, and promptly furnish any information obtained, and if the child be found, cause the detention of the parties having him in custody.

This circular must not be posted up, and care must be exercised, that suspicious persons do not obtain access to it.

Members of the press are specially requested to refrain from publishing the interrogatories hereafter given, so that the parties having the child in custody may not obtain the means of training him regarding his answers thereto.

On the discovery of any child, who shall be suspected of being the lost one, a photograph should be immediately obtained, if possible, and forwarded; and photographs of the parents will be sent for identification by the child.

$20,000 REWARD has been offered for the recovery of the child, and conviction of the kidnappers; all claims to which, however, will be relinquished in favor of the parties giving the information which shall lead to this

21

The Abduction of Charley Ross, the First Kidnapping for Ransom

(1874)

Six-year-old Walter Ross looked ashen, scared. He'd quickly run inside a store to buy some fireworks—he'd been given a quarter to spend and still had four cents left—but when he ran back outside to climb into the carriage he'd arrived in, it was gone.

For little Walter, this was terrifying. He started to cry, which drew the attention of passersby, who ended up helping reunite Walter with his dad at a police precinct a bit closer to home.

His dad, Christian, heaved a sigh of relief but then asked Walter where his brother, Charley was.

Walter looked confused, and replied that of course, Charley was still in the carriage.

In all the hubbub, Walter had considered himself the lost one, but in truth, it was his brother who had disappeared. On July 1, 1874, four-year-old Charley Ross had vanished with two men who had been grooming the boys for days with gifts of candy to ensure they'd leave the front yard of their Philadelphia home without a fuss.[1]

What happened next went down in history as America's first kidnapping-for-ransom case, and it changed attitudes and laws surrounding such crimes—all while remaining a baffling mystery that continues to confound historians to this day.

The Ross family lived on Philadelphia's Washington Lane in an ornate nineteenth-century Victorian Italianate house that was set a way back from

OPPOSITE: An oval portrait of Charley Brewster Ross is attached to a handbill issued by the Pinkerton detective agency in 1874, announcing the details of his abduction and of the $20,000 reward offered. On the back is a description of Charley and of the kidnappers.

The Ross house on Washington Lane in Philadelphia, depicted in an engraving from a book written by his father, Christian, in 1876, titled *The Father's Story of Charley Ross, the Kidnapped Child*.

the road.[2] The country, helmed by President Ulysses S. Grant, was two years shy of celebrating its one-hundredth birthday.

From the outside, it appeared that Christian Kunkel Ross, the patriarch of the Ross family, had done well for himself running a wholesale dry goods dealership called Ross, Shott & Co. on Market Street. The business afforded him his Germantown mansion and household servants—two nannies, a cook, and a gardener. Beneath the successful facade, though, the Rosses were hurting more than their neighbors realized, having taken a big hit the year before in the Panic of 1873, a series of financial crises that set off what was then referred to as the Great Depression—until that title was "stolen" in 1929.

The Ross family was sizable: Christian was married to a woman named Sarah, with whom he would eventually have eight children. Charley was their fifth child, born two years after Walter.

Charley was a friendly boy, described by his father as sensitive: "A word spoken harshly to him would cause his eyes to fill, and the tears to slowly trickle down his cheeks," Christian wrote.[3] The area in which the family lived was generally safe. The kids played outside in the vast front yard, and their parents didn't worry very much about it. One day, when Christian noticed his son Walter carrying a piece of candy, he didn't find it unnerving when he learned the treat had been given to the boy by a stranger. Christian's only thought was: *Gee, that was nice. Someone spotted my cute kids and felt compelled to give them candy.* That happened on June 27, 1874, which was a Saturday. Christian wouldn't think about the incident again for several days.[4]

In the meantime, Christian's wife, Sarah, went on a trip. She hadn't been feeling well and wanted rest and fresh air. She likely needed some rest after the birth of her most recent baby—who was now eight months old—so she and her daughter Sophia headed east for a trip to the beach at Atlantic City, while the rest of the family stayed home. Sarah said goodbye to Walter and Charley and the other children and told them that they'd be joining her at the seashore in just a few weeks. The first few days after Mrs. Ross left were humdrum. Christian continued working while the nannies kept watch over the boys. July 1 was as mundane as the days before it. Before Christian went to work, the boys began badgering him to buy fireworks—the Fourth of July was nearing, after all—and Christian told them to be patient. He went to work, then came home around 6:00 p.m. The maid said the boys were out front playing on the sidewalk, which was typical, so Christian was not concerned. But, as he wrote in his book about the affair, *The Father's Story of Charley Ross, the Kidnapped Child* (1876), they still weren't back by teatime.[5]

It was odd for teatime to come and go without word from the boys, so Christian went outside and walked up and down the road to see if he could find them.[6] A neighbor named Mrs. Kidder caught wind of his search and asked whether the boys would have gotten into a carriage with strangers if they'd been asked. Christian, remembering the candy he'd seen with Walter, said, yes, actually, they probably would. Mrs. Kidder said she saw the boys talking to two men in a carriage, and the boys climbed in and the carriage headed east. The exchange had seemed benign to her, so it hadn't alarmed her, but now that Christian couldn't find the boys, she found it curious.

Christian found it downright disturbing. Worried, he went to the police station and asked for help, but the police didn't share his panic; back then, kidnapping wasn't really a thing. The cops told Christian not to worry, those two guys in the buggy were probably just messing around and they'll let them out on the side of the road. Someone will spot them and bring them back soon, you'll see.

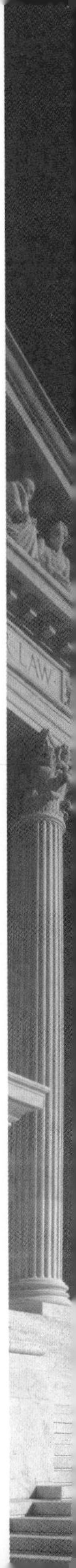

And that did happen—with Walter. But not with Charley.

Once Walter was found clutching the fireworks that he'd been sent off to buy, the gravity of what had happened became painfully clear. Walter shared all the details he could recall. He explained that the two men hadn't felt like strangers to the boys because on three separate days in the previous week, the men had stopped to watch Walter and Charley play, and each time, they plied them with a piece of candy. By the time July 1 rolled around, the boys didn't think twice about accepting a treat from the men. And when the men asked if they'd like a ride in the carriage, Charley responded that he wanted to buy fireworks. The men said of course we can do that, though they wouldn't take them to the closest store on Main Street. "We will take you to Aunt Susie's [as Ross notes in his book, "Susie" was a fictitious person], who keeps a store," they told the boys, "and will give you a pocketful for five cents."[7] Walter and Charley climbed in the carriage. Walter was in the back seat alone, while the two men were up front. Charley was on the knee of the man in the passenger seat.

At first the trip to Aunt Susie's sounded pretty exciting, but the ride seemed to last a really long time and Charley started to cry. He wanted to go home. The men soothed him, saying, we're almost there, which worked for a bit, but Walter was getting a little impatient, too. Finally, the men pulled up to a store, handed Walter a quarter, and told him to grab firecrackers for himself, plus some torpedoes for his little brother. Walter dutifully went in and bought the goodies, spending all but four cents of the quarter.[8] When he stepped outside to return to the carriage, it was gone, as was his brother. Walter was nowhere near home, which was incredibly upsetting, and so a girl approached and asked what was wrong. Finally, someone brought him home, and the whole time, Walter felt like he had made some mistake, he'd gotten lost somehow, when, in reality, he'd been purposefully ditched so that his brother could be taken.

This scenario was incredibly confusing not just for Walter, but for the police, too. What's the point of grabbing two kids, then shooing one away? They got their answer the next day when Christian Ross received his first letter from the kidnappers.

These missives were horribly written with misspellings and awful grammar, and were, in fact, so bad that the police felt they were being

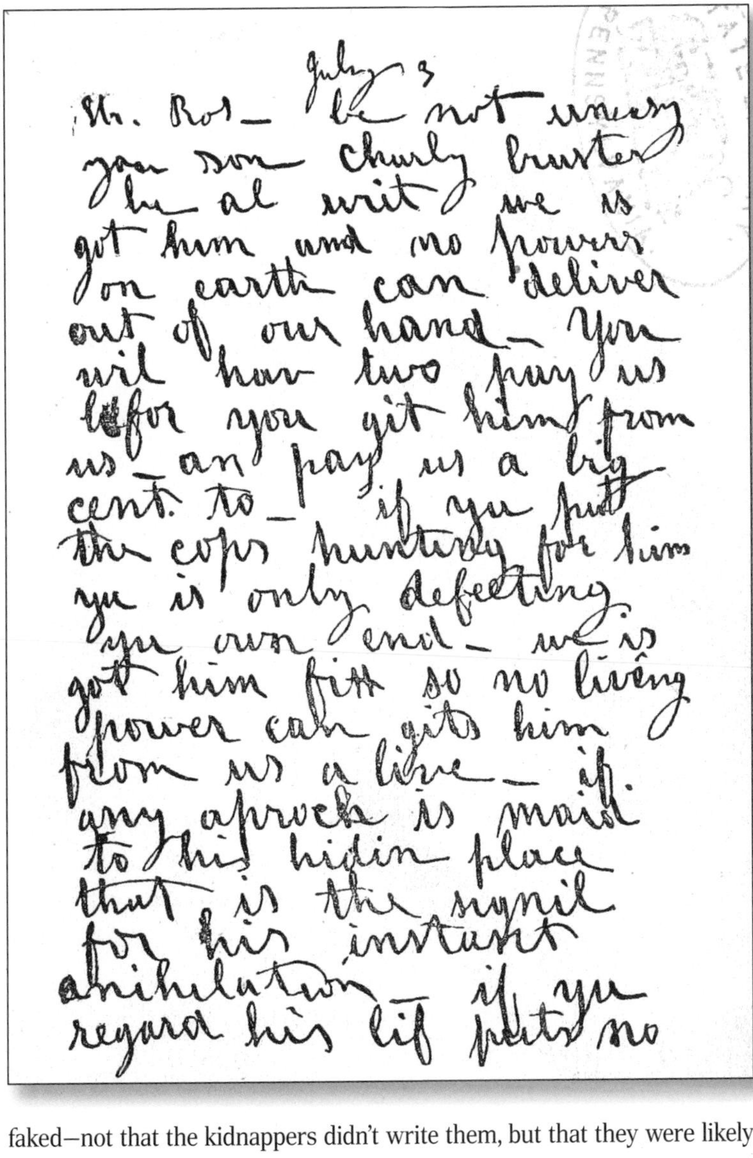
July 3
Mr. Ros— be not uneasy
you son charly bruster
be al writ we is
got him and no powers
on earth can deliver
out of our hand— You
wil hav two pay us
befor you git him from
us— an pay us a big
cent to— if you put
the cops hunting for him
yu is only defeeting
yu own end— we is
got him fitt so no living
power can gits him
from us a live— if
any aproch is maid
to his hidin place
that is the signil
for his instant
anihilation if yu
regard his lif puts no

The first page of the first ransom letter Christian Ross received from the kidnappers, which he reprinted in his book.

faked—not that the kidnappers didn't write them, but that they were likely writing them poorly to help disguise their identities. For example, this is a line in that very first message:

> *be not uneasy you son charley bruster be all writ we is got him and no powers on earth can deliver out of our hand—you will hav two pay us be for you git him from us, and pay us a big cent to.*[9]

An 1874 lithograph depicting Charley Ross; it was used as an illustration in sheet music cover for a song about Charley's abduction written by Dexter Smith, "Bring Back Our Darling."

The spelling was so bad that the letters were difficult to read. The first letter didn't mention a dollar amount, but it made it crystal clear that if the Rosses wanted their son back, they'd have to pay—and pay big. Christian had already alerted the police, and the letter-writers seemed to accept that the authorities would be looking for them. But they also seemed disconcertedly unfazed about it. The letters basically said, go ahead, sic the police on us. You're not going to find us. And even if you did by chance figure out where we're holding Charley, our setup ensures that we'd be alerted to anyone approaching and we'd kill him. Simple as that.

Christian wrote in his book that he was hoping to find Charley without his wife, vacationing in Atlantic City, ever knowing that he had gone missing. This is why the very first mention of a four-year-old abducted in Germantown that appeared in the *Philadelphia Inquirer* on July 3 made no mention of the boy's name. The short piece, titled "Abduction of a Child," didn't even provide a description. It said only that two men drove off with two boys, and that one of the boys had been left at Palmer and Richmond Streets. It concluded: "The detectives are looking into the case."[10]

The next day, another brief ran that, had Sarah Ross seen it, might have caused her to worry. Charley's name still wasn't mentioned, but it described the boy as four years old, with "long, flaxen curls, oval face, and brown eyes. His parents are almost distracted about him."[11]

Actually, Sarah wasn't distracted yet, as she was completely unaware of what had transpired. But soon, Christian went to Atlantic City to break the news to her in person that Charley was not just missing; he had been stolen. This was so novel at the time that it wasn't a felony to kidnap a child, said Meaghan Good, founder of CharleyProject.org, an online database of more than thirteen thousand missing persons cases, named after Charley Ross. Charley's clothes were better protected than his person, she noted: "The police said the best they could do as far as charging the men is to charge them with stealing his clothes. That would actually amount to a life sentence if you did the maximum seven-year sentence for every article of clothing he was wearing."[12]

On July 6, the second ransom letter was received, demanding $20,000 for Charley's release—approximately $530,000 in today's money[13]. As police tried to navigate the uncharted territory of this crime, the kidnappers kept writing. Surely, if their intent had been as they described—a straightforward swap, child for money—it might have gone more smoothly with the aid of a telephone, but it'd be two more years before Alexander Graham Bell made the first phone call.[14] So the communication went like this: A grammatical nightmare of a letter would arrive at the Rosses' home, and it would threaten Charley's life and tell Christian that he was stupid if he thought detectives would be able to help him. It also instructed Christian to reply to the letter with an advertisement in the local newspaper. Ross obliged. Back and forth, they would communicate this way—the kidnappers with a rambling, threatening letter, and Christian with a succinct reply in the newspaper, as requested. It was an agonizingly slow process.

Once Mrs. Ross knew the reality of her son's kidnapping, the story was no longer told in code in the newspapers, and people were outraged upon learning the details. Never had a child been stolen in this country and a bounty put on the poor kid's head. Who would do such a thing? Christian served as the family's spokesperson and made it clear they were all tormented by this awful act, which resonated with loving parents nationwide. The story was *everywhere*. From Philadelphia to Cincinnati, New York to San Francisco, it was splashed on all the newspapers.[15] Unfortunately, the media attention sometimes complicated matters. It was clear from the kidnappers' letters that they were keeping up on the coverage. They would comment on stories that mentioned details or theories or suggested plans to foil the bad guys.[16] One story mentioned that detectives were keeping an eye on the local post office in the hope of spotting the culprit dropping one of the letters in the mail, so the kidnappers relocated.

Whoever had the child was confident that their careful planning would pay off. And it did. For the whole month of July, police not just from Philadelphia, but from all over the East Coast, were heavily involved in the search for Charley. Cops went door to door searching homes. Children even remotely similar in description to Charley were investigated. People came out of the woodwork to offer their help. One wealthy man, learning that the Rosses weren't nearly as well off as the kidnappers obviously believed, offered Christian $20,000 outright to pay the thieves—and he promised no repayment would ever be needed.[17]

But because this was the first kidnapping for ransom, Christian was thinking about more than his unique situation. He assumed that whatever happened in the case would set a precedent for others to come. Christian figured that if he paid the kidnappers off, he would be putting countless other children at risk. On principle, he decided early that he wouldn't do it. He didn't communicate this to the kidnappers, though he did convey reluctance to them in other ways. In one of his personal ads, Christian wrote that he'd negotiate "to the extent of his ability,"[18] implying that he'd pull together money but that $20,000 might be too difficult to amass. In other ads, he insisted that when he handed over the money, Charley must be immediately released to him. The kidnappers replied that this was impossible. They insisted on at least five hours after the money's delivery—and then later upped it to ten and then twelve—to give them time to make sure the bills were not counterfeit or somehow marked to make them traceable, and once they were satisfied the money was clean, only then would they leave Charley somewhere he could be found and safely returned home.

"Both Christian and the police thought that he should not pay the ransom because it would just be like rewarding the criminals for their bad behavior," Meaghan Good said. "It would set a bad example and other people would start kidnapping children for ransom. They also believed that the criminals, once they realized they weren't going to get any money, would just give the boy back, which is touchingly naive."[19]

To buy time, Christian continued making excuses as to why he could not get the money just yet. He also repeatedly asked for proof they actually had Charley. He wanted them to send an article of clothing or a lock of hair. They refused. They deemed it too dangerous, so the only proof they'd give came via information in their letters—descriptions of a ribbon Charley had beneath his Panama hat to keep his hair out of his face, for example. That detail had never been published in the papers. They also relayed some of the lies they'd told Walter in the carriage, like that they were headed to Aunt Susie's place, and said to ask Walter if this wasn't true. Walter confirmed it was.

Christian was satisfied he really was communicating with the kidnappers, but that didn't mean he could trust that they'd release Charley alive. They tried to reason with Christian by assuring him that it would not make sense for them *not* to release his child—otherwise such a scheme would never work on anyone again. It seemed they, too, were thinking about precedent. Their assurances didn't do much to sway Christian, who was already worried that another family would be going through this hell soon if he gave in.[20]

Finally, at the end of July, the day came for Christian to supposedly meet his son's kidnappers. They contacted him with convoluted instructions to take a specific train from Philadelphia to New York, then switch to another train to Albany, getting in the rear car. Along the way he should look out for an "agent" of the kidnappers along the tracks who would wave a white flag and ring a bell (if daylight) or shine a flashlight (if night). They ordered him to stack the ransom money, in bills no larger than ten dollars, in a secured valise. When Christian spotted the flag-waving man described, he was to toss the valise out of the moving train.[21] Christian followed the instructions except he didn't fill the valise with money. Inside it, he put a letter that told the kidnappers he was willing to pay but needed proof they had Charley.[22]

It was a bold choice, one that could have prompted the men to kill Charley, as they'd promised repeatedly in their letters, but Christian never got a chance to learn how they'd respond because the flag-waver never appeared. Christian rode the trains all night, a sleepless two hundred miles, for nothing.

It turned out this was because one of the daily newspapers had made a mistake and reported that Christian was headed to Pottsville, Pennsylvania, to check out a claim that his son was being held there. It was an error that the newspaper quickly corrected—well, quickly for 1874, anyway, when corrections had to wait for the paper's next edition.

When Christian got back from his demoralizing train ride, he placed an ad that said: "Your directions were followed, you did not keep faith."[23] The kidnappers replied quickly, admitting they'd canceled because they thought he'd gone to Pottsville, though they later saw the correction and resumed with new demands in yet more personal ads. The back-and-forth was a nightmare for the family—a roller-coaster ride of hope and despair—as Christian would relay in his book. It was true that people stepped forward to help, but it was also true that other people stepped forward with lies in hopes of getting reward money. The reward had started at $300 in the days after Charley disappeared,[24] but before July was out, the mayor and residents had pledged a pot of $20,000 for the arrest and conviction of the

A detail of the twenty-second letter Christian Ross received from the kidnappers, dated October 31, 1874. It starts off: "Mr. Ross we told you at the beginning of this bisnes [sic] we would deal with none but you. . . . The fate of your child would depend entirely from your actions in dealing with us."

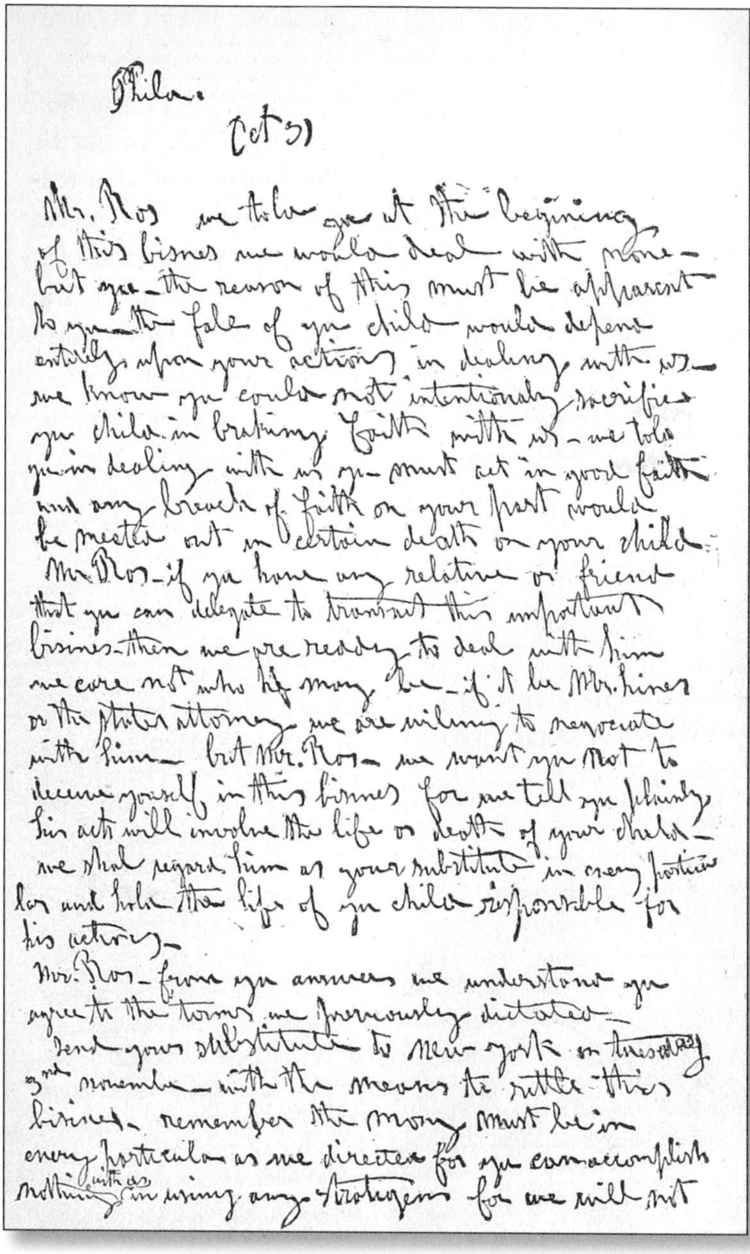

Phila.

Oct 31

Mr. Ros we told you at the begining of this bisnes we would deal with none but you — the reason of this must be apparent to you — the fate of you child would depend entirely upon your actions in dealing with us — we know you could not intentionaly sacrifice you child in braking faith with us — we told you in dealing with us you must act in good faith and any breach of faith on your part would be meeted out in certain death on your child.

Mr. Ros — if you have any relative or friend that you can delegate to ~~transact this~~ important bisnes — then we are ready to deal with him we care not who he may be — if it be Mr. hines or the ~~states~~ attorney we are wiling to negociate with him — but Mr. Ros we want you not to deceive yourself in this bisnes for we tell you plainly his acts will involve the life or death of your child — we shal regard him as your substitute in every particular and hold the life of you child responsible for his actions —

Mr. Ros — from you answers we understand you agree to the terms we previously dictated —

Send your substitute to New York on tuesday 3rd november with the means to settle this bisnes — remember the mony must be in every particular as we directed for you can accomplish nothing with us in using any stratagems for we will not kidnappers, and the safe return of Charley to his family. That the reward matched the ransom seemed to irk the kidnappers. They actually said in one letter that, after realizing Christian Ross wasn't as wealthy as they'd thought, they considered cutting the demand in half, but if the public could scrape together the ransom amount for the reward they could surely scrape it together for the ransom, too. So the price tag remained fixed.

The cranks and con artists of the world came out in full force. One man told Christian that his son was stolen as punishment from God because the Rosses dared to cut their hair, which the man considered a grave sin. Let your hair grow, and God will return your boy, he said.[25] Prisoners came forward to say they knew the culprits and would happily share the details—but only if they were promised early release. Self-anointed clairvoyants and spiritualists shared their visions. Fortune tellers offered their services. Christian said in his book that if there ever had been a time for fortune tellers to prove their powers, it would have been in this case. But it didn't happen.[26]

Finally, an informant came out with some plausible information. A convict said he'd been approached in New York to commit a similar kidnapping of a child from the famously rich Vanderbilt family. The ransom was supposed to be $50,000, but the plan otherwise was just like the Ross kidnapping.[27] They'd find the child in the front yard, lure him with candy or toys, and then secret him away until the money had been paid. The informant had declined because the plan as pitched included the very real possibility of child murder, and though he might have been a criminal, he wasn't willing to kill an innocent child. The informant, Clinton "Gil" Mosher, identified the men as his own younger brother, William Mosher, and Joseph Douglas.[28] Both were petty criminals. Mosher was on the run at the time, having escaped from jail. The men were known to stay in New York, but they had lived in Philadelphia for a spell over the summer. The circumstantial evidence, at least, excited authorities. New York officers worked to find them, updating Philadelphia police every few days. The weeks dragged on, however, and the Ross family's resolve was weakening. They just wanted their boy back. By October, Christian was sick from the stress and Sarah stepped in with her brothers to take over negotiations. She decided to forget about worrisome precedent and pay the ransom. Sarah's brother, Joseph W. Lewis, set up a meeting at a New York hotel to drop the money off on November 18.

He hoped against hope that this would finally end the family's pain, but the culprits never showed, nor did they answer the personal ad the family posted afterward: "We have performed our part to the letter, you have broken faith; we will have no more trifling, action must now be simultaneous."[29]

Then William Westervelt entered the picture. He was the brother-in-law of Mosher—one of the suspected kidnappers—but that's not all he was. Westervelt had been fired as a New York city policeman for graft; he cut a deal with NYPD superintendent George Walling that if he helped get Charley back home by spying on Mosher, he'd not only get the $20,000 reward, but he'd also get reinstated as a cop.[30] Westervelt kept providing information that he said would lead police to Mosher and Douglas, but it never panned out—he was also acting as a double agent, feeding the police's plans back to the kidnappers.[31]

"And then in December," Good said, "it all went to hell."[32]

In the early morning hours of December 14, 1874, police were called to a house in Bay Ridge, Long Island, about a burglary.[33] It escalated into a gun battle, with police shooting two suspects who ultimately proved to be Mosher and Douglas. After the men had been identified, little Walter was brought in to see their corpses. He identified them as the two men from the carriage. One in particular, Mosher, had an identifiable nose[34]—Walter called it a "monkey nose"—because he'd had syphilis and had some of the physical deformities the disease was known to cause. Douglas had been mortally wounded in the shoot-out, but he'd lived just long enough to say that he had been one of the people who had kidnapped Charley Ross. Police demanded to know where the boy was, to which Douglas replied that they would have to ask the other guy that. But the other guy, Mosher, had been killed instantly.[35]

"And so then the family was really just out of luck," Good said.[36]

Walter took a look at Westervelt, too, but said he didn't recognize him, and despite the investigators' certainty that the disgraced policeman had been involved, he told them nothing of value, even when offered immunity to lead them to little Charley Ross. In August 1875, Westervelt went on trial for Charley's kidnapping[37]. Although the jury acquitted him of that charge, he was convicted of conspiracy and sentenced to six years in prison.[38]

No one knows for sure what happened to Charley. Mosher's wife insisted he was alive. She was sure of it, she told reporters in 1875, though she said she'd never seen him herself or where he'd gone. "I know my husband wouldn't

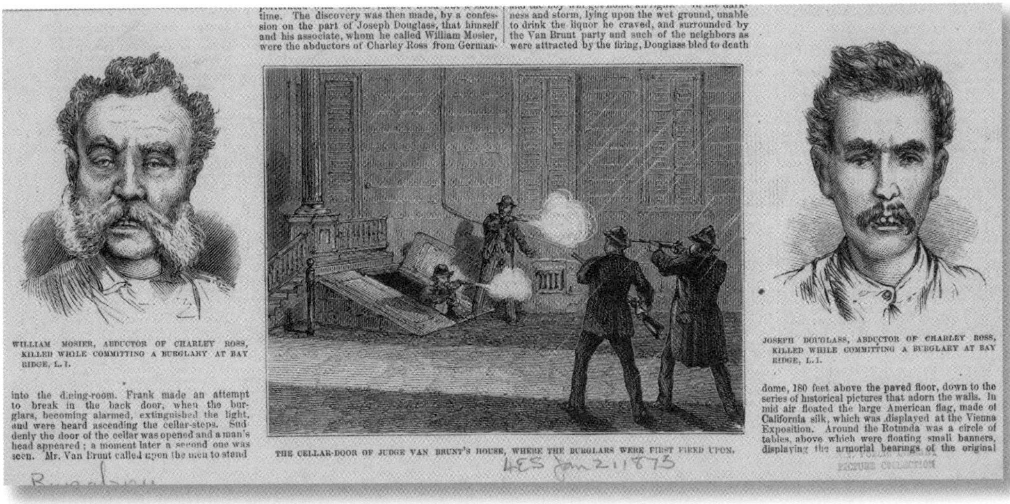
time. The discovery was then made, by a confession on the part of Joseph Douglass, that himself and his associate, whom he called William Mosier, were the abductors of Charley Ross from German-

ness and storm, lying upon the wet ground, unable to drink the liquor he craved, and surrounded by the Van Brunt party and such of the neighbors as were attracted by the firing, Douglass bled to death

WILLIAM MOSIER, ABDUCTOR OF CHARLEY ROSS, KILLED WHILE COMMITTING A BURGLARY AT BAY RIDGE, L. I.

into the dining-room. Frank made an attempt to break in the back door, when the burglars, becoming alarmed, extinguished the light, and were heard ascending the cellar-steps. Suddenly the door of the cellar was opened and a man's head appeared; a moment later a second one was seen. Mr. Van Brunt called upon the men to stand

THE CELLAR-DOOR OF JUDGE VAN BRUNT'S HOUSE, WHERE THE BURGLARS WERE FIRST FIRED UPON.

JOSEPH DOUGLASS, ABDUCTOR OF CHARLEY ROSS, KILLED WHILE COMMITTING A BURGLARY AT BAY RIDGE, L. I.

dome, 180 feet above the paved floor, down to the series of historical pictures that adorn the walls. In mid air floated the large American flag, made of California silk, which was displayed at the Vienna Exposition. Around the Rotunda was a circle of tables, above which were floating small banners, displaying the armorial bearings of the original

On January 2, 1875, *Frank Leslie's Illustrated Newspaper* depicted the scene of the fatal shootout at the summer home of a judge, Charles Van Brunt, which Ross abudctors William Mosher and Joseph Douglas had broken into.

have hurt a hair of his head," she said.[39] Christian and Sarah Ross spent their remaining years chasing down every rumor, responding to every condolence, and sinking far more money into the search for their son than the kidnappers had ever requested. It's clear that they still held out hope: In the 1880 census, six full years after Charley disappeared, it shows that his parents still listed him as part of the household. They reported his age as ten.[40]

The book Christian wrote in 1876 was published to raise more money to keep the search going, which was expensive. In the years that followed, literally hundreds of boys, and then men, stepped forward to say they were Charley Ross. Every time, their stories were looked into, and every time they amounted to nothing. By the time Christian died in 1897, it's estimated he spent $60,000 on the search—well over $2 million in today's money. A month after Christian died, Mosher's nephew, Ellsworth—the informant Gil's son—reported that his father had told him Charley had been killed.[41] Still, Sarah Ross wouldn't give up hope. Her search continued until her death on December 13, 1912, after which more than half of her obituary was dedicated to Charley:

> **The fate of the boy is still wrapped in mystery. A fortune had been spent by Mr. Ross, but to the end of his life in 1897, he neglected no chance to find the missing son. Charley Rosses by the score appeared in every part of the country, and every case was carefully**

Gustave Blair—who claimed to be Charley Ross—shown in a 1939 photograph.

> **investigated, but without result. Since Mr. Ross's death, Mrs. Ross has been untiring in her efforts to investigate every clew, and her hope that before her death she might find her son was unfailing.[42]**

The case continued to hang over Charley's siblings the rest of their lives, too. The year after his mother died, Henry Ross, Charley's older brother, got engaged, and a wire story announced the news. It read:

> **An engagement that recalls the most famous kidnapping mystery in the history of this country was made known yesterday when friends of Miss Jessie Lloyd Gifford, a well-known settlement worker and student of sociological subjects in this city, learned that she will be married to Mr. Henry A. Ross of Philadelphia, brother of Charley Ross, who was kidnapped more than 38 years ago and whose fate has never been learned.[43]**

After Sarah died, Charley's siblings were so jaded by all the false claims that they simply couldn't abide any more of them. But twenty years after her death, they received the most detailed claim yet, when an elderly man who went by the name Gustave Blair stepped forward, professing to be the missing boy.

Blair surfaced in early April 1932. Newspaper reports said Blair's attorney advanced the claim "as part of a campaign to have the immigration authorities allow the gardener's son to cross the American border from Canada to Seattle"—the campaign would be aided if Blair was a native-born American.[44]

Blair said he remembered being stolen and then hidden in a cave for weeks, where he was guarded by two men, one of them a young man named Lincoln Miller. He described being taken to a home and raised by a family in Illinois as Lincoln's brother. He'd been renamed Nelson Miller, after the family's youngest son, who'd recently died. When this new Nelson Miller was older, he'd claimed to have confronted his adopted family about not being related to them, and he said the father had threatened to kill him.[45] Scared for his life, the young man moved to Canada and returned to the States with yet another new name.

After the father died, Lincoln Miller confirmed the story, so Blair had a witness corroborating his story—which none of the previous claimants had had. And some of his story really did align with bits and pieces from the kidnappers' letters. Those missives were so long and rambling that it was easy to overlook the crumbs they left behind, but when comparing Blair's and Miller's tale with the letters, you do see some overlap: Blair said he'd been hidden in a cave, and the kidnappers referred to Charley as being both behind a rock and somewhere sunshine didn't reach. Miller said that he'd traveled two or three days into the wilderness to reach the cave where Charley had been held, and a pair of ransom letters sent three days apart suggested that Charley had indeed been about that distance from Philadelphia. Also, it's notable that if Blair's story were true, it'd mean that Charley eventually had been taken to Illinois; Mosher told friends he'd just returned from Chicago in December 1874.[46]

Blair took his case to a court in Arizona and a judge, for one, believed him. He declared that Blair was legally the long-lost Charley Ross—though the ruling didn't carry much weight. Charley's brother, Walter, was adamant it was yet another lie. "The whole thing is ridiculous," he said.[47] He told a reporter in 1939 that he and his siblings had been harassed by claimants for sixty-five years and had long believed that his brother had died at the kidnappers' hands back in the nineteenth century. He refused to even meet with Blair.

It would take DNA testing to determine if Blair's story really was true or an elaborate lie. An article published in the journal *Pennsylvania History* in 2000 noted that Blair's descendants prepared DNA samples for comparison in the late 1990s, but there's no documentation suggesting that the Rosses ever did.[48] However, the Miller family commissioned a Y-DNA study that determined with 99.99 percent probability that Blair was, in fact, a Miller, meaning he could not have been Charley Ross.[49] "Y-DNA doesn't lie," Rod Miller said in an email to me. "While the disappearance of Charley Ross is still a cold case, at least we know who Charley Ross is *not*. Unfortunately, most modern takes on the kidnapping end with Gustave Blair. The sad correction is Charley Ross is still lost."[50]

Legal Legacy

Not only was the kidnapping of Charley Ross one of the most sensational cases of the nineteenth century, but it's recognized today as America's first kidnapping-for-ransom case.

- When Charley disappeared, stealing a child was such a rare crime that it wasn't even on the law books as a felony—the kidnappers stood to face stiffer penalties for stealing Charley's clothing than for stealing the child.[51] His case led to authorities nationwide taking kidnapping cases far more seriously,[52] but it would not be until 1932 with the Lindbergh baby kidnapping (see chapter 24) that the Federal Kidnapping Act was passed.
- Charley's disappearance also inspired parents to begin teaching their children lessons in "stranger danger." The warning not to take candy from strangers is said to have come directly from Charley's case.[53]

22
The Enduring Mystery of the Villisca Axe Murders
(1912)

The Stillinger girls were supposed to stay with their grandmother overnight, but Lena Gertrude, twelve, and Ina Mae, eight, had performed in a Children's Day program at the local Presbyterian church. The show was going to end late and the small town of Villisca, Iowa, lacked working streetlights.[1] The girls were nervous about walking that late in the dark, so, at the last minute, the husband of the program's organizer got a grand idea: Josiah B. Moore called up the Stillinger household and asked if the two girls could stay at the Moore house instead of at their grandmother's. The Stillinger parents weren't around, but one of their older daughters was, and she said sure. So it was settled: Lena and Ina would be overnight guests, making the Moore house on East Second Street even fuller than usual. The two parents and their four children slept upstairs, while Lena and Ina slept downstairs.

But come the next morning, the household seemed anything but bustling. In fact, a neighbor noticed that no one had roused by 7:00 a.m, which was unusual. Neighbor Mary Peckham noticed that the house was dark, and no one was performing their typical morning chores.[2] The Moores were a farming family, and their days were structured like clockwork. The concerned neighbor called Josiah Moore's brother, Ross, who came to the house and knocked on the door. No answer. He went around to the back door. That, too, was locked up tight. Strangely, he couldn't even peek through the windows because the glass in every one of them seemed to be obstructed.

Finally, he made use of the key his brother had given him for emergencies and walked inside the house. Things were eerily quiet. He walked into the only ground-floor bedroom—the guest room, where Lena and Ina had slept that night—and found the girls so badly bludgeoned that they no longer had faces. Ross rushed from the house and blurted, "Something terrible has happened!"

Police officer Henry "Hank" Horton arrived and searched the rest of the house—a task made all the more daunting because the whole interior was dark—the windows had been covered with bedsheets and clothes, and in 1912, few rural houses had electricity. Horton used a match to illuminate his way, with no guarantee that the killer had already fled.

When he emerged from the house, he uttered, "There's somebody dead in every bed."[3]

The once-sleepy town would never be the same, and not just because it was witness to the most infamous murder mystery in Iowa history, in which a killer armed with an axe brutally slaughtered people in their sleep. Over time, the horrified nation realized the slayings might be the work of a madman traveling the country and killing entire families indiscriminately.

Villisca, Iowa, was then—and remains today—a little town near the southwest corner of the state. It was twice as populated in 1912 compared to now, with about 2,000 residents per the 1910 census, and about 1,130 in the 2020 census. It covers less than two square miles of Montgomery County.[4]

LAST VICTIMS OF MAD MURDERER OF WEST

J. W. Moore, wife and 3 of 4 children who were murdered in bed at Villisca, Ia. Star shows room in which Misses Stillinger, visiting Moores, were killed.

An article on the Villisca axe murders from *The Day Book*, a Chicago daily, June 14, 1912. It depicts the Moore house and family.

In 1912, the Moore family lived in a white, two-story A-frame house that had been built in 1868. The family moved there in 1903 and had been well-respected, well-liked members of the sleepy town. Josiah Moore, often called by his initials J. B., had worked at a local company selling farming equipment, but a few years before the murders, he left that company to form his own. He was a natural with customers so a lot of his clients followed him to his new business, a fact that would raise suspicions later.

Josiah was forty-three years old and married to a thirty-nine-year-old woman named Sarah. The couple had four children between the ages of five and eleven. Sarah

Moore was active in the Presbyterian church, so she often organized events like the Children's Day program. It was one of the many ways the Moore family stayed active in the community.

June 9, 1912, was a warm summer Sunday in Villisca. The program Sarah Moore had helped create was an annual event designed to showcase how much the kids had learned at Sunday school over the year. The children had rehearsed skits, songs, and Bible readings for the evening performance.

As Dave McFarland of the Montgomery County History Center explained in an amateur documentary called *Villisca: A Town Divided*,[5] the program ended around 10:00 p.m. The town didn't have streetlights, but that wasn't because the technology didn't exist.

"There was an argument going on about who was responsible for the streetlights in Villisca," McFarland said, "and the power company had turned the power off to the streetlights."[6]

The Stillinger girls found the unlit streets unnerving and felt it safer to stay at the Moore house. The sisters flanked the Moore's eleven-year-old daughter Katherine in age. As investigators tried to make sense of the horrific crime scene, they became convinced that the sisters had been the last to die—and that Lena, the oldest, had actually been the only victim to awaken before she was slain.

Unlike today, in 1912, most small towns didn't have a real police department. They might have an officer or two, but there was no budget provided for investigations because it was exceedingly rare that a crime warranting an in-depth investigation would take place in any given year.

"We had a town marshal, and we had a sheriff," said Roy Marshall, author of the book *Villisca: The True Account of the Mass Murder that Stunned the Nation* (2003), in the documentary. "Sheriff was purely a political office.... You had no qualifications other than to get votes. There were no training programs." Marshall explained that officers weren't expected to investigate serious crimes back then. "They were peace officers at the time," he said, "there to keep the peace."[7]

Because of that, there was no routine funding for investigations, either. When a big crime occurred, the community donated money to foot the associated bills. That meant that victims with wealthy connections were more likely to have their cases investigated than poor victims. The Moores were well off and had kin in town, so that was a good start. Plus, as word spread throughout the small town about this dastardly crime, residents pitched in plenty, too. Eight people had been killed in their sleep. This was an evil, nightmare-inducing act. They wanted the killer caught—and quickly.

Evidence collecting was relatively primitive at the time. While the English first started using fingerprints as a crime-solving tool in the mid-nineteenth century, America's first fingerprint system wasn't created until the mid-1900s.[8] There was a smattering of experts in the country by 1912; Villisca officials found one about 130 miles due south in Leavenworth, Kansas, and called for him to come consult as quickly as possible.

"The fellow from Leavenworth arrived the next day after the murder had been discovered, and he was drunk when he got there," said Dr. Edgar Epperly on the webcast *CSI Iowa*. Epperly is a historian and Villisca expert who has spent much of his professional career studying this case.[9]

With no other options, officials took the man to a local hotel to sober up. After that, he conducted an examination of the crime scene but uncovered no prints.

"[The scene] had been contaminated," Epperly said. "Maybe a hundred people went through the site."[10]

This wasn't unusual for the time. Lookie-loos arrived in droves after the bodies were discovered, and while Horton, the officer, managed to keep most people out until the bodies had been removed, afterward was another matter. With police so scarce, neighbors not only showed up to crime scenes like this one because they were curious, but they showed up to help solve the crime. There was much more of a community focus, especially in rural areas, and the idea that the town would leave an investigation up to its one part-time officer to solve would have seemed ludicrous. So townspeople—some fascinated for macabre reasons, others earnestly wanting to help—tromped through the house looking for clues. They found clothes and toys strewn about,[11] a bloody handkerchief, and footprints, as well as gouges in the upstairs ceiling where it appeared the killer had swung his axe overhead as he butchered the second-floor victims.[12]

In the attic of the Moore home two cigarette butts were found. No one in the family was known to smoke, so this was noted. On the second floor, every one of the six victims had had their bedding pulled over their heads

"A TERRIFIED TOWN BARRED WINDOWS, BOUGHT GUNS FOR PROTECTION. YOU GO INTO A LOT OF HOUSES, TODAY EVEN, AND YOU'LL SEE DOUBLE-BOLT LATCHES ON DOORS."

before they'd been fatally whacked by what appeared to be the blunt end of an axe. Everyone, that is, except for Josiah. He was covered like the others, but his head had been smashed with the sharp edge of the axe, completely obliterating his face. It appeared no one had stirred from their sleep, which led investigators—and wannabes—to speculate that the killer had perhaps already been inside the home when the family had gone to bed. Those two cigarettes might have been smoked while he waited.[13]

Outside the main house, investigators noticed that inside a detached barn was a pile of hay that looked to have been used recently as someone's makeshift bed. Additionally, a knothole in the wood allowed someone lying down in the hay to keep watch over the house, said Richard Estep, author of *A Nightmare in Villisca* (2020). "And the one girl [Lena] had been moved in the bed, her undergarments removed, and she was sexually posed with a lamp at the foot of the bed."[14]

Back inside the house, the first floor had the most curious details. Every door had been locked, as had every window—save one. As mentioned, the windows had been covered. But more than that, every pane of glass within the doorways had also been covered. Also, mirrors in the house had been covered by cloth or clothing the killer apparently had taken from dresser drawers.[15]

"And then there was a four-pound piece of bacon that was taken from a back room and left leaning against the wall," noted Epperly.[16]

Lena, the older of the Stillinger sisters, appeared to have tried to fend off a blow because she had suffered a defensive wound on one of her arms. This fact devastated her family. While the other victims didn't know what was coming, Lena knew.

"The paper was full of gruesome details," said Darwin Linn, whose family owned the murder house for decades, speaking to Local 5 News in 2002. "A terrified town barred windows, bought guns for protection. You go into a lot of houses, today even, and you'll see double-bolt latches on doors."[17]

Protective gear was in such demand that "you couldn't buy a gun or a padlock for fifty miles in any direction," Linn said. "People took turns staying up at night guarding their family."[18]

News wire services weren't a new phenomenon in 1912—the Associated Press, for example, was founded in 1846—but their use nationwide grew exponentially after the turn of the century.[19] Not only that, but newspapers had become longer, with more pages that needed to be filled. And though it is touted today that true crime is more popular than ever, the fact is that true crime has been regular newspaper fodder since at least the late 1800s; and leaflets and broadsides on local crimes and trials were circulated even as far back as the 1500s in Britain.[20] As such, newspaper editors routinely pulled out-of-state crime stories from the news wire services to run. In the wake of this particular crime, two things were happening at once: more newspapers were using wire services, and they were making more use of crime content from other places. It's because of this that a few keen-eyed people noticed that the details of the Villisca axe murders sounded mighty familiar. Police fielded tips pointing to similar murders along train routes throughout middle and eastern America.

Large police force or no, close to home is where all investigations have always tended to start, so that's where this one started, too. Statistically, murders are most likely to be committed by a killer acquainted with the victims, and while the Moores were well liked, motivation for murder can be easily retrofitted in most situations. The suspicions in this case began with a man named Frank Fernando Jones. Jones had been born in Bath, New York, but had spent most of his life in the Midwest. He'd moved to Villisca in 1882 and, like Josiah Moore, was a successful businessman, albeit not a very popular one. His job was to collect payments on accounts in arrears, though he sold farm equipment, too. In fact, he'd been Josiah's partner before Josiah decided to set off on his own, taking most of their clients with him. Some assumed that Jones must have been furious, though solid evidence of that is scant.[21]

Police questioned whether that was motive enough for murder, though, since Jones wasn't completely reliant on his farming business. He dabbled in a lot of things, including politics. He'd served on the Villisca City Council, then won a seat in the Iowa House of Representatives in 1904. He kept that post until 1909. When the murders occurred, Jones was readying to run for the state senate and had his eye on bigger statewide gigs—maybe even governor one day. Rumors continued despite a dearth of physical evidence, but Jones had a strong enough support system that helped him rise above the suspicions to win the Republican senate seat in 1913.

This case would prove to be a stubborn one, and no one was arrested at the outset. Days turned into weeks, weeks into months. A few years earlier,

the Burns Detective Agency had heralded success in solving the 1910 murder of Marie Smith in Asbury Park, New Jersey (see page 151). In that case, the private investigator sent by Burns solved the case with a doggedness that bordered on obsession. Officials in Villisca were hoping for similar success in the Moore case, but this time around, things went a little differently. The investigator assigned to Villisca was a man named James Newton Wilkerson.[22] In hindsight, he was every bit as dogged as Raymond Campbell Schindler, but nowhere near as principled. And this is the problem with privatized investigative agencies doing police work: if someone unscrupulous is helming the investigation, there's no way to hold that party accountable because he's a contractor rather than a public servant. Things can get messy, especially because there often were rewards attached to solving crimes that private investigators were eligible to receive.

Wilkerson had been born in 1888, so he was just twenty-six years old when he arrived in Villisca in 1914, two years after the murders. He came because the community was outraged that the case hadn't been solved. Soon after he arrived, he signed onto the theory that Frank Fernando Jones must be the killer. And he pushed that narrative hard.

"Wilkerson started a campaign," McFarland said. "It's kind of sad, but it was almost kind of slanderous."[23]

Wilkerson tried to get Jones to confess, and when that effort failed, he publicly claimed that it was because Jones was too slippery a slayer. Then Wilkerson expanded his view, positing that Jones had hired a man named William "Blackie" Mansfield to be the killer. Mansfield was described as a convict, former soldier,[24] and "dope fiend," per Wilkerson.[25] That Mansfield's own family was murdered in similar fashion by an axe-wielding killer did not bolster his claims of innocence. Those slayings happened in July 1914 in Blue Island, Illinois. Killed were Mansfield's wife, his baby, and his wife's parents. Mansfield insisted he played no role, but police scoffed at the notion that the echoing crime scenes could be coincidental.

In 1916, four years after the murders at the Moore house, Mansfield was charged with eight counts of murder. Wilkerson said that neighbors who'd initially reported having seen and heard nothing out of sorts the night of the slayings stepped forward to say they now remembered seeing a man matching Mansfield's description having a conversation about killing the Moores the very night it happened. The man purportedly was planning the crime with other men, including Jones and Jones's son, Albert.[26]

At one point, Mansfield himself confessed. He said Jones had hired him to kill the Moores. But he soon recanted and explained that Wilkerson had offered to share the reward money with him if he helped pin the crime on Jones.[27] As it turned out, Mansfield had a solid alibi for June 9, 1912: he was in another state altogether. Not only that, but the grand jury that weighed Wilkerson's evidence noticed something odd: At the time, investigators would pull together a so-called "dope sheet," which was basically a summary of the evidence they intended to present as a way to streamline the process. But when witnesses listed on the dope sheet testified before jurors, they weren't saying the things that the sheet indicated they would say. If the sheet said one witness would testify that Mansfield confessed outright to her, that witness might actually say the opposite in front of the jury. Once jurors realized the dope sheet was a complete fabrication, charges against Mansfield were dismissed and he never went to trial. Mansfield later sued Wilkerson, the Montgomery County sheriff, and the prosecuting attorney for false arrest.[28]

None of these developments made Wilkerson concede, however. He made it his life's mission to convince as many people as possible that Jones had killed the Moore family. Plenty of people in the community believed him, though another compelling suspect surfaced. This man was the Reverend Lyn George Kelly, who wasn't from Villisca but had attended the Children's Day program the night of the deaths. Though he left the town by train about three hours before the slayings were discovered, he would forever be tied to the horror that happened there.

Kelly had been born in England in 1878 but moved to the United States with his wife in 1904. He'd bounced from job to job, never really settling on a path, and in 1912 was working as something of an apprentice minister. His father had been a minister, and Kelly figured he might be gifted in that arena by birthright. And in a way he was. In the 2004 documentary *Villisca: Living with a Mystery*,"[29] he's described as a confident and articulate speaker—at least, when preaching. Away from the pulpit, he seemed like a mess. He seemed nervous, his eyes darting back and forth in a shifty way, and he spoke so quickly that he'd sometimes drool.

Left to right: An undated photograph of John Montgomery (Sarah Moore's father); Mrs. Kelly; Reverend Lyn George J. Kelly; and Josiah Moore, son-in-law of John Montgomery, who was killed along with his wife, Sarah, and four children in Villisca.

It so happened that on June 9, he'd traveled to Villisca specifically to see the annual church show. When he learned of the murders, he was naturally disturbed. But quickly it seemed Kelly had developed a strange fascination with the slayings—so much so that he returned to Villisca at one point and actually posed as a private investigator to be allowed inside the house. He walked from room to room, taking in every bit of the scene. Afterward, he began telling anyone who would listen about his theories on the case and the killer. That kept up long after he left Villisca, which kept his name in people's minds. Over the years, he moved time and again, preaching in Minnesota, Iowa, Kansas, Oklahoma, and Nebraska. But his thoughts kept returning to Villisca.

As Epperly said, Kelly "became obsessed with the crime."[30]

Kelly wrote letters to the sheriff, to detectives, to prosecutors, to judges. He would not stop speculating about the case. And it didn't help that Kelly himself had what authorities at the time referred to as sexual perversions. For example, he'd been arrested after advertising in the *Omaha World-Herald* for a "girl stenographer typewriter for literary and artistic work. . . . Must be willing to pose for book pictures."[31] It wasn't the job posting that was problematic, but rather his response to a sixteen-year-old applicant. He wrote back to her and said she sounded well-suited for the job, but told her that if she were hired, she'd be posing in the nude. The girl turned the letter over to police, who learned it hadn't been the first time Kelly was accused of trying to get young girls to undress for him. A year after the Villisca murders, he was caught in Carroll, Iowa, trying to convince two thirteen-year-old girls to pose nude for him. Just days *before* the murders, he'd supposedly been spotted peeping into a woman's bedroom window.[32]

All of this seemed potentially relevant, especially because Lena Stillinger had been posed after she was murdered. Her underwear had been removed and her nightshirt had been bunched above her hips, exposing her. Where her legs dangled off the bed, the killer had placed a lantern. Because it appeared the killer had illuminated the girl for purposes of looking at her body, some investigators believed that it seemed to jibe with Kelly's proclivities. He'd tried repeatedly to see young girls naked, and maybe that urge led him to slaughter a family, and the girl, so he could look all he wanted.

The state brought their theory to a grand jury and ultimately charged him with the crime. But there was one piece of physical evidence that didn't fit with Kelly being the killer: the gouged upstairs ceiling. The thinking was that the killer must have been fairly tall, for when he raised the axe to level the fatal blows, the axe scraped the plaster. Kelly was only five-foot-two, meaning he was too short for his upward arcs to hit the plaster overhead.

Then Kelly did something to confuse things further: he reportedly confessed. Back in this era, cops unrepentantly gave suspects the third degree—and at the time, that could mean beatings, psychological tricks—anything to elicit a confession. Which is why it's not surprising that, once out of the interrogation room, Kelly recanted.[33]

He went on trial in 1917 for the five-year-old crime. Every day, the courtroom was packed with spectators, and the divide in Villisca was stark. The state attorney general, Horace Havner, argued his case against Kelly strenuously. Tensions were so high that Havner found himself indicted by a grand jury for "oppression in office" for allegedly intimidating witnesses in the case against Kelly.[34] (Those allegations were championed by Wilkerson, who, it should be noted, ran against Havner in the 1918 election.[35])

As is often the case with politicians, there was probably a reason he pushed so hard, according to Roy Marshall. "For him, being the attorney general was a stepping stone. His ambition was to become governor," Marshall said, "so he grabbed onto this case. If he could get a conviction in the most high-profile murder case in Iowa history, that would be very good for his political career."[36]

ALLEGED AX MURDERER, Who was removed from Red Oak for safe keeping to the county jail at Logan, Ia. yesterday.

REV. LYN GEORGE J KELLY

KELLY TAKEN TO LOGAN JAIL BY SHERIFF'S MEN

KAISER ATTACKS WITH MEN TAKEN FROM RUSS LINE

A clipping from an article in the *Omaha Daily Bee*, May 17, 1917, reporting on Kelly's transfer to the county jail in Des Moines from Red Oak, Iowa, to await trial.

On the other side was Wilkerson, the private eye. He publicly defended Kelly and collected money purportedly for Kelly's legal costs, though, in truth, Wilkerson pocketed most of that money.[37] The fathers of the Stillinger girls and of Sarah Moore supported Kelly, too. There's a photo of the two grieving dads with Kelly and Kelly's wife, a photograph snapped specifically to show that the survivors of the slaying believed Kelly innocent.[38]

The first jury came back deadlocked.[39] So Kelly was tried again the next year. That time, he was acquitted.

No one was ever charged again, so to this day, it's officially an unsolved case. But people have theories. Some believe it was the work of a man named Henry Lee Moore (no relation to the Moore family killed in the case).[40] In December 1912, Moore had been convicted of killing two members of his family—his mother and grandmother—with an axe in Columbia, Missouri. After his arrest, newspapers began attributing the best-known of the axe murders to him because he was Midwest-based and because they desperately wanted an answer. Not everyone believes Moore killed anyone outside of his family. For example, authors Bill James and his daughter, Rachel McCarthy James, said there's no evidence to suggest that Henry Lee Moore rode the rails, and they're certain the real killer did. In *The Man from the Train*, the authors describe grisly axe murder after axe murder across the country, far beyond Villisca—crimes that began in 1898 and stopped in 1912. Their theory is that a single killer, probably who worked as an itinerant lumberjack, was hopping trains to go where the jobs were—and had a side hobby of familicide. Moore didn't fit the description because 1) he wasn't known to leave the Midwest region, and 2) his grandmother wasn't in bed when she was killed. She'd been bludgeoned while in a rocking chair, wide awake. It didn't fit the pattern. Henry Moore more likely tried to pattern his slayings after the by-then-known serial killer in hopes of getting away with it.

The Jameses sifted through countless newspapers looking for any crimes that seemed remotely similar to the one in Villisca. They then documented those cases and spelled out which elements were the same, which were different, and which they believe were part of a series of slayings committed by one man. Their reasoning was simple: many of the Villisca details were repeated in other crimes, and whoever killed the Moore family didn't seem to be a novice. As McCarthy James said, "This guy had a lot of practice, especially by Villisca. He was very, very good at killing large groups of people."[41]

Newspapers in 1911 and 1912 had started tying some of the Midwest slayings together, but McCarthy James assumed that the spree was indicative of a practiced killer going through a frenzied period. Most serial killers don't start out hot and heavy. They start with a single crime that's far less polished than their later work will be. So McCarthy James worked backward, taking special note of specific commonalities. In the end, she and her father determined that crimes sharing most of the following characteristics were likely committed by their so-called Man from the Train:[42]

- **The murders were committed not just near railroad tracks, but near junctions where multiple rail lines merged.**
- **Lumberjacking or mining were the main industries of the area.**
- **The crimes took place in very small towns with little, if any, police presence.**
- **Entire families were killed in a single attack.**
- **The victims' faces were often covered after the attack, usually by their bedding.**
- **The murders happened within ninety minutes of midnight, after the household had gone to sleep.**
- **The killer didn't use the sharp side of the axe, but rather smashed in his victims' skulls with the blunt side.**
- **The murder weapon was one the killer found either at the victims' own home or at a neighbors' home, and the killer left the axe behind upon leaving.**
- **Frequently, there were prepubescent females among the victims, and when there were, the girls would have been clearly singled out and often posed.**
- **The killer covered windows and locked or jammed the doors when he left.**
- **Lanterns inside were often moved from their usual locations.**
- **Robbery was never a motive—and, in fact, money was often left untouched right out in the open, almost as if to prove this was no robbery.**

Because these are fairly detailed similarities, the Jameses believe that the odds of two or three of these overlapping would be slim enough, but to have most overlap? They say, statistically, it's more likely that the same killer was responsible for each. That's a sobering thought, especially when considering that police in many of the cases were certain someone local was the killer, and several of the cases resulted in convictions of now-seemingly innocent suspects. Some of those people were executed. Several were lynched.

McCarthy James said that though some police investigators believed there was likely a madman riding the rails and killing families, when such a murder happened in their own towns, they'd always look for a local killer.

"Serial killers have always existed, and we've always created myths to deal with them," she said.[43] The concept of random serial killings is too terrifying for the public to contend with—or to accept as a satisfying explanation for a motive to a crime. "Even today we see people wanting an answer, a specific answer that is satisfying, that makes sense, that makes them feel safe again," McCarthy James said.[44]

The Jameses are confident that of the 40 or so murders they researched, the same killer is responsible for 14 of them, which, if true, would make his body count 59, making him one of the most prolific serial killers in American history. The Jameses suspect connections with up to 25 more slayings, though they're less certain about those. If their suspicions were true, it would mean this man killed more than 100 people in a 14-year span.

The father-daughter duo believes the killer was a man named Paul Mueller, which was sometimes misspelled as Muller or Miller. Mueller was a German emigrant who had been employed as a farmhand by a family called the Newtons near Brookfield, Massachusetts. That whole family was murdered in January 1898 the same way as the Moores were in Villisca. Found dead in their beds were Francis D. Newton, 45; his wife Sarah, 38; and their 10-year-old daughter, Ethel.

From a January 11, 1898 story in the *Boston Globe*: "The autopsy held this afternoon on the bodies demonstrated the brutality of the assault. Although an axe was used viciously, in no case were the blows struck with the blade, but all with the back of the blade."[45]

Suspicion immediately fell on the farmhand. Newspapers nationwide ran stories about the slayings for days as a manhunt for Mueller got underway. His background was a mystery, with him having been born overseas, there were no photos or even illustrations of him ever provided, and the descriptions people gave were pretty vague.

"He had weirdly spaced teeth, a bunch of scars, kind of an unpleasant disposition of a grumpy expression all the time," McCarthy James said.[46] "He was between five-foot-four and five-foot-five; pretty trim; about 155 pounds; and had long greasy, dark hair and a poorly trimmed mustache. Occasionally he wore a beard. Believed to be about thirty-five years old, he had little feet and a scar running from his wrist to his little finger and another above his right eye. He also walked with a distinctive sailor's gait."[47]

If Mueller really was the Villisca murderer, it was close to his final kill. The last murder that seems plausibly attributable to Mueller was the slaughter of the Pfanschmidt family near Payson, Illinois, on September 27 or 28, 1912. Killed were Charles Pfanschmidt; his wife, Mathilda; their fifteen-year-old daughter, Blanche; and a young schoolteacher named Emma Kaempen who was boarding with the family.[48] The only surviving Pfanschmidt was a son named Ray, who had been away working on a railroad excavation job in the nearby town of Quincy. Ray was convicted in 1913 for the slaying; a key part of the prosecutor's evidence was that two bloodhounds had tracked Ray's scent from the house along a route to Quincy. The case was appealed, and the conviction was overturned in 1914 by the Illinois Supreme Court.[49] This helped set a precedent in Illinois that the behavior of tracking dogs cannot be used to establish guilt, as "neither court nor jury can have any means of knowing why the dog does this thing or another."[50] The son was released, and the case remains unsolved to this day.

After the Pfanschmidt slaying, the Jameses believe that Mueller might have died or maybe landed in prison. Or perhaps he was unnerved by the attention the slayings were generating and went back to Germany. Regardless, theirs is just one of many theories that have been circulated in the 110 years since the Villisca axe murders, making the crime one of the most enduring mysteries in American history.

Legal Legacy

Part of the enduring impact of the Villisca axe murders was that it underscored the importance of preserving crime scenes in investigations.

- Amateur sleuths had "trampled" through the Moore house, potentially tainting evidence,[51] and some townsfolk walked through the house as well. Some even snagged souvenirs from the scene, reportedly including a chunk of J. B. Moore's skull.[52] Once news of the sloppiness spread, it started a slow-moving trend toward better protecting crime scenes and preserving evidence.
- While the English had started using fingerprints as a crime-solving tool in the mid-nineteenth century, America's system wasn't created until 1903. When Iowa officials summoned one of the few fingerprint experts in the country to Villisca from Leavenworth, Kansas, he arrived drunk, highlighting the need to have more people trained in the technique.[53]

23
The Murder of Mary Phagan
(1913)

One spring day in 1913, thirteen-year-old Mary Phagan went to fetch her paycheck. Her job, in this era before federal child labor laws, was repetitive and mindless: inserting rubber erasers into eraser tips at the National Pencil Co. on Forsythe Street in Downtown Atlanta. The next day, her name was splashed in newspapers alongside headlines such as "Body of Girl Found in Cellar."[1] Nationally, the case would ultimately have three major and entirely distinct legacies: it would spark laws protecting child workers from exploitation; it would play a major role in the second incarnation of the Ku Klux Klan, after its suppression by the federal government in 1871; and it would focus attention on anti-Semitism in the United States. Mary's family could never have anticipated that these consequences would come to be associated with her and her brief life span.

Mary was born in Alabama, the last of her parents' four children. The oldest was Benjamin, born in 1893. Then came Ollie in 1894, followed by Charlie in 1896. Mary was born in 1899.[2] That same year, her twenty-six-year-old father, William, died.[3] Mary's mother, Frances, remarried soon after to a man named John Coleman, and moved the family to Atlanta. While this new marriage must have provided the family some stability, they were struggling financially. Every bit helped, which is why Mary found work at the local pencil company, the wages from which she'd bring home to her parents.

April 26, 1913, promised to be an exciting day in Atlanta because a huge parade was planned to celebrate Confederate Memorial Day. The Civil War had ended only forty-eight years earlier, and there were still Confederate veterans alive in Georgia who would be participating in the event. The *Atlanta Constitution* ran briefs in the days leading up to the event, such as this one, describing the kind of fanfare expected: "The members of Allen Turner chapter, U.D.C., are planning an interesting and appropriate program to be carried out on Confederate Memorial Day. There will be included in the program one or two addresses for the occasion. The local chapter has been organized only a short time and there is much enthusiasm being manifested in its work here, as well as in the program for the 26th."[4]

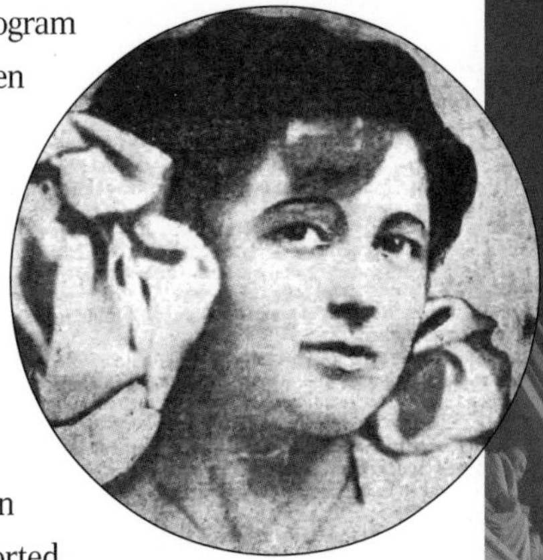

An undated photo of Mary Phagan before 1913.

Mary ate her usual breakfast of cabbage and bread and hopped on the streetcar to go to work so she could collect her pay.[5] Her boss was a man named Leo Frank, who was in his office when she arrived. He gave her the $1.20 she was owed and later said that was the last time he saw her. Newspapers on April 28 reported that Mary Phagan's body was found by a night watchman around 3:30 a.m. in the pencil company's cellar. Mary, wrongly reported at first to be fifteen years old,[6] was filthy with a gaping wound in the back of her head, bruises and cuts all over her body, and some cloth knotted around her throat.

Tied to the cloth was a short piece of rope, which police believed had been used to lower her body into the basement through a small hole in the floor above. Physicians who were called to the scene declared it death by strangulation. There were two odd notes left beside her body that seemed to be scrawled on scrap paper. Barely legible, one read: "Mam that negro hire down here did this. I went to make water and he push me down that hole. A long sleam tall negro."[7] Later in the note, it referred to the man in question as the "night witch," which authorities took to mean "night watchman."

At first, it seemed feasible that this death note was written by Mary because the floor around her was littered with pencils that also seemed to have fallen from the small hole above. But Mary's stepfather said the handwriting didn't match. Mary wasn't a highly educated girl at thirteen, but she had attended some schooling and this writing was too simplistic to be hers. Police immediately went about collecting clues. They realized the cloth around her neck was torn from her underclothing. They found a lead pipe near her body, which they thought might have been used to beat her. Police canvassed the area for witnesses and interviewed the night watchman who reportedly found Mary's body. He was a Black man named Newt Lee, who was immediately suspected of the crime—not just because he'd found the body but also because the note accompanying Mary seemed to implicate him. Lee said he'd heard a scream shortly after midnight, but because the day had been such a ruckus with the parade and partiers, he didn't investigate it. Lee was arrested under the then-legal blanket charge of suspicion despite his insistence he had nothing to do with it. Police learned from witnesses that Mary had been spotted around 12:30 in the morning—three hours before her body was found—with a white man named Arthur Mullinax. He, too, was arrested on a charge of suspicion.[8]

The story of Mary's death was huge news, and thanks to wire coverage, was featured in newspapers in thirty states around the country. This was national news even before any outlet had produced an image of her with her big innocent eyes and a girlish bow in her hair. The general reaction was that she was just so young, and so undeserving of this kind of shocking violence. This was a child whose only major achievement so far in life was that she had earned rave reviews playing Sleeping Beauty in a church performance the year before.

At the time, "Atlanta was in the midst of a newspaper war," said author Steve Oney, who wrote a book about the case titled *And the Dead Shall Rise: The Murder of Mary Phagan and the Lynching of Leo Frank* (2003). "There were three independent newspapers in Atlanta at the time: the *Atlanta Journal*, the *Atlanta Constitution*, and the *Atlanta Georgian*, which was owned by William Randolph Hearst. The Hearst paper especially "went wild with this story," Oney said during a 2014 presentation.[9]

Police of course had questions for Mary's boss, Leo Frank, the superintendent of the pencil factory, who struck them as nervous. He was a twenty-nine-year-old Jewish man of slight stature who lived with his wife, Lucille. Frank was a quiet, rational, well-educated mechanical engineer who graduated from Cornell University. He had numerous outside interests: chess, photography, poker, tennis. In 1912, he had served as president of the Atlanta chapter of B'nai B'rith, a Jewish fraternal organization.[10] Police didn't immediately read his nerves as guilt, but they noted it as they listened to Frank's description of his last encounter with Mary, whom he said he'd seen just briefly when she requested her pay. He had no idea what happened after that, he said.[11]

Arthur Mullinax, one of the first suspects, was the streetcar driver who regularly drove Mary to work. He was twenty-eight and supposedly a bit of a flirt. Mary was described as a bit mature for her age—perhaps accounting for the initial misreporting of her age—but she was still a few months shy of fourteen and far too young for Mullinax. Newt Lee, the man who'd found her body, had no alibi because he was at the factory doing his job, and while that meant he was at the scene of the crime, the notes found near Mary's body seemed at odds with Newt being guilty. Why would he have planted messages pretending to be written by Mary that implicated himself? Police also looked at a friend of Mary's who had previously worked at the pencil factory with her and had been there that day, according to other workers. James Milton Gantt had first met Mary and her family about ten years prior when she was four years old and her mother was still known as Mrs. Phagan rather than Mrs. Coleman.[12]

After Mary's father died and her mother remarried, they moved away from the Marietta area where Gantt lived and into the city, where he and Mary would eventually reconnect as coworkers. Leo Frank had reportedly fired Gantt in early April because the payroll was short two dollars (almost double Mary's weekly wage—about sixty dollars today), and Gantt had worked as the paymaster. The day of Mary's murder, Gantt, who was in his early twenties, asked to go into the building around 6:00 p.m. because he'd left some shoes there that he wanted to pick up.[13] Because of Gantt's unexpected appearance at the plant that specific day—plus his known friendship with Mary—he was added to the list of suspects and held not on a charge of suspicion this time, but on a charge of murder.

Leo Frank, c. 1910.

In the first days after Mary's death, newspapers floated the names of four people of interest: Mullinax, Lee, Gantt, and Frank.[14] It was also mentioned in at least one newspaper report that two other Black employees were being held at the police station, too, though their names weren't published.[15] Despite that, it was still Leo Frank who was gaining traction as a suspect. The late 1800s had brought an influx of Jewish immigrants to the country from Eastern Europe, prompting a wave of nationalism, nativism, and anti-Semitism, in which Jewish people were often cast as "others."

As antsy as the public was to get this horrid crime solved, some counseled caution. On May 2, 1913, the *Atlanta Constitution* ran a story titled "Keep an Open Mind."[16] It began:

> **Notwithstanding all that has happened since the finding of the murdered body of Mary Phagan, nothing has yet been developed that in any way fixes the crime on any individual. Several arrests have been made, and in the excitement incident to the affair, suspicion has been directed from one person to another as the kaleidoscope has turned on the investigation. All of which goes to show that the public is often constrained to reach hasty and frequently unwarranted conclusions.**

The piece reasoned that not everyone who had been named as a potential suspect could be guilty, so people needed to be patient to avoid blaming an innocent man. "Nothing can be more unjust nor more repugnant to the popular sense of justice than to convict even by hearsay an innocent man."

"NOTHING CAN BE MORE UNJUST NOR MORE REPUGNANT TO THE POPULAR SENSE OF JUSTICE THAN TO CONVICT EVEN BY HEARSAY AN INNOCENT MAN."

As police waded through the suspects, they began to whittle down the list. Arthur Mullinax was said to have flirted with Mary and seemed to gravitate toward teenage girls despite being nearly thirty. In fact, it was eventually a teenage girl who provided him with an alibi. A sixteen-year-old named Pearl Robinson said Arthur couldn't have killed Mary because the two of them went to supper and the theater, and when they parted, he went straight home.[17] Gantt was eliminated as well, because of a supposedly solid alibi, though the details weren't published. Once the list was whittled down to three Black men and one Jewish man, concerns began to grow about mob justice.

"Troops Called Out in Phagan Murder," ran a wire headline on May 2, 1913.[18] What wasn't as widely reported that day was something that had happened the previous day. Yet another man, a factory worker named Jim Conley, had been arrested in connection with the murder. Conley was spotted trying to wash some stains from a shirt that were later identified as bloodstains—the most incriminating evidence found to date. Conley had a few conflicting explanations at first, but he eventually offered one that detectives liked: He said that the blood was Mary Phagan's. He had helped hide her body, he said, but he hadn't killed her. That had been done by the man who had forced him to help: Leo Frank.

Conley explained that he wrote those grammatically nightmarish letters found by Mary's body on Frank's orders.

"He told the police that Leo Frank dictated those notes to him to pin the crime on yet another Black man; that Leo Frank was in the habit of seducing young women at the pencil factory; and that Conley had served as Leo Frank's guard" during his illicit rendezvous, Oney said in a webcast.[19] Mary Phagan fought back, Conley claimed, leading to her death. Conley's statements changed everything. The detectives on the case went from casting a broad net with seemingly endless possibilities to zeroing in on Frank, despite evidence that undercut the theory. Leo Frank was "the ultimate New York Jew living in the South, and that brought out a lot of anti-Semitism that lay beneath the surface," said Mark Moskowitz, southern regional director of the Anti-Defamation League, in a *USA Today* webcast.[20]

Just two months after Conley's arrest, Leo Frank went on trial as prosecutors presented a problematic case in a packed courtroom left with standing room only. Conley was the state's star witness. He had worked as a sweeper at the factory and provided details so graphic that the judge reportedly cleared the courtroom of women and children for him to testify. According to Conley, Frank was a sexual deviant who preyed on girls. For whatever reason, Frank had chosen Conley to be his wingman and lookout, he said, and routinely invited young women into his office where he entertained them. The morning of April 26, Frank set his sights on Mary for a "chat." Conley agreed to keep watch. A little while later, he said he heard Frank whistle for him to come into his office. Conley said Frank was unhinged when he walked in, so nervous he was "shivering."[21] During his testimony, Conley stood and demonstrated by shaking his knees and arms.

He said Frank's eyes were large—"they looked funny and wild"—and he was so rattled that he had to lean on Conley to stand upright.[22] He explained that little Mary Phagan hadn't been interested in chatting and that Frank had struck her and left her in the machine room. He sent Conley in to get her, and Conley said that when he approached, he saw the dead girl on the floor, her arms outstretched. Frank told him to wrap up the body and hide it in the basement. But when Conley found it difficult to carry Mary's 125-pound frame, Frank helped get her body onto an elevator. He bribed Conley to keep his mouth shut and supposedly muttered, "Why should I hang?"[23] Conley then said Frank instructed him to write the notes implicating Newt Lee as the killer.

This would all be quite damning if there had been solid corroboration for it, but there wasn't. More than twenty character witnesses testified on Frank's behalf, and those who testified against him usually had little worse

Leo Frank and his wife, Lucille, in the courtroom for his murder trial, Atlanta, August 1913.

to say than Frank made the girls uncomfortable with his nervous mannerisms. Several people, both young workers and contemporaries, said Frank had a stuttering, clinical sort of personality, but that was normal for him. Prosecutors accused those who testified of lying or being bribed by Frank.

"This is a good example of why we need lawyers," said former Georgia governor Roy Barnes at a conviction integrity news conference in August 2019. Barnes, who has studied the case over the years, added, "A lawyer should stand up against passion and prejudice. There were some good lawyers in this case, but unfortunately, they did not control the mob."[24]

Almost all those who testified that Frank seemed guilty had something to gain from his conviction—most notably Newt Lee, who was second in the line of suspects. Even with so much on the line, Lee's most damning testimony was that Frank had called him the day of the murder and asked how the plant was doing when he normally wouldn't have. It was hardly a smoking gun. Defense lawyers tried to shake Conley's testimony, but aside from acknowledging that he told inconsistent statements, he held to his story.

Frank testified on his own behalf, and it likely hurt his case beyond repair. He was such a smart man, so matter of fact, that he spent a big chunk of time talking about the work he'd been doing that Saturday.[25] This was complicated, boring work involving finances and orders and other matters the jury just didn't understand or care about. He described Mary coming into his office and asking for her pay, but he said he didn't really know the girl. She had to tell him her employee number, after which she took her pay from the cash box and slid it into an envelope, on the outside of which he wrote her employee number. Mary apparently paused before she left and asked if the metal for her department had arrived yet. Frank said no, and she left. Pressed on why he seemed so nervous when police told him of the death early the next morning, Frank said the explanation was simple. He'd been yanked from bed and shown Mary's body at the morgue. He testified, "Gentlemen, I was nervous. I was completely unstrung. Imagine yourself called from sound slumber in the early hours of the morning, whisked through the chill morning air, without breakfast to go into that undertaking establishment, have the light suddenly flashed on a scene like that. To see that little girl on the dawn of womanhood so cruelly murdered, it was a scene that would have melted stone. Is it any wonder I was nervous?"[26]

The investigators had embraced Frank as a killer in part because he hadn't been terribly cooperative after he was accused of the murder early on. He said they had tried to put words into his mouth that he knew weren't true. When Lee didn't implicate himself, they tried to convince Frank to meet up with Conley, to see if the two of them discussing what had happened that night might clear up some inconsistencies in Conley's story. Frank refused. Not only did that sound like a bad idea to him, period, but the cops tried to arrange it when his lawyer wasn't around. The investigators interpreted that refusal as a sign of guilt. Why would an innocent man not want to clear the record? Frank said he only refused because he didn't want things to get twisted around. He testified, "I knew that there was not a word that I could have uttered that they would not deform and distort and use against me."

Governor Barnes said the courthouse during the trial was a madhouse. "The Fulton County courthouse was on Marietta Street at the time. There were no air conditioners, so the windows would be open and there was a mob down below." A spectator watching the action in the courtroom would sit in an open window and relay the testimony to the crowd below. "And the mob would either groan or cheer. It's reported that when the jurors would walk up the street to go to the trial . . . the mob would scream, 'Hang the Jew or we'll hang you!' That mob had power."[27]

Though the evidence presented was objectively weak, Leo Frank was convicted of killing Mary Phagan and sentenced to death on August 26, 1913.[28]

He was to be hanged. Back in the last century, just as today, the American judicial system featured a robust and complicated appeals system, which Frank put to use. The case was appealed five times.[29] In April 1914,

The packed courtroom at the Fulton County courthouse in Altlanta on the first day of the Leo Frank trial, July 28, 1913. The night watchman, Newt Lee, far right, can be seen on the stand as he is being questioned by prosecutor Hugh Dorsey. Leo Frank is sitting directly in front of the judge, Leonard Roan.

when Frank's lawyers appealed the hanging that was scheduled for later that month, the County court denied the request. Frank's lawyers appealed the ruling to the Georgia Supreme Court. The state's high court affirmed the trial. Frank's lawyers then appealed to the federal district court of North Georgia. Denied again. Next, Frank's lawyers appealed to the Supreme Court and got another denial. At this point, Frank's execution was set for June 1915. Three weeks before it was scheduled, Frank's lawyers filed an appeal for clemency with the Georgia prison commission, hoping to have his death sentence commuted.[30] That appeal was yet again denied. But finally, at long last, someone sided with Frank. On June 20, 1915, just two days before the scheduled hanging, Georgia governor John Slaton announced he had pored over the files, devoured the transcripts, and reviewed all the evidence. And he was convinced Frank was innocent. In his last day in office, Slaton commuted the sentence from death to life in prison. Slaton worried the reaction to his decision might be dramatic, so he warned his wife, Sally, who supported him.

Slaton had the encouragement of some unlikely players, like L. S. Roan,[31] the judge who had presided over the case, who said he had serious doubts about Frank's guilt, and Jim Conley's attorney, William Smith, who had come to believe Conley was the killer. But even though Slaton believed Frank was innocent, he didn't upend the system altogether. He simply took death off the table. He wanted to see the man live and have a chance to clear his name. As such, he ordered Frank to be moved from a prison in Fulton County to another in Milledgeville, in hopes of avoiding a lynch mob attacking him. On July 18, 1915, a prisoner named William Green slashed Frank's throat in an attempt to kill him. Luckily, two prisoners nearby happened to be doctors; they were able to stop the bleeding and save his life.[32]

On August 16, 1915, though, a mob came to Milledgeville. A caravan of some twenty-eight armed men—including former governor of Georgia, Joseph Mackey Brown; Eugene Herbert Clay, former mayor of Marietta; E. P. Dobbs, mayor of Marietta; and other prominent Georgian leaders and professionals arrived in Milledgeville and

A 1912 photograph of John Mackey Brown, who served as governor of Georgia from 1909 to 1911, and then from 1912 to 1913. Brown was a member of the mob who kidnapped Frank from prison and lynched him on August 16, 1915.

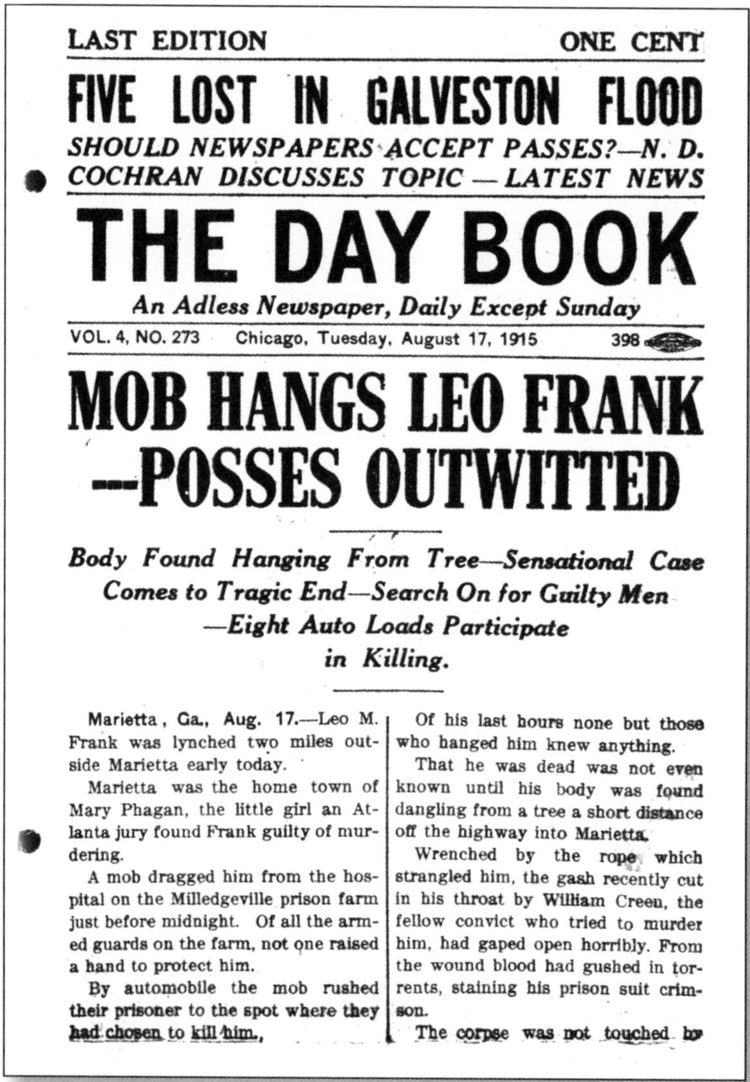

LAST EDITION ONE CENT

FIVE LOST IN GALVESTON FLOOD

SHOULD NEWSPAPERS ACCEPT PASSES?—N. D. COCHRAN DISCUSSES TOPIC — LATEST NEWS

THE DAY BOOK

An Adless Newspaper, Daily Except Sunday

VOL. 4, NO. 273 Chicago, Tuesday, August 17, 1915 398

MOB HANGS LEO FRANK —POSSES OUTWITTED

Body Found Hanging From Tree—Sensational Case Comes to Tragic End—Search On for Guilty Men —Eight Auto Loads Participate in Killing.

Marietta, Ga., Aug. 17.—Leo M. Frank was lynched two miles outside Marietta early today.

Marietta was the home town of Mary Phagan, the little girl an Atlanta jury found Frank guilty of murdering.

A mob dragged him from the hospital on the Milledgeville prison farm just before midnight. Of all the armed guards on the farm, not one raised a hand to protect him.

By automobile the mob rushed their prisoner to the spot where they had chosen to kill him.

Of his last hours none but those who hanged him knew anything.

That he was dead was not even known until his body was found dangling from a tree a short distance off the highway into Marietta.

Wrenched by the rope which strangled him, the gash recently cut in his throat by William Creen, the fellow convict who tried to murder him, had gaped open horribly. From the wound blood had gushed in torrents, staining his prison suit crimson.

The corpse was not touched by

The front page of the Chicago *Day Book*, August 17, 1915.

surrounded the prison.[33] They cut the telephone lines, surprised some guards, drained police vehicles of gas, and kidnapped Frank. They drove for hours back toward Marietta, where Mary had spent her childhood, and asked if Frank had any last requests. He said he had one: that his wedding band be returned to his wife, Lucille, who had stood by him and never doubted his innocence. The mob then wrapped a rope around Frank's neck and hanged him from a tree.

When word spread of the hanging, crowds arrived to gawk at the corpse. Photographs were taken of this slight man, his head dangling back in an unnatural way, his hands still cuffed in front of him, the people who killed him posing with his body. One of the pictures was turned into a souvenir postcard. Some of the county's most prominent people were pictured in the crowd–including the current sheriff and his predecessor.

Every murder has ripple effects that extend far beyond the original victim and their family. This one sparked enormous change on numerous fronts. Soon after Frank's lynching, the two-year-old Anti-Defamation League, founded by B'nai B'rith, catapulted into a national force against anti-Semitism and hate; and on top of Stone Mountain, Georgia, the Ku Klux Klan rallied and reformed as an homage to the Knights of Mary Phagan.

In 1982, seventy years after Mary was killed, a witness stepped forward with new information.[34] Alonzo Mann had been Frank's office boy in 1913 and had testified in Frank's trial, but only about his boss's general demeanor, which he said was affable. He told reporters of *The Tennessean* that he also should have been called as a witness to the crime. Alonzo said he had seen Jim Conley alone shortly after noon, carrying Mary's body through the factory lobby toward a ladder that led to the basement. He said he didn't step forward earlier because Conley had threatened him and because he had told his parents about what he had seen, and they insisted he forget it and not get involved, so he didn't. While it was impossible to prove Alonzo's story nearly seven decades after Mary's death, most historians believe that Jim Conley was the killer and that he had pinned it on Leo Frank.

Jim Conley served just one year in jail for being an accomplice after the fact. There's no official record of his death, but it's believed he lived at least another forty years. The state of Georgia never granted Frank a full pardon in Mary's death, but in 1986, officials at least recognized that the state had failed to protect him and thus stole his chance to continue fighting to clear his name.

"The pardon and parole board did that on the procedural basis that he was not afforded a fair trial," Barnes said. "I think that the evidence is more than sufficient to show that he did not commit the crime."

No one was ever charged in Leo Frank's lynching.

Legal Legacy

In addition to acting as a catalyst in the expansion of two organizations on opposite sides of basic decency—the Anti-Defamation League and the Ku Klux Klan—the murder of Mary Phagan also sparked the reform of child labor laws.

- An April 30, 1913 *Atlanta Constitution* story quoted Dr. A. J. McKelway of the Southern Sociological Congress: "If children . . . were not forced to work, Mary Phagan might be living. Think of the heavy toll which she undergoes and the physical conditions under which she labors. Why is it that such is allowed in our fair land?"[35] It was a sentiment echoed on editorial pages nationwide.
- The Phagan case, in addition to organizations such as the National Child Labor Committee (1904) and the work of sociologist and photographer Lewis Hine, led to Congress in 1906 passing some of the first child labor laws; while they were challenged by Southern states and overturned, these laws marked the beginning of the end of the practice.[36]

24

The Lindbergh Baby Kidnapping

(1932)

Betty Gow went to each of the three windows in the little boy's bedroom to make sure the shutters were closed and locked for the night, but one set gave her trouble.

The house was a new and expensive construction being built by one of the most famous couples in the world, yet the wood on these shutters was warped. Betty, the boy's nanny, called his mother, Anne, and the two women tried together to force the latch closed, but they just couldn't do it. They gave up, and Betty left that one set unlocked, put the toddler in his crib, and waited in the room until she could tell by his breathing that he'd fallen asleep.

Two and half hours later, she kept to another of her nightly routines: She went to check on the baby. Quietly padding into his bedroom, she intentionally left the lights off so as not to startle the boy. But as soon as she'd crossed the threshold, she knew something was wrong. She couldn't hear little Charlie's breathing. She inched closer and peeked inside the crib. It was empty.[1]

Betty rushed down the hallway, where Anne had been taking a bath. Anne didn't have the baby, so Betty's thoughts jumped to Charlie's father. He'd been known to play jokes on his staff before. One time, he'd even hidden Charlie in a closet for half an hour, playing dumb while Betty scoured the place looking for the child.[2] Maybe he was pulling her leg again? She rushed downstairs to his study and blurted: "Do you have the baby?"

Charles Lindbergh Sr. looked confused. "Isn't he in his crib?"

"No," Betty said. Lindbergh darted up the stairs, saw the empty crib for himself, and said to his wife: "They've stolen our baby."[3]

The date was March 1, 1932, and the kidnapping of little Charlie Lindbergh would set off a media firestorm like never seen before in US history, changing laws across the nation. While it eventually resulted in a controversial conviction, the full story of what happened that night remains a mystery to this day.

Aviator Charles A. Lindbergh was beyond merely famous in 1932. Five years prior, he'd flown the *Spirit of St. Louis*—a single-engine, high-wing monoplane—from New York to Paris, making him the first person to successfully complete a nonstop, transatlantic flight. This was huge news. Wilbur and Orville Wright had made their historic Kitty Hawk, North Carolina, debut only twenty-four years earlier in 1903—for 12 seconds and 120 feet. Lindbergh pulling off 33.5 hours and 3,600 miles with no copilot proved beyond question that aviation was on the cusp of changing the world.

When Lindbergh landed in Paris, some 150,000 people thronged the airstrip.[4] Back home, he received two million letters and telegrams congratulating his achievement, and four million people attended a ticker-tape parade in New York City in his honor. It was a public response unlike any other—one that certainly caught Lindbergh more than a little off guard. He came home a national hero and an incredibly rich man. A hotel owner named Raymond Orteig had, in 1919, offered a $25,000 prize to the first person to do what Lindbergh did. Even though it took some eight years for him to do it, Lindbergh was awarded that $25,000—which would be about $430,000 in 2023. Not only that, but he released an autobiography called *WE* within three months of the flight that became a wildly popular bestseller, and he wrote a number of articles for newspapers. All of this made him a millionaire, even before adjusting for inflation. Lindbergh was more famous than any of the country's politicians, actors, or athletes. He was routinely described as the most famous man in the world, not just in America.

Charles Lindbergh with the *Spirit of St. Louis* in the background, in late May 1927 after his historic flight.

That popularity hadn't waned by the time he married writer Anne Morrow two years after his flight in May 1929. Nor had it diminished when the couple welcomed their first-born son, Charles Jr., on June 22, 1930—which also happened to be Anne's twenty-fourth birthday.

Charles A. Lindbergh Jr., celebrating his first birthday on June 22, 1931.

Charles Lindbergh had earned a few nicknames in his lifetime—"Slim," courtesy of his friends before he was famous, and "Lucky Lindy," courtesy of the press afterward. When he departed on that history-making flight, newspapers also referred to him as "The Lone Eagle." Charlie Jr. got his own nicknames—"Little Lindy" and "The Eaglet." The word *paparazzi* dates to the 1960s, but the way press photographers hungered for every tidbit surrounding the Lindbergh family is a reminder that feeding the public's obsession with looking at celebrities began far earlier.

A photo appeared on front pages nationwide in July 1930 beneath the headline "First Photo of Charles A. Lindbergh Jr."[5] After that debut, the coverage didn't abate. The press pounced on little Charlie's every move—Charlie playing in his backyard, Charlie cuddling his mother, Charlie's first family portrait, Charlie celebrating his first birthday. (At that milestone, reporters made a point to say that the famed aviator's firstborn hadn't himself been on a plane yet.)

Most of the coverage was well intentioned, even fawning. But not all of it. By 1932, the country was still mired in a brutal depression that was nowhere near over, and here were the Lindberghs—a family with so much money and a little boy who would want for nothing his whole life. Apparently, someone decided Lindy's luck should run out.

The Lindberghs were in the process of building a house that, come spring 1932, was still under construction. The family was eager to move but because the place wasn't quite ready yet, they only stayed there on the weekends. The new house was in Hopewell, New Jersey, on Sourland Mountain, but during the week, the family stayed at the fifty-six-acre Morrow estate, Next Day Hill, in Englewood, New Jersey.[6] That's where they should have been the night of March 1, a Monday, but little Charlie had a cold and Anne thought it'd be better for him to stay put a little longer in the new house, which they called the Highfields.

This is one of the confounding aspects of the kidnapping: Whoever kidnapped Charlie seemed to have known that the family had changed their usual routine at the last minute. Also odd was the fact that the kidnapping happened while everyone was home, including Charles Sr. He'd been expected to give a talk that evening, but he uncharacteristically forgot about the event and came home from the day's other appointments at around 8:00 p.m. He shouldn't have been home, and yet he was working in his study just beneath his son's nursery when the kidnapper struck.

After Betty alerted the family to Charlie's disappearance, Lindbergh ordered a butler to call the police while he grabbed a rifle. He rushed outside to look for the kidnapper but found no one. A white envelope had been left in Charlie's room. Inside it was a poorly written note that was hard to decipher in spots but the gist of it was clear: Charlie was being held for a $50,000 ransom. Lindbergh was warned not to involve the police, but he didn't even read the note until the cops arrived, so that ship had sailed.

Word about the brazen kidnapping spread first throughout the area, and then the world. As a news report declared at the time: "Not a single bed is overlooked, not a single suspicion unverified in the search for the most famous baby in the world."[7] Search parties scoured the Highfields property. Strangers drove in from all over the country either to help or, more often, just to gawk.

"The cops had to say, 'Please stay away because we're afraid you might find some evidence and destroy it,'" said A. Scott Berg, an author whose biography *Lindbergh* (1998) won a Pulitzer Prize in 1999. "But you couldn't stop people that night. Just torchlights everywhere. From five miles away, you could see the lights surrounding the Lindbergh house."[8]

The ransom note that was left in baby Charlie's room the night of the March 1, 1932, kidnapping; it was made public in September 1934 by the New Jersey State Police.

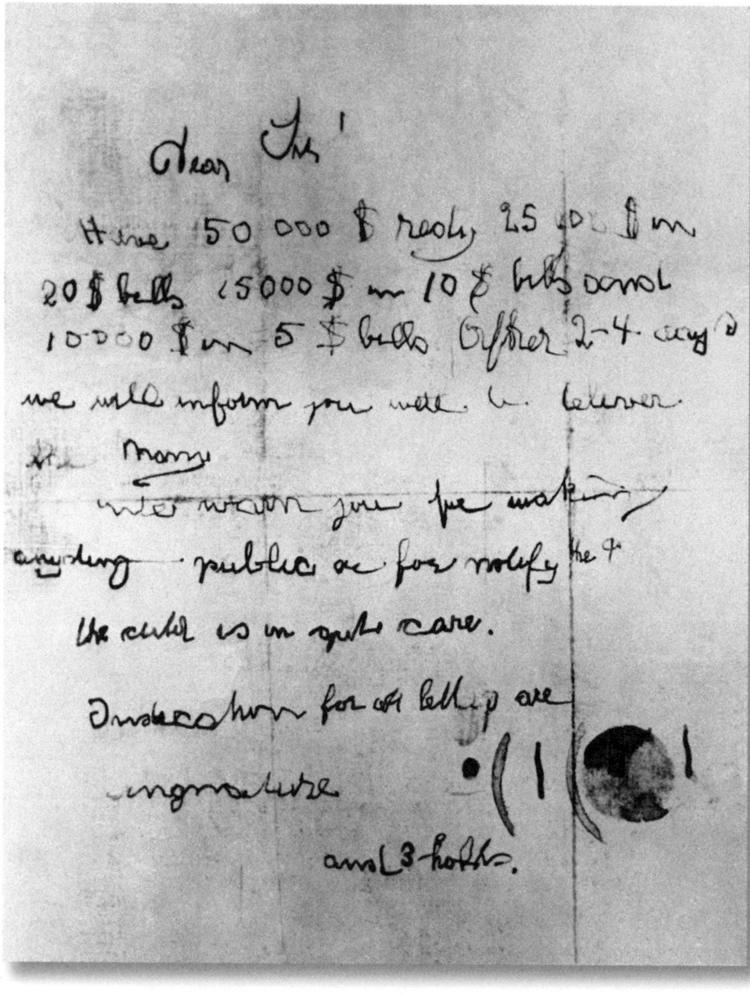
Dear Sir!

Have 50 000 $ redy 25 000 $ in
20 $ bills 15000 $ in 10 $ bills and
10 000 $ in 5 $ bills After 2–4 days
we will inform you were to deliver
the mony.

We warn you for making
anyding public or for notify the Po
the child is in gute care.

Indication for all letters are
singnature
and 3 holes.

The new house, a $50,000 mansion, was being built on 390 acres set far back from the public road. It was no coincidence that its construction was coming to an end at the same time the due date for Anne's second pregnancy was nearing. The whole point of the place was that it was hard to reach and secluded—something the Lindberghs desperately wanted so they could raise their growing family away from the prying eyes of the public.

In the aftermath of the kidnapping, police cataloged the clues found by officers and volunteers.

About seventy-five feet away from the house, a janky, homemade ladder had been abandoned. It had been built in three sections, but only two sections had been connected together—which made sense when propped against the house. With two sections, the ladder reached just below Charlie's nursery window; with three, the ladder would've overshot the window.

Beneath that window were two deep grooves in the earth, which was soft due to recent rain. The discarded ladder fit perfectly in those grooves. Also, one of the rungs on the ladder was broken—which made sense when Lindbergh Sr. mentioned that while he worked in his study, he at some point heard a loud bang. He described it as the sound of an orange crate in the kitchen maybe toppling off a chair. He'd paused his work and listened for more, but all was quiet and he'd shrugged it off. In hindsight, it would seem that he'd heard the kidnapping in progress but didn't realize what was happening.[9]

Footprints led away from the ladder. Police tried to make a plaster cast of those prints, but they weren't typical shoe prints. It appeared that whoever had left them had worn socks on top of their shoes, or maybe tied their feet in burlap or other material, in order to undermine their evidentiary value. The effort worked. Police could get a general sense of the foot size, but that was it.[10]

What they could see, though, was where the footprints led. Investigators followed them away from the window until they passed the discarded ladder and disappeared at the road. Dogs brought in to track the smell stopped there, too, which meant that whoever made the prints likely climbed into a car and drove away.

Going back to the scrawled note left in Charlie's bedroom, it seemed perfectly clear what had happened: the worries the Lindberghs had had about the public's infatuation with them had proved more than justified. Someone stole their child and was keeping him hostage until the ransom was paid.

Investigators at the Lindbergh estate in Hopewell, New Jersey, reconstructing details of the 1932 kidnapping, December 7, 1934. The ladder shown is suspected to be the one used in the crime.

Charles Lindbergh decided right away that he'd cooperate. Anything, he said, to bring Charlie home.

As soon as the news broke, the busybodies came out in such numbers that the many players were hard to keep straight. Some were certainly aiming to be helpful. Their hearts hurt for these worried parents, and they wanted to do what they could to help. But some of the attention came from people who were only a step or two away from the kidnappers themselves, morally speaking. For example, from his jail cell in Chicago, notorious gangster Al Capone offered to help the day after the abduction, announcing a reward of $10,000 for the safe return of the Lindbergh baby and the capture

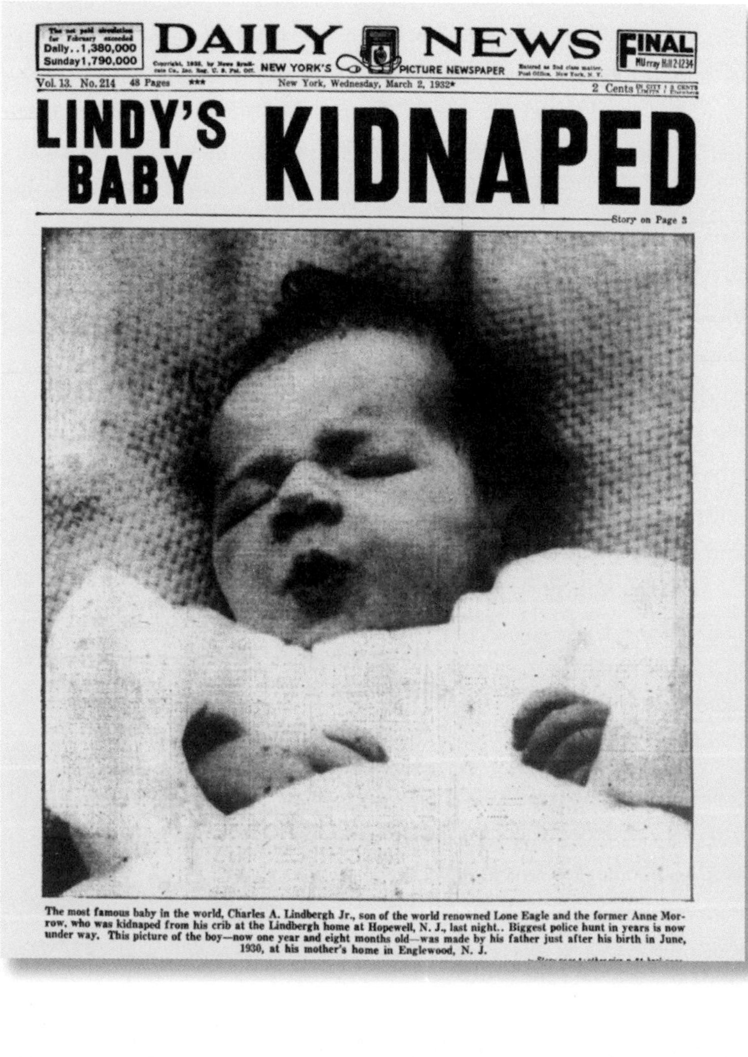
Daily..1,380,000
Sunday 1,790,000
DAILY NEWS
NEW YORK'S PICTURE NEWSPAPER
FINAL
MUrray Hill 2-1234
Vol. 13. No. 214 48 Pages ★★★ New York, Wednesday, March 2, 1932★ 2 Cents

LINDY'S BABY KIDNAPED

Story on Page 3

The most famous baby in the world, Charles A. Lindbergh Jr., son of the world renowned Lone Eagle and the former Anne Morrow, who was kidnaped from his crib at the Lindbergh home at Hopewell, N. J., last night.. Biggest police hunt in years is now under way. This picture of the boy—now one year and eight months old—was made by his father just after his birth in June, 1930, at his mother's home in Englewood, N. J.

The kidnapping was one of the biggest stories of the twentieth century, and made headlines in newspapers from coast to coast and beyond; here, the front page of the *Daily News*, March 3, 1932.

of his kidnappers.[11] Capone said: "It's the most outrageous thing I ever heard of. I know how Mrs. Capone and I would feel if our son were kidnapped and I sympathize with the Lindberghs." But there was a catch. Capone had just months earlier been sentenced to eleven years in prison for tax evasion and was being held in the county jail pending his appeals. "If I were out of jail," he said, "I could be of real assistance."[12]

Charles Lindbergh welcomed any help but said he wouldn't help spring Capone even if it saved a life. Still, Capone's offer sparked a theory: maybe the kidnapping had been the work of the criminal underworld. Lindbergh attorney Henry Breckinridge thought this scenario especially likely. He suggested to the Lindberghs that they accept an offer from a bootlegger and con man named Morris Rosner, who had long been connected to the New York underworld.[13] Charles Lindbergh agreed, and Rosner came to the Hopewell home, where he was filled in on every detail known thus far. Rosner demanded to work out of the Lindbergh's house so that he'd have the most current information possible about the crime, and he insisted that police not follow him as he made his connections. His primary goal, he said, was to save the baby, not lead cops to the captors. This was fine by Lindbergh, who kept insisting that the police stand down, a request to which they oddly acquiesced. Lindbergh told the gung-ho cops that aggressively going after the kidnappers would put little Charlie's life in danger, so the focus first had to be on getting the boy back. Then they could do whatever they needed to do to find the culprits.

Through Rosner, Lindbergh met two other princes of New York's underbelly: Salvatore "Salvy" Spitale and Irving Bitz,[14] two men "known only as Broadway racketeers."[15] The Lindberghs authorized the two criminals to act as their go-betweens in pursuing tips from the sordid streets. "We will also follow any other methods suggested by the kidnappers that we can be sure will bring the return of our child," the couple said in a news release.[16] The idea was that whoever stole Charlie might want to keep their distance from Lindbergh—and law enforcement—so instead, he could deal with these two fellow criminals instead. It's hard to say how sincere Spitale and Bitz had been when first offering to help, but in statements to the press they insisted their intentions were pure. "As the father of two children, I told the representatives of the Lindbergh family that I was concerned with only one thing—to recover the child, alive and in good health," Spitale said.[17]

Regardless, their involvement soon became a joke to law enforcement and the underworld alike, as the duo set up a makeshift office in a bar behind the *New York Daily News* building. Before long, Spitale soon told a reporter that he wished he'd never gotten mixed up in the kidnapping. He didn't like the attention, nor did he like that newspapers were running not just photos of him, but of his wife and kids.[18]

Inside the Lindbergh home, the couple's staff was questioned. Some investigators were sure that someone working for the Lindberghs had to have either intentionally or unwittingly given away information that helped the kidnapper—like the fact that one window shutter didn't lock properly. Everyone on staff denied this. Most had worked for Anne's parents at their estate before working for the Lindberghs, so they had been loyal to the family for years. Still, the police interrogations were so harsh that one employee eventually poisoned herself after telling a coworker that the cops would never interview her again.[19]

Meanwhile, on March 12, Rosner the bootlegger announced he'd received assurances that the baby was alive and well and would be safely returned to his parents.[20] This was a huge relief to both parents, but especially to Anne. Through reporters, she had pleaded with the kidnappers to take good care of Charlie. She even gave instructions on what to feed him because of his cold. She said he needed orange juice, cooked cereal and vegetables, and two tablespoons of stewed fruit. Rosner said that his informants specifically referenced Anne's diet requests. They promised that little Charlie was being cared for just as his mother had asked.

Meanwhile, more ransom notes arrived. One expressed annoyance that police were involved despite the original note's warning not to involve law enforcement. One note said that because of all the intense publicity in the case, the kidnappers would have to hold Charlie longer until the fervor subsided. That meant they would probably have to hire an additional person to pull off the job, so the ransom demand was upped from $50,000 to $70,000.[21]

Each of the ransom notes—there would be fifteen in total—bore a unique symbol at the bottom to make it clear they were the real deal and not some copycat nonsense. The symbol was a pair of overlapping circles on the insides of which were short, squiggly lines. Three holes were punched in the paper—one on either side of the design, and the third one smack dab in the center in the overlap portion. That middle hole was also encircled in red.[22] It was a tough design to replicate, helping ensure the Lindberghs could spot any forgeries. The handwriting in the notes was also unique. Handwriting experts opined that the writer had likely been raised as a German speaker based on misspellings that seemed to point to German as the writer's native language. For example, *good* was repeatedly misspelled as g-u-t-e. The German word for *good* is *gut*.

While the underworld characters entrusted to solve the case kept spinning their wheels, another apparent do-gooder wrote a letter to the editor of the *Bronx Home News*. In the letter, he offered to act as intermediary between the kidnappers and the Lindberghs. John F. Condon was a seventy-one-year-old Bronx resident who'd taught in New York City schools for some four decades. He was self-important and boisterous and just the type of guy to insert himself in the biggest story in the country. The day after his offer ran in the paper, he received a letter in a long, white envelope. He later described how he felt realizing the message had been sent from the kidnappers and authorized, on their end, anyway, for him to be the intermediary with the Lindberghs: "I could feel the rush of blood from my face, an emptiness in the pit of my stomach, and a heavier hammering of the heart than is good for a man in his seventies."[23] When Condon reached out to the Lindberghs, they didn't pay him much mind—until he mentioned the strange interlocking circles at the bottom of the letter he'd received. After learning that, the Lindberghs asked him to come to Hopewell.

It was decided that Condon needed a code name, so he used his initials—JFC—to come up with the moniker "Jafsie."[24] In his first media address, he called the kidnapping "the most dastardly crime of modern time" and vowed that the baby would be returned in short order.[25] This was nearly two weeks after the kidnapping. The Lindberghs were hopeful that little Charlie was okay despite not having seen any proof of life because of the assurances given to them by the ransom letters. The couple got the $70,000 ready in the specific denominations that had been outlined in one of the many ransom notes. Most of the bills were in small denominations, which was going to make tracing them tricky. Even though the FBI recorded every serial number, they'd be hard pressed to get cashiers to inspect $5 and $10 bills when they were so incredibly common. The tacked-on $20,000 was in bigger bills,

though, which investigators hoped would be easier to trace.[26] Plus, some of the money was supplied not in the paper dollars we use today, but in gold certificates. In 1932, the US was still on the gold standard, and many people who were untrusting of banks after the crash of 1929 began hoarding money in gold certificates. This would become important later.

On March 11, "Jafsie" placed ads in the *New York American* and the *Bronx Home News*. The next day, he got a visit from a man named Joseph Perrone, a taxi driver who'd been stopped by what looked to be a fare only to be asked to deliver an envelope to John F. Condon. Inside the envelope was a note to go to a vacant hot dog stand near Woodlawn Cemetery in the Bronx, where he received another note that instructed him to go to the cemetery for a

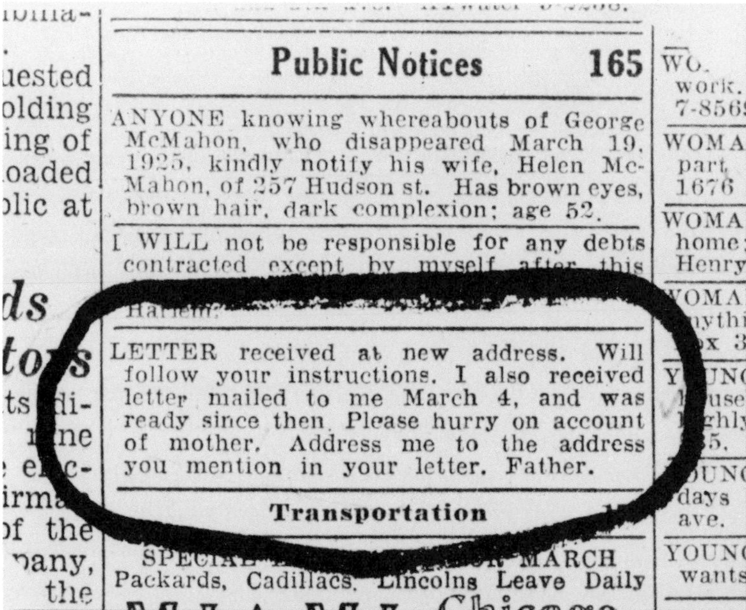

Public Notices 165

ANYONE knowing whereabouts of George McMahon, who disappeared March 19, 1925, kindly notify his wife, Helen McMahon, of 257 Hudson st. Has brown eyes, brown hair, dark complexion; age 52.

I WILL not be responsible for any debts contracted except by myself after this ...

LETTER received at new address. Will follow your instructions. I also received letter mailed to me March 4, and was ready since then. Please hurry on account of mother. Address me to the address you mention in your letter. Father.

Transportation

SPECIAL ... MARCH
Packards, Cadillacs, Lincolns Leave Daily

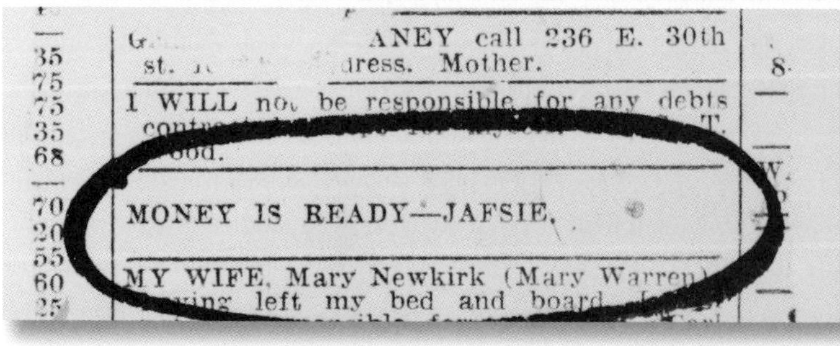

... ANEY call 236 E. 30th st. ... dress. Mother.

I WILL not be responsible for any debts ...

MONEY IS READY—JAFSIE.

MY WIFE, Mary Newkirk (Mary Warren) ... left my bed and board ...

Two notices placed in New York City newspapers in March 1932: the top note was an appeal from Lindbergh to the kidnappers; the bottom note was signed by the alias JAFSIE, which John Condon used during his negotiations with the kidnappers.

meeting. There, Condon encountered a man who was identified as "John." The man, who would forever be dubbed Cemetery John, was described as having what sounded like either a German or Scandinavian accent. He told Condon that there were five people involved in the kidnapping—a gang of three men and two women.[27] This meeting wasn't the ransom drop, though. Condon said he needed proof that this man he was meeting actually had Charlie. He also tried to convince John to hand over Charlie at the same time he received the ransom money, but the kidnapper said no, the gang would not allow it. Instead, John said, once he got the money, the Lindberghs would be notified of Charlie's location within eight hours. The meeting ended with John promising to send the sleep suit Charlie had been wearing the night of his kidnapping as proof he had the child.[28]

On March 16, the suit arrived. It was a Dr. Denton sleep suit, a one-piece, footed pajama that went high to the neck in an almost mock turtleneck. Advertisements of this item claimed kids slept better in them because they were made with unbleached cotton blended with soft wool, creating a hygienic knit fabric. Charlie had been wearing one atop a flannel nightshirt. He'd also had thumb guards on, which were metal devices meant to keep children from sucking their thumbs. Once Condon got the sleep suit in the mail, he rushed it to Charles, who examined it closely. Despite the suit having been recently laundered, which seemed odd, Charles said, yes, this is the sleepwear my son was wearing when he disappeared.[29]

It seemed Cemetery John was the real deal, but after that first meeting, the letters slowed. What would be the eighth note came on March 21, saying the baby was fine, "insisting with compliance on all the terms."[30] Days slipped by without a word, and Charles Lindbergh, antsy to feel like he was doing something productive, would take meetings with pretty much anyone who claimed to be able to help. Finally, on March 30, a letter arrived that said it's time. In fact, it said, if the ransom isn't paid by April 8, the price goes up to $100,000 instead of the $70,000 where it now stood.[31]

Condon placed ads in the same two newspapers: "Money is ready—Jafsie." On April 1, he received the tenth ransom note, instructing him to get the money together for the next evening.

Condon had a box made of wood matching the dimensions that one ransom note had described—a curiously specific 14 × 7 × 6 inches.[32] He

shoved the money inside, and Charles Lindbergh drove him to St. Raymond's Cemetery in the Bronx. Condon grabbed the box crammed with money and then, as he was about to leave the car, peeled off all of the fifty-dollar bills—which basically comprised the entire $20,000 that had been added on to the original demand. Condon told Lindbergh that he was sure the kidnapper would be satisfied with $50,000 and he wanted to save Lindbergh some money if he could help it.[33]

With $50,000 in hand, Condon walked toward the cemetery while Lindbergh waited near the car. At first, he encountered no one. He started to get worried he'd been stood up, but then, a voice called out, "Hey, doctor." It was loud enough that Lindbergh could hear it, and he noticed the voice had an accent.[34]

All along, Condon had made things a bit more dramatic than necessary, and the money drop was no exception. He demanded to get a written receipt. He later said that was to verify that the handwriting matched the many ransom notes he'd received, but whatever the reason, it slowed down the meeting. Finally, after Cemetery John handed over a receipt, Condon passed along the wooden box of money. Cemetery John opened it and counted it, at which point Condon explained they could only get their hands on $50,000—and Cemetery John agreed to accept it. Condon had been right; $20,000 less than demanded had been accepted without hesitation. Condon noticed another man lurking behind Cemetery John in the shadows during the transaction. Then Cemetery John handed Condon an envelope that he said contained Charlie's whereabouts, though he said that no one should open the envelope for eight hours. Naturally, Lindbergh was in no mood to wait. Once Condon got back to Lindbergh's car, they ripped open the envelope. The note inside said the baby was on a boat called the *Nelly* off the Elizabeth Islands near Cape Cod. Well, actually, it said it was on the "boad Nelly." Again, the ransom writer wasn't the best speller.[35]

The search for Charlie began. Lindbergh got an airplane ready, and he and some volunteers began searching the waters near Cape Cod.[36] Anytime he spotted a boat, he would swoop down and check it out. Sometimes volunteers on boats below would question the various skippers. None had Charlie aboard. Days passed. Condon placed an ad in a newspaper asking: "What is wrong? Have you crossed me? Please, better directions—Jafsie."

But there would be no better directions provided. There'd be no further contact from the kidnappers at all. Condon had been played. A month would pass before anything new would develop in the case, and when it did, the whole nation was heartbroken. On May 12, two months after Charlie's abduction, two truckers, Orville Wilson and William Allen, pulled off the side of the road to make a pitstop on their way to deliver a truckload of lumber to Hopewell.[37] Allen tromped through some brush so he wouldn't be seen relieving himself—and came upon the decomposed remains of a small child, who was soon identified as Charlie.[38]

The autopsy suggested that Charlie had probably died the very night of the kidnapping.[39] He had a fractured skull, and while it was difficult to properly examine him because he had been outside for so long, the coroner said the inside of the skull showed that there had been a hemorrhage.[40] The theory was that whoever stole him had built a ladder that could handle his weight, but not the added weight of the baby. One of the rungs had broken, after all. Maybe Charlie was dropped at that point, killing him. Maybe the kidnapper tore off his sleep suit because he figured someone would demand proof that he had the baby and he needed to keep the ruse going to secure his payoff. Or

Journalists and spectators watch as a young man points to the spot where Charlie's body was found in a shallow grave, near Mount Rose, New Jersey, on May 12, 1932, four-and-a-half miles away from the Lindbergh estate.

maybe the kidnapper never had plans to keep a twenty-month- old baby alive and hidden for weeks on end. Maybe the plan always was to kill him.[41]

Whatever had happened, Charlie was dead. His parents were devastated. And now the police were set loose to find the killer. After Charlie's body was found, bits of the ransom money started popping up around New York. A $5 bill would show up in a store. Maybe a $10 in another store. The trouble was, though, most of the time, no one really noticed those denominations until well after the spender was gone. They were too small to stand out. Condon had peeled off the largest bills—the $20,000 in $50 bills—which infuriated police when they learned of it. Condon might've been trying to save the Lindberghs some money, but he'd eliminated the easiest-to-trace bills in doing so. Plus, the Lindberghs didn't need to save money. They were wealthy beyond most people's imagination. While the tens and fives didn't stand out to salesclerks receiving them, the gold certificates did, especially once 1933 hit, which is when President Franklin Roosevelt took the United States off the gold standard and recalled all gold. The gold certificates were supposed to be turned in and converted to legal tender.

This didn't happen all at once. Gold certificates were still accepted by plenty of merchants, but they were becoming rare enough that it stood out when someone used one, which helped ensure that federal investigators might get a few physical descriptions of the person who'd presented the certificates.

Meanwhile, FBI agents had painstakingly analyzed the wood used on the kidnap ladder and managed to figure out that it'd been sold at a hardware store in the Bronx. The bills that showed up always seemed to be in that area, too.[42]

Two and a half years passed like this. Then, on Saturday, September 15, 1934, a manager at a gas station on Lexington Avenue and 137th Street, Walter Lyle, was paid with a $10 gold certificate by a man whose license plate he jotted down on the bill. Lyle and his assistant brought the bill to a bank, which alerted the police. The certificate did, indeed, prove to be one of the marked bills. When authorities checked the license plate number Lyle provided, the tag came back registered to a man named Richard Bruno Hauptmann.[43]

In the 1930s, there wasn't criminal profiling like there is today, but the investigators in this case had made some inferences based on pieces of evidence. Beyond feeling certain the kidnapper was German, they'd felt it likely that he was a carpenter and that he lived in or near the Bronx. Hauptmann checked all those boxes. He was married with a young son—Manfred Hauptmann had been born about two years after Charlie was killed. Bruno Hauptmann worked odd jobs and, in fact, hadn't worked at all for more than a year—and yet, when police visited, they noticed surprisingly expensive furniture throughout the house. But what really piqued investigators' interest was when the taxi driver, Perrone, told them about the businesses he'd seen Hauptmann visit, and several of the businesses had reported getting ransom bills.[44] Police figured this couldn't be a coincidence, so they questioned Hauptmann, who denied any involvement. Then they searched his house and found money hidden everywhere—money with serial numbers matching the ransom dough. Some money was hidden in a can buried beneath the garage. More was shoved into auger holes cut into 2×4 beams.

Then they found a wall in Hauptmann's son's bedroom that had a phone number and address scrawled on it in pencil.[45] The contact info happened to belong to John F. Condon, aka Jafsie. Hauptmann said he'd gotten the money from a friend and business associate named Isidor Fisch, who'd conveniently died earlier that year. He hid the money because he'd found it in a box Fisch had given him to watch and figured that Fisch's family might come back for it. He didn't want that, so he concealed the money and kept its existence hidden from his wife, Anna.

Investigators didn't buy it. The carpenter was arrested and charged with murder in what promised to be the highest-profile and most sensational trial in American history. The evidence presented against Hauptmann included several eyewitnesses beyond Perrone identifying him as someone connected to the kidnapping years earlier, plus handwriting experts who testified to overlaps between Hauptmann's known handwriting and the ransom letters, as well as FBI experts who said they could match the wood used to build the kidnapper's ladder with wood found at the Hauptmann house. Hauptmann insisted that he'd played no role in the kidnapping, knew nothing about it, and simply had been given the money that the police recovered at his home from his now-dead friend Fisch. While all this evidence was surely compelling, it was likely Lindbergh's own testimony that sealed Hauptmann's verdict.

Bruno Richard Hauptmann, center, being arraigned in Bronx County, New York, October 11, 1934, on a charge of extorting $50,000 in ransom money from Charles Lindbergh. The charge was dismissed so that an extradition warrant could be served on Hauptmann after the state of New Jersey indicted him for the murder of Charles Jr.

"Lindbergh himself took the stand," A. Scott Berg said, "and was asked if he recognized the voice of the man" to whom Condon had handed the ransom money years earlier. "Even though it was just a few syllables, and it was from a hundred yards away in the night, [Lindbergh claimed] that he recognized that voice." To the press, and more important, to jurors, it was as though "God himself had said, 'That's the man who stole my baby,'" Berg said.[46]

On February 13, 1935, Bruno Hauptmann was convicted of murder. His lawyers' appeals failed, and on April 3, 1936, he was executed in the electric chair at the New Jersey State Prison in Trenton. He was pronounced dead at 8:47 p.m.[47]

Forty years later, a journalist named Anthony Scaduto wrote a book called *Scapegoat: The Lonesome Death of Bruno Hauptmann* (1976), in which he argued vehemently that Hauptmann was innocent. He said that anti-German sentiment clouded the case from the start, that eyewitnesses had lied, and that the police had withheld physical evidence.[48] Hauptmann's wife, Anna, also kept insisting her husband had nothing to do with the kidnapping. She said she routinely heard people screaming, "Kill the German!"[49] during the trial. And, when you look at newspaper coverage from the time, it is pretty clear that reporters were certain he was guilty by the way they framed the stories. One said Hauptmann "fit the picture." "He is thrifty, close-mouthed, stoical. It is wholly conceivable that the mystery surrounding the actual perpetration of the crime will never be cleared up, for Hauptmann belongs to the type which never talks, never breaks down."[50] In 1981, at age eighty-two, Anna sued the state of New Jersey for "wrongfully, corruptly, and unjustly" trying and executing her husband.[51] She wanted to clear his name, she said then. She didn't win her suit, but she did manage to help turn the Hauptmann conviction into a controversial one.[52] Some websites are dedicated to the conspiracy theory that Lindbergh himself killed his own son—or that Charlie never died at all. Easily a dozen people stepped forward claiming to be baby Lindbergh over the years, including, infamously, a Black woman.[53]

Berg believes two things can be true at once: Hauptmann might have endured a sham trial while also being guilty. "There is no doubt in my mind that Bruno Richard Hauptmann committed the crime, that he kidnapped the baby. I am just as certain that this man got a truly unfair trial. He was a condemned man from the very beginning."[54]

Legal Legacy

The handling of the Lindbergh investigation continues to stir controversy to this day. Among the criticisms:

- Police seemed to defer to Charles Lindbergh far more than would be considered appropriate in modern times. They allowed him to work with liaisons to the "underworld" and insist that police share tips. Colonel H. Norman Schwarzkopf, commander of the New Jersey State Police, not only obeyed Lindbergh's commands, but said, "There is nothing I wouldn't do for Colonel Lindbergh—there is no oath that I wouldn't break if it would materially help his well-being."[55]
- Curious choices in the case have left openings for theories, of both the plausible and conspiratorial varieties, to flourish—including one that posits that "Cemetery John" was a Hauptmann accomplice named John Knoll who'd fled the Bronx during Hauptmann's trial.[56]

25

The Tylenol Murders

(1982)

On June 5, 1986, a seemingly healthy man named Bruce Nickell, age fifty-two, came home from work with a throbbing headache. He did what most people would do in that situation: He went to his kitchen, where he and his wife, Stella, kept their painkillers, and grabbed some headache medicine.

It was a rough headache, so Bruce took four pills at once and waited for the drug to kick in. He watched a little TV, went for a short walk near his home in Auburn, Washington, and then called out to his wife.

"Babe?" he said. "I feel like I'm going to pass out."[1] And then he did pass out. He was dead a few hours later.

Less than a week later, on June 11, a forty-year-old mother of two woke up for her job at a bank near Seattle, Washington. Sue Snow felt fine, but she had a morning routine that included popping a couple of Excedrin because it contained caffeine and it was akin to her morning coffee. Fifteen minutes later, her fifteen-year-old daughter found her sprawled on the bathroom floor. "Mom's eyes were open and her fingers were bent and locked up," said Snow's daughter, Hayley Klein, in a 1997 episode of the TV show *Forensic Files*. "She was having a hard time breathing."[2] Like Bruce, Sue Snow never regained consciousness and died within hours.[3]

Because Bruce Nickell was a recovering alcoholic in his fifties with health issues, no toxicology screen was done, so the medical examiner ruled his death natural. Official cause: pulmonary emphysema. Sue Snow's death was unexpected enough that it triggered additional tests, which showed she'd died of acute cyanide poisoning. It turned out that she and Bruce Nickell had taken Excedrin pills from the same lot number, sparking panic and prompting store owners across the country to pull the painkiller off its shelves. Excedrin's parent company, Bristol-Myers, sprang into action, pulling all Excedrin capsules from store shelves across the country and warning people not to use any they'd already bought.[4]

For much of the country, this felt like a horrible case of déjà vu—because it wasn't the first time people had died from using an over-the-counter painkiller. To fully understand these two deaths from 1986, and to grasp how authorities caught the killer, it's helpful to back up to a crisp autumn morning four years earlier, when seven other people who took over-the-counter pain medication died in Chicago.

That story began on Wednesday, September 29, 1982, when twelve-year-old Mary Kellerman woke up for school but felt a cold coming on.[5] The seventh grader told her parents she felt crummy, and they gave her permission to stay home from school. Mary went to the bathroom upstairs and took an Extra-Strength Tylenol to ease her symptoms. Her father, in his first-floor bedroom, heard a loud thud, then ran upstairs to find his daughter sprawled on the bathroom floor.[6]

Around the same time on the other side of town, Adam Janus also woke up feeling ill. The twenty-seven-year-old father decided he was too sick for work, so he took the day off as supervisor of the Elk Grove Village post office. He swung by a pharmacy to get some medicine, made lunch for his young children, and popped two Extra-Strength Tylenol. Then he, too, collapsed.[7]

Both Mary and Adam would be rushed to nearby hospitals, where they died soon after. The two were just the beginning of a wave of victims in a case that terrified the country, sparked dozens of copycats, and led to new Federal Drug Administration (FDA) regulations that are still in place today.

Though both Mary and Adam died on the same day, no one made any connection between the cases at first. Despite Adam's age, the medics who arrived thought he'd had a heart attack. Mary's death was harder to explain, but she'd woken up feeling sick, so medics assumed her collapse was related to that. An autopsy was ordered, but the doctors already assumed the ruling would come back as something natural—a heart attack, maybe, or a stroke. Those things *can* happen to twelve-year-olds, too.

After hearing that Adam collapsed, his whole family had rushed to Northwest Community Hospital, where doctors tried in vain to revive him. Thomas Kim, the medical director of the intensive care unit, shook hands

with Adam's younger brother, twenty-five-year-old Stanley. Kim offered his condolences before signing off on the death being caused by a heart attack.[8]

As Kim wrapped up his shift later in the day, he got jarring news: Stanley Janus, the brother he'd just talked to a few hours earlier, had been rushed to the hospital. So had Stanley's nineteen-year-old wife, Theresa. Kim had seen both earlier, and while they'd naturally been upset at the time, they'd still seemed healthy. Theresa had complained of a headache, and Stanley had some chronic back pain, but neither said anything to suggest their symptoms were severe. Stanley died soon after arriving; by the end of the day, Theresa was barely clinging to life.

Kim was flummoxed: *What the hell was going on here?*

He paced his office, turning the cases over in his mind. Then it hit him: Just before each of these people collapsed, they had complained of abdominal pain and dizziness, after which their hearts stopped. These were symptoms of potassium cyanide poisoning.[9] Kim ran some blood tests and confirmed his hunch.[10] He had figured out the *what*, but he still had no clue about the *why* or the *how*.

A casket is carried out of the Basilica of Saint Hyacinth church in Chicago, after the funeral mass for Adam, Stanley, and Theresa Janus, October 5, 1982.

Meanwhile, people kept dying. A thirty-one-year-old woman named Mary MacFarland got a headache as she was working at a telephone store in the mall and took some Tylenol. Within minutes, she was on the floor. Another woman named Mary Reiner, twenty-seven, was recovering from giving birth to her fourth child. Though the baby boy was just six days old, Mary had powered through grocery shopping with her mother-in-law and picked up Tylenol on her doctor's orders.[11] Soon after, Reiner's young daughter watched medics wheel Mary from the house on a stretcher.[12]

Investigators scrambled to find some link between the victims. Mary Kellerman was a seventh grader at Jane Addams Junior High in Schaumburg. She loved babysitting and horseback riding and, based on her obituary, was an only child. She didn't know any of the other victims, and neither did her parents.

The Januses were connected, of course, but only to each other. Adam was married with two young children in Arlington Heights. His brother, Stanley, and his wife had been married less than a year.

Mary MacFarland was a single mother with two young sons and a steady job at Illinois Bell. She took the Tylenol while at work and collapsed in front of her coworkers.

Mary Reiner was a stay-at-home mom with a loving husband named Ed. She liked playing softball and the drums, was an amazing cook—especially of Irish food, a nod to her ancestry—and loved being a mom.

It took twelve hours between the time the first body fell and when authorities realized that Tylenol was the only common denominator. And the connection wasn't made by a doctor. Two firefighters—Arlington Heights fire lieutenant Philip Cappitelli and Elk Grove Village firefighter Richard Keyworth—had been listening to their emergency radios on their day off and noticed that dispatchers were taking calls about people collapsing all over the city. They'd also noticed that at least in the Kellerman and Janus cases, emergency responders happened to mention that the victims had taken Tylenol. Keyworth called Cappitelli and said, "This is a wild stab, but maybe it's Tylenol."[13] Their theory reached Dr. Kim. And the next day, the whole world knew that the over-the-counter pill meant to kill pain was actually killing people.

One news story read: "The Food and Drug Administration today advised consumers nationwide to stop using Extra-Strength Tylenol

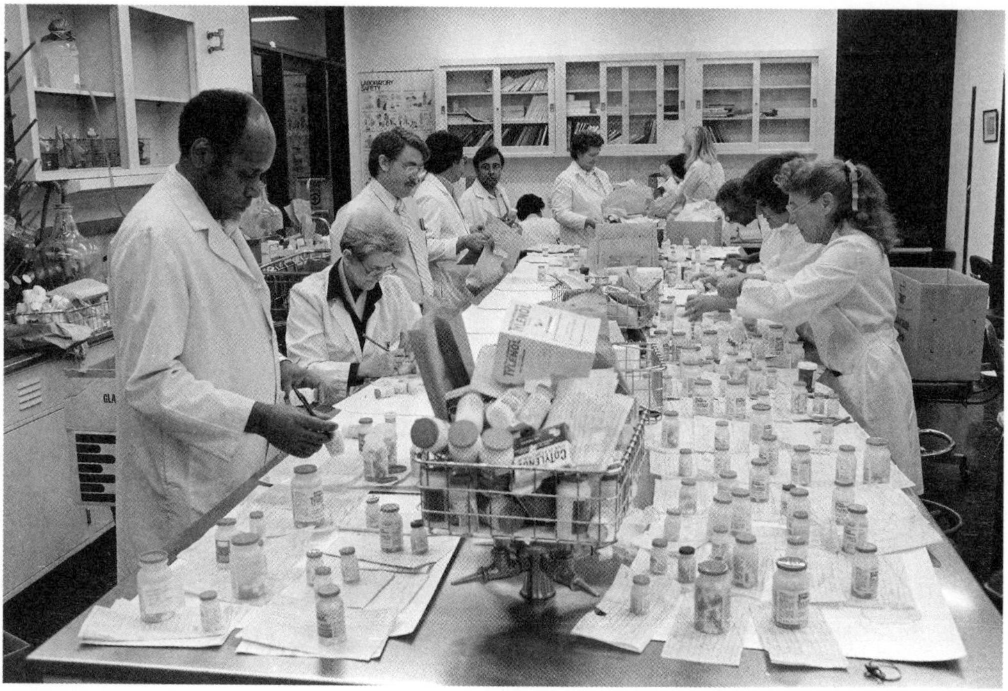

Chicago City Health Department employees test Tylenol for cyanide content at a city laboratory, October 4, 1982.

capsules after officials disclosed a second batch of cyanide-tainted pain reliever had been found. The poison-tainted medicine is linked to as many as five deaths."[14]

Inside of random Tylenol bottles throughout Chicago were capsules that looked just a little bit different than the others. The capsules, which had powdered medicine inside, had been carefully split open, refilled with poison, and resealed again. Only someone paying close attention would have seen that the markings on the outside of the capsule were slightly misaligned and the powder on the inside was brown, not white. News reporters got the message out quickly: "Cyanide-laced capsules linked to area deaths" read an October 1 jump head from the *Chicago Tribune*.[15] A sidebar reported: "Stores around nation pull Tylenol capsules." Here's another terrifying headline: "Cyanide Deadly Just to Touch."[16]

Tylenol was produced by McNeil Consumer Products Company, which fell under the umbrella of Johnson & Johnson, a Cincinnati-based company that was facing a public relations nightmare they never could have anticipated. They didn't know what was happening. They checked the production line, which was made a lot easier by their practice of saving a random sample of pills from every lot produced. The samples were clean, meaning the cyanide wasn't being added during production. Tylenol itself was not killing people. Someone had either bought or stolen bottles from individual stores, tampered with the product, and then put it back on the shelves for someone to buy. By morning, there had been five deaths, and Theresa Janus was on life support. On Friday, October 1, she officially became victim number six.

That evening, thirty-five-year-old Paula Prince was supposed to meet her sister for dinner, but she hadn't shown up. At first, her sister assumed she was running late, but after a while, she started to get worried. She telephoned Paula's home, but no one answered. Then she called the police. Paula, a flight attendant, had last been seen after working a flight from Las Vegas to O'Hare International Airport in Chicago. On her way home, she stopped at a Walgreens at about 9:30 Wednesday night. A surveillance camera captured her buying a bottle of Tylenol. Police had to piece together what happened next from the crime scene: It appeared Paula had gone to the bathroom to start taking off her makeup as she readied for bed. Judging by the open Tylenol bottle on the vanity, she'd taken a pill or two. An investigator later said: "By the time she got to the threshold of the door, she was dead."[17]

She probably took the medicine that very night, but no one knew she had died until two days later. She was victim number seven. The panic continued. Police searched desperately for a culprit, which seemed like it shouldn't be too difficult. After all, they had found surveillance images of Paula buying the Tylenol; they hoped it would be just as easy to find footage of someone planting the bottle on the shelf. But first, authorities needed the deaths to stop.

With the body count linked to cyanide-laced Tylenol at seven, companies involved with making Tylenol were just as panicked as the public. Johnson & Johnson pulled together a public relations team that included Alan Hilburg, a consultant.

"We didn't have a crisis plan," Hilburg later said in a talk about the experience. "We created a strategy literally over thirty-six hours that said our first responsibility is to those who use the product, so pulling the product off the shelf was an easy one. Next come employees, next come the communities in which our plants live. Our final responsibility is to stockholders. So,

we pulled all the Tylenol off the shelf simply because it was the right thing to do."[18]

It was also an expensive thing to do.

"We pulled 330 million tablets off the shelf," Hilburg said. "We went from 30 percent market share to zero overnight."[19]

Cyanide is a chemical compound that can be produced naturally by bacteria, fungi, and algae; and the pits of some edible fruits contain a chemical called amygdalin, which when digested can release cyanide—but those aren't the parts of the fruits that people eat. Potassium cyanide—which was found in each of the Chicago victims—is extremely toxic; exposure to it leads to rapid poisoning, with symptoms like headaches, dizziness, and vomiting. It can cause seizures and slow one's heart rate. Eventually, it can stop the heart altogether. In acute cases, all the symptoms accelerate. The victims were doomed the second the gelatin casing on those Tylenol capsules dissolved.[20]

Tracking cyanide is difficult because it is commonly sold and used for commercial purposes.[21] It's used in professional capacities in jewelry manufacturing, mining, and some forms of photography, and it can also be an effective insecticide (although its use is now limited).[22] Without any initial leads or suspects and with Tylenol pulled from the shelves, the story began petering out. Then Johnson & Johnson received a letter. It began:

> **Gentlemen: As you can see, it is easy to place cyanide (both potassium and sodium) into capsules sitting on store shelves. And since the cyanide is inside the gelatin, it is easy to get buyers to swallow the bitter pill. Another beauty is that cyanide operates quickly. It takes so very little. And there will be no time to take countermeasures.**[23]

The letter writer demanded $1 million wired to a specific Chicago-based bank account. In exchange for the money, the killings would stop.[24]

At first, the letter was largely dismissed as a hoax. After all, it was incredibly easy for police to track the bank account holder. What idiot would kill people, then send a letter to police giving away their identity? The account holder was quickly determined to be a man named Frederick McCahey, and the account itself had already been closed.[25] McCahey came in voluntarily for questioning, and the police were satisfied that he had nothing to do with either the extortion letter or the cyanide poisonings. But his interview did lead authorities down an interesting path. McCahey had owned a business in Chicago called Lakeside Travel. In April 1982, the business was struggling. Paychecks to a number of employees bounced, angering them. Among the angered workers was a bookkeeper named Nancy Richardson.[26] Her paycheck had been for $512, which she cashed at a currency exchange, which in turn had filed a lawsuit against her a few months after the check was returned for insufficient funds.[27]

Lakeside's workers tried to recoup their pay by filing a claim with the Illinois Department of Labor. Nancy Richardson was especially aggressive on this front, arguing that if the business accounts were drained, then her former boss's personal accounts should cover the wages. She got into an argument with McCahey about it, which her husband, Robert Richardson, soon joined. The confrontation escalated until McCahey threatened to fire Nancy.

That's why when McCahey was dragged in for questioning about an extortion letter tied to one of his bank accounts, the Richardsons came to mind. Authorities agreed the couple seemed suspicious enough to investigate further. For starters, their names weren't Nancy and Robert Richardson. They were really James and LeAnn Lewis and had been using aliases. In the early 1970s, they had run an accounting firm called J & L Business Tax Service.[28] Records show they had a five-year-old daughter named Toni who died in 1974, and using aliases was second nature to them. They also went by countless other surnames, including Wagner.[29] They'd bounced from one job to another, changing names more often than most people change the oil in their cars.

Once authorities started looking at McCahey, they started looking for the Richardsons, who in turn led them to the Lewises, who'd already left Chicago for New York. Investigators learned that James Lewis had lived in Kansas City at some point and had run-ins with the police,[30] so they asked for his fingerprints. That's how they learned that he'd previously been charged with murder. In 1978, a seventy-two-year-old man named Raymond West went missing for three weeks before he was found, decomposed with his legs removed, in his attic.[31] Lewis had been this man's accountant and during the weeks West was missing, acted suspiciously enough that he drew the attention of the authorities. The cops arrested Lewis and searched his home and found seemingly damning evidence: Lewis had forged a check for $5,000 from one of West's accounts.[32]

But the murder case was riddled with technical mistakes. The grand jury indictment didn't use the word *felonious*, which made it invalid.[33] A judge also ruled that the police had searched Lewis's home improperly and hadn't read him his rights. Finally, the dismemberment and decomposition made it tough to tell exactly how the old man had been killed, so the case against Lewis was dismissed, despite a *Kansas City Times* report in 1979[34] describing the evidence against Lewis as substantial: there was the forged check, Lewis had made contradictory statements to police, and detectives even found ropes and overhand knots in Lewis's station wagon that matched the ropes and knots hanging from a rafter in the victim's attic. Because that evidence wasn't admissible, the prosecution had no case.[35] Lewis was free to continue living his life.

If the Lewises thought decamping to New York would protect them from the police, they were wrong. Unlike the death of Raymond West, the Tylenol poisonings were a nationwide story, so the manhunt was nationwide, too. On December 13, 1982, James Lewis was arrested inside a New York City public library, where he was reading the Chicago papers to keep tabs on the Tylenol investigation.[36] Lewis admitted to the extortion attempt, but he denied having anything to do with the killings. He further denied his wife had anything to do with either. Despite having learned about Lewis's ties to the Raymond West case back in 1978, officials were still leaning toward the letter being a hoax—meaning that they suspected Lewis had simply seen an opening to extort a company while also casting suspicion on a man who'd done his wife wrong, but then Lewis said something interesting. According to an Associated Press report, he "gave investigators a detailed account of how someone could buy medicine, use a special method to add cyanide to the capsules, and return them to store shelves."[37]

The *Kansas City Times* also reported that Lewis was a partner in an import scheme with an Indian-born pharmacist who taught Lewis how to make pills and capsules.

Police apparently tried to build a murder case against Lewis, but the best the feds managed was an indictment for the extortion, for which Lewis spent more than twelve years in prison.[38] His wife was never charged, and in the decades since his release from prison, no further suspects have been identified in the Tylenol poisonings despite the feds having tried to come at the case a few different ways. They even searched Lewis's Boston home in 2009.[39] Nothing came of it, and the case remains officially unsolved. As recently as 2022, Lewis continued to deny playing a role in the deaths.

"Have you been harassed over something for forty years that you didn't have anything to do with?" he asked a *Chicago Tribune* reporter working on an anniversary project about the deaths. Lewis added that while Tylenol's involvement in the case has long been lauded, he believed they were allowed too much access to, and input in the investigation. "What have you done on that story about J & J's destruction of all the evidence? They burned several million capsules."[40] Lewis died on July 9, 2023, at age seventy-six.[41]

But while the seven Chicago cases don't have satisfying resolutions, the broader story continued. For starters, Johnson & Johnson quickly changed how it packaged its pills, adding tamper-resistant packaging such as aluminum foil over the top of the medication and a childproof cap. Soon after, the

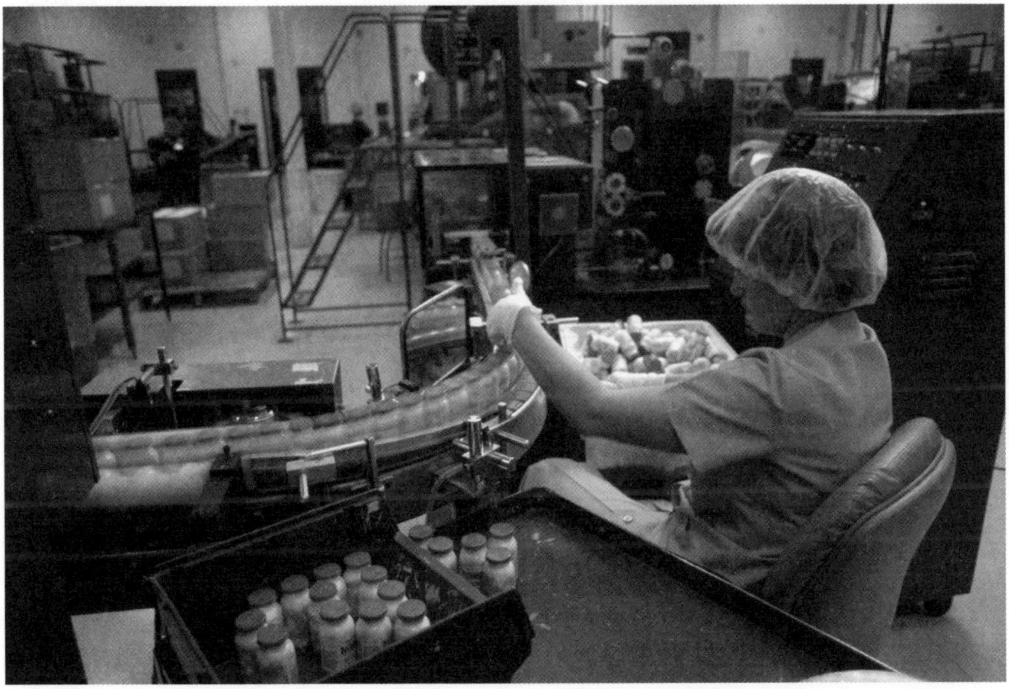

A worker checks the newly implemented safety seals on Tylenol bottles in 1984, after Johnson & Johnson's re-release of Tylenol capsules.

FDA required that all over-the-counter consumer drug products have similar packaging, paving the way for widespread use of blister packs and shrink seals.[42]

In 1983, Congress passed what had been nicknamed the "Tylenol bill," which made it a federal offense to tamper with consumer products. Still, even after Tylenol returned to the shelves and the immediate panic subsided, a smattering of false confessions and copycats were reported across the country. A story from October 1982 by United Press International gave a rundown:[43]

- **A twenty-year-old disgruntled hospital employee named Jerome Howard was arrested after FBI officials said he threatened to poison patients with laced Tylenol unless he was paid $8,000. He claimed credit for the Chicago-area killings, but authorities said no evidence supported the claim and his name hasn't been publicly raised in connection with the case for more than forty years.[44]**
- **Another man, Jerome Oman of Chicago, got upset that a ham he'd bought was spoiled, so he claimed he was the Tylenol killer in hopes of getting a phone operator to give him the unlisted number of the Dubuque Packing Co., which sold him the ham. He was charged with disorderly conduct and cleared as the killer. An investigator said Oman "was just very upset over a ham not being up to par."**
- **An anonymous letter sent to a newspaper in DeKalb County, Illinois, claimed that cyanide had been placed in one gallon of apple cider from a specific orchard, so authorities warned not to drink that cider. No tainted gallon was ever found.**
- **And in Sheridan, Wyoming, nineteen-year-old Jay Adam Mitchell died of unexplained cyanide poisoning, though it was never formally linked to Tylenol and investigators never found a connection to the Chicago cases.**

By 1986, it seemed clear that whoever poisoned the people in Chicago had gotten away with it, and another copycat surfaced in New York. Twenty-three-year-old Diane Elsroth died after taking two capsules from a bottle of

Extra-Strength Tylenol at her boyfriend's house in Yonkers. Authorities searched nearby stores in Bronxville, where the bottle had been bought, and found another tainted bottle as well.[45] Once again, tainted Tylenol was on front pages nationwide. According to a newscast:

> **Investigators were briefly sidetracked when three suspects arrested in another case were found with a copy of an extortion letter addressed to the Bronxville Police Department. The letter demanded $2 million to halt the Tylenol tampering, but investigators are convinced the group had nothing to do with the poisonings.[46]**

They were also convinced the mini-outbreak had nothing to do with the one four years earlier. Like Chicago, that case is unsolved. Authorities' failure to solve the Chicago and New York poisonings made them that much more determined to figure out just what happened to Bruce Nickell and Sue Snow, the two Excedrin-takers from the Seattle area.

When Bruce died, his passing didn't make headlines or draw much notice. But a week later, Sue's did. While performing an autopsy, assistant medical examiner Janet Miller opened Sue's chest cavity and noticed the faint, telltale outdoor of bitter almonds, which she recognized as "such a distinct odor," as she said on *Forensic Files*. "It's like when you're driving down the road and you smell a skunk. That's a very distinct odor and you say, 'Oh, a skunk was near here.' It just leaves an impression in your brain that you don't forget."[47]

After tests confirmed cyanide poisoning, authorities had to figure out how it got in her system. That's when Sue's twin sister, Sarah, noticed Excedrin capsules in Sue's house.

"She never took capsules," Sarah later said.[48]

Sue was recently married. Her husband, Paul Webking, had been married three times before and was a gruff guy and a trucker. Suspicion fell on him straight away, which wasn't eased when, soon after Sue's death, he married for a fifth time. He was still being investigated when Stella Nickell contacted police to alert them that her husband, who had died a week earlier than Sue, had taken Excedrin as well. She brought in that bottle plus one other and, as she suspected, some of the capsules had indeed been

Stella Nickell is taken from the federal courthouse in Seattle May 9, 1988, by US Marshall Jerry Moore. She was convicted in Seattle of causing the deaths of her husband and another woman by lacing their Extra-Strength Excedrin with cyanide.

tampered with. Paul Webking had no connection with the Nickells at all, and authorities worried that maybe there was another random killer picking up where the Chicago and New York killers had left off. They pulled all Excedrin from the shelves and found tainted capsules inside two more bottles. Each of the capsules contained 700 milligrams of cyanide, which is four times the amount you need to kill an average human.

When the FBI analyzed the cyanide more closely, they noticed that there were some tiny foreign particles mixed in with it. Scientists analyzed it and determined it was algae killer—like the type you'd use in a fish tank. They didn't know what that meant, but they took note.

Stella Nickell, meanwhile, was ruffling feathers. Certain that her husband had been murdered, she demanded answers.

Stella had had a rocky start in life, giving birth to a daughter named Cynthia when she was sixteen. When Bruce died, Stella was forty and had stayed out of trouble for a while, but in her twenties, she'd been arrested several times—including for fraud in 1968 and for forgery in 1971.[49] She was divorced when she met Bruce, and the two hit it off right away. They both liked to party, and Stella was a bar-hopper, so Bruce's hard drinking was just fine with her. After they married, though, Bruce decided to sober up. He entered rehab and quit drinking. Stella was less than pleased to lose her drinking buddy, and she began complaining bitterly about Bruce to her now-grown daughter, nicknamed Cindy. She told Cindy that Bruce had become a bore.

In the fall of 1985—about nine months before Bruce died—Stella had taken out a $40,000 life insurance policy on Bruce. That was his second policy—he had another for $31,000, though that amount would be increased by $105,000 if he died accidentally. Stella wasn't eligible for that extra amount, though, because Bruce's cause of death was supposedly natural.[50]

When police realized how much money was contingent on Bruce's death being unnatural, they began to get curious. Most of the time, people aren't murdered at random. They are murdered by people they know. It struck investigators that of the five tainted Excedrin bottles discovered in Washington State, two had been bought by Stella Nickell. Stella asked the coroner's office to reclassify Bruce's death, after which authorities suggested she take a polygraph. She said no thanks. They continued to press her about clearing her name so she could be exonerated. Eventually, investigators wore her down. Stella took a polygraph, and she supposedly failed. That on its own wouldn't have done much since polygraphs have controversial reputations, but it seems the failed test prompted Stella's daughter to come forward. She told police that her mom had not only complained about Bruce Nickell for five years, but she'd talked at length about killing him. Cindy also mentioned that her mother had long been fascinated by the 1982 Tylenol deaths.[51]

The way Stella likely saw it, those had been the perfect crimes. And the New York copycat just a couple of months before Bruce died would have confirmed her thinking. The police then zeroed in looking for evidence, which wasn't hard to find. Stella had gone to the library to research effective poisons. Detectives pulled those books and found Stella's fingerprints all

over the *C* section—as in, *c* for cyanide.[52] The signature on Bruce's latest life insurance policy did not match his known samples. It had been forged.[53] Stella had written a letter to a creditor in which she said she'd been having marital problems but they were about over and Bruce would no longer be around. She wrote that five days before he died. And finally, those tiny foreign particles found in the cyanide analyzed from the tainted Excedrin bottles had been the exact brand of algaecide that Stella had bought for her fish tanks at home. Nickell has long maintained her innocence, pointing to rewards collected by several people who testified against her, including her daughter. In 2022, however, she took responsibility for the deaths in a handwritten petition to the US District Court in Seattle, asking for an early release due to ailing health. She wrote: "I am accused of 'not knowing the moral wrong I committed.' Nobody knows better than I the depth of my heinous offense and how deeply it goes against the 'accepted standards of conduct.' I am most remorseful for being responsible for the loss of two human lives."[54]

It seemed that Stella Nickell had gotten away with murder. With the pulmonary emphysema diagnosis, she was free and clear and $71,000 richer. But that wasn't enough for her. She wanted the $105,000 she would get if her husband's death hadn't resulted from natural causes, so she tampered with five bottles in all—two in her own home, and three on store shelves.[55] Sue Snow just happened to buy one of those three. Because of the Tylenol deaths in 1982 and the laws that came after them—making tampering with consumer products a federal crime—Stella faced federal charges, becoming the first person ever to be convicted of violating the Federal Anti-Tampering Act. She went on trial in 1988, at which her own daughter testified against her. The jury deliberated almost five days before finding Stella guilty.[56] Her sentence was surely a bitter pill to swallow: she received two ninety-year sentences, one for each of her victims, and three ten-year terms for product tampering.

Legal Legacy

The unsolved Tylenol murders continue to fascinate and spark theories—including one that notes that the inventor of the first tamper-evident bottle submitted his patent applications six days before the murders and was a man who worked in the Chicago area—but its repercussions are less mysterious:[57]

- The 1982 deaths sparked the FDA to work with Johnson & Johnson to develop tamper-proof packaging, including foil seals. The company also introduced "caplets," a tablet that was far harder to tamper with than powder-filled capsules.[58]
- In 1983, Congress passed the Federal Anti-Tampering Act, making it a federal offense to tamper with consumer products.[59]
- In 1989, the FDA also established federal guidelines for manufacturers on packaging all over-the-counter "human drug products" in tamper-evident packaging.[60]

Acknowledgments

This book could not exist without the hundreds of journalists and authors cited within its pages, some of whom granted me interviews and even forwarded primary source documents. Please look at the endnotes section. It represents so much legwork by a wide array of players spanning hundreds of years—journalists who worked to quote accurately, describe candidly, and document thoroughly. I did my best to cite every source I used, but know that once I delve into old newspapers, I disappear for hours to absorb as much as possible and get to know the story as completely as I can. The main sources are cited, but I'm sure there are some I missed.

I want to give special thanks to the people who granted interviews for my podcast *Crimes of the Centuries*, upon which this book is based. Each one of these amazing researchers and writers shared their insight, passion, and enthusiasm to bring these stories and people to life for me. Specifically, I want to send heartfelt thanks to: Paula Uruburu, Emerson Baker, Kate Moore, Harold Schechter, Kate Winkler Dawson, Meaghan Good, Alex Tresniowski, Peter Lucia, Benjamin Saulsberry, Paula Fass, and Carolyn Morrow Long. Long, who did exhaustive research for her book on Madam Delphine LaLaurie, went above and beyond when I had a follow-up question for this book, going so far as to send me dated lists of the enslaved people bequeathed to LaLaurie by her parents. While the topic at hand was heartbreaking, Long's gesture was a moment of professional generosity I will treasure.

I owe enormous gratitude to the exemplary Pulitzer Prize–winning journalist Amy Wilson, who had served as my trusted editor on seasons 1 through 4 of the *Accused* podcast. Amy retired from the *Cincinnati Enquirer* just as I began writing this book and graciously read everything I sent her. She also alerted me to the existence of a nearly century-old booklet of trial transcripts housed at the University of Cincinnati, which was invaluable in the section on the Snooks-Hix affair. Most of all, though, Amy was my cheerleader when my energy began to flag, which happened more times during this project than I'd like to admit. I owe her drinks.

The book would not exist at all without the *Crimes of the Centuries* podcast, which, as I mentioned in my foreword, was birthed in the pandemic and I daresay kept me as close to sane as was ever going to be possible. I'm forever grateful to Patrick Hinds and Steve Tipton of the Obsessed Network for believing in the show, as well as the people who have worked on its production over the past few years: Natalie Grillo, Amy Sapp, Jennifer Swiatek, Garrett Tiedemann, and Madeleine Poston (my littlest sister). My dad Bruce Hunt has been a big supporter of—and musician for—*COTC*, too.

I also need to thank the amazing listeners of the show, who make me feel dorky and unworthy with their unwavering praise. I worked hard to dig deeper, fact-check more thoroughly and tell these stories differently so that you'd find something worthwhile even if you're an avid listener of the podcast.

To do that, I had enormous help from Barbara Berger, my editor at Union Square & Co. She pushed back on details and sources to ensure that this is as reliable an anthology as possible. To put it plainly, it is not easy to confirm details from decades and even centuries past, and Barbara helped me find and solidify sourcing when things felt shaky. Also on the Union Square front, thank you to: cover designer Igor Satanovsky, interior designer Kevin Ullrich, production editor Michael Cea, photo editor Linda Liang, managing editor Christine Stambaugh, and production manager Sandy Noman.

Finally, thanks goes to Dan Milaschewski of United Talent Agency, who helped me shore up my book pitch and find this project a home.

Notes

Preface

1 "Dodging the 'Flu,'" [KS] *Parsons Daily Eclipse*, Oct. 17, 1918, https://rb.gy/q7o90.
2 "London, Yarmouth, August 9," *Maryland Gazette*, Dec. 5, 1750, https://rb.gy/jpkxy.
3 "Shocking Murder!!, Norwich, Feb. 26," *Lancaster Intelligencer*, Mar. 12, 1800, https://rb.gy/7an4b.

1: Lessons Learned from the Salem Witch Trials

1 Emerson W. Baker, *A Storm of Witchcraft: The Salem Trials and the American Experience* (New York: Oxford Univ. Press, 2015), Kindle.
2 Baker, *Storm of Witchcraft*.
3 Harry S. Stout, *The New England Soul: Preaching and Religious Culture in Colonial New England* (New York: Oxford Univ. Press, 1986).
4 Baker. *Storm of Witchcraft*.
5 Sometimes spelled Soolard or Soolart; see Ancestry.com.
6 See Ancestry.com.
7 DOB is 1650 according to Ancestry.com.
8 Spelled "Osburne" on the warrant, see https://bit.ly/3VkQNnq; other variations include Osborn and Osburn.
9 Baker, Storm of Witchcraft; Malcolm Gaskill, Univ. of East Anglia, "The Salem Witch Trials," Bill of Rights Inst., https://bit.ly/426y4Oo; Nathan Dorn, "Evidence from Invisible World in Salem," Library of Congress (hereafter LOC) Blogs, In Custodia Legis, Aug. 20, 2020, http://bit.ly/3MbtA4s.
10 Salem Witch Trials, Documentary Archive and Transcription Project, Univ. of Virginia, examination of Sarah Osborne, as recorded by John Hathorne, https://salem.lib.virginia.edu/n95.html.
11 Baker, *Storm of Witchcraft*.
12 Ibid.
13 Gwynn Guilford, "Germany Was Once the Witch Burning Capital of the World. Here's Why," Jan. 24, 2018, Quartz, https://bit.ly/42dUHAF.
14 British Library, "King James VI and I's *Demonology*, 1597, https://bit.ly/3OLRLaT; James Sharpe, *The Bewitching of Anne Gunter: A Horrible and True Story of Deception, Witchcraft, Murder, and the King of England* (New York: Routledge, 2000); Baker, *Storm of Witchcraft*.
15 Brian P. Levvack, "Possession, Witchcraft, and the Law in Jacobean England," *Washington and Lee Law Review* 52 (3), Winter 1996, https://bit.ly/3M4UL0l.
16 Sometimes spelled "Procter"; see WikiTree at https://www.wikitree.com/wiki/Proctor-736.
17 "Samuel and Mary Sibley Home," *Salem Witch Museum*, https://bit.ly/3B44MEB. Accessed May 18, 2023.
18 Baker, *Storm of Witchcraft*.
19 Ibid.
20 Ibid.
21 Thomas, Ann (Sr.), and Ann (Jr.) Putnam Home, *Salem Witch Museum*, https://bit.ly/3HNAeL4. Accessed May 18, 2023.

2: The Dream Team Representing Levi Weeks

1 "Columbian Intelligence," *Farmer's Museum or Literary Gazette*, Jan. 6, 1800, https://bit.ly/41So8Za.
2 J. M. Beattie (1991), "Scales of Justice: Defense Counsel and the English Criminal Trial in the Eighteenth and Nineteenth Centuries," *Law and History Review* 9 (2), 221–67. *JSTOR*, https://doi.org/10.2307/743649.
3 Levi Weeks, and William Coleman. *Report of the Trial of Levi Weeks, on an Indictment for the Murder of Gulielma Sands*... (New York: John Furman, 1800); https://bit.ly/3OTcxoS.
4 Ibid.
5 Ibid.
6 Ibid.
7 Ibid.
8 Ibid.
9 Ibid.
10 Ibid.
11 Ibid.
12 David J. Krajicek, "Woman Down the Well," *Daily News*, Jan. 7, 2001, https://bit.ly/41Qzkor.
13 "Henry Brockholst Livingston," Oyez, https://bit.ly/3P2AIBA.
14 "History of Our Firm," *JP Morgan Chase & Co.* https://bit.ly/3IcdeG3.
15 Weeks and Coleman. *Report of the Trial of Levi Weeks*.
16 Ibid.
17 Ibid.
18 Ibid.
19 Paul Collins. *Duel with the Devil: The True Story of How Alexander Hamilton Teamed Up to Take on America's First Sensational Murder Mystery* (New York: Crown, 2013), Kindle.
20 Weeks and Coleman. *Report of the Trial of Levi Weeks*.
21 "A Woman's Curse," *Lincoln Evening Call*, May 4, 1890, https://bit.ly/42zLmmU.
22 Untitled on trial of Richard D. Croucher, *Lancaster Intelligencer*, July 16, 1800, https://bit.ly/3HOI07q.

3: Daniel Sickles's Claim of Temporary Insanity

1 "Dreadful Tragedy: Shocking Homicide at Washington," *NY Times*, Feb. 28, 1859; https://bit.ly/3WECcDH.
2 "Francis Scott Key," National Park Service, https://bit.ly/3OmZcVV.
3 Chris DeRose, *Star Spangled Scandal: Sex, Murder, and the Trial that Changed America* (Washington, DC: Regnery History), Kindle.
4 Ibid.
5 W. A. Swanberg, *Sickles the Incredible* (New York: Charles Scribner's Sons, 1956), https://bit.ly/43trSkg.
6 DeRose, *Star Spangled Scandal*.
7 "The Tragedy at Washington," *Middlebury Register*, Mar. 9, 1859, https://bit.ly/44G3KfK.
8 "Women Working, 1800–1930," *Curiosity Collections*, https://bit.ly/42k7Zfh. Accessed May 18, 2023.
9 DeRose, *Star Spangled Scandal*.
10 Ibid.

11 Ibid.
12 Ibid.
13 Ibid.
14 Ibid.
15 "The Washington Tragedy," *NY Daily Herald*, Mar. 2, 1859, https://bit.ly/42ruIWE.
16 DeRose, *Star Spangled Scandal*.
17 "The Madison Place Murder," [Washington, DC] *Evening Star*, Apr. 20, 1859, https://bit.ly/3HQxr3X.
18 "Horrible Affair in Washington," *Buffalo Evening Post*, Mar. 1, 1859, https://bit.ly/3B6QtPy.
19 DeRose, *Star Spangled Scandal*.
20 *The National Cyclopedia of American Biography*, vol. 3 (New York: James T. White, 1893); bit.ly/3ogUWMA.
21 DeRose, *Star Spangled Scandal*.
22 "Phillip Barton Key Shot By Daniel Sickles," *Wisconsin State Journal*, Feb. 28, 1859, https://bit.ly/42tMzvK.
23 "Murder in Washington," *Boston Evening Transcript*, Feb. 28, 1859, https://bit.ly/44HoIef.
24 See Ancestry.com.
25 "Taps is Sounded for Last Great Gettysburg Hero," *Daily Oklahoman*, May 4, 1914, https://bit.ly/3LD5AVU. (Note: His age is wrong here because he often lied and said he was born in 1825 when it was 1819/1820.)

4: The Slaying of Stanford White and the Trial of the Century

1 "A Real Roof Garden," *Passaic Daily News*, June 23, 1906, https://bit.ly/3B5gIp0.
2 Evelyn was born Florence Evelyn; her mother was named Evelyn Florence. The daughter transposed her name for professional purposes when she became a model, but they are called Evelyn and Mrs. Nesbit here for clarity.
3 Paula Uruburu, *American Eve: Evelyn Nesbit, Stanford White, the Birth of the "It" Girl, and the Crime of the Century* (New York: Penguin, 2008), Kindle.
4 Ibid.
5 Ibid.
6 Ibid.
7 Author interview with Paula Uruburu, November 2020.
8 "Beautiful Girl Model," *Marion Star,* Mar. 23, 1901, https://bit.ly/41hk7MS.
9 "New Type of Beauty," *Parsons Daily Sun,* May 11, 1901, https://bit.ly/3B37yd9.
10 Uruburu, *American Eve*.
11 "A Woman's Theater," *Evansville Journal,* Nov. 2, 1902, https://bit.ly/42DKlu5.
12 Evelyn Nesbit, *The Story of My Life* (Unknown: John Long, 1914).
13 Evelyn Nesbit, *Prodigal Days: The Untold Story of Evelyn Nesbit* (New York: Julian Messner, 1934).
14 Uruburu, *American Eve*.
15 Ibid.
16 "The Washington Tragedy," *NY Daily Herald*, Mar. 2, 1859, https://bit.ly/3OgYdqa.
17 Cecilia Rasmussen, "Girl in Red Velvet Swing Longed to Flee Her Past," *LA Times*, Dec. 11, 2005; https://bit.ly/3osQGdu.
18 Uruburu, *American Eve*.
19 Ibid.
20 *National Cyclopedia of American Biography* (New York: James T. White & Co., 1893), https://bit.ly/3OnkpPj.
21 "I Could Love a Million Girls," lyrics by Edgar Allan Woolf, 1906, for the musical *Mam'zelle Champagne*; Baylor Univ. Arts and Special Research Center, https://bit.ly/3L2oklR.
22 "Recapitulation of Important Events in Thaw Murder Trial," *Winnipeg Tribune,* Feb. 26, 1907, https://bit.ly/44BzdQb.
23 Ibid.
24 Ibid.
25 "Thaw Jury Locked Up for the Night," *Poughkeepsie Eagle-News,"* Apr. 11, 1907, https://bit.ly/3nMW5LP.
26 Ibid.
27 "Thaw's Escape is the Twentieth from Matteawan," *NY Times,* Aug. 24, 1913, https://bit.ly/3nxxJ93.
28 "Trenton Christens New Flying Field," [Camden, NJ] *Evening Courier-Post,* Oct. 26, 1929, https://bit.ly/3HKCe72.
29 Simon Baatz, *The Girl on the Velvet Swing: Sex, Murder, and Madness at the Dawn of the Twentieth Century* (New York: Little, Brown, 2018). Kindle.
30 "Newbit Girl's Mother Speaks," *Green Bay Press-Gazette,* July 6, 1906, https://bit.ly/3M6j9i2.
31 "Evelyn Newbit Thaw, Red Velvet Swing Girl," *Newsday* [Suffolk Ed.], Jan. 19, 1967, https://bit.ly/3NPrmsf.
32 "3 Into 2 Just Won't Go," *Daily News*, Mar. 16, 1980, https://bit.ly/42dyzH2.
33 Uruburu, *American Eve*.
34 Ibid.
35 Find a Grave, "Evelyn Nesbit," https://bit.ly/44Dv8ec.

5: The Coerced-but-True Confession in the Hix-Snooks Case

1 "Com. Mathot's Victory," *Brooklyn Daily Eagle*, Nov. 3, 1903, https://bit.ly/3VGbVV2.
2 Melvin Hix, "Further Contributions to the Interesting Discussion . . . ," *NY Times,* Apr. 14, 1906, https://bit.ly/3M3hU3g.
3 "State Teachers Hear Shop Talks," *Hartford Courant*, Oct. 25, 1913, https://bit.ly/3NOCt4B.
4 "Road Sign Brings New York Couple Here to Reside," *Bradenton Herald*, Aug. 1, 1923, https://bit.ly/3HKDUxm.
5 *The Murder of Theora Hix. The Uncensored Testimony of Dr. Snook . . . August 1929* (Franklin Cty. Ohio Court of Common Pleas, 1929).
6 Mark Gribben, *The Professor & the Coed: Scandal & Murder at the Ohio State University* (Charleston, SC: History Press, 2010), Kindle.
7 *Murder of Theora Hix*.
8 Ibid.
9 *Cty. of Riverside v. McLaughlin*, Justia. https://bit.ly/3nxzRO5. Accessed May 18, 2023.
10 *Murder of Theora Hix*.
11 "Columbus Neighborhoods: Infamous Columbus Characters," WOSU Public Media, Columbus historian Doreen Uhas Sauer at 9:48, https://bit.ly/43UQJgZ.
12 Gribben, *Professor & the Coed*.
13 "Professor, State Employe [sic] Held in Murder of Girl," *Dayton Daily News*, June 15, 1929, https://bit.ly/42yXsgl.
14 Gribben, *Professor & the Coed*.
15 *Murder of Theora Hix*.
16 Ibid.
17 *Gideon v. Wainwright* (1963); Justia, https://bit.ly/3oCCQVX.
18 *Murder of Theora Hix*.
19 "Gold Medalist's Murderous Act Still Horrifying," *Akron Beacon Journal*, May 16, 2010, https://bit.ly/3BnA3CR.
20 *Murder of Theora Hix*.

21 "Body of Dr. Snook, Buried Secretly to Avoid Crowds," [Holyoke, MA] *Transcript-Telegram*, Mar. 1, 1930, https://bit.ly/3nGURBU.
22 Ibid.
23 "Dr. James Howard Snook," Ohio Exploration Society; https://bit.ly/3HPURWX. Accessed May 18, 2023.

6: How the Shirtwaist Factory Fire Changed Industry Standards

1 "Remembering the 1911 Triangle Factory Fire," Testimonials, Cornell Univ., https://bit.ly/428kIli.
2 "Abolish Sweatshops, Pleads Inspector Story," *Brooklyn Daily Eagle,* Oct. 4, 1900, https://bit.ly/3oBOkcg.
3 Janus Adams, "Triangle Fire's Tragic Lessons Still Matter Today," *Newsday,* Mar. 11, 2011, https://bit.ly/43eIe0n.
4 "Shirtwaist Kings," *American Experience*, PBS, 2011, https://to.pbs.org/3piPqt9.
5 "Triangle Fire," *American Experience*, PBS, Season 23, ep. 8, YouTube video, https://bit.ly/460f8DB.
6 "Clara Lemlich Sparks 'Uprising of the 20,000,' November 22, 1909" Jewish Women's Archive, https://bit.ly/3P73SPW.
7 Gustavus Myers, *The History of Tammany Hall* (New York: Gustavus Myers, 1901), https://bit.ly/3LFx2Cf.
8 David Von Drehle, *Triangle: The Fire That Changed America* (New York: Grove Atlantic, 2003), Kindle.
9 "Complete Transcript of Triangle Fire," Cornell Univ. Library, p. 1868, https://bit.ly/3NpbRXc.
10 Jack Gottschalk, *Firefighting* (New York: DK Publishing, 2002).
11 Von Drehle, *Triangle*.
12 Ibid.
13 Ibid.
14 Ibid.; "The Triangle Shirtwaist Fire: The Disaster that Changed the Workplace Forever," Geographics, Apr. 28, 2021, YouTube video, https://bit.ly/42Ca2uB; Christine Seifert, *The Factory Girls: A Kaleidoscopic Account of the Shirtwaist Factory Fire* (Minneapolis: Lerner), Kindle.
15 Eileen Reynolds, "Traces of an American Tragedy: Inside the Former Triangle Shirtwaist Factory," NYU News Story, Mar. 19. 2015, https://bit.ly/3oVw8dr.
16 "Triangle Shirtwaist Survivor Son Talks," *Daily News*, YouTube video, 2:13, Mar. 20, 2011, https://bit.ly/3qGcVgJ.
17 William G. Shepard, "Jumping to Eternity," *Kansas City Globe*, Mar. 27, 1911, https://bit.ly/3OKZplM.
18 "Fixing the Blame for Horror Fire," *Mount Vernon Argus*, Mar. 28, 1911, https://bit.ly/4377gi7; Von Drehle, *Triangle*.
19 "Factory Fire Dead Now 142," *NY Sun,* Mar. 27, 1911, https://bit.ly/3WyOmhD.
20 David Von Drehle interview in "Triangle Shirtwaist Factory Fire," History Center, on Mr. Campbell's Social Studies YouTube video, 2015, https://bit.ly/3J9iCdm.
21 Mel Stuart, dir. *The Triangle Factory Fire Scandal*, Alan Landsburg and Don Kirshner Prod., 1979.
22 "New York Factory Investigating Commission," US Dept. of Labor, https://bit.ly/3NpX92g.
23 Social Security History, "Frances Perkins," https://bit.ly/3NnIHYI.

7: The Radium Girls' Fight for Workplace Safety

1 "Poisoned While They Chatted Merrily at Their Work," *SF Examiner.*, Feb. 28, 1926, https://bit.ly/42bNC39.
2 "United States Radium Corporation," Wikimedia, last modified Jan. 17, 2023, https://bit.ly/3CIloCV.
3 "The Radium Girls," *Medical Bag*, Jan. 1, 2014, https://bit.ly/3nu9tof.
4 Shellie Carol-Chik, "Radium Girls: The Ghost Girls with Glowing Haloes," Old Bridgewater Historical Soc., YouTube video, July 24, 2019, https://bit.ly/3NqGR9o.
5 Ad titled "Important to Arthritis Sufferers Concerning Radium Treatment," *LA Times*, Jan. 8, 1928, https://bit.ly/3C0uNoK.
6 Ad titled "The New Weapon of Curative Science Radium Mesothorium," *LA Times*, Jan. 22, 1928, https://bit.ly/3WzlLss.
7 Kate Moore, reading *The Radium Girls* at Seattle Town Hall, YouTube video, May 19, 2017, https://bit.ly/3oTDwX8.
8 Kate Moore. *The Radium Girls: The Dark Story of America's Shining Women* (Naperville, IL: Sourcebooks, 2017), Kindle.
9 "Poisoned Mother Concludes Plea," *Daily Illini*, Feb. 12, 1938, Illinois Dig. Newspaper Collections, https://bit.ly/3nI3dZQ.
10 Carole Langer, dir. and prod., *Radium City*, 1987.
11 Ibid.
12 "Poisoned While They Chatted Merrily at Their Work," *SF Examiner*, Feb. 28, 1926, https://bit.ly/42bNC39.
13 Ibid; Moore, *Radium Girls*.
14 Bert M. Coursey (Feb. 2022). "The National Bureau of Standards and the Radium Dial Painters," *Jour. of Research of the Nat'l Inst. of Standards and Tech.* 126 (126051), https://doi.org/10.6028/jres.126.051.
15 Ibid.
16 "US Starts Probe of Radium Poison Deaths in Jersey," *Brooklyn Daily Eagle*, June 19, 1925, https://bit.ly/3BZiR6U.
17 Ibid.
18 Kate Moore, "The Forgotten Story of the Radium Girls," BuzzFeed, May 5, 2017, https://bit.ly/3piUmyb.
19 Moore, *Radium Girls*.
20 Ibid.
21 "Radium Paint Takes Its Inventor's Life," *NY Times*, Nov. 15, 1928, https://bit.ly/3IF5KLK.
22 "Statement by the Radium Dial Company," *Streator Times*, June 9, 1928, https://bit.ly/3N0RkZ8.
23 "Radium Paint Takes Its Inventor's Life."
24 Moore, *Radium Girls*.
25 Stephanie Szuda, "Too Ill to Visit," *Streator Times*, Nov. 15, 2010, https://bit.ly/3oyXAOi.
26 "'Radium Water' Held Cause of Golf Star's Poisoning," *Pittsburgh Press*, Apr. 1, 1932, https://bit.ly/3IEcZnm; "The Radium Water Worked Fine Until His Jaw Came Off," *Lateral Science*, Dec. 14, 2017, https://bit.ly/3qhCSCN; Moore, *Radium Girls*.
27 "Radium Blamed for Death," *Latrobe Bulletin*, Apr. 1, 1932, https://bit.ly/436APA8.
28 "'Radium Water' Held Cause of Golf Star's Poisoning," *Pittsburgh Press*, Apr. 1, 1932, https://bit.ly/3IEcZnm.
29 Moore, *Radium Girls*.
30 Ibid.
31 Ibid.
32 "Doomed to Die Woman Collapses," *Ottawa Journal*, Feb. 11, 1938, https://bit.ly/45vQr1Q.
33 Carol-Chik, "Radium Girls."
34 "Doomed Woman Hopes Others May Be Aided," *Enid Daily Eagle*, Apr. 6, 1938, https://bit.ly/3ozp2LH; "Seven Doomed Women Testify at Bedside of 8th," *Minneapolis Star*, Feb. 11, 1938, https://bit.ly/3MZ4cPe.
35 "$3,000,000 Gas Rate Raises Voided," *St. Louis Globe-Democrat*, Feb. 23, 1939, https://bit.ly/43qFgFM.

36 Author interview with Kate Moore, Dec. 2019.
37 Rebecca Hersher, "Mae Keane, One of the Last "Radium Girls," Dies at 107," *All Things Considered*, NPR, Dec. 28, 2014, https://bit.ly/43rrnHt.

8: The Bath Massacre: America's Deadliest School Attack

1 "The Deadly Virus: The Influenza Epidemic of 1918," NARA, https://www.archives.gov/exhibits/influenza-epidemic/.
2 Ibid.
3 Harold Schechter, *Maniac: The Bath School Disaster and the Birth of the Modern Mass Killer* (New York: Little A, 2021).
4 Ralph Goll and Donald F. Scram, "The Strange Case of the Village Hitler and the Slaughtered Innocents," *Detroit Free Press*, May 16, 1943, https://bit.ly/3MBXw8u.
5 Dan Austin, "The Day Detroit Lost U-M to Ann Arbor," *Detroit Free Press*, Mar. 18, 2015, https://bit.ly/431w2A1.
6 Arnie Bernstein, *Bath Massacre* (Ann Arbor: Univ. of Michigan Press, 2009), Kindle.
7 "Sixty Lawyers Graduate," *Detroit Evening Times*, June 19, 1909, https://bit.ly/45vQVoG; Schechter, *Maniac*.
8 Author interview with Harold Schechter, May 2022.
9 Bernstein, *Bath Massacre*; Grant Parker, *Mayday: History of a Village Holocaust* (Lansing, MI: Liberty Press). https://bit.ly/45xo5Eo.
10 Schechter, *Maniac*.
11 Bernstein, *Bath Massacre*.
12 Schechter, *Maniac*.
13 Linda A. Cameron, "Agricultural Depression, 1920–1934," MNOpedia, https://bit.ly/3ILkbxY.
14 Ali, Malik et al., *The 20th Century: A Moving Visual History*, https://bit.ly/3N0L16x.
15 Schechter, *Maniac*.
16 Ibid.
17 Ibid.
18 Ibid.
19 Ibid.
20 *US Bureau of Public Records Report* (Washington, DC: US Govt. Printing Office, 1923) https://bit.ly/3WGl3tl.
21 "Swenhart Answers Pyrotol Questions," *Iron Cty. Miner*, Aug. 15, 1924, https://bit.ly/42cw4UD.
22 Ralph Goll and Donald F. Scram, "The Strange Case of the Village Hitler and the Slaughtered Innocents," *Detroit Free Press*, May 16, 1943, https://bit.ly/3MBXw8u.
23 Schechter, *Maniac*.
24 Ibid.
25 BookTV, "Arnie Bernstein, author of *Bath Massacre: America's First School Bombing*," YouTube Video, 8:02, June 11, 2009, https://bit.ly/3IJCyn4.
26 Rachel Greco, "Bath School Bombing: Oldest Surviving Student Recalls 'How Awful It Was,'" *Detroit Free Press*, May 11, 2017, https://bit.ly/3OILyfP.
27 Schechter interview.
28 Ibid.
29 "Estimate 35 Dead as Blast Destroys School," *Battle Creek Enq.*, May 18, 1927, https://bit.ly/3WGiYxM.
30 Edward Main, "Tear Gas Is Latest of Crime Weapons," *Detroit Free Press*, Mar. 10, 1929, https://bit.ly/3oDocO3.
31 Newspapers.com search of Bath massacre stories and references in 1999 after the Columbine massacre had 98 results, such as this one: "1927 School Bombing Recalled After Colorado," *Springfield News-Leader*, May 2, 1999, https://bit.ly/3BVqMSJ.

9: The Legacy of Kitty Genovese's Lonely Murder

1 Robert D. McFadden, "Winston Moseley, Who Killed Kitty Genovese, Dies in Prison at 81," *NY Times*, Apr. 4, 2016, https://bit.ly/43vwRB6.
2 "Kitty Genovese," History.com, May 21, 2021, https://bit.ly/42QXCiJ. Accessed May 27, 2023.
3 James D. Solomon and Jessica Robinson, dir. *The Witness*, Five More Minutes Productions, 2015.
4 Kansas City Public Library, "Kitty Genovese: The Murder, the Bystanders, the Crime that Changed America," YouTube Video, 29:08, Mar. 11, 2014, https://bit.ly/43brLtK.
5 Dan McCue, "Killer of Kitty Genovese Dies in NY Prison," Courthouse News Service, Apr. 5, 2016, https://bit.ly/45CgDrM.
6 Jeff Pearlman, "Infamous '64 Murder Lives in Heart of Woman's 'Friend,'" *Newsday* and *Chicago Tribune*, Mar. 12, 2004, https://bit.ly/3MFgL0G.
7 McCue, "Killer of Kitty Genovese Dies in NY Prison."
8 A. M. Rosenthal, *Thirty-Eight Witnesses: The Kitty Genovese Case* (New York: McGraw-Hill, 1964; Open Road Media Kindle Ed., 2015).
9 Brent Curtis, "Woman Recalls Partner's Brutal Murder," *Rutland Herald Online*, Mar. 14, 2004, https://bit.ly/3MYYVHl. Accessed May 27, 2023.
10 Thomas Pugh and Richard Henry, "Queens Barmaid Stabbed, Dies," *Daily News*, Mar. 14, 1964, https://bit.ly/3MFhuiq.
11 Rosenthal, *Thirty-Eight Witnesses*.
12 Ibid.
13 Martin Gansberg, "37 Who Saw Murder Didn't Call the Police," *NY Times*, Mar. 27, 1964, https://bit.ly/45wBigG.
14 McFadden, "Winston Moseley."
15 Robert Mayer, "Moseley Convicted of Barmaid Slaying," *Newsday* [Nassau Ed.], June 12, 1964, https://bit.ly/3BYOLjP.
16 Solomon and Robinson, *The Witness*.
17 Solomon and Robinson, *The Witness*; Thomas Pugh, "Moseley Lawyer Convinced Client Is Slayer of Girl," *Daily News*, Apr. 3, 1964, https://bit.ly/3WAQTrm.
18 Rosenthal, *Thirty-Eight Witnesses*.
19 McFadden, "Winston Moseley."

10: The Mass Hysteria of the Satanic Panic

1 Matthew LeRoy and Deric Haddad, *They Must Be Monsters: A Modern-Day Witch Hunt* (San Diego, CA: Manor, 2018), Kindle.
2 Ibid.
3 Robert W. Stewart and Austin Scott, "5 on School Staff Held in Molestations," *LA Times*, Mar. 22, 1984, https://bit.ly/45MjIWj.
4 LeRoy and Haddad, *They Must Be Monsters*.
5 Ibid.
6 Lee Coleman, "McMartin PreSchool Case: Exposing the 'Experts,'" Psychiatry and Society, YouTube video, 14:47, Oct. 16, 2018, https://bit.ly/461ZWG2.
7 Charles J. Brainerd and Valerie F. Reyna, *The Science of False Memory: An Integrative Approach* (New York: Oxford Univ. Press, 2005).
8 Ibid.
9 Ibid.
10 LeRoy and Haddad, *They Must Be Monsters*.
11 David Shaw, "Reporter's Early Exclusives Triggered a Media Frenzy," *LA Times*, Jan. 20, 1990, https://bit.ly/3C2mF7n.

12 Ibid.
13 Muriel Dobbin, "Victims Tell Abuse Tales to Puppets," *St. Louis Post-Dispatch*, Apr. 8, 1984, https://bit.ly/43wKxLW.
14 Ibid.
15 Missy Hughes, dir. *Uncovered: The McMartin Family Trials*, Oxygen, 2019, https://bit.ly/3P4KtPL.
16 Murray Dubin, "Boy, 7, Testifies in School-Sex Case," *Phila. Inq.*, Jan. 23, 1985, https://bit.ly/45zJ0Xd.
17 "Sample Interviews by Investigators with Former Students of the McMartin Preschool," Univ. of Missouri-Kansas City, https://bit.ly/3N1yP6S. Accessed May 27, 2023.
18 Ibid.
19 Kyle Zirpolo, "I'm Sorry," *LA Times*, Oct. 30, 2005, https://bit.ly/43aFLnM.
20 Ibid.
21 LeRoy and Haddad, *They Must Be Monsters*.
22 R. C. Summit (1983). "The Child Sexual Abuse Accommodation Syndrome," *Child Abuse and Neglect* 7, 177–93, https://bit.ly/41QLm1T.
23 "Transcript: The Preschool Sex Abuse Case that Changed How Molestation Is Investigated," RetroReport, Mar. 5, 2014, https://bit.ly/45ydngK. Accessed May 27, 2023.
24 Hughes, *Uncovered.*
25 Richard Beck, *We Believe the Children: A Moral Panic in the 1980s* (New York: PublicAffairs, 2015).
26 "Frances Keller," Univ. of Michigan's National Registry of Exonerations, https://bit.ly/3BZDyzk. Accessed May 27, 2023.
27 "McMartin Preschool: Anatomy of a Panic," RetroReport, YouTube video, 2014, https://bit.ly/3PbvTG2.
28 Margaret Carlson, "Six Years of Trial by Torture," *Time*, Jan. 29, 1990, https://bit.ly/3oCDIK7.
29 Linda Deutsch, "McMartin Defendants Not Guilty on 52 Counts; 13 Others Declared Mistrial," Associated Press, Jan. 18, 1990, https://bit.ly/429NKQr.
30 LeRoy and Haddad, *They Must Be Monsters*.
31 *McMartin v. Children Inst. Internation ABC* (1989), Court of Appeal, 2nd Dist., Div. 5, CA, https://bit.ly/3N1LCVG. Accessed May 27, 2023.
32 LeRoy and Haddad, *They Must Be Monsters*.
33 Melissa Harris-Perry (Host), "Investigating the Legacy of the McMartin Child Abuse Trial," *Takeaway*, Sept. 10, 2015, https://bit.ly/42fiMGG. Accessed May 27, 2023; Brainerd and Reyna, *Science of False Memory*.

11: Delphine LaLaurie's Horrific Torture Chamber

1 "The Fire Museum & Educational Center," Nola.gov, https://bit.ly/3ITBb4Z.
2 Author interview with Carolyn Morrow Long, Oct. 2020.
3 Carolyn Morrow Long, *Madame Lalaurie: Mistress of the Haunted House* (Gainesville, FL: Univ. Press of Florida), Kindle.
4 Long interview, Oct. 2020.
5 Long, *Madame Lalaurie*.
6 Ibid.
7 Long, *Madame Lalaurie*; Gilbert C. Din, *Spaniards, Planters, and Slaves: The Spanish Regulation of Slavery in Louisiana, 1763–1803* (College Station, TX: Texas A&M Univ. Press, 1999).
8 Victoria Cosner Love and Lorelei Shannon, *Mad Madame Lalaurie: New Orleans' Most Famous Murderess Revealed* (Charleston, SC: History Press, 2011), Kindle.
9 Long interview, Oct. 2020.
10 Newspapers.com entries, 2022 search for term "ran away from the subscriber."
11 Long interview, Oct. 2020.
12 Love and Shannon, *Mad Madame Lalaurie*.
13 George Washington Cable, *Strange True Stories of Louisiana* (New York: Charles Scribner's Sons, 1889); http://bit.ly/3EIhfjI.
14 "Understanding the Louisiana Divorce Process," Betsy A. Fischer, LLC, Louisiana Family Law, https://bit.ly/43Achjv. Accessed May 27, 2023.
15 Long, *Madame Lalaurie*.
16 Ibid.
17 "Revisited Myth #53: Kitchens Were Separated from the Main House in Colonial Days . . . ," History Myths Debunked, https://bit.ly/3q8E1wt.
18 Cable, *Strange True Stories of Louisiana.*
19 "New Orleans, April 10," *Vicksburg Whig*, Apr. 24, 1834, https://bit.ly/3OLLwUq.
20 "From the New Orleans Bee, April 11," *Phila. Inq.*, Apr. 26, 1834, https://bit.ly/43wqwW6.
21 "New Orleans, April 10," *Vicksburg Whig*, Apr. 24, 1834, https://bit.ly/3OLLwUq.
22 Long, *Madame Lalaurie*.
23 Ibid.
24 "The New Orleans Bee of the 11th Instant . . . ," *NY Evening Post*, Apr. 26, 1934, https://bit.ly/3MF50Hx.
25 Long, *Madame Lalaurie*.
26 "Turns from Society to Devote Life to Feeding New Orleans Destitute," *Gaffney Ledger*, Mar. 28, 1929, https://bit.ly/43p3Arq.
27 Love and Shannon, *Mad Madame Lalaurie*.
28 "A New Orleans Legend," *Carolina Watchman*, July 26, 1883, https://bit.ly/43xOz71.
29 "The Haunted House," *Louisiana Times-Picayune*, Mar. 13, 1892, https://bit.ly/438lK0V.
30 Ibid.
31 Long, *Madame Lalaurie.*
32 Natalie Zacek, "Holding the Whip-Hand: The Female Slave-holder in Myth and Reality," *Jour. of Global Slavery* 6 (1), Jan. 29, 2021, https://bit.ly/3MXDUwU. Accessed May 27, 2023.
33 Ibid.
34 Emily Abbott, "The Abolitionist Press," HuronResearch.ca, https://bit.ly/429eu3F. Accessed May 27, 2023; John J. Dunphy, "Abolitionist Newspapers Were 19th-Century Social Media," *Telegraph,* Mar. 18, 2022, https://bit.ly/45BAZB4.

12: The Slaying of Marie Smith, and the Black Man Nearly Lynched for It

1 Author interview with Alex Tresniowski, Jan. 2021.
2 Alex Tresniowski, *The Rope: A True Story of Murder, Heroism, and the Dawn of the NAACP* (New York: Simon & Schuster, 2021), Kindle.
3 "Missing School Girl Sought by Playmates," *Asbury Park Press*, Nov. 10, 1910, https://bit.ly/3qkQRYw.
4 "History of Asbury Park," Asbury Park Historical Soc., https://bit.ly/3qLt4RK.
5 "Asbury Park Is Aroused Over Negro," *Perth Amboy Evening News*, Nov. 14, 1910, https://bit.ly/3oxmDRG.
6 Tresniowski interview, Jan. 2021.
7 Tresniowski, *The Rope*.
8 "Story of Girl's Murder, and Continuous Search for Slayer," *Asbury Park Press*, Mar. 15, 1911, https://bit.ly/3osj3IJ.

9 "Gypsies May Have Kidnapped Girl," *Buffalo Times*, Nov. 12, 1910, https://bit.ly/3N0GVfZ.
10 "Drag Lake for Missing Girl," *Pittston Gazette*, Nov. 12, 1910, https://bit.ly/3owJXz7.
11 "Child Slain by Fiend," *Baltimore Sun*, Nov. 14, 1910, https://bit.ly/45MqBH9.
12 Ibid.
13 Ibid.
14 Ibid.
15 Ibid.
16 "Lynchings by Year and Race," Univ. of Missouri-Kansas City School of Law, https://bit.ly/3MCKK9M. Accessed May 27, 2023.
17 Tresniowski, *The Rope*.
18 Tresniowski interview, Jan. 2021.
19 "Inquest Indicates Girl was Murdered Where Found," *Asbury Park Press*, Dec. 2, 1910, https://bit.ly/3C06NCo.
20 Tresniowski, *The Rope*.
21 "Police at Standstill in Schoolgirl Murder," *Asbury Park Press*, Nov. 17, 1910, https://bit.ly/3oHIINo.
22 Tresniowski, *The Rope*.
23 "Axe Found in Deal Lake," *Monmouth Democrat*, Dec. 1, 1910, https://bit.ly/3MZ8tSJ.
24 "Monmouth County Courts," *Monmouth Inquirer,* Apr. 6, 1911, https://bit.ly/3qdBNfo.
25 "Confesses He Murdered Girl Where Body was Discovered," *Asbury Park Press*, Mar. 16, 1911, https://bit.ly/3MXmIYn.
26 "City Employs Ace Detective in Jail Death," *Tennessean*, July 30, 1947, https://bit.ly/3IK7za6.
27 Author interview with Peter Lucia, Jan. 2021.
28 Ibid.
29 "Release of Murder Suspect Improbable," *Asbury Park Press*, Dec. 8, 1910, https://bit.ly/3OINIMl.
30 "Confesses He Murdered Girl," *Asbury Park Press*.
31 Ira Wolfert, "Another New Jersey Murder," *Star Tribune*, May 10, 1936, https://bit.ly/438rJml.
32 Tresniowski, *The Rope*.
33 Wolfert, "Another New Jersey Murder," *Star Tribune*.
34 Tresniowski, *The Rope*.
35 Ibid.
36 Ibid.
37 Michele Galen, "1910 Murder a Detective Classic," *Asbury Park Press*, Mar. 16, 1986, https://bit.ly/3OJClUz.
38 "'Complete Detective' About Ray Schindler," *Lewiston Sun-Journal*, Dec. 30, 1950, https://bit.ly/43NdELp.
39 "Towne Booms Clark in Dinner Speech," *Brooklyn Daily Eagle*, May 4, 1912, https://bit.ly/3MVPrg5.

13: How the FBI Helped End the Osage Nation Murders

1 David Grann, *Killers of the Flower Moon: The Osage Murders and the Birth of the FBI* (New York: Doubleday, 2017), Kindle.
2 Ibid.
3 "1920s American Car Ownership Report," OldMagazineArticles .com, Feb. 1922, https://bit.ly/3C0ot0E.
4 "Telephone History Part 2: Early Years," Greatest Achievements, https://rb.gy/sw69s.
5 "Extension Would Make Osages Rich," *Wichita Beacon*, Jan. 2, 1921, https://bit.ly/42jltr2.
6 Ibid.
7 Grann, *Killers of the Flower Moon*.
8 "Statistics of Income from Returns of Net Income for 1923," IRS, https://bit.ly/44dXjQ7.
9 "Lo's Little Joke," *Decatur* [IL] *Herald and Review,* Apr. 9, 1921, https://bit.ly/3MGZaW6.
10 Jennifer Penland, "Black Gold and Greed: The Tragedy of the Osage Murders," YouTube Video, 2:29, https://bit.ly/3NqePuD.
11 Storytellers' Studio, "Best Selling Author, David Grann, Talks about Killers of the Flower Moon," YouTube Video, 10:20, https://bit.ly/42FWzSm.
12 Grann, *Killers of the Flower Moon*.
13 Ibid.
14 Don Whitehead, "The FBI Story," *Austin American-Statesman*, Jan. 16, 1957, https://bit.ly/3qcV5l6.
15 "'King of the Osage' Formerly Lived in Jefferson County," *Waurika News-Democrat*, Feb. 12, 1926, https://bit.ly/3IL6QWt.
16 Whitehead, "The FBI Story," *Austin American-Statesman*.
17 Grann, *Killers of the Flower Moon*.
18 Ibid.; "Slew Rich Indian," *Osage Journal and Osage Cty. News*, Mar. 5, 1926, https://bit.ly/3BXmwlJ.
19 "Find Two Bodies," *Osage Journal and Osage Cty. News*, June 3, 1921, https://bit.ly/43rMUzG.
20 "Offer Reward for Slayer of Indian Woman," *Ponca City News*, June 6, 1921, https://bit.ly/45LynB0.
21 "He Implicates Another," [Bartlesville, OK] *Morning Examiner*, July 24, 1921, https://bit.ly/3Mzjrgx.
22 Grann, *Killers of the Flower Moon*.
23 "Alleged Forger Says He Killed Woman," *Fort Worth Star-Telegram*, July 23, 1921, https://bit.ly/3ILS2Xr; Grann, *Killers of the Flower Moon*.
24 "Makes Decision in Indian Estate Case," *Pawhuska Journal-Capital*, July 11, 1924, https://bit.ly/3qdpsId.
25 Grann, *Killers of the Flower Moon*; "Willie Stepson Dead," *Hominy News-Republican*, Mar. 17, 1922, https://bit.ly/43aGKEs.
26 "William Stepson Dies Suddenly," *Osage Chief,* Mar. 3, 1922, https://bit.ly/3ILkfh0; "Coroner's Verdict Is Returned," *Osage Chief*, Apr. 28, 1922, https://bit.ly/3OLQQam.
27 "Mysterious Murder Victim Identified," *Sioux City Journal*, Aug. 12, 1922, https://bit.ly/3OHH6hi.
28 "Muskogeean Slain; Robbery Motive?" *Okmulgee Daily Times*, Aug. 12, 1922, https://bit.ly/3osoqYp.
29 Grann, *Killers of the Flower Moon*.
30 Roy Buckingham, "'Curse of Gold' on Osage Indians," *Modesto News-Herald*, Nov. 18, 1923, https://bit.ly/45xsGGF.
31 Grann, *Killers of the Flower Moon*.
32 Ibid.
33 Ibid.
34 Ibid.
35 "Conviction of William Hale Is Reversed," *Morning Examiner*, Mar. 28, 1928, https://bit.ly/3oycSme.
36 Oklahoma Educational Television Authority, "Reign of Terror–Murder and Mayhem in the Osage Hills," YouTube Video, 15:55, https://bit.ly/42C2SpW.
37 "Mann Act," Cornell Law School Legal Info. Inst., https://bit.ly/3MVxL2Q.
38 "Largely Forgotten Osage Murders Reveal a Conspiracy Against Wealthy Native Americans," *Fresh Air*, NPR, Apr. 17, 2017, https://bit.ly/3ozg7dk.
39 "Link M'Bride Case with Osages," *Muskogee Times-Democrat*, Mar. 12, 1925, https://bit.ly/3MG8kSQ; "Alleged Slain Bank Robber Wanted Here," *Osage Journal*, Dec. 18, 1924, https://bit .ly/438s08V; "Largely Forgotten Osage Murders"; "U.S. Ready to Push Osage Murder Cases," *Daily Oklahoman*, Nov. 13, 1925, https://bit.ly/3MGBDoB; R. Scott Decker, "Today in Security

History: Special Agent White," ASIS International, Oct. 28, 2019, https://bit.ly/3IIvEya.

40 "Death Halts Wren's Hunt for Frome Women Killers," *El Paso Herald-Post*, Apr. 14, 1939, https://bit.ly/45rpQTs; Grann, *Killers of the Flower Moon*.

41 Ad titled "Moose Round-Up and Buffalo Chase," *Hominy News-Republican*, May 21, 1920, https://bit.ly/425KfuB.

42 Grann, *Killers of the Flower Moon*.

43 "Former County Attorney Killed," *Caddo Cty. Tribune*, July 5, 1923, https://bit.ly/43aI9ec; Grann, *Killers of the Flower Moon*.

44 "Rich Ranchman Is Charged in Osage Cases," *Daily Ardmoreite*, Jan. 4, 1926, https://bit.ly/3Wz7BYp.

45 Grann, *Killers of the Flower Moon*.

46 Ibid.

47 "State Stories," *Blackwell Daily News*, Aug. 29, 1921, https://bit.ly/3OHI5y0.

48 Storytellers' Studio, "Best Selling Author, David Grann."

49 Grann, *Killers of the Flower Moon*.

50 Ibid.

51 "Mollie Burkhart Given Divorce," *Pawnee Courier-Dispatch*, Sept. 29, 1927, https://bit.ly/43dhvkQ.

52 Oklahoma Educational Television Authority, "Reign of Terror."

53 "Witnesses in Osage Case Tell of Plot," *Blackwell Journal-Tribune*, Mar. 16, 1926, https://bit.ly/43fDo2X.

54 Jon D. May, "Osage Murders," Oklahoma History Center, https://bit.ly/3MQUBsE. Accessed May 27, 2023.

55 Grann, *Killers of the Flower Moon*; Act of June 18, 1934 (Indian Reorganization Act), https://bit.ly/3CaiGFK.

56 US Dept. of Justice Archives, "A Historic Settlement with the Osage Tribe of Oklahoma," Oct. 21, 2011, https://bit.ly/44UaXsF.

14: The Legacy of the Scottsboro Boys

1 Larry Dane Brimner, *Accused!: The Trial of the Scottsboro Boys—Lies, Prejudice, and the Fourteenth Amendment* (New York: Calkin Creek, 2019), Kindle.

2 "Scottsboro Timeline," PBS, https://bit.ly/3CcXb7n. Accessed May 27, 2023.

3 "How Bad was the Great Depression? Gauging the Economic Impact," Federal Reserve Bank of St. Louis, https://bit.ly/43u4d3b. Accessed May 27, 2023.

4 Errol Lincoln Uys, *Riding the Rails: Teenagers on the Move During the Great Depression* (Boston: T. E. Winter & Sons, 2014), Kindle.

5 "Scottsboro: An American Tragedy—Full Transcript," *American Experience*, PBS, https://bit.ly/3WBru0e. Accessed May 27, 2023.

6 "SPLC to Alabama Lawmakers: Remove White Supremacy from State's Jim Crow-Era Constitution," Southern Poverty Law Center, Sept. 12, 2021, https://bit.ly/3oHNvhQ. Accessed May 27, 2023.

7 "Mann Act," Cornell Law School Legal Information Inst., https://bit.ly/3MVxL2Q.

8 "I.L.D. Says Women Are True Parents," *Chattanooga News*, Jan. 15, 1932, https://bit.ly/43aqKSG.

9 Brimner, *Accused!*; Emory Univ., "The Scottsboro Boys," YouTube video, 7:40, 2012, https://bit.ly/3XIrNlE.

10 Emory Univ., "The Scottsboro Boys."

11 "Third Negro," *Cincinnati Enquirer*, Apr. 9, 1931, https://bit.ly/3N1ObrG.

12 "Set Trial Date for Attackers of White Girls," *Chattanooga Daily Times*, Mar. 27, 1931, https://bit.ly/3oCNSuf.

13 Ibid.

14 Ibid.

15 "Trial Excerpt of Victoria Price," Famous Trials, https://bit.ly/3IWlt9j.

16 "Set Trial Date for Attackers of White Girls," *Chattanooga Daily Times*, Mar. 27, 1931, https://bit.ly/3oCNSuf.

17 "The Women on Trial," *Scottsboro: An American Tragedy*, PBS, https://bit.ly/42q9IyS. Accessed May 27, 2023.

18 "The NAACP and the Scottsboro Trial," *American Experience*, PBS, https://bit.ly/3BntnEC; "Brand Role of Socialists as Aid to Bosses in Fighting the Jobless and Preparing Imperialist War," *Daily Worker*, Apr. 30, 1931, https://bit.ly/3N2oQhD.

19 Brimner, *Accused!*

20 Emory Univ., "The Scottsboro Boys."

21 Brimner, *Accused!*

22 Ibid.

23 Ibid.

24 Ibid.

25 Ibid.

26 "Riotous Throng Hails Leibowitz," [Brooklyn, NY] *Times Union*, Apr. 11, 1933, https://bit.ly/3BZ4IXd.

27 Ibid.

28 Brimner, *Accused!*

29 "Who Were the Scottsboro Boys?," *American Experience*, PBS, https://bit.ly/3BFjTVz.

30 Emory Univ., "The Scottsboro Boys."

31 Ibid.

32 Patterson was the defendant who'd escaped to Michigan in 1948, after serving 17 years of a 75-year sentence. He was the only codefendant not to have been paroled. Michigan refused to extradite him. He wrote a book called *Scottsboro Boy* in 1950, which he was selling copies of at a saloon when a fight broke out. Multiple people pulled knives, and a man named Willie Mitchell was stabbed to death. Patterson maintained his innocence and the first jury deadlocked. The case was retried, and the second jury found him guilty of manslaughter. He died in prison two years later of cancer at 39. "Who Were the Scottsboro Boys?," PBS, https://bit.ly/3BFjTVz/.

33 Of the several times aspects of this case were appealed to SCOTUS, in one instance a justice recused himself because of his past affiliation with the Ku Klux Klan; see: "Supreme Court Upholds Term of Patterson," *Southern Star*, Oct. 28, 1937, https://bit.ly/3OGI8tU; Justice Hugo Black "eventually became a strong supporter of civil rights," according to the Free Speech Center: Richard L. Pacelle Jr., "Hugo Black," https://bit.ly/43s5vfr. Accessed May 27, 2023.

34 Abby Ohlheiser, "Alabama Grants Posthumous Pardons to the Scottsboro Boys," *The Atlantic*, Nov. 21, 2013, https://bit.ly/43pmC0W.

35 Janae Pierre, "Remembering Sheila Washington, Who Told the Story of the Scottsboro Boys," *All Things Considered*, NPR, Feb. 4, 2021, https://bit.ly/3WSlqBr.

36 "ACLU History: The Tragedy of the Scottsboro Boys," ACLU, https://bit.ly/3oP8oHZ. Accessed May 27, 2023.

37 Ellis Cose, "The Saga of the Scottsboro Boys," ACLU, July 20, 2020, https://bit.ly/3Nc49Qq; Hollace Ransdell, "Report on the Scottsboro, Ala. Case," ACLU, May 27, 1931, https://bit.ly/3p0uPtX.

38 *Powell v. Alabama*, Oyez, https://bit.ly/3J8CKfE. Accessed May 27, 2023.

39 Brimner, *Accused!*.

15: The Galvanizing Murder of Emmett Till

1 "Brave Testimony," *American Experience*, PBS, https://bit.ly/4254Pes.
2 Beauchamp, Keith, dir. *The Untold Story of Emmett Louis Till*, 2005, YouTube Video, 4:32, https://bit.ly/3NqjZXC.
3 "The Attack on Greenwood," Tulsa Historical Soc. and Museum, https://bit.ly/43CopQr. Accessed May 27, 2023.
4 "Corn Products Refining Co.," Encyclopedia of Chicago, https://bit.ly/43CoDHh. Accessed May 27, 2023.
5 "The Murder of Emmett Till," *American Experience*, PBS, YouTube Video, 8:03, Sept. 6, 2022, https://bit.ly/3OE1srS.
6 Ancestry.com: 1930; Census Pl.: Summit, Cook, IL; p16B; Dist.: 2193; FHL microfilm: 2340237.
7 Beauchamp, *Untold Story of Emmett Louis Till*.
8 Devery S. Anderson, *Emmett Till: The Murder That Shocked the World and Propelled the Civil Rights Movement* (Jackson: Univ. Press of Mississippi, 2015), Kindle.
9 Ibid.
10 Ibid.
11 Emma Brown, "Judge Orders Mississippi School District to Desegregate, 62 Years after *Brown v. Board of Education*," *Wash. Post*, May 16, 2016, https://bit.ly/45yFY5G.
12 Kathy Eyre, "Mississippi Still Far from Accepting Interracial Marriage," Nov. 28, 1987, https://bit.ly/43WUPFg.
13 "History of Lynching in America," NAACP, https://bit.ly/45Kqdsj. Accessed May 27, 2023.
14 Horace R. Cayton, and St. Clair Drake, *Black Metropolis: A Study of Negro Life in a Northern City* (Chicago: Univ. of Chicago Press, 2015).
15 Cayton and Drake, *Black Metropolis*.
16 Mamie Till-Mobley and Christopher Benson, *Death of Innocence: The Story of the Hate Crime that Changed America* (New York: Random House, 2011), Kindle.
17 LOC, "Civil Rights History Project: Wheeler Parker," YouTube Video, 1:07:30, June 23, 2014, https://bit.ly/43CxsBc.
18 Beauchamp, *The Untold Story of Emmett Louis Till*.
19 Ibid.
20 Till-Mobley and Benson, *Death of Innocence*.
21 Ibid.
22 Beauchamp, *The Untold Story of Emmett Louis Till*.
23 Ibid.
24 William Bradford Huie, "The Shocking Story of Approved Killing in Mississippi," *American Experience*, PBS, https://bit.ly/3qixuPP.
25 "Till Almost Missed Train to Murder in Mississippi," [Wilmington, DE] *Morning News*, Sept. 24, 1955, https://bit.ly/45w2QTj.
26 "'Insult' Kidnaping of Youth Charged," *Cincinnati Post*, Aug. 30, 1955, https://bit.ly/3ozjj8O.
27 "Charges Pair Kidnaped Boy," *Des Moines Register*, Aug. 30, 1955, https://bit.ly/3WKhS3V.
28 Anderson, *Emmett Till*.
29 "Jury Finds Half-Brothers Innocent of Boy's Murder," *Enid Morning News*, Sept. 24, 1955, https://bit.ly/3C0vD52.
30 Till-Mobley and Benson, *Death of Innocence*.
31 Anderson, *Emmett Till*.
32 Margalit Fox, "Willie Louis, Who Named the Killers of Emmett Till at Their Trial, Dies at 76," *New York Times*, July 24, 2013, https://rb.gy/k8zx3; "The Murder of Emmett Till," *American Experience*, PBS, Apr. 15, 2023, https://bit.ly/3WZy8OJ.
33 "The Murder of Emmett Till," *American Experience*, All Arts, PBS, https://bit.ly/3WMAe4g.
34 "Huff Fears Plot to Free Accused," *New York Age*, Oct. 22, 1955, https://bit.ly/3OM0FFh.
35 John Edgar Wideman, *Writing to Save a Life: The Louis Till File* (New York: Scribner, 2016).
36 "The Shame of Mississippi: A Story That Is Not Ended," *Virginian-Pilot*, Nov. 11, 1955, https://bit.ly/3MDLfQX.
37 William Bradford Huie, "The Shocking Story of Approved Killing in Mississippi," *American Experience*, PBS, https://bit.ly/3qixuPP. Accessed May 27, 2023.
38 Timothy B. Tyson, *The Blood of Emmett Till* (New York: Simon & Schuster, 2017).
39 Author interview with Benjamin Saulsberry, Nov. 2021.
40 Justin Gamble and Jacquelyne Germain, "Unpublished Memoir of Emmett Till's Accuser Raises New Questions," CNN, July 19, 2022, https://bit.ly/3IKmQrP. Accessed May 27, 2023; Adeel Hassan, "Emmett Till's Enduring Legacy," *NY Times*, Apr. 27, 2023, https://bit.ly/425611q; Chuck Johnson, "Grand Jury Declines to Indict Carolyn Bryant Donham," CNN, Aug. 10, 2022, https://bit.ly/3IG2n7i. Accessed May 27, 2023.
41 Hassan, "Emmett Till's Enduring Legacy"; Ed Pilkington, "'Emmett Till Was My George Floyd': John Lewis Makes Final Rousing Call for Progress in Essay," *Guardian*, July 30, 2020, https://bit.ly/3OJ1sXG.
42 Anderson, *Emmett Till*.
43 H.R. 55—Emmett Till Antilynching Act, Congress.gov, https://bit.ly/3OPEnlZ.
44 Bureau of Justice Assistance, "Emmett Till Cold Case Investigations and Prosecution Program," US Dept. of Justice, https://bit.ly/3OO93nO.

16: How an Orthopedic Shoe Felled Criminal Genius Edward Rulloff

1 Carol Kammen, "Scoundrel of a Century," *Ithaca Journal*, Apr. 2, 1994, https://bit.ly/3OJZR3N.
2 *Life, Trial and Execution of Edward H. Ruloff: The Perpetrator of Eight Murders, Numerous Burglaries and Other Crimes* . . . (Philadelphia: Barclay & Co., 1871).
3 Ancestry.com, New Brunswick, CAN., Marriages, 1789–1950. Original data: Provincial Archives of New Brunswick, CAN.
4 Kate Winkler Dawson, *All That Is Wicked: A Gilded-Age Story of Murder and the Race to Decode the Criminal Mind* (New York: Penguin, 2022), Kindle.
5 Canadian History: Pre-Confederation, "Chap. 10. Societies of British North America to 1860," BCcampus Open Pub., https://bit.ly/43KbXhJ.
6 Author interview with Kate Dawson, Nov. 2020.
7 Priscilla Amelia (Howard) Rulofson, WikiTree, Dec. 26, 2022. https://www.wikitree.com/wiki/Howard-12329.
8 Dawson, *All That Is Wicked*.
9 "Remarkable Murder Trial," *Lloyd's Weekly Newspaper*, May 31, 1857, https://bit.ly/3WBkUYi.
10 Dawson, *All That Is Wicked*.
11 Ibid.
12 Dawson interview.
13 Dawson, *All That Is Wicked*.
14 "Rulloff Case Stirred Tompkins County, Nation Just 100 Years Ago; Master Criminal Never Punished for Murder of His Wife and Child," *Ithaca Journal*, June 23, 1945, https://bit.ly/426vmrH.
15 "Ancient Ledger, Containing Record of Rulloff Case, Found in Old Jail," *Ithaca Journal*, Aug. 5, 1933, https://bit.ly/3qefDK6.
16 Dawson interview.

17 "Remarkable Murder Trial," *Morning Chronicle*, May 25, 1857, https://bit.ly/45MQVkr.
18 Amasa Junius Parker, *Reports of Decisions in Criminal Cases Made . . . in the Courts of Oyer and Terminer of the State of New York* (Albany, NY: Gould, Banks, 1855).
19 Parker, *Reports of Decisions in Criminal Cases*.
20 "A Remarkable Murder Trial: The Case of Edward H. Rulloff," *Buffalo Weekly Republic*, May 12, 1857, https://bit.ly/43rRX38.
21 "Samuel Thomson," Wikipedia, Sept. 24, 2021, https://bit.ly/42CcyRz. Accessed Sept. 24, 2021.
22 "Ancient Ledger, Containing Record of Rulloff Case, Found in Old Jail," *Ithaca Journal*, Aug. 5, 1933, https://bit.ly/3qefDK6.
23 Parker, *Reports of Decisions in Criminal Cases*.
24 Ibid.
25 Dawson, *All That Is Wicked*.
26 Parker, *Reports of Decisions in Criminal Cases*.
27 Ibid.
28 Dawson, *All That Is Wicked*.
29 Dawson interview.
30 *Life, Trial and Execution of Edward H. Ruloff*.
31 Ibid.
32 Antero Pietila, "In Need of Cadavers, 19th-Century Medical Students Raided Baltimore's Graves," *Smithsonian Mag.*, https://bit.ly/3oSidF4. Accessed May 27, 2023.
33 Parker, *Reports of Decisions in Criminal Cases*.
34 Carol Kammen, "Scoundrel of a Century," *Ithaca Journal*, Apr. 2, 1994, https://bit.ly/3OJZR3N.
35 Ibid; "Remarkable Murder Trial," *Morning Chronicle*, May 25, 1857, https://bit.ly/45MQVkr.
36 "Rulloff, the Binghamton Murderer—Facts Connected with the Killing of His Wife and Child—Rulloff's Flight, Arrest, and Attempted Escape," *Richmond Dispatch*, Jan. 19, 1871, https://bit.ly/45ueuhL.
37 Gordon Linkon (1952), "The Corpus Delicti. Confession Problem," *Jour. of Criminal Law, Criminology, and Police Science*, 43 (2), https://doi.org/10.2307/1139263.
38 Fether's Counsel Would Free Him on Habeas Writ," *Buffalo Courier*, Aug. 18, 1919, https://bit.ly/3P0YcXV.
39 "Edward H. Rulloff . . ." *Vermont Phoenix*, Mar. 5, 1846, https://bit.ly/43q3Ozj.
40 Dawson interview.
41 Carol Kammen, "Scoundrel of a Century," *Ithaca Journal*, Apr. 2, 1994, https://bit.ly/3OJZR3N.
42 Dawson interview.
43 "Rulloff Case Stirred Tompkins County," *Ithaca Journal*.
44 Peter Levins, "When Justice Triumphed in Execution of Brutal Murderer," *Knoxville Journal*, July 25, 1943, https://bit.ly/3WFoW1V; Dawson, *All That Is Wicked*.
45 Dawson, *All That Is Wicked*.
46 Richard W. Bailey, *Rogue Scholar: The Sinister Life and Celebrated Death of Edward H. Rulloff* (Ann Arbor: Univ. of Michigan Press, 2003).
47 Ibid.
48 Joe Lemak, "Mark Twain Day by Day: The Day Mark Twain Defended a Serial Killer," Apr. 29, 2021, https://bit.ly/3qnJhws. Accessed May 27, 2023.
49 Ibid.
50 Bailey, *Rogue Scholar*.
51 *Life, Trial and Execution of Edward H. Ruloff*.
52 "Rulloff Executed," *Vermont Chronicle*, May 27, 1871, https://bit.ly/3qgBvoh.
53 Dawson interview.
54 "Big Mind Does Not Mean a Big Brain," [Brantford, Ont., CAN] *Expositor*, June 29, 1932, https://bit.ly/3oF8rWL.
55 "Big Mind Not Always Housed in Big Brain, Study Proves," [Elmira, NY] *Star-Gazette*, Apr. 7, 1932, https://bit.ly/3qadoY9.
56 N. Scott Trimble, "Come See the Massive Brain of a Serial Killer at Cornell," Oct. 7, 2016, https://bit.ly/3Nax9rP.
57 *Ruloff v. the People*, 18 NY 179 (NY 1858), https://bit.ly/3N6LAf9.
58 Dawson, *All That Is Wicked*.

17: The Beheading of Pearl Bryan

1 Frank Rolandelli Jr., "Mystery in Pearl Bryan Murder Still Unsolved," *Indianapolis Star*, Mar. 7, 1937, https://bit.ly/43ax7pg.
2 "Jackson's Trial," *Jackson Cty. Banner*, Apr. 30, 1896, https://bit.ly/3qadOOd.
3 Author interview with Andrew Young, Aug. 2020.
4 "Jackson's Trial," [Hillsboro, OH] *News-Herald*, Apr. 30, 1896, https://bit.ly/42dLBmO.
5 "A Gruesome Recital," *Indianapolis Journal*, Mar. 19, 1897, https://bit.ly/43axj7Y.
6 Sorcha Pollak, "Size 8 is the New 7: Why Our Feet are Getting Bigger," *Time*, Oct. 16, 2012, https://bit.ly/3WKAVer.
7 "Jackson's Trial," *Jackson Cty. Banner*, Apr. 30, 1896, https://bit.ly/3qadOOd.
8 "She Has a New Story," *Indianapolis Journal*, Feb. 11, 1896, https://bit.ly/3qdDF7V.
9 Andrew Young, *Unwanted: A Murder Mystery of the Gilded Age* (Yardley, PA: Westholme, 2016), Kindle.
10 *The Mysterious Murder of Pearl Bryan, Or: The Headless Horror . . .* (Cincinnati: Barclay & Co., 1897), Kindle.
11 "Deliberate Murder," *Indianapolis Journal*, Feb. 7, 1896, https://bit.ly/3C0Edkf.
12 Eric Bernsee, "Historian Tippin Shares Mountains of Research into Pearl Bryan Tragedy," *Banner Graphic*, June 26, 2017, https://bit.ly/3ozDPGm.
13 "Scott Jackson Happy," [Louisville, KY] *Courier-Journal*, Apr. 26, 1896, https://bit.ly/45xzVON.
14 "Deliberate Murder," *Indianapolis Journal*, Feb. 7, 1896, https://bit.ly/3C0Edkf.
15 Young, *Unwanted*.
16 Ibid.
17 "Story of a Crime," *Indianapolis News*, Feb. 6, 1896, https://bit.ly/3MFmnbf.
18 *Mysterious Murder of Pearl Bryan*.
19 Albert Vinton Stegman Jr., "Pearl Bryan Murder," Campbell Cty. Historical Soc., https://bit.ly/3C9KtWR.
20 Young, *Unwanted*; "All Excitement . . . ," *Journal and Tribune*, Feb. 12, 1896https://bit.ly/46cYzVt.
21 Young interview.
22 "The Main Facts Still Hidden," [Knoxville, TN] *Journal and Tribune*, Feb. 7, 1896, https://bit.ly/435TkVo.
23 *Mysterious Murder of Pearl Bryan*.
24 Ibid.
25 "Scott Jackson Trial," *Rushville Republican*, Apr. 24, 1896, https://bit.ly/3MFxQaL.
26 Ibid.
27 "Pretty Girls," *Journal and Tribune*, Feb. 24, 1896, https://bit.ly/3MClAYD.
28 "Without Remorse," *Journal and Tribune*, Feb. 9, 1896, https://bit.ly/439NNNL.
29 Young, *Unwanted*.

30 "Suicide Theory," *Journal and Tribune*, Feb. 11, 1896, https://bit.ly/3IKztTo.
31 "She Gave Her Drugs," *Indianapolis Journal*, Feb. 10, 1896, https://bit.ly/3IL68bx.
32 "Identifies the Suspect," *Chicago Chronicle*, Feb. 12, 1896, https://bit.ly/3IFDusv.
33 "Crowd at Jackson's Trial," *Chicago Chronicle*, Apr. 26, 1896, https://bit.ly/3BXdjcW.
34 "Were Seen Together," *Shelby Cty. Democrat*, June 5, 1896, https://bit.ly/43x4DFM.
35 "Jackson's Trial, [Hillsboro, OH] *News-Herald*, Apr. 30, 1896, https://bit.ly/42dLBmO.
36 Young, *Unwanted*.
37 Peter Levins, "The Case of the Narrow Shoe," *Atlanta Constitution*, Sept. 11, 1949, https://bit.ly/3qeiwKW.
38 Young interview.
39 Levins, "Case of the Narrow Shoe."
40 "She Gave Her Drugs," *Indianapolis Journal*.
41 "Poison," *Cincinnati Enquirer*, Feb. 7, 1896, https://bit.ly/3N0ndkk.
42 "Jackson's Trial," *Jackson Cty. Banner*, Apr. 30, 1896, https://bit.ly/3qadOOd.
43 "Jackson's Case," *Kentucky Advocate*, Apr. 24, 1896, https://bit.ly/3MCP2Oj.
44 "Bloody Clothes," *Buffalo News*, Apr. 28, 1896, https://bit.ly/3qdEwFF.
45 "Walling Testifies," *Jackson Cty. Banner*, June 11, 1896, https://bit.ly/3MDeaVg.
46 "Poison," *Cincinnati Enquirer*.
47 "Liberty Was Theirs to Take," *Cincinnati Enquirer*, May 17, 1896, https://bit.ly/3N03AZJ.
48 "Met Their Doom," *Topeka State Journal*, Mar. 20, 1897, https://bit.ly/3OFzSun.
49 Ibid.
50 "Actors in the Great Pearl Bryan Tragedy," *Cincinnati Post*, Mar. 20, 1897, https://bit.ly/3osMxGp.
51 Young interview.
52 "Actors in the Great Pearl Bryan Tragedy," *Cincinnati Post*.
53 Joan Christen and James McDonald, *The Perils of Pearl Bryan: Betrayal and Murder in the Midwest in 1896* (Bloomington, IN: AuthorHouse, 2012).
54 "Hanging of Scott Jackson and Alonzo Walling," Kentucky Historical Society, https://bit.ly/3NAeTbz.

18: Leopold and Loeb: The Evidence that Felled Them

1 Univ. of Michigan, "Notable Alumni," https://bit.ly/45wQGtx. Accessed May 27, 2023.
2 Fergus Mason, *The Perfect Crime: The Real Life Crime that Inspired Hitchcock's* Rope (Stranger Than Fiction Book 5 (Anaheim, CA: Absolute Crime, 2020), Kindle.
3 Univ. of Michigan, "Richard Loeb: UM Alumni Card," 1936, https://bit.ly/45CMGYz. Accessed May 27, 2023.
4 Mason, *Perfect Crime*.
5 Author interview with Paula Fass, Sept. 2020.
6 Simon Baatz, "Leopold and Loeb's Criminal Minds," *Smithsonian Magazine,* Aug. 2008, https://bit.ly/3C12M0q.
7 US School Yearbooks, 1880–2012, Univ. of Chicago, 1923, https://bit.ly/3qiTzhb. Accessed May 27, 2023.
8 Federal Highway Administration, State Motor Vehicle Registrations by Years, https://www.fhwa.dot.gov/ohim/summary95/mv200.pdf. Accessed May 27, 2023.
9 Mason, *Perfect Crime*.
10 Ad titled "Buy a Used Car," *Arizona Republic*, Feb. 13, 1924, https://bit.ly/3ORmZ06l; ad titled "He's Driving a Better Car Than I Am Now," *Capital Journal*, Oct. 1, 1924, https://shorturl.at/bBDQX.
11 John Theodore, *Evil Summer: Babe Leopold, Dickie Loeb, and the Kidnap-Murder of Bobby Franks* (Evanston, IL: Southern Illinois Univ. Press, 2007), Kindle.
12 Sears Archives, "Store History – Chicago, Illinois," https://bit.ly/3C7SXxA. Accessed May 27, 2023.
13 Theodore, *Evil Summer*.
14 Mason, *Perfect Crime*.
15 "Excerpts from the Psychiatrist ('Alienist') Testimony in the Leopold & Loeb Hearing," Univ. of Missouri-Kansas City, https://bit.ly/42BhSEV.
16 Ibid.
17 Tijana Radeska, "Nietzsche 'Supermen' Who Talk to Teddy Bears," *Vintage News,* July 29, 2017, https://bit.ly/3IFtHCQ.
18 Theodore, *Evil Summer*.
19 Erik Rebain, *Arrested Adolescence: The Secret Life of Nathan Leopold* (Blue Ridge Summit, PA: Rowman & Littlefield, 2023).
20 Theodore, *Evil Summer*.
21 Maurine Watkins, "'Dick Innocent,' Loebs Protests; Plan Defense," *Chicago Tribune*, June 1, 1924, https://bit.ly/3My9Giy; Theodore, *Evil Summer*.
22 "Chicago's Student Murderers First to Mar Honor of Two Families of High Standing," *St. Louis Post-Dispatch*, June 3, 1924, https://bit.ly/3ozF3RY; "14-Hour Night Shift Rolled Up Profits for Millionaire Parents of Slayer Leopold," *Daily Worker*, Aug. 7, 1924, https://bit.ly/3N043uX; Maureen M'Kernan, "Leopold Family a Big Factor in City's Business," *Chicago Tribune*, June 1, 1924, https://bit.ly/3C2WoGI.
23 Ancestry.com, Florence Foreman Leopold, Cook County, Illinois Death Index, 1908–88 [database].
24 Mason, *Perfect Crime*; "Scarcity of Jewel Setters Makes Supply of Watches Less than Demand," *Chicago Tribune*, Mar. 8, 1903, https://bit.ly/45rPLdI; Jacob Franks Is Married," *Chicago Tribune*, Feb. 18, 1906, https://bit.ly/3IKHPL7; Ibid; Paul Augsburg, "Jacob Franks Thinks Slayers of Son Insane," *Chicago Tribune*, June 1, 1924, https://bit.ly/3qbMCyC.
25 Author interview with Paul Durica, Sept. 2020.
26 "Leopold & Loeb," Chicagoology, https://bit.ly/3NcQBnJ. Accessed May 27, 2023.
27 Theodore, *Evil Summer*.
28 "Crowe Makes Public Long List of Franks Witnesses," *Chicago Tribune*, July 23, 1924, https://bit.ly/45CNfBF.
29 Theodore, *Evil Summer*.
30 "Slasher Tells Own Story of Killing Loeb in Prison," *Pittsburgh Sun-Telegraph*, Jan. 29, 1936, https://bit.ly/3IMdc82.
31 Frederick A. Mackenzie, *Twentieth Century Crimes* (Boston: Little, Brown, 1927).
32 "Kidnap Rich Boy; Kill Him," *Chicago Tribune*, May 23, 1924, https://bit.ly/3WzG0Gt.
33 "Crowe Lashes Loeb, Leopold as Cold Blooded, Cautious, Cruel Murderers," *Chicago Tribune*, July 24, 1924, https://bit.ly/3oIbu0m.
34 Richard Loeb, "Loeb-Leopold Murder of Franks in Chicago May 21, 1924," Journal of Criminal Law and Criminology 15 (3): May 1924–February 1925, https://bit.ly/42a9Fr0.
35 Ron Grossman, "The Original Affluenza Case," *Chicago Tribune*, https://bit.ly/3MY8Ywm.
36 Theodore, *Evil Summer*.
37 Durica interview.

38 "The Confessions of Richard Loeb and Nathan Leopold," Crime-Archives, https://bit.ly/42glcT0. Accessed May 27, 2023.
39 Baatz, "Leopold and Loeb's Criminal Minds."
40 Theodore, *Evil Summer*.
41 "The Confessions of Richard Loeb and Nathan Leopold," CrimeArchives.
42 James Doherty, "Kidnaped [sic] Boy Died Fighting," *Chicago Tribune*, May 24, 1924, https://bit.ly/43nhpHe.
43 Ibid.
44 "Franks Death Letter Like Current Story in Magazine," *Chicago Tribune*, May 24, 1924, https://bit.ly/3Wzxp6J.
45 "Franks Murder One of Famous Chicago Crimes," *Chicago Tribune*, Jan. 29, 1936, https://bit.ly/43dHTeo.
46 Theodore, Evil Summer.
47 Nathan F. Leopold, *Life Plus 99 Years* (New York: Doubleday, 1958).
48 Theodore, *Evil Summer*.
49 Leopold, *Life Plus 99 Years*.
50 Fass interview.
51 Theodore, *Evil Summer*.
52 Maurine Watkins, "'Dick Innocent,' Loebs Protests; Plan Defense," *Chicago Tribune*, June 1, 1924, https://bit.ly/3My9Giy.
53 "Youth Retain Friends' Faith During Their Long Ordeal," *Chicago Tribune*, May 31, 1924, https://bit.ly/43sN6yO.
54 Loeb, "Loeb-Leopold Murder of Franks in Chicago May 21, 1924."
55 Univ. of Michigan, "Clarence Darrow, 1877–78," https://bit.ly/3MPAxGR. Accessed May 28, 2023.
56 "Clarence Darrow Is Dead in Chicago," *New York Times*, Mar. 14, 1938, https://bit.ly/43b7a96.
57 "Closing Argument: *The State of Illinois v. Nathan Leopold & Richard Loeb*," Univ. of Missouri-Kansas City, Aug. 22, 1924, https://bit.ly/3NcaECP. Accessed May 28, 2023.
58 Ibid.
59 Fass interview.
60 "Closing Argument: *State of Illinois v. Nathan Leopold & Richard Loeb*."
61 "Taxi Driver's Charge is Denied by Leopold," *Omaha World-Herald*, Jan. 6, 1927, https://bit.ly/46l1Ulg.
62 "Loeb and Leopold Flatly Deny Charges of Drivers," *Altoona Tribune*, Jan. 6, 1927, https://bit.ly/42cq4eg.
63 Julia M. Klein, "Five Things: It Was Leopold, Not Loeb," *Chicago*, Sept. 14, 2022, https://bit.ly/3MFp4cR.
64 "Measles Hits Loeb While Leopold Goes Under Knife," *San Francisco Examiner*, May 27, 1925, https://bit.ly/42bIiN1.
65 "Richard Loeb Slashed with Razor; Dies," [Mattoon, IL] *Journal Gazette*, Jan. 28, 1936, https://bit.ly/45C5RS0.
66 Michael Hannon, "Leopold and Loeb Case (1924)," Univ. of Minnesota Law Library, May 2010, https://bit.ly/3WH03D0. Accessed May 28, 2023.
67 Mason, *Perfect Crime*.
68 "Convict Day Cleared in Loeb Killing," *Decatur Herald and Review*, June 5, 1936, https://bit.ly/3C0n1LC.
69 Leopold, *Life Plus 99 Years*.
70 Mason, *Perfect Crime*.
71 Lily Rothman, "The 'Affluenza' Defense Is Older Than You Think," *Time*, Feb. 9, 2016, https://time.com/4206296/affluenza-leopold-loeb/.

19: Nannie Doss: The Giggling Grandma

1 "Tulsa Death Case Probed," *Tulsa World*, Nov. 4, 1954, https://bit.ly/3oxatIH.
2 Ancestry.com, US Veterans Admin. Master Index, 1917–40.
3 Ancestry.com, 1920; Census Place: Cabanal, Carroll, AR; Roll: T625_55; p4A; Dist. 52
4 FamilySearch.org, Wilma Jean Doss, Mar. 6, 1942–Apr. 12, 1945, KCGM-Q6C, https://bit.ly/3MQmL8i.
5 National Archives at St. Louis, MO; Records of the Selective Service System; Group No. 147.
6 "Madison County Native Dies in Tulsa Oct. 10," *Madison Cty. Record*, Oct. 21, 1954, https://bit.ly/3N2eRsH.
7 "Tornado Worst Disaster in Madison County History," *Madison Cty. Record*, Apr. 19, 1945, https://bit.ly/3MGAwVG.
8 Ibid.
9 Some records spell it "Hazle"; https://www.wikitree.com/wiki/Hazel-213.
10 Author interview with Tori Rose, Sept. 2020.
11 Ancestry.com, 1940; Census Place: Straight Mountain, Blount, AL; Roll: m-t0627-00005; p8B; Dist. 5–19.
12 *Nannie Doss: Serial Killer—The Giggling Granny*, True Crime; Bus Stop Reads Book 13 (Goldmineguides.com, 2015), Kindle; "Nannie Doss," Encyclopedia of Alabama, https://bit.ly/462yrME.
13 Ryan Green, *Black Widow: The True Story of Giggling Granny Nannie Doss* (Ryan Green, 2019), Kindle.
14 Rose interview.
15 Joseph Geringer, "Nannie Doss: Lonely Hearts Lady Loved Her Man to Death," Crime Library, https://bit.ly/43DZNY6.
16 Michael Newton, *Bad Girls Do It! An Encyclopedia of Female Murderers* (Port Townsend, WA: Loompanics Unlimited, 1993).
17 Ken Raymond, "Great-grandmother's Murders Led to Medical Examiner System," *Oklahoman*, June 26, 2005, https://bit.ly/3BW7xsd.
18 Ancestry.com, "Sam L. Doss," OK Cty. Marriage Records, 1890–1995.
19 "Crimes of Passion," *St. Louis Globe-Democrat*, Jan. 13, 1957, https://bit.ly/43nYJr2; note: some sources cite Oct. 10 as the day Sam died.
20 Ibid.
21 Rose interview.
22 "Crimes of Passion," *St. Louis Globe-Democrat*.
23 "Giggling Widow Chilly; Her Cell to be Warmer," *Greenville News*, Dec. 1, 1954, https://bit.ly/43dJwsw.
24 "Grandma Admits Poisoning 4 Husbands," *Chillicothe Gazette*, Nov. 29, 1954, https://bit.ly/3IMlaOh.
25 "'Lonely Hearts' Widow Confesses She Killed Four Husbands," *Statesville Record and Landmark*, Nov. 29, 1954, https://bit.ly/3IMg2K5.
26 Ancestry.com, AL, US Cty. Marriage Records, 1805–1967.
27 "Nannie Doss' Prospective Groom 'Mighty Proud She Didn't Come,'" *Knoxville Journal*, Dec. 19, 1954, https://bit.ly/3OFkCO9.
28 Ancestry.com, "Florine Braggs," US Find a Grave® Index, 1600s–Current.
29 Ancestry.com, 1940; Census Place: Straight Mountain, Blount, AL.
30 Ancestry.com, AL, US Deaths and Burials Index, 1881–1974.
31 Ancestry.com, 1940; Census Place: Matthews, Chatham, NC; Roll: m-t0627-02888; p62A; Dist. 19–20.
32 Ancestry.com, "Viola Lenoria Lanning," US Find a Grave® Index, 1600s–Current.
33 Ancestry.com, "Arlie Jackson Lanning," NC, US Death Indexes, 1908–2004.
34 "More Poisoning Victims Sought," *Daily Oklahoman*, Dec. 5, 1954, https://bit.ly/3MYlSL0.

35 CDC, *Medical Examiners' and Coroners' Handbook on Death Registration and Fetal Death Reporting*, 2003 Revision, https://bit.ly/3ozHIeq. Accessed May 28, 2023.

36 "Emporia Poison Charges Filed," *Wichita Beacon*, Dec. 2, 1954, https://bit.ly/3OK7pn9.

37 Ancestry.com, "Richard Lewis 'Chief' Morton Sr.," 1910; Census Place: Tiger, Okmulgee, OK; Roll: T624_1267; p6A; Dist. 0155; FHL microfilm: 1375280; "Mrs. Viola Pearl Morton Dead," *Emporia Weekly Gazette*, Mar. 20, 1952, https://bit.ly/3ORq8Ns.

38 Michael Farrell, *Criminology of Serial Poisoners* (Cham, SWITZ.: Springer Nature, 2018).

39 Ancestry.com, "Louisa H. Hazel," NC, US Death Indexes, 1908–2004.

40 "Arsenic Deaths Probed in Tulsa," *Wichita Beacon*, Nov. 27, 1954, https://bit.ly/42at6zQ.

41 "Reticent Widow Investigated in Arsenic Deaths," *Great Bend Tribune*, Nov. 27, 1954, https://bit.ly/3OJiIvF.

42 Alana Biggers (Reviewer), "What Is Arsenic Poisoning," *Medical News Today*, reviewed Jan. 4, 2018, https://bit.ly/43DcC4u.

43 Traci Pedersen, "Facts About Arsenic," LiveScience, July 28, 2016, https://rb.gy/wb7av.

44 "Reticent Widow Investigated in Arsenic Deaths," *Great Bend Tribune*, Nov. 27, 1954, https://bit.ly/3OJiIvF.

45 Rose interview.

46 Robert Rousek, "The Case of the Giggling Grandma," *St. Louis Post-Dispatch*, Dec. 31, 1954, https://bit.ly/3oDekUz.

47 Bill Sansing, "Tulsa Woman Chills Police in Reciting Poison Details," *Sacramento Bee*, Nov. 29, 1954, https://bit.ly/3MGXpZi.

48 "Emotionless Doss Woman Proves Enigma to Probers," *Tulsa World*, Nov. 29, 1954, https://bit.ly/425tuj2.

49 "Grandmother Signs Statements Admitting She Killed 4 of 5 Husbands with Rat Poison," (Racine, WI) *Journal Times*, Nov. 29, 1954, https://bit.ly/43tl5XD.

50 "Poisoner Turns to Memoirs," *Miami Herald*, Dec. 4, 1954, https://bit.ly/3OMpdOr.

51 "4-Time Widow Under Suspicion," *Tennessean*, Nov. 28, 1954, https://bit.ly/3qhhr56.

52 "Wholesale Mate Killer Is Charged," *Pasadena Independent*, Nov. 30, 1954, https://bit.ly/3qbPFXA.

53 Green, *Black Widow*.

54 "Nanny Doss," Murderpedia.org, https://bit.ly/3qpxqhp. Accessed May 28, 2023.

55 "Long Jail Stay Ahead," *Kansas City Star*, Dec. 16, 1954, https://bit.ly/3oB1aY8.

56 John Clayton, "Widow Admits Poisoning 4 Mates, Still Says her 'Conscience Is Clear . . .'," *Tulsa World*, Nov. 29, 1954, https://bit.ly/3qdSszz.

57 "Okla. Widow Loses Smile When Arraigned in Poisoning of Four Husbands," *News and Observer*, Nov. 30, 1954, https://bit.ly/3MCmAvW.

58 "Life Term Given Nannie Doss in Death of No. 5," *Sapulpa Daily Herald*, June 2, 1955, https://bit.ly/3MB89IB.

59 "Husband-Poisoner Nannie Doss Still Smiles but Wants to Die," *Muskogee Daily Phoenix and Times-Democrat*, May 13, 1957, https://bit.ly/43uX0Qh.

60 "Coroner Reform Is Overdue," *Rocky Mount Telegram*, Dec. 2, 1954, https://bit.ly/3MY6n5I.

61 CDC, North Carolina Coroner/Medical Examiner Laws, https://bit.ly/3P8P9DZ. Accessed May 28, 2023; Marcella Fierro, "Comparing Medical Examiner and Coroner Systems," Inst. of Medicine (US) Committee for Workshop on Medicolegal Death Investigation System (Washington, DC: National Academies, 2003), https://www.ncbi.nlm.nih.gov/books/NBK221913/; "What Is the Difference Between a Medical Examiner and a Coroner?" Washoe Cty. Regional Medical Examiner's Office, https://bit.ly/42lVXRJ. Accessed May 28, 2023.

62 L. Kay Gillespie, *Dancehall Ladies: The Crimes and Executions of America's Condemned Women* (Lanham, MD: Univ. Press of Amer., 1997).

63 Randy Hanzlick, "Overview of the Mediciolegal Death Investigation System in the United States," Inst. of Medicine (US) Committee for Workshop on Medicolegal Death Investigation System (Washington, DC: National Academies, 2003), https://rb.gy/kfa3s; Hanzlick (Dec. 1, 2014), "A Synoptic Review of the 1954 'Model Postmortem Examinations Act,'" *Academic Forensic Pathology* 4 (4), https://bit.ly/3OFP1fl. Accessed May 28, 2023.

20: Kirk Bloodsworth and American's First DNA Exoneration

1 Robert Engelman, "Help Find Missing Children, Reagan Asks," *Knoxville News-Sentinel*, Mar. 8, 1985, https://bit.ly/3OJhtg5.

2 Eduardo Medina, "Man Convicted in 1984 Murder of 12-Year-Old Girl, *Dayton Daily News*, Nov. 3, 2022, https://bit.ly/3WG2pC8; "Former Idaho Governor Candidate Convicted of Murder of Colorado Girl," *Idaho Statesman*, Nov. 2, 2022, https://bit.ly/3WF3NEW.

3 Tim Junkin, *Bloodsworth: The True Story of the First Death Row Inmate Exonerated by DNA* (Chapel Hill, NC: Algonquin, 2004), Kindle.

4 Ibid.

5 "The Real Killer," *Daily News*, Mar. 19, 2000, https://bit.ly/3IFHPMj.

6 Junkin, *Bloodworth*; Rob Hiaasen, "The Second Life of Kirk Bloodsworth," *Baltimore Sun*, July 30, 2000, https://bit.ly/3N0rjsI.

7 Laura Buchanan, "Former Death Row Inmate Speaks at MCC," [Madisonville, KY] *Messenger*, Oct. 29, 2015, https://bit.ly/3OFP9Lx.

8 Junkin, *Bloodsworth*.

9 Ancestry.com, "Casimira E. Sponaugle," US Index to Public Records, 1994–2019.

10 Margaret Sponaugle Obituary, *Baltimore Sun*, Nov. 7, 1979, https://bit.ly/3C26S8o.

11 Author Frank Weber blog post, "Bloodsworth: A Man Unfairly Convicted and Sentenced to Death Is Saved by DNA," https://bit.ly/3BWKnSu. Accessed May 28, 2023.

12 Junkin, *Bloodsworth*.

13 Elizabeth Hudson and David Michael Ettlin, "Rosedale Girl, 9, Is Found Murdered; Police Seek Man She Reportedly Met," *Baltimore Sun*, July 26, 1984, https://bit.ly/3qeExJA.

14 Junkin, *Bloodsworth*.

15 Maria Bovsun, "Until Proven Innocent," *Daily News*, Feb. 4, 2007, https://bit.ly/3WFMjIH.

16 Robert J. Norris, "The 'New Civil Rights': The Innocence Movement and American Criminal Justice," dissertation, SUNY Albany School of Criminal Justice, 2015, https://bit.ly/3WT3g2t. Accessed May 28, 2023.

17 Junkin, *Bloodsworth*.

18 "You Judge the Law: Death Penalty Errors," *Casper Star-Tribune*, Mar. 6, 1994, https://bit.ly/3C27Ots.

19 Junkin, *Bloodsworth*.

20 Maria Bovsun, "Until Proven Innocent," *Daily News*, Feb. 4, 2007, https://bit.ly/3WFMjIH.

21 Techa Johnson, "Mistaken Identity," essay, Southern New Hampshire Univ., June 15, 2020, https://bit.ly/432yRRn; David J. Kramer blog post, "Eyewitness Misidentification: The Scary Truth," David J. Kramer Law Firm, May 9, 2018, https://bit.ly/43cAuft. Accessed May 28, 2023.
22 Stephanie Hanes, "'84 Investigation Quick to Overlook the Culprit," *Baltimore Sun*, May 22, 2004, https://bit.ly/3OJFEv2.
23 Kirk Bloodsworth, "Kirk Bloodsworth Speaks at Christ School," YouTube video, 46:12, Sept. 23, 2003, https://bit.ly/43yQvMJ.
24 Junkin, *Bloodsworth*.
25 Gregory Bayne, dir., *Bloodsworth: An Innocent Man*, 2015, https://bit.ly/43y5iHq.
26 Junkin, *Bloodsworth*.
27 Ibid.
28 Bayne, *Bloodsworth*.
29 Ibid.
30 Idaho Public Television, "Dialogue: 'An Innocent Man,'" YouTube video, 28:51, Feb. 21, 2016, https://rb.gy/ewh4r.
31 Junkin, *Bloodsworth*.
32 Real Responders, "DNA Evidence Brings Killer to Justice (The New Detectives)," YouTube video, 50:34, June 7, 2021, https://bit.ly/3OU2VdH.
33 Bayne, *Bloodsworth*.
34 Junkin, *Bloodsworth*.
35 Tony Pipitone profile, LinkedIn, https://rb.gy/tenxu. Accessed May 28, 2023.
36 Real Responders, "DNA Evidence Brings Killer to Justice."
37 Junkin, *Bloodsworth*.
38 Ibid.
39 Ibid.
40 Raju Chebium, "Kirk Bloodsworth, Twice Convicted of Rape and Murder, Exonerated by DNA Evidence," CNN, June 20, 2000, https://bit.ly/3MYFoXM.
41 Junkin, *Bloodsworth*.
42 "Man Convicted of Murder Gets New Trial," *Baltimore Sun*, Aug. 3, 1986, https://bit.ly/3qc9qOK.
43 Robert A. Erlandson, "Bloodsworth Declines to Testify at 2nd Trial in Slaying," *Baltimore Sun*, Apr. 4, 1987, https://bit.ly/3BYx6IT.
44 Junkin, *Bloodsworth*.
45 Ibid.
46 Real Responders, "DNA Evidence Brings Killer to Justice."
47 Ibid.
48 Louis B. Cei, "DNA Test Rescued Wrongly Convicted Man," *Richmond Times-Dispatch*, Oct. 10, 2004, https://bit.ly/3oEox31.
49 Bayne, *Bloodsworth*.
50 Idaho Public Television, "Dialogue: 'An Innocent Man,'" YouTube video, 28:51, Feb. 21, 2016, https://bit.ly/3OWUT3J.
51 Stephanie Hanes, "Guilty Plea Closes '84 Case of Rosedale Girl's Murder," *Baltimore Sun*, May 21, 2004, https://bit.ly/3IM7XoC; Junkin, *Bloodsworth*.
52 Kendall Green, "Walter Lomax, State Law's Namesake, Weighs in on Potential Compensation for Syed," WMAR-TV Baltimore, Oct. 13, 2022, https://bit.ly/3qdKq9O; Jessica Anderson, "Charges Dropped After Man Served 38 Years in Murder," *Baltimore Sun*, Apr. 3, 2014, https://bit.ly/3OHsnmu; Maryland State Dept. of Corrections inmate locator reported Ruffner was housed at Eastern Correctional Institution East, https://bit.ly/3MQKMuy. Accessed May 28, 2023.
53 "Baltimore County Accepts Plea Deal in 1984 Murder of Rosedale Girl, 9," [MD] *Daily Record*, May 20, 2004, https://bit.ly/3N1ACsA.

21: The Abduction of Charley Ross, the First Kidnapping for Ransom

1 Heather Thomas, "The Kidnapping of Little Charley Ross," LOC, Apr. 23, 2019. https://bit.ly/42ru7DI
2 Thomas Everly, "Searching for Charley Ross," *Pennsylvania History: A Journal of Mid-Atlantic Studies* 67 (3) (2000): 376–96. https://www.jstor.org/stable/27774275.
3 Christian K. Ross, *The Father's Story of Charley Ross, the Kidnapped Child* . . . (Philadelphia: John E. Potter, 1876), https://bit.ly/3MCxZNG.
4 Ibid.
5 Ibid.
6 Ross, *Father's Story*.
7 Ibid.
8 Ibid.
9 Carrie Hagen, "The Story Behind the First Ransom Note in American History," *Smithsonian Mag.*, Dec. 9, 2013, https://bit.ly/43pb528.
10 "Abduction of a Child," *Phila. Inquirer*, July 3, 1874. https://bit.ly/45NuI5o.
11 "About Town," *Phila. Inquirer*, July 4, 1874. https://bit.ly/43KX7aJ.
12 Author interview with Meaghan Good, CharleyProject.org, Oct. 2020.
13 Ross, *Father's Story*.
14 "The First Telephone Call," America's Story from America's Library, https://bit.ly/3WLL0b3. Accessed June 4, 2023.
15 Ross, *Father's Story*.
16 Norman J. Zierold, *Defy All the Devils: America's First Kidnapping for Ransom* (New York: Open Road Media, 2018), Kindle.
17 Ibid.
18 "Another Charley Ross," *St. Albans Advertiser*, Dec. 31, 1875, https://bit.ly/3MRlw7s.
19 Author interview with Good, Oct. 2020.
20 Zierold, *Defy All the Devils*.
21 "Forging the Fetters around Westervelt," *Reading Times*, Sept. 11, 1875, https://bit.ly/3MRmCA6.
22 Ross, *Father's Story*.
23 Ibid.
24 "Another Charley Ross," *St. Albans Advertiser*, Dec. 31, 1875, https://bit.ly/3MRlw7s.
25 Ross, *Father's Story*.
26 Ibid.
27 Zierold, *Defy All the Devils*.
28 Ibid.; "Another Charley Ross," *St. Albans Advertiser*, Dec. 31, 1875, https://bit.ly/3MRlw7s; H. M. Egbert, "The Kidnapping of Charley Ross," *Sedgwick Pantagraph*, June 13, 1918, https://bit.ly/45JvArW.
29 Egbert, "The Kidnapping of Charley Ross."
30 Zierold, *Defy All the Devils*.
31 Hagen, "The Story Behind the First Ransom Note in American History."
32 Good in discussion with author, Oct. 2020.
33 "Charlie Ross," *Intelligencer Journal*, Dec. 14, 1874, https://bit.ly/42gYzAo.
34 "Charley Ross," *NY Daily Herald*, Dec. 15, 1874, https://bit.ly/3MSlVH3.

35 Steven Casale, "1874 Kidnapping of Charley Ross was the First of its Kind," *Metro Philadelphia*, Jan. 28, 2016, https://bit.ly/3IXBqMt.
36 Good interview.
37 "Charley Ross," [Lancaster, PA] *Daily Evening Express*, May 17, 1875, https://bit.ly/3qpftj7.
38 "The Ross Abduction," *Pittsburgh Daily Post*, Sept. 21, 1875, https://bit.ly/45MP3rS.
39 "Is Charley Ross Alive?" *Phila. Times,* Sept. 5, 1875, https://bit.ly/43mG0w6.
40 Ancestry.com, 1880; Census Place: Phila., PA; Roll: 1181; Page: 487D; Dist. 454.
41 "Fate of Charley Ross," [KS] *Larned Weekly Chronoscope*, July 16, 1897, https://bit.ly/43sUyKM.
42 "Mrs. Christian K. Ross," *Lancaster New Era*, Dec. 14, 1912, https://bit.ly/3CbEr88.
43 "Brother of 'Charley' Ross," [Baltimore, MD] *Evening Sun*, Apr. 25, 1913, https://bit.ly/43ICz2m.
44 "Gardener Claims to be Kidnaped Charlie Ross," *Daily News*, Apr. 4, 1932, https://bit.ly/43EqVWu.
45 "Carpenter Named as 1874 Kidnap Victim," [Ont, CAN] *Windsor Star*, May 9, 1939, https://bit.ly/43kh2NR.
46 Everly, "Searching for Charley Ross."
47 "Insists Blair Isn't Brother," *Windsor Star*, May 9, 1939, https://bit.ly/3CdkKg8.
48 Everly, "Searching for Charley Ross."
49 Rod and Larry Miller, "Charley Ross—Gustave Blair—Nelson Miller," https://charleyross.com, Accessed June 4, 2023.
50 Rod Miller email to author, Mar. 9, 2023.
51 Good interview.
52 Fass interview.
53 Kathryn Canavan, *True Crime Philadelphia: From America's First Bank Robbery to the Real-Life Killers Who Inspired Boardwalk Empire* (Guilford, CT: Lyons Press, 2021).

22: The Enduring Mystery of the Villisca Axe Murders

1 Bill James and Rachel McCarthy James, *The Man from the Train: Discovering America's Most Elusive Serial Killer* (New York: Scribner, 2017), Kindle.
2 Ed Epperly, "Villisca Murders: A Real-Life Whodunit," *Cedar Rapids Gazette*, Sept. 28, 1986, https://bit.ly/45IFAld.
3 James and James, *Man from the Train*.
4 "Jones-Wilkerson Case Still On," *Adams Cty. Free Press*, Dec. 2, 1916, https://bit.ly/43BzuSp.
5 E. Dana Durand, "Thirteenth Census of the United States Taken in the Year 1910," Statistics for Iowa, https://bit.ly/3MT2QEq; "Total Population in Villisca Iowa," US Census Bureau, https://bit.ly/3WW5IVJ.
6 Mattingly Overton Overton Prod, *Villisca: A Town Divided*, YouTube video, 1:07:17, Oct. 5, 2015, https://rb.gy/6hv8f.
7 Ibid.
8 Ibid.
9 "The American System of Fingerprint Classification," NY State Div. of Criminal Justice Services, https://bit.ly/3IUbTno. Accessed June 4, 2023.
10 CSI Iowa, *The Villisca Axe Murders*, YouTube video, 1:01:12, Nov. 25, 2012, https://rb.gy/8959j.
11 Ibid.
12 Edgar V. Epperly, *Fiend Incarnate: Villisca Axe Murders of 1912* (Moline, IL: Fourth Wall, 2021), Kindle.
13 James and James, *Man from the Train*.
14 Joe Turner, "Unsolved Villisca Axe Murders of 1912," Historic-Mysteries.com, Jan. 4, 2021, https://bit.ly/3qun3co. Accessed June 4, 2023.
15 City of Longmont Colorado, "Investigating Haunted Places w/Richard Estep," YouTube video, 57:03, Oct. 12, 2018, https://rb.gy/nw9c0.
16 James and James, *Man from the Train*.
17 CSI Iowa, *Villisca Axe Murders*.
18 "KCCI Archive: Iowa's Infamous Villsca Axe Murder was Renovated in 1996," KCCI-TV, YouTube Video, 1:48, Apr. 23, 2022, https://rb.gy/duh5m.
19 Darwin Linn, "Villisca Axe Murder House Interview with Darwin Linn," Kline Studios Production, YouTube Video, 13:38, Nov. 27, 2013, https://bit.ly/3CcclLm.
20 "Associated Press, News Agency," *Britannica*, July 20, 1998, https://bit.ly/3C9kjnh.
21 Pamela Burger, "The Bloody History of the True Crime Genre," *JSTOR Daily*, Aug. 24, 2016, https://bit.ly/3CcrQ4H. Accessed June 4, 2023.
22 James and James, *Man from the Train*.
23 Ibid.
24 Mattingly Overton Overton Prod, *Villisca: A Town Divided*.
25 "The Villisca Murder," *Adams Cty. Free Press*, June 21, 1916, https://bit.ly/3OWF5OE.
26 Epperly, *Fiend Incarnate*.
27 "More of Jones Case," *Adams Cty. Free Press*, Nov. 29, 1916, https://bit.ly/42m0lAi.
28 Ibid.
29 "Mansfield to be Closely Guarded," *Des Moines Register,* June 18, 1916, https://bit.ly/3Pcett9.
30 Kelly and Tammy Rundle, prod., *Villisca: Living with a Mystery*, 2007, https://www.villiscamovie.com.
31 CSI Iowa, *Villisca Axe Murders*.
32 Epperly, *Fiend Incarnate*.
33 Ibid.
34 James and James, *Man from the Train*.
35 "Atty. General Is Indicted," *Iowa City Press-Citizen,* Sept. 5, 1917, https://bit.ly/3IVUf2R.
36 "The Voters Take a Hand," *Sioux City Journal,* June 12, 1918, https://bit.ly/3OVsR8P.
37 Mattingly Overton Overton Prod, *Villisca: A Town Divided*.
38 James and James, *Man from the Train*.
39 Edgar V. Epperly, "Villisca Axe Murders: the True Story: Part 5," Epperly's Blog, Dec. 1, 2010, https://bit.ly/42nVK0k.
40 James and James, *Man from the Train*.
41 "Thinks Lee Moore Ax-Murderer of 25," *Columbia Missourian*, May 9, 1913, https://bit.ly/3oQuYjt.
42 Author interview with Rachel McCarthy James, Mar. 2021.
43 James and James, *Man from the Train*; Author interview with Rachel McCarthy James, Mar. 2021.
44 James interview.
45 Ibid.
46 "Killed for $40," *Boston Globe,* Jan. 11, 1898, *https://bit.ly/43mxYDq*.
47 James interview.
48 Ibid.
49 "Charred Bodies of 4 Found in Burned House," *Cairo Bulletin*, Sept. 30, 1912, https://bit.ly/3OSM7DS; "'Axman' Murders Another Family," *Chicago Tribune*, Sept. 30, 1912, https://bit.ly/42rpuJM.
50 *People v. Pfanschmidt* (1914), https://cite.case.law/ill/262/411/.
51 Ibid.

52 Don Allen, "Villisca Ax Murders a 33-Year Mystery," *Des Moines Register*, Jan. 28, 1945, https://bit.ly/3MPBOOf.
53 Epperly, *Fiend Incarnate*.
54 CSI Iowa, *Villisca Axe Murders*; Bethany Dale, "A History of Fingerprinting," Imprint Project, https://rb.gy/msclk. Accessed June 4, 2023.

23: The Murder of Mary Phagan

1 "Body of Girl Found in Cellar," *Nashville Banner*, Apr. 28, 1913, https://bit.ly/3IQTXtZ.
2 Ancestry.com, "Mary Anne Phagan," US Find a Grave® Index, 1600s–Current.
3 Ancestry.com, "William Joshua Phagan," US Find a Grave® Index, 1600s–Current.
4 "Memorial Day at Royston," *Atlanta Constitution*, Apr. 22, 1913, https://bit.ly/3C9TDTd.
5 "Mary Phagan Murder—Leo Frank Trial (Bryan County Now)," *Savannah Now*, Aug. 1, 2016, https://bit.ly/42jF8a5. Accessed June 4, 2023.
6 "Atlanta Girl Is Murdered," *Chattanooga Daily Times*, Apr. 28, 1913, https://bit.ly/42liePF.
7 "The Night Witch Did It," Famous Trials, https://rb.gy/c7srl. Accessed June 4, 2023.
8 "Killed Young Girl," [Charlotte, NC] *Evening Chronicle*, Apr. 28, 1913, https://bit.ly/42oGfFF.
9 GBH Forum Network, "And the Dead Shall Rise," Breman Museum, YouTube video, 40:24, Mar. 27, 2014, https://rb.gy/rv75n.
10 Michael Feldberg, "The Lynching of Leo Frank," *My Jewish Learning*, https://bit.ly/43psQyu. Accessed June 4, 2023.
11 "Testimony of Leo Frank," Famous Trials, https://rb.gy/rcvki.
12 "Second Installment of Testimony Against Leo M. Frank," *Washington Times*, Jan. 24, 1915, https://bit.ly/43IAfbA.
13 "Frank 'Guilty' and 'Innocent,' Say Two Experts," *Washington Times*, Apr. 4, 1915, https://bit.ly/3CbGqJz.
14 "JNo. M. Gantt Held in Phagan Killing," *Macon Telegraph*, Apr. 29, 1913, https://bit.ly/43ruX4H; "Frank Is Being Drawn into Net in Murder Case," *Montgomery Times*, May 1, 1913, https://bit.ly/3NdsKnC.
15 "Pinkertons Hired to Assist Police Probe the Murder of Mary Phagan," *Atlanta Constitution*, Apr. 29, 1913, https://bit.ly/3OPl50d.
16 "Keep an Open Mind," *Atlanta Constitution*, May 2, 1913, https://bit.ly/43DL4Mf.
17 "Murder Still Mystery," *Natchez Democrat*, May 1, 1913, https://bit.ly/43FCZGL.
18 "Troops Called Out in Phagan Murder," *Macon Telegraph*, May 2, 1913, https://bit.ly/3IXgNQG.
19 Country Fried Cryptid, "The Murder of Mary Phagan and the Lynching of Leo Frank," YouTube Video, 20:37, https://bit.ly/3MR4jej. Accessed June 4, 2023.
20 *USA Today*, "Leo Frank's Lynching Remembered 100 Years Later," YouTube video, 3:30, https://bit.ly/45FK3VX.
21 "Testimony of Jim Conley," Famous Trials, https://bit.ly/3WOEQXA.
22 Steve Oney, *And the Dead Shall Rise: The Murder of Mary Phagan and the Lynching of Leo Frank* (New York: Knopf, 2004).
23 "Others Will Be Charged in New Bribery Charges Intimates Chief Lanford," *Atlanta Constitution*, May 25, 1913, https://bit.ly/3Cdbxo6.
24 Jennifer Brett, "After More Than 100 Years, Will Leo Frank be Exonerated?", *Atlanta Journal-Constitution*, Aug. 22, 2019, https://bit.ly/3NlRGd3.
25 "Girl's Body 'Sight Enough to Drive a Man to Distraction,' Says Frank in Plea," *Washington Times*, Mar. 7, 1915, https://bit.ly/3WSqlCm.
26 Ibid.
27 Mercer Law School, "Former Georgia Gov. Roy Barnes," YouTube video, 50:59, Nov. 13, 2019, https://rb.gy/m8abt
28 "Frank Fights for Life Now Forfeit," *Lincoln Journal Star*, Feb. 25, 1915, https://bit.ly/42CB317.
29 "Leo Frank Trial (1913)," Famous Trials, https://www.famous-trials.com/leo-frank.
30 "Cobb County Protests Clemency for Frank," *Atlanta Constitution*, June 1, 1915, https://bit.ly/42h2r4o.
31 "Judge L. S. Roan," *Chattanooga Daily Times*, Mar. 24, 1915, https://bit.ly/3MQrl5b.
32 "Leo Frank's Throat Cut by Convict; Famous Prisoner Near Death," *NY Times*, July 18, 1915, https://bit.ly/43B6nOk. Accessed June 4, 2023.
33 Jerry Klinger, "The Lynching of Leo Frank, the Commutation of Gov. John Slaton," Jewish American Society for Historic Preservation, https://bit.ly/3WMRmXE. Accessed June 4, 2023.
34 Frank Ritter et al, "An Innocent Man Was Lynched," *Tennessean*, Mar. 7, 1982, https://bit.ly/43DGZaS.
35 "Murder Analyzed by Dr. M'Kelway," *Atlanta Constitution*, Apr. 30, 1913, https://bit.ly/3IUvjZo.
36 "Keating-Owen Child Labor Act (1916)," NARA, https://bit.ly/3N98SlN.

24: The Lindbergh Baby Kidnapping

1 Alice Cogan, "'Anne, They've Stolen Our Baby . . .' Betty Gow's Story Hushes Crowd," [Brooklyn, NY] *Times Union*, Jan. 7, 1935, https://bit.ly/45FKUWF.
2 Lloyd C. Gardner, *The Case That Never Dies: The Lindbergh Kidnapping* (New Brunswick, NJ: Rutgers Univ. Press, 2004), Kindle.
3 Gardner, *Case that Never Dies*; Cogan, "'Anne, They've Stolen Our Baby.'"
4 "New York-to-Paris Flight," Charles Lindbergh House and Museum, https://rb.gy/lvzba.
5 "First Photo of Charles A. Lindbergh, Jr." *Alton Evening Telegraph*, July 10, 1930, https://bit.ly/3OVIZau.
6 Gardner, *Case That Never Dies*.
7 Critical Past, "Newsreel 'Nation Aroused at Revolting Kidnapping of Lindbergh Baby . . .' YouTube video, 2:21, https://bit.ly/3oOnKg8.
8 Morven Museum & Garden, "A. Scott Berg Lecture on the Lindberghs," YouTube video, 1:32:23, Nov. 6, 2017, https://bit.ly/45Dk7tQ.
9 "Col. Lindbergh's Evidence at Bruno Hauptmann Trial," *Windsor Star*, Jan. 4, 1935, https://bit.ly/3C9bwll.
10 Gardner, *Case That Never Dies*.
11 Ibid.
12 "Al Capone Posts Sum to Spur Search," *Salt Lake Tribune*, Mar. 3, 1932, https://bit.ly/3CdcnkK.
13 Raymond Crowley, "Babe Near Home Experts Believe," *Deseret News*, Mar. 9, 1932, https://bit.ly/3IV1N5D.
14 Gardner, *Case That Never Dies*.
15 "Intermediaries Known Only as Broadway Racketeers," *St. Louis Post-Dispatch*, Mar. 7, 1932, https://bit.ly/3oCk0yg.
16 "Lindberghs Dickering with Kidnappers, Authors Two Members of NY Underworld to Act as Go-Between in Negotiations," *Phila. Inquirer,* Mar. 6, 1932, https://bit.ly/43BDu5n.
17 Ibid.

18 William Cook, *The Lindbergh Baby Kidnapping* (Mechanicsburg, PA: Sunbury), Kindle.
19 Ibid.
20 "Investigators Say Babe Alive, Well," [Elmira, NY] *Star-Gazette*, Mar. 10, 1932, https://bit.ly/3qogQP8.
21 Cook, *Lindbergh Baby Kidnapping*.
22 Mike Stewart, *State vs. Hauptmann, Vol. I: The Lindbergh Baby Kidnapping and Murder Trial Transcripts* (Mike Stewart, 2017), Kindle.
23 Gardner, *The Case That Never Dies;* John Francis Condon, *Jafsie Tells All! Revealing the Inside Story of the Lindbergh-Hauptmann Case* (New York: Jonathan Lee, 1936).
24 Gardner, *Case That Never Dies*.
25 British Pathé, "USA: Dr. J. F. Condon Who Met Kidnappers of Lindbergh Baby (1932)," YouTube video, 3:03, https://bit.ly/3oKZATI.
26 Gardner, *Case That Never Dies*.
27 FBI, "Lindbergh Baby Kidnapping FBI Files," Internet Archive, https://bit.ly/3oFxTM6. Accessed June 4, 2023.
28 Gardner, *Case That Never Dies*.
29 Ibid.
30 FBI, "Lindbergh Baby Kidnapping FBI Files."
31 Gardner, *Case That Never Dies*.
32 Cook, *Lindbergh Baby Kidnapping*.
33 Ibid.
34 Mike Stewart, *State vs. Hauptmann, Vol. I: The Lindbergh Baby Kidnapping and Murder Trial Transcripts* (Mike Stewart, 2017), Kindle.
35 Ibid; FBI, "Lindbergh Baby Kidnapping FBI Files"; Cook, *Lindbergh Baby Kidnapping*.
36 Gardner, *Case That Never Dies*.
37 Cook, *Lindbergh Baby Kidnapping*.
38 "Start Probe of Norfolk Angle of Kidnaping Case," [San Pedro, CA] *News-Pilot*, May 12, 1932, https://bit.ly/3qpcUgT.
39 William A. Kinney, Lindbergh Ransom Bills Identified, *Paterson Evening News*, Jan. 17, 1935, https://bit.ly/42sOro5.
40 "Body Found Near Road to Hopewell," *Hartford Courant,* May 13, 1932, https://bit.ly/43nJHld.
41 Gardner, *Case That Never Dies*.
42 Stewart, *State vs. Hauptmann*.
43 "Lindbergh Baby Kidnaping Nears Solution," *Jacksonville Daily Journal*, Sept. 21, 1934, https://bit.ly/3WOn8DA.
44 Cook, *Lindbergh Baby Kidnapping*.
45 "Lindbergh," *Sayre Headlight*, Sept. 20, 1934, https://bit.ly/3WMTvma.
46 Morven Museum & Garden, "A. Scott Berg Lecture on the Lindberghs," YouTube video, 1:32:23, Nov. 6, 2017, https://bit.ly/45Dk7tQ. Accessed June 4, 2023.
47 Samuel G. Blackman, "Bruno Dies in Electric Chair for Lindbergh Baby Murder," *Paterson Morning Call*, Apr. 4, 1936, https://bit.ly/3qpmbWl.
48 Neil Genzling, "Anthony Scaduto, an Early Biographer of Dylan, Dies at 85," *NY Times*, Dec. 13, 2017, https://bit.ly/43m8DJM.
49 "Prosecutor Says Bruno has been Proved Murderer," *Cedar Rapids Gazette*, Feb. 11, 1935, https://bit.ly/3qrxIV9.
50 "Lindy Identifies Suspect's Voice," *Buffalo Evening News*, Oct. 9, 1934, https://bit.ly/3IVZ8Jf.
51 Tom Zito, "Aging Widow Seeks Balm for Old Sorry in the Lindbergh Case," *Courier-Journal*, Oct. 16, 1981, https://bit.ly/3IV3cJr.
52 "Anna Hauptmann, Wife of Man Convicted in Lindbergh Murder," *LA Times,* Oct. 20, 1994, https://bit.ly/3OULXff. Accessed June 4, 2023.
53 Mark J. Price, "The Lindbergh Maybe," *NY Times*, July 30, 2000, https://bit.ly/3OZYdvb.
54 Morven Museum & Garden, "A. Scott Berg Lecture on the Lindberghs."
55 Gardner, *Case That Never Dies*.
56 Rupert Cornwell, *Independent Mag.,* Oct. 20, 2012, https://bit.ly/42hyHo4.

25: The Tylenol Murders

1 "She Denies Poisoning Husband," *Battle Creek Enquirer*, Apr. 28, 1988, https://bit.ly/3qlPfxP; Gregg Olsen, *Bitter Almonds: The True Story of Mothers, Daughters, and the Seattle Cyanide Murders* (New York: St. Martin's, 2007).
2 Jane Ridley, "A Mom Randomly Died After a Woman Laced Bottles of Excedrin with Cyanide to Cover Up Her Husband's Murder," *Insider*, Nov. 9, 2022, https://bit.ly/45KykVW. Accessed June 4, 2023.
3 Richard Monahan (director), *Forensic Files,* Season 2, episode 9, "Something's Fishy." Aired Nov. 27, 1997, https://www.imdb.com/title/tt1472366/.
4 Lee May, "Bristol-Myers to Remove All Shell Capsules," *LA Times*, June 21, 1986, https://bit.ly/45MaJ7h. Accessed June 4, 2023.
5 Jerry Crimmins, "2 Firemen Tied Drug to Deaths," *Chicago Tribune*, Oct. 1, 1982, https://bit.ly/3WKZU1n.
6 William Mullen, "The Hunt," *Chicago Tribune*, Oct. 2, 1983, https://bit.ly/3qsJFde.
7 Ibid.
8 Ibid.
9 "Poisoned Pills Kill 5 in Chicago," *Indianapolis Star*, Oct. 1, 1982, https://bit.ly/3IXDeoN.
10 William Mullen, "The Tylenol Trail: A Year Later, Police Plod On," [Moline, IL] *Dispatch*, Oct. 2, 1983, https://bit.ly/3Ney4Yg.
11 Marianne Taylor et al, "Antidote to Sniffles Results in a Tragedy," *Chicago Tribune*, Oct. 1, 1982, https://bit.ly/3NbNr3m.
12 Retro Report, "A Trusted Pill Turned Deadly. How Tylenol Made a Comeback," YouTube video, 8:40, Sept. 16, 2018, https://rb.gy/0q0hh. Accessed June 4, 2023.
13 Jerry Crimmins, "2 Firemen Tied Drug to Deaths," *Chicago Tribune*, Oct. 1, 1982, https://bit.ly/3WKZUln.
14 Martin Zimmerman, "Suspect Bottles of Tylenol Found in Mississippi," [Jackson, MS] *Clarion-Ledger*, Oct. 2, 1982, https://bit.ly/42o0Fli.
15 Jack Houston et al, "5 Deaths Tied to Pills," *Chicago Tribune*, Oct. 1, 1982, https://bit.ly/42h5gCw.
16 "Cyanide Deadly Even to Touch," *Chicago Tribune*, Oct. 2, 1982, https://bit.ly/43KXnGN.
17 "Revisiting Chicago's Tylenol Murders," *Chicago Mag.*, Sept. 21, 2012, https://bit.ly/3qp41E4.
18 GIBS Business School, "Managing the Tylenol Crisis," YouTube video, 3:16, Feb. 13, 2014, https://rb.gy/2la3p.
19 Ibid.
20 "Cyanide: Exposure, Decontamination, Treatment," CDC, https://bit.ly/45OCVqm. Accessed June 4, 2023.
21 "Potassium Cyanide: Systemic Agent," CDC, https://bit.ly/3OVO1nh. Accessed June 4, 2023.
22 "Cyanide: Exposure, Decontamination, Treatment," CDC.
23 *Federal Reporter* (Eagan, MN: West Publishing Co., 1986).
24 Clyde Haberman, "How an Unsolved Mystery Changed the Way We Take Pills," *NY Times,* Sept. 16, 2018, https://bit.ly/3NlVjQd.

25 "The Chicago Tylenol Murders," Icebox blog, Penn State, Mar. 18, 2021, https://bit.ly/43o1NDF. Accessed June 4, 2023.
26 Janet Cawley, "Suspect Denies Poisonings," *Orlando Sentinel*, Oct. 31, 1982, https://bit.ly/42h68qM.
27 Stacy St. Clair et al., "Unsealed: The Tylenol Murders Part 4," *Chicago Tribune*, Oct. 16, 2022, https://bit.ly/42m6YTc.
28 Michael Bauer, "Refunds Up in '75 But So Are Taxes," *Kansas City Star*, Mar. 5, 1975, https://bit.ly/3OPpW1r.
29 Stacy St. Clair et al., "Unsealed: The Tylenol Murders Part 4."
30 "Former Tylenol Suspect Denies Role in Slayings," *Tyler Courier-Times Telegraph*, Feb. 19, 1984, https://rb.gy/zhujr.
31 Stacy St. Clair et al., "Unsealed: The Tylenol Murders Part 4."
32 Ibid.
33 Joy Bergmann, "A Bitter Pill," *Chicago Reader,* Nov. 2, 2000, https://bit.ly/45G4mm9.
34 Richard A. Serrano, "Mysterious Death Case Dismissed," *Kansas City Times*, Oct. 18, 1979, https://bit.ly/3WL0YSV.
35 "Pair Sought for Questions," *Wichita Eagle,* Oct. 15, 1982, https://bit.ly/3qpeRtJ.
36 "FBI Captures Tylenol Suspect in Library," *Greenwood Commonwealth*, Dec. 14, 1982, https://bit.ly/3WQvpqx.
37 "Suspect in Tainted-Tylenol Case Leaves Prison," *Macon Telegraph*, Oct. 14, 1995, https://bit.ly/3WSvbzw.
38 "FBI Reviewing Case of Tylenol Killer," CBS News, Feb. 4, 2009, https://bit.ly/3IQQc7W. Accessed June 4, 2023.
39 "Federal Agents on Wednesday Searched the Home . . ." *Charlotte Observer*, Feb. 4, 2009, https://bit.ly/43kkgkh.
40 Christy Gutowski et al., "Movement in the Tylenol Murders," *Chicago Tribune*, Sept. 22, 2022, https://bit.ly/42vobtC. Accessed June 4, 2023.
41 Michael Levenson, "James W. Lewis, Suspect in the 1982 Tylenol Murders, Dies at 76," *NY Times*, July 10, 2023; updated July 11, 2023; https://www.nytimes.com/2023/07/10/us/james-lewis-tylenol-poisonings-dead.html.
42 Alok Patel et al., "How an Unsolved Murder Mystery Changed Our Pill Bottles," CNN, Aug. 24, 2018, https://bit.ly/43oghmO.
43 "One Tylenol Lead Dissolves as Claim is Traced to Bad Ham," *Buffalo News*, Oct. 11, 1982, https://bit.ly/3NbFc7D.
44 "Tylenol Leads Keep Washing Out," UPI News Archive, Oct. 10, 1982, https://bit.ly/3qpoWHb. Accessed June 4, 2023.
45 James Feron, "A Year Later, Few Clues in Tylenol Poisoning," Feb. 8, 1987, https://bit.ly/3WR9pfa.
46 "Tylenol Tampering Coverage, February 1986," News Active 3, YouTube video, 37:29, https://rb.gy/gakxu. Accessed June 4, 2023.
47 Monahan, *Forensic Files,* "Something's Fishy."
48 Ibid.
49 Erik Godchaux, "Auburn Poisoning Lead Found in Library," *News Tribune,* Mar. 3, 1988, https://bit.ly/3OUzt7x .
50 "Poisoning Evidence Released," *Spokesman-Review,* Mar. 3, 1988, https://bit.ly/3qvATLh.
51 Monahan, *Forensic Files,* "Something's Fishy."
52 Ibid.
53 Tim Klass, "Fingerprints on Poison Book Match Those of Accused Cyanide Killer," [Bremerton, WA] *Kitsap Sun*, Mar. 3, 1988, https://bit.ly/3MRwbPw.
54 Mike Carter, "Stella Nickell, Serving 90 Years for Planting Poisoned Pills, Killing 2, Seeks Release from Prison," *Seattle Times*, May 10, 2022, https://bit.ly/3oQCFGn.
55 "Woman Convicted of Killing Two in Excedrin Tampering," History Channel, https://bit.ly/3qwYFGI. Accessed June 4, 2023.
56 Timothy Egan, "Woman Convicted of Killing 2 in Drug Tampering," *NY Times*, May 10, 1988, https://bit.ly/3WQtnqx.
57 Bruce Reading, email to author, Feb. 13, 2023; Efrem M. Ostrowsky, US Patent No. 4,478,343, Issued Oct. 23, 1984, https://rb.gy/08qhd.
58 Dr. Howard Markel, "How the Tylenol Murders of 1982 Changed the Way We Consume Medication," *PBS NewsHour*, Sept. 29, 2014, https://rb.gy/so7rx. Accessed June 4, 2023.
59 Criminal Resource Manual 1401–1499, "1448. Tampering with Consumer Product—The Offenses," US Dept. of Justice Archives, https://bit.ly/3qiiQYW.
60 "CFR—Code of Federal Regulations Title 21," US Food & Drug Admin., https://bit.ly/3OVAcVV. Accessed June 4, 2023.

Picture Credits

Alamy: Alpha Stock: 54; Everett Collection Historical: 183; Gado Images: 24 right; Historic Collection: 300; The Picture Art Collection: 136; Philip Scalia: 204; Science History Images: 71, 83; ZUMA Press Inc.: 72

AP: 178, 240, 244, 261, 308, 309, 317, 320; Atlanta Journal Constitution: 298; The Daily News: 114; Charlie Knoblock: 326; Gary Stewart: 334; Mark Wilson: 259

Art Resource, NY: The New York Public Library: 275

Bridgeman Images: Prismatic Pictures: 92

Everett Collection: 176, 231, 314; CSU Archives: 306

Fenimore Art Museum: 199

Getty Images: AFP/MLADEN ANTONOV: 260; Archive Photos/Chicago History Museum: 227; Archive Photos/Bob Riha Jr.: 130; Bettmann: 97, 108, 109, 118, 129, 131, 157, 161, 163, 174, 188, 189, 221, 237; Corbis Historical/Leif Skoogfors: 331; Los Angeles Times/Lacy Atkins: 121; New York Daily News Archive: 173, 232, 310; Tribune News Service/Chicago Tribune: 187, 324

Courtesy of Hathi Trust: 206, 209

Imagn/USA TODAY NETWORK: © The Columbus Dispatch: 63; © Columbus Evening Dispatch: 69; © Des Moines Register: 286; © Indianapolis Star: 212

Courtesy of Internet Archive: 1, 7, 142, 195, 264, 267, 272, 293

Kentucky Historical Society: 217

Courtesy of Kheel Center: 77

Courtesy of Library of Congress: 9, 24 left and middle, 25, 27, 28, 31, 33, 40, 46, 165, 262, 268, 288, 301, 302, 305; Bain News Service Photograph Collection: 58, 295; Detroit Publishing Co.: 2, 145; Carol M. Highsmith: throughout (Supreme Court), vi, 356, 358; Historic American Buildings Survey: 132; New York World-Telegram and the Sun Newspaper Photograph Collection: 48, 51, 276

Courtesy of National Archives: 79

Courtesy of Newspapers.com: 90, 155

Courtesy of Northwestern University Libraries/ Charles Deering McCormick Library of Special Collection and University Archives: 191, 223

Courtesy of New York Public Library: 17, 22, 192

Ohio State University Archives: 60, 62

Redux Pictures/The New York Times: 117; Eddie Hausner: 116

Courtesy of UCLA/Los Angeles Times Photographic Archive, Library Special Collections, Charles E. Young Research Library: 127

Courtesy of University of Virginia Libraries: 4, 8

Courtesy of Wikimedia Commons: 14, 86, 89, 105, 110, 279; Kheel Center: 82; Library of Congress: 74

OPPOSITE: Remnants of the demolished county jail in Marion, Illinois (1913-71), displayed inside the Williamson County Historical Society's museum.

Index

OPPOSITE: A cellblock in the Missouri State Penitentiary in Jefferson City, 2021. Opened in 1836 and now a museum, it was the oldest continually operating prison west of the Mississippi until it was decommissioned in 2004.